The Sonic Self

Advances in Semiotics

Thomas A. Sebeok, general editor

The Sonic Self

Musical Subjectivity
and Signification

Naomi Cumming

Indiana University Press
Bloomington and Indianapolis

Royalties from the sale of this book go to the Naomi Helen Cumming
Foundation, a non-profit educational trust to encourage
young scholars in their pursuit of music studies.

This book is a publication of Indiana University Press
601 North Morton Street, Bloomington, IN 47404-3797 USA

http://iupress.indiana.edu

Telephone orders 800-842-6796
Fax orders 812-855-7931
Orders by e-mail iuporder@indiana.edu

Chapters 2 and 3 appeared previously in a different form as
"Musical Signs and Subjectivity: Peircean Reflections,"
*Transactions of the Charles S. Peirce Society: A Quarterly Journal
in American Philosophy* 35(3), Summer 1999, 437–474.

The paper used in this publication meets the minimum requirements of American National Standard for Information Sciences—Permanence of
Paper for Printed Library Materials, ANSI Z39.48-1984.

Design and composition by Julie Allred, B. Williams & Associates
Music engraving by Evan Conlee, Con Brio Music Typesetting

Manufactured in the United States of America

Library of Congress Cataloging-in-Publication Data
Cumming, Naomi.
The sonic self : musical subjectivity and signification / Naomi Cumming.
p.   cm. — (Advances in semiotics)
Includes bibliographical references and indexes.
ISBN 0-253-33754-2 (cl : alk. paper)—
ISBN 0-253-21393-2 (pa : alk. paper)
1. Music—Semiotics.   2. Music—Philosophy and aesthetics.
3. Musical analysis.   I. Title.   II. Series.
ML3845.C86 2000
780'.1'4—dc21   00-040917
1   2   3   4   5   05   04   03   02   01   00

Contents

Contents

Examples

Tables

Foreword

~

David Lidov

$\mathcal{N}$AOMI CUMMING completed *The Sonic Self* just a few months before her sudden and unexpected death at the age of thirty-eight. She was wrapping up revisions of her manuscript then and had only some illustrations to sketch out.[1]

For anyone who knows Naomi Cumming's earlier work, the book bears witness to an immense intellectual evolution, an achievement that became possible for her, but not less extraordinary, because she had won a prestigious Australian Research Council, Queen Elizabeth II Fellowship at the University of Melbourne, permitting her full-time research for five years. She decided midway through the fellowship that she wanted to be expert in philosophical debate and changed her academic residence from music to phi-

---

[1] The manuscript which Naomi left did not include any analytical diagrams. The voice-leading reductions in Chapter Seven are the work of Robert Wannamaker, principally, and myself.

losophy so as to receive the whole brunt and the full benefit of criticism from colleagues in that discipline. This book is the first full fruit, and sadly the last, of her disciplinary crossing.

The two special technologies of academic philosophy and academic music theory could have combined as a double barrier to communication, but Naomi Cumming, after encountering skepticism in the first stages of her research, developed a strong sense of mission about building a bridge between music and philosophy for students. The last time I saw her, she said emphatically that was the main point of the book.

I am not convinced that this was really its whole purpose for her or for us, but *The Sonic Self* does build a bridge, because it is exceptionally lucid. Two-thirds of it may be read and understood by persons who have no training in music theory, and what such readers will have to skip is not essential to the intelligibility of the overall argument.[2] *All* of the book can be read and understood by musical scholars who have no prior training in philosophy — even, I think, the "hard part" she saved for the Appendix. Sartre once remarked in admiration of Husserl that he could "make philosophy from a glass of wine." This book, too, displays the quintessentially philosophical craft of extracting important questions from the most commonplace kinds of thought and experience. *The Sonic Self* deals with controversial problems in

---

[2] I hope there will be many readers who are not musicologists. Perhaps a couple of pointers would be useful. In the text there is often a very quick interplay between the notion of music as representing a personal voice and the music-theoretical terms of "voice leading" and "structural voice", terms based on the same idea but now almost as a dead metaphor. These technical terms refer to syntactic connections between notes that are adjacent in the musical scale but separated in time. Readers who are not musicologists should also be alerted to two usages that, though not exactly technical, are idiosyncratic "code words" in the field. "Authentic" always refers to the 20th-century academic reconstruction of 18th-century performance practice, although the author's own analysis will frequently allow us to reflect that authenticity in a more general sense (e.g., emotional authenticity, honesty) may be a very different issue. Similarly, "romantic" always stands for the predominant 20th-century performance style for 19th-century music, a style which may not be immediately allied to the aesthetic or philosophical entailments of "romanticism" in literary or cultural-historical studies.

musical aesthetics and music theory—the mental content of interpretation, the contribution of musical structure to musical affect, the premises of judgment and valuation.

I met Naomi in 1994 at a meeting of the International Association for Semiotic Studies in San Francisco. Though my publications were not highly conspicuous, one or two had reached her halfway around the world in Australia, and she sought me out on that account. It made a flattering encounter for me, and lead to four years' conversation, mostly by e-mail and by an exchange of all our prior publications, for the next years. She had then become very disenchanted and disheartened with her own work in musicology (very astute work, as I later learned, in the analysis of music theoretical concepts and aesthetics). She was seriously reconsidering whether she ought to redirect her studies to theology, an area of passionate interest to her, but she also expressed the thought that what I and a few others were doing with musical semiotics might swing the balance the other way. I didn't want to take sides on the big question and simply said what any graduate research supervisor might have said to any young scholar: if she wanted to do something with music theory or musicology that would be truly and adequately her own, she'd better figure out how to connect it to what she found personally important.

She did just that, quite spectacularly. A year or so later she had written her essay on the musical theology of the "Erbarme Dich" aria of the St. Matthew Passion—an essay that was published in 1997 by *Music Analysis* and won the Society of Music Theory "best article" award for that year. Although she did finish the present, magnificent and very whole book, we ought to keep in mind that her lifetime research was interrupted early and was incomplete. Situating *The Sonic Self* in relation to the "Erbarme Dich" article, a turning point for her, can clarify what she accomplished while also suggesting further where the work was leading and also how others might hope to continue it.

The first part of the earlier article is concerned with the theoretical stance which warrants semiotic analysis for music. Much of *The Sonic Self* may be read as an elaboration of that first part, which in retrospect still seems brilliant but now may appear just a sketch. Her starting point was the observation that an engaged listening to music inevitably entails a play of imagination that neither score analysis nor historical contextualization can account for unless we recognize music as a domain of signs.

Although she had adopted the general terms of a Peircean framework before to address this issue, the book reveals for the first time how fully immersed in Peirce's work Naomi Cumming had become and how fully persuaded by it she was. Peirce's semiotics develops in several directions, of which two play salient roles here. The less important of these two for her work is what most of us know best, Peirce's construction of the sign as a triadic relation among representamen, object and interpretant. The more important for her is his triadic system of categories (qualities, events and regularities, to sketch it on a shirt cuff). She draws a line of argument that, to my knowledge, has never previously entered musicology. She shows how Peirce's work, to distinguish the security of knowledge we can enjoy regarding each of his categories of phenomena, bears on musical knowledge. She shows that while relativity is the only intellectually honest option regarding some types of musical judgment, it is a logical mistake to be sidetracked by doubt about certain of our own intuitions of musical meaning.

The dynamo of this study is the author's detailed attention to intuition — a concept she unfolds with a Kantian and Peircian understanding that all perception is interpreted. Her analysis of musical intuition empowers her to return in the last chapter to another theme she had announced in the earlier article. It concluded with a warning to music listeners and music scholars against a facile relativity, against the "premature assumption of ironic distance." But whereas there she had been content to discredit the negative of her proposition, in *The Sonic Self* she achieves a more positive demonstration that indifference in attentive listening is really impossible. She shows that we can allow no discontinuity between sensuous and formal listening, between individual and social interpretation, or between abandonment to music and critical reflection on it. In the end, transcending her own adroit constructions of value relativity, she leaves us nowhere to hide from the seriousness of musical engagement. Whatever tack we take, she has raised the stakes for musical analysis.

But the earlier article on "Erbarme Dich," also reminds us of work Naomi Cumming still had left to do, or to put it more positively, the work which she has now shown us how to do. Readers will see for themselves many pathways that extend *from* the book. *The Sonic Self* does not undertake sustained, thorough exegesis of single works. (Yet, her discussion of the Adagio of the Bach G minor Sonata for unaccompanied violin is arguably quite complete.) The book is more concerned to introduce and demonstrate its own tools, quite a sufficient task; the examples it summons to that end are certainly rich enough to show the worth of those tools. Right there, we are offered mines of opportunity, and her own recent work — for example, her exemplary studies of Reich and Sculthorpe — as well as the Bach article begin to suggest the wide range of music to which her techniques are pertinent. But I want once more to draw attention to her own point of departure.

Distant as I am personally from her private beliefs (invisible in the present work), I remain inspired by the seriousness they motivated her to achieve in musicology. A student of mine who heard Naomi lecture on Bach remarked to me that the "new musicology" had tackled politics, gender, economics, colonialism and much else, but seemed to not to have the nerve yet to deal with personal religious experience (as opposed to its institutional vestments) as a factor in the Western musical tradition. He appreciated her insistence that the capacity of music for spiritual expression is a musicological issue. Although she adopted a deliberately neutral personal stance in *The Sonic Self*, I hope and expect that this book, in some respects a prolegomenon, will instigate further study in a vein that I think she has revived for us regarding specifically our spiritual reception of music. I believe this is a task to which she would have returned. Her final injunction in *The Sonic Self*, again invoking Kant, is that we recognize the work of music in constructing soul, and that is what she has shown us how to do.

The Sonic Self

Introduction

1. Musical Initiations

In his book, *Musical Elaborations,* Edward Said (1991) argues that musical performances are extreme occasions, where virtuosic soloists intimidate a submissive crowd into a state of angst at knowing their performative inferiority. In many phases of my life, playing the violin has been an extreme occasion —but not of this kind. At first it was not so much the act of playing that impressed itself upon my memory. Of more formative importance was the extreme effort taken to make lessons possible. Playing music was worth a sacrifice. It was a central value in life. Neither impediments of health nor of geography were allowed to get in its way.

My violin lessons commenced in a conservatorium on "Black Heath," in South London. The place was so named, I was told, because many people had died there during the medieval Black Death. Even the nursery tune, "Ring o' Roses," could recall that historical panoply of death to my mind. It was an instructive story. ("Ring, a ring o'roses, a pocket full of posies, a-tissue! a-tissue! they all fell down!") Fear of a "death of cold" was apparently not far from my parents' minds when I went to lessons, as I was a severely asthmatic child. In midwinter I was carried from the house covered in a blanket, like a canary, to emerge blinking in the violin teacher's room, having tried hard to obey instructions not to breathe while being transported through the cold night air.

A few years later, as an immigrant in a small logging town in the hills of southeast Victoria (Australia), I was driven to violin lessons fifty miles away, across the "black spur"—the southernmost tip of the Great Dividing Range that runs down the eastern coast of Australia. It was a treacherous, winding road, through forested country, with strange-looking tree ferns on either side. I arrived carsick and disoriented, to play out of tune.

A year after immigration, I was sent to boarding school in a provincial city (Geelong). There I found that no other child had ever seen a violin. Playing was an oddity and a source of social alienation, like my British accent.

a. Discovering a Voice in Sound

As a teenager, and a day-girl once more, I was invited to join a master class being held by a newly arrived master in Melbourne. It was then that I met Claude Dunand.[1] Or rather, I *heard* him first. A robustly sarcastic and nasal laugh emanated from the stairs, as I stood trembling in the audition room. When its owner walked in, I was startled by his appearance and tried to hold back tears of fright as I delivered a Handel sonata, with minimal sound. Dunand, I soon learned, was a French-Egyptian graduate of the Paris Conservatory and Juilliard, leader of the second violins in the Melbourne Symphony Orchestra. A devoted Romantic in the French school, his tradition was that of Mischa Elman, a Parisian violinist acclaimed for a sensuous, personal sound. His whole demeanor was frightening and bizarre to me: emotional, intense, demanding, expressive. The affront he gave me was such indeed that, for a year, I could not speak in his presence, though he became my teacher during that time. "Does she want to become a violinist?" he asked my mother (I was always the third person in the conversation) " . . . then it requires commitment . . . but I think we can do it!" To live, for Dunand, was to play the violin, and no compromise was to be allowed of me. One incident in a lesson, during that first year, is symptomatic of how he taught. I was playing the Concerto in E Minor by eighteenth-century Italian violinist Pietro Nardini (1722–1793), a work now known to have been arranged by a nineteenth-century composer from two of Nardini's sonata movements. Dunand, seated in his armchair, suddenly became animated as I reached a slow section and, leaning forward, made the motions of a "vibrato" with his left hand in the air. "Emote! Emote!," he said, with an urgency in his soft and nasal voice that made great expressiveness seem imperative (despite the restrained conventions for playing works of this style). "Emote!," I had discovered by careful induction, was the verb from "emotion" and meant "more vibrato!" This term, which Dunand used often, was familiar neither in its etymology nor its lived application. Having no idea, then, of what emotion was connected with "emoting," I found that I could satisfy Dunand's demand just the same by increasing the frequency of my vibrato. So it was that I discovered emotion as a quality of sound.

My backwardness in expression led Dunand to describe me as having "no personality." (The mute are often regarded as deaf as well. He would ask my mother, "Is she stupid? Does she speak?") One day, after a lesson, he advised that I should be encouraged to "fall in love" as the necessary solution to my interpretive lack. From sadly crooning his way through a piece of Kreisler, he turned around to protest my social recalcitrance (to my mute embarrassment). Listening, I felt an impulse to rebel, though I had no inkling of how I could comply with his commands. He could not force me towards an experience of emotions I did not know, this much I recognized, but neither could I resist the strength of his desire to initiate me into a Romantically expressive world, through the violin. Eventually he did succeed, to some degree. Although I at first knew nothing of what Romanticism was, Dunand's playing itself was a revelation of sensuality, of emotional nuance. I observed him often with an awed sense of incapacity and tried to emulate his style.

One of the consequences of encountering Dunand was that I acquired a beautiful violin, a gift (and parental sacrifice) I could not deserve. Before even meeting the instrument, I read in a note from the London dealers: "It has a 'black velvet' sound." When I began to play it, the sound of this new violin seemed to draw from me something I did not know I possessed. It was as if the violin had the potential to become the voice I lacked.[2] This was quite a discovery, not made fully in a moment of time but over a couple of years. Yet understanding or realizing this potentiality was not without some difficulty. Dunand's command to "emote!" carried expectations he could not articulate. They were, however, hinted at in his spontaneous response to

3

a passage from a new publication, a popular book on the violin by Yehudi Menuhin (with William Primrose). With sardonic amusement, expressed in his nasal laugh, Dunand pointed out a passage where Menuhin writes of images of the violin's body, comparing it to that of a female bodily shape. In this passage, he draws his reader unexpectedly into a moment of musical intimacy and wonders whether a woman could ever know such love for an instrument she perceives as her own "voice":

> Its shape is in fact inspired by and symbolic of the most beautiful human object, the woman's body. . . . The varnish of a Stradivarius or Guarnerius evokes the sun caught in the silken texture of human skin. And like the female human voice, the violin combines the entire soprano and contralto range. I have often wondered whether psychologically there is a basic difference between the woman's relationship to the violin and the man's. . . . Does the woman violinist consider the violin more as her own voice than the voice of one she loves? Is there an element of narcissism in the woman's relation to the violin . . . ? (Menuhin and Primrose, 1991: 7–8)

Dunand denied Menuhin's sensuality as madness. He could not do otherwise, so blatantly did it describe a sensibility that was well-known to him, yet nuanced with a sense of restraint and propriety. What he sought, somehow, was an identification of his students with the sound of the violin as a voice that could be expressive of their own passion, and yet a cultivated distance that would allow them also to draw out the best in the violin's tone, in a critical stance that recognized it as more than a projection of their subjective states.

Whether Dunand's view of a violinist's relationship to his or her instrumental "voice" was gendered is hard to tell, but the gendered relationship depicted in Menuhin's ode of admiration to his violin is so remarkably obvious as to elicit a cascade of questions when reread in the 1990s. Does attraction to the violin's physical beauty need to be read as a male prerogative? Does a woman's singing always indicate a narcissistic fondness for the sound of her own voice? And if not, why would it be so on the violin? Could not a state of identification with the violinistic sound be felt by men, who take this instrument as their "voice"? Why is a state of "identification" by a male violinist with his feminized voice so strongly to be denied, through protestations of loving its "otherness"? If, in women, a violinistic "singing" confirms a perceived propensity to self-admiration, what is to be said of men's showmanship? Menuhin's naive reflections are offensive in the 1990s due to his simplistic construction of gendering in binary terms. More questions could easily be asked. Could a woman not appreciate (or even love) a voice that is feminine, yet recognize it as not merely a projection of herself? Does any artist maintain only one position in relation to his or her sound? Whatever the gender of the player, a relationship with the violin's sound can include the idea of projecting a "voice" that is one's own, and also of standing apart to listen to the sound as the "voice" of another. It was this intensity of listening, identification, and relationship that Dunand taught.

b. Performance as Self-Formation

My continued training in a performance school was to make me aware that playing the violin was not just "expressing myself" but working with the demands of a style. If Menuhin's general suspicion of narcissistic tendencies was right, and female performers were prone to lack a distance from the violin that would allow them to respect the violin's musical utterance as other than a projection of their own "interior" states, an increasing awareness of musical style could begin to correct this propensity. At college, I joined a Baroque ensemble conducted by a well-known harpsichordist, ignorant of the changes in performance style that it would demand. The first command was "do not vibrate!" I had to curtail the "switched-on vibrato" of a Romantic style and learn a new performance art where variations in the use of the bow and spontaneous ornamentation were the principal sources of expressivity. Competencies practiced in the morning for nineteenth-century concerti were to be discarded in the evening for playing Henry Purcell.

⌐◡

In my third year of undergraduate study, I moved to a performance school in another state, headed by "Démon Sebistik," a well-respected European violinist and pedagogue. I had been attracted there by a summer school, in which Sebistik impressed me with an understanding of technique. Students of stringed instruments would gather in a lecture theatre and present technical problems, which would be solved by communal criticism. Such analysis of technique was new and fascinating to me, but as I sat there taking notes I did not guess that my demeanor of silent observation was itself observed. I was to be confronted on my return. My attitude of detachment had caused offense. "Where is the book?" Sebistik asked, in my first class as a student, "Weren't you taking notes for it in the summer?" His laugh was disarmingly dry.

I did not often take private lessons with this teacher but encountered him primarily in the "technique class," or at performance class, or in the corridors. Even so, he had a profound influence on me. At first I could glean little of his educational methods, but I later found out he had absorbed some ideas of a pre-Soviet Russian mystic, George Ivanovich Gurdjieff.[3] It is in the nature of Gurdjieff's philosophy to retain an aura of mystery, as part of a spiritual tradition with roots in Sufism, a mystical branch of Islam (see Gurdjieff, 1974; Nicoll, 1984; Ouspensky, 1977), and Sebistik certainly used this "mystery" to advantage, seeking surreptitiously to influence the development of a student's character by manipulating his or her technique, creating calculated "dramas" with barbed and cryptic comments in the communal "technique class."[4] Within the perspective of this philosophy, the role of a teacher could be construed as creating the conditions for a "crisis" where an habitual mode of approach could be seen as weak in some respects, or a preconceived virtue in performance opened up to question as an inhibiting strait-jacket. "Up is down and down is up!" was one of the mottos repeated often in my first summer school. It meant not only that a movement in one part of the arm would have a compensating effect somewhere else in the body, but that positive aspects of character could have their "down" side. The habit of disarming students by making cryptically personal remarks was some indication of this belief. "You are a judge!" he might say, in the middle of class. "You see yourself as a priest" or "Of course, you are the analyst!" My tendency to rational analysis was the most obvious object of "correction": a compulsive reliance on reflective activity at the expense of "instinctual response."[5] When I once made the mistake of venturing a response to a theoretical question ("It's an inverted triad!"), I was to be derided with faintly sardonic praise. Sebistik, it seemed, wished to elicit insight by placing students in situations where the apparent strength of a rational mind could be revealed as incapacity, a blindness to the triviality of their own thought, or its masking of other sides of character. He took my violin one day, to demonstrate with, and dropped it audibly on the hard desk in front of him. My attachment to the instrument was heard by all. No rational defense could at that moment hide my instinctive cry of pain. He laughed and did it again. A training exercise can be cruel.

Sebistik's prompting of his students to confront their weaknesses did not need to take a consistently verbal form but could be enacted in the "technique" class, as it was with the dropping of my violin. Such small incidents could be taken as mere accidents, but a more systematic approach to change was being enacted there. Radically change a student's basic technique, and you have also altered his or her expressive medium. Because the string's sound is directly tactile in origin, and is commonly invested with expressive weight, a manipulation of the position and motion of the hands is more than a technical change. To reorient a violinist's hands on the violin is to change his or her mode of touch, of movement, of forming a vibrato to enliven a note. Making these changes requires an adjustment in how the musician experiences him- or herself as forming "expressive" sound, and as able to realize scores that require it. Times of technical change are like times of handicap, when the body loses competence in carrying through a desired task. Jonathan Dunsby has pointed out the reality of the loss experienced by a performing musician who has "'lost' their technique" (1995: 35). He draws attention to its strong emotional tone. The "loss" I have described as involved in technical reconstruction can be regarded as temporary, leading to new gains, and is often required of a professional in training. Well-handled, it need not be invidious (see Havas, 1961: 63), but my experience of change was not so benign. Most difficult was the display of handicaps publicly during the "technique class." It was through this relatively innocuous means that my teacher furthered my confrontation with expressive lack, and of fear in a public space. No display of rational competency in musical analysis could serve to hide the lack.

c. Does the Self Form the Sound, or the Sound the Self?

The modes of teaching used by Dunand and Sebistik could be seen as a species of "folk psychology." In neither case did they have an explicitly formulated or coherent set of ideas about the relationship between a performer's emotional states and the sounds produced on the violin. They did not espouse any recognized psychological theory about development in adolescents and young adults. Nor were any articulate notions of social and cultural conditioning applied when they made comments on a student's eccentric habits of self-expression. Despite this, their actions implied an informal "theory" of personal character, or "identity," and its expression in sound. Of most interest, philosophically, is the contrast between the views taken by these teachers of the relationship between emotional experience and musical expression. For Dunand, the performer's emotional life had first to be developed and then to be expressed "through" the violin. Invasive conversations and an incitement to introspection were the result. For the other teacher, whose ideas were more sophisticated even if vague, a student's subjective states could be manipulated directly by altering his or her technical means of producing expressive sound. He rarely entered into direct discussion of the emotions he heard embodied in a work, but instead focused on features of its execution, to create an expressive result.

Most striking in each case was that the teachers extended their role beyond the transmission of technical skills, or even of formal and stylistic understanding, to include a challenge to emotional life, and rationality, in the name of musical interpretation. Each believed that for a performer to communicate music's expressive content he or she would require a specific kind of emotional understanding, particularly when playing works in a Romantic style. To be trained as a violinist was then not simply to learn the violin, but to be "formed" as an interpreting musician, in a disciplined process that demanded confrontations with personal expressive lack. Dunand's way of confronting this lack was simply naive. Sebistik's approach was more calculated. As they could not fully articulate the relationship of bodily states, emotional experience, and qualities of sound, all these teachers could do was to push students to a point of crisis, making them confront the gap between any "interior" state they might feel in contemplating a work, and the expressive content heard by others in their performances. Neither introverted self-analysis nor a momentous effort to produce the sound in the "right" way could be successful in bridging this gap, though both activities would be engaged in at length by students in the solitary practice rooms. Somehow a connection was supposed to "happen" in a moment of spontaneous combustion, where interiority made its way into sound.

When visiting London in 1991 I stopped at a subway station and heard for the first time a repeated and weighty injunction from a stern male voice, coming from on high, "Mind the Gap! Mind the Gap!" He could have been a prophet of fundamental ontology. How can you name that place between intention and "sensible" form? How can you name that spot where you would like your illuminating presence to be seen, when your appearance attracts nothing but a transparent stare? How can you name the terror of a dream when you think you sing, but no sound will come from your violin? How do you "mind the gap" you cannot find? It took a moment's recollection to notice that the platform was a step away.

2. Subjects and Subjectivity

This book is concerned with aspects of subjectivity as it is experienced in music and by musicians of the Western European Classical tradition, with particular reference to solo works for the violin. The idea of subjectivity can be divided up in many ways, but only three need be mentioned at this point: those of music, musician, and listening interpreter. To a musician, it is hardly news that subjectivities may be attributed to music itself: tones of voice, with their emotional connotations, appearing in sound; affective states, suggested by gestural action, heard in the shaping of a melodic segment; aspects of willed direction found in the impetus of tonal harmony. The musician's work is to master these potentialities on a given instrument and to work with them in accordance with the requirements of a style, drawing out the possibilities of a composed musical moment by making his or her own choices of sound, emphasis, and tempo. Something of the musician's own "character" will be heard in the choices he or she makes, in the patterns of emphasis that constitute a performance style. So it is that his or her own "subjectivity" appears. The performing musician becomes the first listener to his or her own sounds, somewhat privileged by a knowledge of his or her own intentions. Other listeners bring to the moment their own experiences with this or other styles in order to critically appraise what they hear.

It is worth pausing, at this point, to consider further what might constitute a performer's "identity," as appraisals of music are finally insipid if they fail to account for the contributions made by performers in realizing sound. Identity could be thought of, in a preliminary and somewhat superficial manner, as having an outward and an inward face. On the outward side, it is the perceptible result of an individual's patterned choices within a social domain, those characteristic manners of forming sound or gesture that distinguish him or her from the "crowd"—a personal "style" (Meyer, 1989: 4).[6] Understanding identity as personal "style" is consistent with the standpoint on selfhood found in the social psychology of George Herbert Mead and with the philosophical standpoint of Charles Peirce, whose exploration of signs constitutes the impetus for much of this book. It also reflects a twentieth-century philosophical move against Cartesian solipsism. Identity cannot be located in some "inner" space, which is known through introspection alone. Nor is the subject isolated in his or her private "be-ing." The "self" is not, as Descartes implied, an ineffable mystery, formed by its own private thoughts, existing alone as the reflective spectator on events in the world, skeptical of its own impressions. Rather, "selfhood" is an intrinsically social, interactive, and mobile experience. "Subjects" are formed by participation in the social media of gesture, language, or music—media that provide a repertoire of possible choices—within which they achieve their personal "style." This, then, is the outward face of identity, a publicly observable thing. Without this face, it would not be possible to "see" evidence of identity in gestural mannerisms or to "hear" it in the characteristic timbral choices of musicians performing on an instrument.

In addition to an "outward" aspect, the problem of individuated identity may become a topic for reflexive self-awareness, for musical performers as for subjects in the social world. This question of inner identity need not be construed as altogether mysterious, to be discovered introspectively. Consider that it is possible to know oneself as an agent of choice, and to reflect upon patterns of choosing. Looking at my musical performance, I can interrogate the factors that constrain my choices of timbral nuance, making articulate those unexamined "beliefs" that manifest themselves as inhibitions in the production of sound. I might, for example, follow a train of thought like this: "Why are certain sounds so difficult for me to produce on the violin, in their grating harshness or overt sensuality? Is this a stylistic constraint? (They could, indeed, be outside the sonorous range of a Baroque composition.) Or is it a more personal difficulty? A Romantic work calls for these sounds, but I seem to be held back by restrictive 'beliefs,' which allow only some forms of expression." It is when I become aware of the "outward" face of my musical identity, as a pattern of actions, that I can begin to question how I am constrained in my performance. What is the ideology that governs me? What is the domain of my choice? How free am I? These are musical questions, and yet they are an allegory of broader questions about the expressivity of social life. Noticing those sounds I "cannot" make, I begin to gain awareness of those scarcely articulate "beliefs" that present themselves as inhibitions to a convincing performance of a work. I see that my musical inhibitions and social ones are not entirely unconnected. The "outward" identity, of choices audible in sound, reflects a pattern of belief, desire, and inhibition that constitutes an "inner self"—what it is to be "me."

A more concrete example will make this clear. An invitation (from Dunand) to produce a sensuous warmth of tone, in performing works by French composers such as Claude Debussy or Ernest Chausson, seems to contradict my "very British" socialization to restricted expressivity, with the "beliefs" (about the value of restraint) which that entails. By asking me to entertain the possibility of more sensuous qualities in sound, the music is able to touch on a repression of the sensuous in the ascetic traditions to which I have been exposed. At the moment I "see" that there is a conflict between my more or less articulate beliefs about French Romantic or Impressionistic style and the less apparent "beliefs" of my socially inhibited culture, I can choose to set aside the inhibiting factors, at least as they impinge on my performance in this artistic realm. I thereby gain not only an increased awareness of myself, as subject to conflicting ideologies and an agent of choice within them, but I gain the possibility of entering a sound world that was closed to me before. It may not be an immediate entry, as habits of expression are not simply undone, and working to enter a new sound world takes time and practice. Even so, the possibility of greater freedom is there. In the process of questioning my musical capacities, I gain a self-reflexive knowledge, a new ability to refute the beliefs implicit in my social behavior, and a possibility of entering freely into an expressive domain that had been "foreign" to me. On its "inward" side, self-identity is minimally a reflexive awareness of one's own patterns of choice, and the beliefs that govern them. For a musician, it includes a knowledge of the self as having the effective power to answer the expressive demands of different stylistic genres, entering imaginatively into new worlds.

One caveat should be addressed here. It may technically be disputed that unarticulated and socially enforced "beliefs" are beliefs in the normal sense at all (DeBellis, 1995; Stich, 1983). For now I will use the term "belief" to refer to relatively stable but informal views, held by an individual or social group, of how some aspect of experience is, or ought to be, organized. Whether the construction of socially normative behavior is made conscious and articulate or not, it can be said to exist in the mind of an individual if it acts to inhibit his or her range of behavior. One notable aspect of the beliefs I have been mentioning is that they carry an evaluative weighting. Conflicts of belief carry with them conflicts of valuing. A felt opposition between the musical sensuality that is sanctioned in certain styles, and a socialization to restraint, is not merely a problem that I personally have had to resolve, but an indicator of a cultural conflict between two different contexts of valuing. Music may be seen as giving "permission" for sensual content to be expressed, though it is transgressive of some rules for "public" social behavior.

Identity has so far been described as the outward and inward side of choices made among musical sounds, as signifying different attitudes in a social domain. But there is still something more to consider in understanding the apparently "inward," or personal, domain of subjectivity. Something fundamental determines what it is like to be a performing self, whether as a musician or simply as an actor in society. This is that I know myself as some-*body*, an acting *body*. I know how an action on the violin "feels." I know "what it is like" to experience my body as a sounding medium in a social space. Speaking in a whisper invites a sense of intimacy, but if my violinistic sound fails to penetrate beyond the first rank of seats in a hall, I get bare tolerance instead. "An insipid personality." I know the sonic feedback from the space, as well as the lack of attention from listeners who cannot hear. The qualities of aural projection and movement in the space are certainly observable and may be read as symptomatic of my social self-positioning—a lack of dominance, a desire to withdraw. At the same time, there remains something of "what it is like" for me, as an embodied and sounding subject, to be in that space. The philosopher of mind, Thomas Nagel, inquired in a well-known article (1974) whether questions of self-knowledge should ever be asked in a manner that calls for an introspective reply. In his title, he asked "What Is It Like to be a Bat?" (Nagel, [1974] 1979).[7] His way of framing the question is felicitous. By drawing attention to the problem of knowing "what it is like" to experience the world as an actor in another kind of body—that of a bat—he raises the issue of what it is like to experience subjectivity as embodiment at all. Subjective identity includes an awareness of the feelings evoked by one's own patterns of movement and sound in a public space. The self-reflexivity developed by a performing musician has to be such that she can take an awareness of herself as a sounding body in an acoustic space, and work to take control of her audible relationship to that space, accounting for its size and reverberant properties. A violin's "whisper" needs to be heard at the back of the hall, so any reluctance to project the sound can only be put aside. I take the feeling "this is like being engulfed by space" and turn it into a sense of filling the space around with a subtle but penetrating sound. In the process of changing my relationship to space, I discover a new possibility of "self," a new construction of my embodied position and relative dominance. No one can know "what it is like" to experience my particular body, working with my particular violin, in this particular space, unless I give my own first-person report. Even so, the subjective experience that I report is one of relationship to a shared venue and publicly perceptible sounds. Dominance and timidity can be heard in the dynamic of sound. Relative degrees of "warmth" or sensuality can be construed from the quality of its production. The bodily sense that I consider, from a first-person perspective, to be uniquely mine, turns out to be subject to ready interpretation, as a sense of "space," and of controlling movement or sound within it, gained in the process of being socialized and musically trained.

3. A Philosophical Outlook

The questions raised by my student experience of the violin concerned the place of the sensuous and emotional in sound and their relationship to more formal modes of understanding. These questions required a specific kind of philosophy in order to be addressed, one that would take account of the practical experience of being a musician, a person engaged directly with a demanding instrument, the mastery of which was to be formative of social identity in a given domain, and also of an important aspect of emotional life. It would need to make sense of the demand made so habitually by teachers of the violin, that the production of sound and shaping of melodic segments be "expressive" and yet stylistically appropriate. At the same time, this philosophy would need to account for the fascination of abstract forms, their felicitous possibility of being used as a means of withdrawal into a separate "world," away from expressive demands, even while those Romantically inclined teachers strove so hard to elicit expressivity. As the teachers' desire for a particular kind of sound spoke of values that could not be ignored, values that were partial in their nature, and yet were propounded as an "absolute," the philosophy would also need to account for how musical sounds are socially located, evaluated, and controlled.

The perplexities raised by a musician's training cannot be resolved entirely in a first exploration of semiotic philosophy. Even so, the philosophical approach developed in this book does set out a direction towards answering some of them. It has been influenced in important respects by Peirce's philosophy, and reflects both his pragmaticism and his central interest in the play of signs. A further influence is that of feminists in music theory (Guck, Kielian-Gilbert) who have had the courage to address topics that were formerly excluded from the domain of theoretical thought. This philosophy is, then, pragmatic and semiotic while also engaging with some topics that have been raised by feminist theorists. The further rationale for taking this kind of approach will be outlined briefly below.

a. Pragmaticism

Why pragmaticism, if not in response to the formation and interpretation of signs as a practical activity? Music is an action in sound within a social and stylistic context. Though a listener might like sometimes to contemplate it passively, letting it "wash over" her, it is just as likely that he or she will be actively engaged in the production and anticipation of sounds. Whether performing or not, engagement with music involves an active response, even when bodily movements are suppressed. Musical aestheticians have often avoided reflection on this aspect of musical experience, in the belief that anything a performer or listener *does* is somehow external to "the music itself." Peirce's philosophical "pragmaticism" offers an antidote to this tendency, by locating thought about signification within the context of a concern with *practice*—in his case, that of a scientist working with instruments of various kinds. His "pragmatic" approach finds that the meaning of an idea (a "symbol") can be understood by looking at "the general modes of rational conduct . . . which would ensue upon the acceptance of the symbol" (Wiener, [1958] 1966: 204).[8] Peirce's "pragmaticism" has sometimes been confused with the American pragmatism that developed when his philosophy was popularized by others (that is, a businesslike concern to identify what "works" and to implement it for profit). What is meant by pragmaticism is something more methodologically basic than that. To illustrate this, it could be asked how a pragmatic approach might influence the analysis of such ideas as "musical space." The belief that ordinary language will reveal the essential attributes of "space" has led more than one philosopher to the conclusion that musical "space" does not (literally) exist, as the claimed characteristics of movement in that space bear little relation to the behavior of moving objects in visually perceived space (Scruton, 1997). Pragmaticism does not need to draw this conclusion, because its starting point is praxis rather than an idealization of some concept, such as "space," as having a fixed set of attributes. Instead of seeking to fix the essential nature of some idea through an analysis of language alone, privileging visual perception and its linguistic description over other modes of perception and reasoning (see Richard Rorty in *Philosophy and the Mirror of Nature,* 1979), a pragmatic approach seeks to locate uses of language within a given set of practices which determine the meaning of the terms used. The possibility of movement in musical space is presumed in even the most basic descriptions of music, and need not be subject to skeptical questioning. Other descriptive habits, commonly thought of as "metaphorical," are similarly basic to musical experience. A musician's act of forming a "gesture," in the shaping of a melodic moment (or a listener's act of hearing that gesture in sound) need not, for example, be taken as evidence of delusional thinking, but of a developed practice in which it is understood that the expressive shaping of human movement can be heard in sound, even without the reinforcement of visual cues. The practice of *hearing* a shaping as gestural needs to be taken as a starting point, before it is presumed that the description is false, or that it must be explained as an aural translation or visual experience—a matter of appearances (Davies, 1994). A change in modes of conduct may not necessarily result from reflections such as these, but the ideas do have the potential to be embodied in performance.

b. Semiotics: Music as a Play of Signs

Another characteristic of this philosophy is that it is "semiotic." By this I mean that it presents sounds not merely as acoustic phenomena, but as capable of carrying connotations, for example, of human "subjective" qualities, such as those intimated in voice, gesture, or actions suggestive of willfulness. It should be noted that semiotic interpretation differs, in important ways, from a perceptual or cognitive theory of music. A semiotic analysis does not start from ideas developed in cognitive psychology (for example, ideas of grouping), then seek to show how they can be musically instantiated. Nor does it start with presuppositions about the nature of "mind"—an entity conceived of by dualists as distinct from "body"—then proceed to treat musical experience as entirely "cerebral" (based on cognitive acts without bodily enactment). Instead, it starts with the terms used by musicians, and those in a musical community, to describe music-as-signifying, taking seriously the "understanding" involved in kinesthetic activity, as well as that found in more abstract forms of pattern recognition. Peirce believed that his theory of signs could be used as the basis for *forming* a psychological theory, rather than as an addendum to any existing one. An interesting consequence of his giving priority to signs, rather than to a preconceived notion of mind, is that any tendency to mind/body dualism is effectively disarmed. (Chapter 2 discusses in some detail how his argument is worked out.) The same consequence may be observed in musical semiosis (that is, the activity of musical signs). Observations of musical signs suggest an integrated musical mind/body. The musical "mind" is not a distinct entity engaged in the cognition of abstract patterns, and isolated absolutely from actions of the body, if common metaphors such as those of "gesture" are taken as evidence. Images of embodiment appear as common modes of musical understanding (see Lakoff and Johnson, 1980; Johnson, 1987), alongside metaphors for language, such as "phrase" (Kirnberger, 1979 [1773]; London, 1996).

The art historian, Norman Bryson, argues that a semiotic approach to the interpretation of visual art has advantages over a "perceptualist" view, such as that advocated by Ernst Gombrich, because signs are consensually formed and, as a result, the act of recognizing them does not involve making guesses about the artist's state of mind: "An ability to recognize an image neither involves, *nor makes necessary inference towards,* the isolated perceptual field of the image's creator. It is, rather, an ability which presupposes competence within social, that is, socially constructed, codes of recognition" (Bryson, 1991: 65). A similar argument can be made of musical signs, but in order to be carried through, the discussion needs to be situated within an identifiable speech community (Bakhtin, 1986), where a degree of mutual understanding between participants in dialogue about music can be assumed. Rather than talking in absolute terms of "music," "voice," or "gesture," as if they meant the same thing in all contexts, this book will take as its primary focus the Western European repertory of works for violin (solo, accompanied, or in ensemble). Coherent strands of tradition, in which common terms are used, can be identified as continuing from the eighteenth century until the present day. Identifiable communities in the present can also be readily located, through the study of magazines devoted to the promotion of performance or the criticism of new CDs. Violinists of varying professional standing, and listeners of differing degrees of connoisseurship, all have access to this kind of literature. What I offer is by no means a comprehensive study of critical reception related to the violin, but a philosophical reflection on signs, in which violin music and its criticism forms a thread of continuity.

As Bryson suggests, a semiotic philosophy has the advantage of not forc-ing any unwarranted separations between the "psychological," as a set of private feelings or states, and the "culturally conditioned," "social," or "historical." A topic that will here be pursued, for example, is that of a vio-lin's sound as capable of eliciting descriptions suggestive of emotionality: "warmth," "harshness," or "purity." These descriptive terms make sense within the musical discourse surrounding performances on the violin, but they may be heard by some as indicators of a subjective response on the part of the listener and critic who uses them, that is, as of merely "psychological" interest. An understanding of signs does not allow such a peremptory sepa-ration of the psychological from the culturally shared. What is "heard in" the sounds, under these descriptions, has been heard according to a learned code of recognition. Judgment of what kind of sound is "neutral" will vary between the sub-traditions of performance, but despite this, the recognition of sounds as bearing qualities that mark them as "expressive" is not a matter of private feeling alone. If a "feeling" is involved, it is one whose interpreta-tion has been culturally entrained. It does not make sense, then, to say that interpretations of tonal "warmth" or "coolness" are "merely subjective," as if they derived from the psychological states of the listener, because these terms have been socially negotiated, through time, as having a designated range of meanings. This is not, however, to claim that criteria of correctness in description have been rigidly fixed, or that the states of mind held by musical listeners are entirely the puppets of stylistic conditioning. No pretense need be made that the terms of musical description are fully determined by habits of discourse, so that only one choice of words to characterize a performer's sound would be correct. What traditions of discourse provide is a range of descriptions that can be understood as having a recognizable degree of "fit" with a given sound. The "code of recognition," as Bryson puts it, situates the musical sound within a tradition of musical experience, distinguishing it from an uninterpreted aural phenomenon. When individual listeners describe their recognition of sounds as signifying certain qualities, they have not undergone experiences of music that trap them in a private and fictional world, but show evidence of a musical understanding that is intersubjectively intelligible.

The question might be pressed further, as to what place phenomenology could have within an understanding of music as a play of signs. Is not an interest in "sound qualities" really an interest in musical phenomena? To reinforce an answer that has already been suggested, Peirce's approach to signs does not rule out a consideration of "how things seem" to a musician or listener, but it does exclude a concern with sounds as pure, uninterpreted phenomena in those styles (excepting, for example, that of John Cage) where the loading of sound with interpretable meaning is presumed. If a sound seems "warm," it is already situated within a style and culture, as an intrinsically interpreted phenomenon. Instead of "bracketing out" a knowledge of performance style, as the classic method of phenomenology might suggest, Peirce's semiotic philosophy encourages an attention to "how things seem" in the ordinarily interpreted world.

A number of writers (Haraway, 1988; Merrell, 1997) have warned of the dangers of "doing the God trick." One who tries this trick assumes a universal perspective, access to an interpretive position that is historically and geographically unsituated, unlimited by the circumstances of a given life. Instead of acknowledging his or her own situation and source of interest in a topic, a culprit of this trickery presents the illusion of transcending prejudice and presenting the object of study "as it is," apart from any presuppositions he or she might bring to it. The examples discussed in this book are limited deliberately to a repertory of Western violin music, my own relationship to traditions of its performance having been stated. In this way, I seek to make clear that this is not a "God's-eye view" but a study born of perplexities in the experience of performing. Peirce's philosophy of signs does, nevertheless, seek generality. It has the potential to be applied to signs of all kinds and contexts, irrespective of who the interpreter might be, and a theory of musical semiotics based on this philosophy may similarly have features that suggest generality of application to music of many traditions. Those parts of this book that introduce the general principles of Peirce's thought do so in a way that leaves open the possibility of their application to many repertories other than the one discussed.

chapter one

~

Signs of Subjectivity

1. Physical Disciplines and Signs

I would like to start with a question so simple (and rhetorical) as to appear silly: What distinguishes a performing musician from an athlete in a performance sport? The music theorist, Jonathan Dunsby (1995), expresses great irritation at how "sport-think" has infected musical instruction. Barry Green's popular self-help manual for musicians, *The Inner Game of Music* (1987), is the immediate impetus for his annoyance. In his terms, it "perpetuates mindless musical truisms, no doubt unintentionally, but causing turbulent distraction to the thoughtful reader" (Dunsby, 1995: 32). This is unusually strong language for Dunsby, and it reflects the depth of his concern that in seeking to remove obstacles to effective motor performance, Green promotes a false anxiety among musicians about "conceptual intrusion" in their performances. Dunsby believes that such fears engender a resistance to analytical approaches to music, which are a necessary part of any informed interpretation. A preliminary question to consider, in looking at musical performance, might then be what distinguishes it from a purely physical performance.

a. Why Pay Attention to Performative Acts?
Action as Identity

Whatever the dangers of getting too impressed with the analogy between sport and music, it cannot be denied that physical training is an important part of the formation of a musician. Traditional performers entrain their bodies, through many years of practice, to the formation of culturally sanctioned sounds. For the act of performance to be understood, and the signification of musical works to be interpreted, the musician's preparation for performance (both short- and long-term) is, I believe, a good place to start, as it is in this preparatory time that "habitual" modes of expressive action are formed as responses to particular styles. (Following Charles S. Peirce, I will later argue that habits themselves can be read as an indication of beliefs about style.) Paying attention to a performer's physical activity is important also in counteracting the sense of sound as disembodied, a sense that can come from listening to "piped" music without a knowledge of its physical source, or to CDs whose technically altered perfection has removed the sounds of a performer's breath or of the obtrusive scraping of a bow on the strings. It is obvious that musical sounds are not, in origin, an impersonal or accidental event, that they do not come to exist in the disembodied medium of a CD without the action of a performer's body, but technological intervention can induce a partial forgetfulness of this fact. Evidence of the temporary amnesia — or complicity in technical illusion — is easy to find in the nasty surprise that a "live" performance can bring to someone who has heard a performer only in recordings. A reviewer, having heard Midori perform in the large and acoustically unfriendly spaces of the Barbican Concert Hall in London, said: "On this evidence the Midori who sells all those CDs is a creation of the microphone and the Sony engineers. Heard 'live' (10 March), she has a small, rather wiry tone with an E-string sonority that is close to a whistle" (Potter, 1996a: 734). Notice that it is "Midori" who is created through her sound. By altering the balance, dynamic level, and quality of her sounds, the engineers have effectively created for her a musical "body" and identity, at least in Potter's experience. They are able to effect this illusion because the characteristics of sounds are the aural "marks" of bodily actions. A violinist's perceived "strength" reflects the tension of her muscles, the weight of the arm as it is allowed to fall in the movement of a bow, the degree of friction in an "attack." Although a listener's attention, when playing a CD, may not be directed to bodily actions—certainly if they are not themselves a performer —the impression of a "personality" can be gained subliminally through the markers in sound of what seem to be the performer's characteristic physical responses. Sonic illusion is not, then, the innocent cleaning up of a musical surface, but the construction of a personality.

~

If altering sounds can change perceptions of a musical identity, such as that promoted under the name "Midori," the connection between sound quali- ties and perceived subjective content in music cannot be dismissed as trivial. Looking at this from the reciprocal point of view of a performer in training, learning the physical actions to form sounds is the most direct means avail- able for constructing a musical identity. It is not a matter of first having some special personal qualities and then projecting them through the instru- ment, in a sound with some mysterious "depth," but a matter of producing sounds that will create that illusion. Kató Havas, well known for her success in cultivating beauty of sound, writes as follows:

> It is a fallacy to think that the purity and sweetness of tone, that quality which has the power to move us so much, depends on depth of soul or feeling, talent, or goodness knows what else, of the individual player. How often do we come across a violinist who, as a human being, has no artistic qualities, has in fact less sensibility than the average person, but who has such a beautiful tone that we are unable to resist its spell, the moment he begins to play. Yet there are others who have all the neces- sary artistic qualities, as far as personality is concerned, but because they lack this tone, they are unable to move us. No—as I discovered over and over again, a warm and beautiful tone has nothing to do with talent or individual personality. It is not the outcome of hours and hours of prac- tise and perseverance. *It is merely putting the right pressure, on the right spot,*

at the right moment! And the result is instantaneous. (Havas, 1961: 3–4, my italics)

Creating "a beautiful tone," through a well-balanced physical adjustment to the instrument, is central to creating the impression of musical personality. The "sonic self" is thus conceived. It is not a previously existing element of personality, but a creation that comes into being with sound.

b. Creating Music as a Sign

An intuitive grasp of what distinguishes a performance which demonstrates musical "understanding" from one that demonstrates a merely technical achievement may be attained by examining the language used in reviews of performances, and, I will argue, the distinguishing mark is an appreciation of sound as sign—not as the product of musical athleticism, or even acrobatics. The reviews found in popular performers' magazines, such as the British publication, the *Strad,* or the United States publication, *Strings,* are useful indications of the evaluation commonly given to virtuosity when it is pitted against an expectation of interpretive individuality. Because these writings are not philosophically self-conscious, they give a fair representation of what might be a "popular" way of listening, at least by a musically educated and alert listener. Colorful descriptive terms are used to discriminate what are felt to be the subjective qualities of a sound. For the critic, there is no pressing need to distinguish who this subjectivity belongs to, to question whether it is embodied *in* the sound, or merely projected. It is not even a matter for self-consciousness that the descriptions betray a marked gendering, with female violinists judged more obviously on the emotional connotations of their sound than are their male counterparts. Comments on the quality of a violinist's sound and on his or her personal character are also mixed with great freedom, alongside descriptions of qualities heard as intrinsic to a theme or composer's style. An important point to note in this mêlée of evaluative response is that, within a limited musical community such as that defined by the readership of the magazines, references to subjective qualities as belonging to sounds in some (undefined) way are perfectly intelligible. An ability to discriminate between performances that succeed in conveying a "subjective" character from those that fail is also a common achievement of the critics, and one that is presumed to be accessible to their audience.

~

It goes without saying that a violinist is not merely a sonic acrobat, and works for violin not merely the vehicle for an exercise in showmanship, although the pleasures of virtuosity are easily recognized in a concerto or caprice. Unlike the skills of an athlete, the technical skills of a musical performer hold a subsidiary role. This might seem so naively obvious that reviewers would not need to draw attention to it, yet a glance at a few reviews of live performances, or of newly released CDs by aspiring violinists, quickly establishes that the enticements of technical virtuosity are real, and that a failure to appreciate the "artistic" limitations of virtuosity is not uncommon even among players who have achieved some measurable success.

Jennifer Laredo, reviewing for the *Strad,* reports on Marat Bisengaliev's recital in the Wigmore Hall:

> The second half of the concert was a compendium of technical devices —up-bow staccato, left-hand pizzicato, artificial harmonics and double-stopping. The considerable challenges presented . . . posed no significant problems for him. However, I would have preferred to see a willingness to take musical risks instead of negotiating technical obstacles; it seemed that the pieces were *delivered rather than interpreted.* (1996: 829, my italics)

Further evidence that an immature performer might think of "technique" as the capacity to execute the notes of a composition accurately and at optimal tempo is provided by an American violinist, Zvi Zeitlin, in his report on an incident during a teaching tour of China:

> In Shanghai, I asked a 13-year-old boy, who had just concluded a fast, vapid performance of Paganini's "Nel cor più non mi sento," whether he liked the piece. "Yes," he replied. "Why do you like it?" I asked. "Because it is difficult," he replied. "Is that the only reason?" "Well, it's Paganini," he answered. I then explained to him that "Nel cor più" was a popular aria by Giovanni Paisiello. (Zeitlin, 1995: 27)

Despite the student's prodigious technical ability, he had no grasp of "the singing element" in the piece, implicit in its adoption of an aria. Another violinist, Vadim Repin, fares little better in a review of his newly released recording of Tchaikovsky's Violin Concerto. Again the problem is a failure to "sing."

> One aches for the risks and surprises which are often eloquent of genuine musical thought. That the playing is to be tidy and fastidious but routine is apparent from the start of the Tchaikovsky. . . . What is more baneful is the feeling that the soloist has not got properly to grips with the music's inner life. There is hardly anything right about the first few moments of the Canzonetta. The theme needs to sing but Repin's extreme *sotto voce*—robs the material of its plangency. (Joseph, 1996: 750)

By using metaphors of "song" and of "life" when describing what they seek in the violin's sound, the critics identify the liveliness of singing—a distinctively human act, which has its own subjective qualities—as having the potential to be heard in an instrumental sound. That a potential songfulness is markedly offensive in its absence is evident in their intense lack of enthusiasm for mere virtuosity in the performance of these Romantic works. The critics' passion in critique could even suggest their confrontation with an existential "nothingness" in Sartre's sense (1956). An absence of "life" in "singing" is a palpable absence, an affront. Not only is a quality of *sound* perceived to be lost, but that very element which would allow the music to realize its own "inner life." The critic feels a longing for a quality that is absent. It is as if the *music itself* has been robbed of what *belongs to it,* provoking an almost moral fervor in the admonition that "singing" is the only mode in which the themes can be rightly realized. If a performer is to convey the "life" belonging to the work, he or she needs to use the right kind of "voice"—not too soft *(sotto voce)* in Tchaikovsky's style. It is the quality of sound that conveys the "life" of the theme.

This critical language suggests that music is not perceived as a "material" thing, which could be described adequately without recourse to terms applied more usually to living beings. Nor is its "life" and potential for "singing" simply a projection made by some individual whose "reality testing" leaves much to be desired. The "life" heard as belonging to a work in performance can be shared between educated critics and listeners, forming part of a discourse that is well understood. As a metaphor, the "life" of a sound (or its cognates) is common, not a private whim. Musical sound is not heard as sound alone, but as possessing a subjective quality. Two levels have already been identified at which this subjectivity may be perceived. First, it is a quality of sound, realized in performance. Second, it is something called out by the requirements of the work—the subjective potentialities of its style which, if absent, will not allow the work to "live." At neither of these levels is it the performer's state of mind or personality that is a primary concern. Subjective qualities are heard as inhering in the sounds, and belonging to them, without any necessary reference to the performer's subjective states. What, then, is the relationship between the "living" sound of a violin, if it is realized well, and the character of the one who performs? It has been seen that "Midori" is formed in her sound, as acts of manipulating timbre create the illusion of character. Her identity as a musician cannot be known apart from the sounds she makes. Not all reviewers are, however, able to make comments on the qualities of sound without making oblique references to the performer's personal character. The sound can seem quite transparently to be a communication of the performer's inner life, of some hidden quality intrinsic to her. An impressed reviewer of Miriam Fried's very successful CD of the Sibelius Violin Concerto comments, for example, on her "*full-bodied* playing of the Violin Concerto [as] the real attraction." "[I]t is *opulent* in tone, southern in its *radiant warmth*" (Conway, 1996: 833). The unexpectedness of her timbral choices for this Finnish work reveal a new aspect of the well-known theme. Does Conway hear the "opulence" and "radiant warmth" in the tone and theme alone, or is he thereby conveying his perception of Fried's gender and ethnicity? A more obvious inductive leap from sound quality to personal character is found in the review of a CD by the youthful (sixteen-year-old?) Chinese prodigy, Sarah Chang, in which she features Vaughan Williams' *The Lark Ascending,* among well-known virtuoso showpieces. Her sound—and character—is heard as having a "very special, winning innocence," eliciting an expression of hope from the reviewer that she may "preserve it forever"—like Peter Pan? (Sainati, 1996: 750).

In the reviews of Fried and Chang, the character of a work is said to have been revealed in a way that also says something of the soloists' personal character. In the earlier examples, a perceived absence of "singing" frustrated the reviewers, who heard only empty virtuosity, and a lack of "character" in performance. In these cases, a surprise in hearing something unexpected in the quality of a violinistic "voice"—and an awareness that it could have been otherwise—informs the favorable perception of personal character. *The performer's individuality is thus expressed in the moment that she becomes the vehicle for giving "character" or "life" to the work.* Her character in performance is inseparable from the sounds she makes, as appropriate to the style of the work, or even transforming its perceived limitations unexpectedly (as Fried does when she plays Sibelius with a "warm" tone). Whether the "character" conveyed in performance is any reflection of the performer's own character "outside" the work of performance is not a matter to be guessed at casually. It may be that the surprising voluptuousness or engaging innocence of these performances does not have an arbitrary relationship to the performer who has interpreted it, and it is certainly assumed by the critics that a woman's maturity or youthfulness has been conveyed by Fried and Chang on their CDs. That responses of attraction or delighted and wistful engagement are not gender-neutral in the male reviewers' response to these perceived qualities is also obvious. It can be maintained, nonetheless, that "warmth" and "innocence" are qualities perceived in sound as attributes of a strong vibrato by contrast to pure and unadorned sound production, and that they are supplemented by images of the performer as she presents herself. A reductionist account, attributing the perception of particular qualities in "singing" to projections based on images of a performer's gender, ethnicity, or age, is not justified, even when it is acknowledged that the social and commercial context of performance promotes the formation of such images.

In summary, Midori, Chang, and Fried are active, performing subjects who may readily be named as individuals, independently of their performances. These same names may, however, be used to convey the personal qualities that individuate them in performance. "Midori," "Chang," and "Fried" are *heard* in their sounds as performance identities. This interpretive identity can only exist in the way that they form sounds with interpretive nuance, and is not identical with their personalities *outside* the arena of performance—though, as has been seen above, these kinds of "Subject" may be confused. In naming the performers "Midori," "Chang," and "Fried" as having an individual character discernible in their performances, a new level of Subject appears, emerging from the interaction of performer and a text that forms part of a performance tradition. The subjective identity heard in performances is not fully contained as part of "the work" but seems to point back to the person performing it, as a reflection of their interpretive character. A further investigation of the relationship between a performing "subject" and the "subjective character" (or particular quality of singing) posited by performance traditions as appropriate to a style is thus warranted at this point.

2. A Semiotic View of Musical Subjectivity

In order to find a language for describing an area of artistic activity whose creations are neither purely material nor purely mental, it is helpful to turn to the theory of signs developed by Charles Sanders Peirce. In order to deal with a musical work in performance, "text" will be given an extended sense, as a sounding rendition of a musical score according to the dictates of a performance tradition. The fruitfulness of Peirce's semiotic philosophy can be found in the many discriminations it allows between different kinds of musical signification, but at this point, a preliminary concern is with the structure he gives to the sign itself. This structure may be illustrated by reconsidering the practical exercise of producing sound on the violin, then giving it a quality of "singing" in playing a "cantilena" style.

In a technical exercise, a performer's attention is to the movement of her body in making sound. She feels the weight of the bow in her hand and arm, becoming sensitive to its changing weight as it moves across the string. She notices the altered tension in her wrist, according to the angle of the bow on the string, and experiments with the different effects on the sound that are created by varied speed, or modified distance from the bridge. In this exercise, playing with the qualities of the sound is an end in itself, and bodily awareness is its means. Now she switches to playing the slow movement from W. A. Mozart's Violin Concerto in G Major, and her aim changes, to make the sound "sing" in a stylistically appropriate way. This modest interpretive goal is not only one approved of by modern critics; it also accords with the guidelines given by Mozart's father, Leopold, who asked in his violin treatise, "Who is not aware that singing is at all times the aim of every instrumentalist," going on to comment that "one must always approximate to nature as nearly as possible" ([1756] 1948: 101–102). If traditionally established aspirations to creating a "song-like" character are to be carried out, attention in playing can no longer be on physical movements alone. Bodily movement has to become a vehicle for creating sounds that call to mind something they do not "literally" possess, the qualities of a singing voice. In Peirce's terms, the material qualities of the sound are the sign vehicle, by which it comes to represent (to be a "representamen" or "sign"). The vocal grain it achieves is its "object," what it stands for. A third element is, however, required to account for this counter-factual relationship. Without interpretation, no material sound produced by a non-human instrument can be heard as a voice. In the third logical position there is, then, an "interpretant." It acknowledges two things: the conventions that allow a violin's sound to be heard as vocal in some contexts, and the act of recognition in a particular moment of listening. What transforms a dead, mechanical performance into a "live" one is the creation of sound as a sign — in this case, a sign for "singing" in an appropriate tone. (In the following chapters, the kinds of signs will be differentiated.)

∽

This description of the Peircean sign will be elaborated in later chapters, as more specific instances are brought up. For now, though, I return to the role of the violinist in producing these signs. If the "singing" of the cantabile melody belongs to it, as part of a stylistic tradition, the movements of the violinist's body are simply a vehicle for the production of these cultural signs. Even when a "naturalness" of sound has been most effectively achieved, taking Leopold Mozart's comment seriously, it is not a simple transference of the violinist's notion of a "singing voice" into the strings. *What counts as the "natural" character of singing is determined by performance tradition.* The violinist's body is entrained, or habituated, to produce a certain kind of sound, according to the tradition they follow. For a "modern-style" player this entails a continuous vibrato and an even tone, achieved by managing the weight of the bow. For a violinist trained to follow Leopold Mozart's instructions, less vibrato and more variation in the strength of sound might be expected ([1756] 1948: 99, no. 8). In either case, repetitive practice establishes patterns of action that allow standardized significations, such as a "natural singing tone," to be reliably reproduced. To push the point a bit further, it could be said that *a culturally determined sign (or set of signs) is imprinted in the trained body.* Just as Western

ballet dancers and actors in the Indian *Kathakali* (Schechner, 1990) or European Baroque traditions (Barnett, 1987) train their bodies in highly determined sets of actions, which have a specific emotional connotation, in-
strumentalists train their bodies to produce culturally defined expressive
characteristics. "Freedom" of self-expression, in a given performance, is constrained by the choices available in the style (to paraphrase Meyer, 1989).

3. Expressive Individuation and Uncertainty

a. Soloists as Individuated

Leopold Mozart is highly critical of the violinists of his time who sought
prematurely to become soloists without first being able to "interpret rightly
the taste of various composers, their thoughts and expressions" as part of a
unified ensemble ([1756] 1948: 216, no. 4). He reveals, in a pejorative tone,
that would-be soloists distinguished themselves by a lack of concern for
ensemble, due to an heightened interest in the indulgence of their own
"fantasy."

> But what an orchestra is like which is composed entirely of solo players,
> I leave to be answered by the composers whose music has been per-
> formed by them. Few solo players read well, because they are accus-
> tomed to *insert something of their own fantasy* at all times, and to look after
> themselves only, and but rarely after others. (ibid.: 217, no. 4)

He does, however, exempt from damnation those "great virtuosi who, be-
sides their extraordinary art in the playing of concertos, are also good orchestral violinists" (ibid.: 217, footnote). After competence in interpreting
stylistic "thoughts and expressions" has been achieved, it is expected, in this
tradition of violin performance, that a solo player will give something more
to individuate him- or herself from the rank-and-file players. How, then, is
this personal "fantasy" projected in sound? If a performer wishes something
of individual character to emerge, he or she cannot simply stand back and
say "I am giving an authentic reproduction of standardized stylistic gestures." The imperative of individuation is felt even most strongly in modern
competitions, where a soloist is seen to fail if he or she does not inject some
individuality into performance, seeming to reveal something of his or her

personality. A young competitor in the 1996 Leopold Mozart Violin Competition is, for example, criticized for being too "correct": "She had a small sound and an overly 'correct' approach—there was nothing particular to object to, but neither was there very much sign of originality or imaginative artistry" (Duchen, 1996: 519). The chairman of the jury, the Dutch violinist Herman Krebbers, explained that:

> In principle, if you go to a competition you have to show that you are a soloist. *It's a matter of personality, of charisma*—that is one of the most important things. In every competition I listen for whether there is someone who has *something to say, good or bad, with personality.* And in our music world, the *personality will win.* Always. (Duchen, 1996: 518, my italics)

In the way it is expressed here, it would be easy to imagine that "personality" is something possessed by the performer, who transmits it through the instrument in a direct act of communication. It then takes on an almost magical aura, named in many ways. Krebbers describes another candidate in the competition as having "lacked that essential *magnetism*" although he "played beautifully, with a great deal of intelligence" (Duchen, 1996: 518). He was judged to be a "marvelous concertmaster" but not a soloist. His precise lack remains frustratingly undefined.

The taint of mystery left by Krebbers around the means to a performer's artistic success is also potent for Dunsby, when he reflects that "the performer is, when all is going well . . . in the same artistic twilight as the 'inspired' composer and the 'captivated' listener." Secrets of success lie in an inarticulate domain, unnamable even by performers. The knowledge hidden in silence, Dunsby says, is called "artistry" and it is with a note of great seriousness that he pronounces a judgment that "a fear of losing it is built into the core of Western musical life" (1995: 35). That impotence which accompanies recognition of a potential for loss will be known to all performers, who cannot hold onto the "hidden knowledge" of artistry as if it were an articulate code, or a material entity. Dunsby is both shrewd and laconic in observing this fear. Performers appear to him as inherently anxious, aware of the potential for a negation of their past prowess, and constantly responsible for its maintenance, without the surety of success. Sounds of Sartrean existentialism emerge in this consciousness that the "artistry" of a performing "self" is an ephemeral notion, requiring continuous recreation in ongoing acts of performance, yet never sure. The fear of losing such a mysterious power has real poignancy when placed against a recognition of performers' responsibility towards their audiences. The means to gain an accolade of "artistry" cannot be prescribed along with technical exercises, and retaining it is placed beyond the artist's control. To perform, then, is to take a risk of losing the "artistic" self.

By elevating such an anxiety in the face of potential loss to the status of a core experience among Western performers, Dunsby is making a very strong claim about performers' tenuous hold on their artistic identities. Is his statement hyperbole? Or does it identify an intractably problematic aspect of what it is to be a musical performer in the Western tradition—or other traditions of music?

b. Musical Self-Knowledge and Formation through Signs

The nature of an anxiety about holding onto an ill-defined capacity for expressive effectiveness may be made less mysterious by looking at music as a semiotic medium. Irrespective of how the soloist him- or herself *feels* in a successful performance, the only place to look for evidence of distinctive subjective qualities is in the patterns of expressive nuance that reflect both spontaneous and calculated choices. Conversely, the only way to project those personal qualities that seem to be of an "inner" nature is to attend to shaping the material aspects of musical signs. If Peirce's anti-Cartesian view is taken, that "there is no possibility of distinguishing modes of consciousness apart from their immediate objects," it will be pointless to look for "artistry" by gazing inwards (see chapter 2). His approach to signs as the content of consciousness will, if taken seriously, warn against an introspective approach to understanding that elusive "fantasy," "personality," "magnetism," or "artistry" which distinguishes a solo player. It is just pointless to look for an "essence of artistry" apart from the forms that signs may take. A performer's self-knowledge is not a direct intuition of an observing "I," but a sense of an integrated self as emerging from tangible signs: the self-as-gesturing and the self-as-articulating structure, among other things. The "self" cannot, then, be created by a direct act of projection through the music, but can only emerge through the shaping of signs. Subjective identity in performance, however named, is not something that can be directly controlled.

An examination of what it is to prepare a moment in performance may throw some light on how elements of subjective character can emerge through the manipulation of sound. When a violinist is engaged in preparing him- or herself for a performance, having mastered the technicalities of producing the notes accurately and at a plausible tempo, what they have to work with directly is still a tangible thing: "the notes," the material aspect of the musical sign. The very act of playing with the nuances of notes can allow the violinist to discover new expressive possibilities, or nuances of emotion, in the music. As a result she may also recognize "herself" as extending her expressive range. An example will make this clear. I want to play the opening two bars of Tartini's Violin Sonata in G Minor, posthumously entitled "Dido's Lament" ("Didone Abbandonata"), and I experiment with the degree of detachment between the notes of the descending semitone (*see* Example 1.1). As a "modern" violinist, I have previously played these notes as connected, leaning strongly on the first, but then I hear that the Baroque violinist, Elizabeth Wallfisch, plays it differently, with a slight detachment between them. Played that way, the motive "feels" halting, stuttering, more uncertain in its movement. (These terms apply no less to its expressive affect.) In trying to play it this way, I discover something about the expressive possibility of the motive, and also about my own emotional capacity as the agent of its formation. Repetition of the motive with its chosen gestural

Example 1.1. Opening two bars, Violin Sonata in G Minor, "Dido's Lament", by Giuseppe Tartini.

shaping will increase the likelihood of its sounding in performance with precisely the required nuance. In informal terms, the success of a performance in conveying "individual" expression or "artistry" depends on the degree to which this gestural shape has been mastered, not only as a technical movement, but as an expressive shaping.

What it is to "understand" gesture in the latter sense can be grasped by looking at a violinist's technical formation as including an element of affective learning through the internalization of gestural patterns suitable for different musical styles. In a well-known remark, "I cry, therefore I feel sad," the psychologist, William James (1967), drew attention to the symptom or bodily expression of an emotion as the mode of its being. He might seem to have contradicted a common intuition of "sadness" as an inner state, but a consideration of further instances makes the priority of a visible "sign" over an inner state more plausible. The case of tentative motion is a good illustration. I do not know what it is to feel tentative by virtue of some direct intuitive insight, but rather by experiencing my body as carrying through its directed motion in a halting, interrupted fashion. My speaking voice can also halt and stutter. In noticing an involuntary impulse to move in this way, I realize I am nervous or inhibited. In some cases, an observation of the movement may precede awareness of an emotional state, as James' remark implies: "My movement is jerking, therefore I must be tentative in expressing my purpose." When I experiment with interrupting the motion between two melodic notes, I can in a similar way "discover" something of tentativeness. Part of the discipline of learning to perform is discovering how to produce such a state in a voluntary, controlled manner. When it is involuntary and uncontrolled, jerky, interrupted playing is merely a symptom of the performer's failure to overcome "performance nerves." Deliberately produced, the jerky motion is evidence of the performer's capacity both to evoke and to control a state of tentativeness, through manipulation of its observable signs. The performing "self" is thus formed in practice through the mastery of kinesthetic signs.

c. An Actor's Divided I as Formed over Signs

To be engaged in an act of performance that requires the exercise of highly developed skills is neither to assume a state of forgetfulness towards one's own bodily actions nor to be absorbed by consciousness of them. One of the most accomplished actors (Padmanathan Nair) in the highly disciplined Indian dramatic tradition, *Kathakali,* states that "a good actor is the one who understands the character very well, thus becoming the character itself," and goes on to emphasize that "we should not forget ourselves while acting. While acting, half of the actor is the role he does and half will be himself" (Schechner, 1990: 36). The ethnologist, Richard Schechner, interprets this remark quite simply, saying that "the half actor who 'does not forget' himself is the knower, the half who 'becomes the character itself' is the feeler" (ibid.: 37). In a vivid description of Laurence Olivier, playing the role of Othello, he illustrates how a passionate immersion in a role is not incompatible with—or even dramatically possible without—the maintenance of another level of consciousness, monitoring activity.

> How is what the elephant does [in a circus performance] different from what Laurence Olivier did when, in blackface, as Othello, raging "Down, strumpet!" he takes up the pillow to murder Desdemona? The difference is that Olivier's knowing half knows he is just acting and as such controls his gestures so that he does not injure the actress playing Desdemona. Even more, Olivier feels and does not feel rage against that actress. Olivier is absorbed in the task of "performing-the-actions-that-communicate-to-himself-and-to-his-audience-the-emotions-required." The whole bundle is necessary in order to understand this kind of acting. (ibid.: 38)

Olivier puts aside his character as a person, external to the play, when taking up the role, but he does not thereby lose his capacity to monitor the violent gestures he is enacting. The "monitoring" capacity described by Schechner is like that developed in many disciplined practices of performance—not a form of self-assessment but a dispassionate observational mode allowing control even when "passion" is being expressed. Schechner is led to describe an "I," who "stands outside observing and to some degree controlling" (ibid.: 37) as a part of the self that exists in addition to the thinking and feeling parts. He does not purport to be offering a philosophical account of consciousness, but a pragmatic set of observations about the different kinds of awareness experienced by an actor, and the account needs to be fleshed out more systematically. Taken at an intuitive level, his account is nonetheless suggestive. The seeing "I" who takes on a monitoring role, and is implicit in the act of performing, may commonly be recognized by an actor engaged in reflection, after an experience. It is known in looking back that a degree of control was enforced by the "self," even though the self who was fully engaged in the act of monitoring could not, in the process, also reflect on its own activities. The "I" (eye) at its center is blind—as Viktor Frankl put it so neatly. I *am* in an act of which I cannot be self-reflexively aware until it is over. I *am* in a moment of risk and its monitoring, as the subject of more than one level of consciousness.

d. The Anxiety of Uncontrolled Signs

An integrating "self" can be imagined as undertaking the task of monitoring events, as in Schechner's picture of the detached and self-aware "I," distinct from the thinking and feeling parts of the actor. This "self" is not, however, an empty figure, standing apart from all signified content. Rather, it is a level of self-awareness that is made possible through the control of each aspect of the performance, and which emerges into consciousness only in retrospect. It could be claimed, more broadly, that the musical "self" who is able to undertake this complex task in performance is a self who has literally been "formed" by the entrainment of his or her body/mind to the production of musical signs, and who is able to realize these signs in moments of spontaneity—where risk is ameliorated by a formed capacity for non-inhibiting control.

In the light of this discussion, it is possible to gain a new perspective on the problem raised by Dunsby (1995), of a performer experiencing anxiety about a potential loss of the "artistry" they have so carefully developed. It is impossible to generalize about the causes of anxiety, but an important one must be a fear of the potential for lost control in performance. In musical performance the potential for loss is not merely technical. There may certainly be a breakdown in manual dexterity, and the demands of technical mastery cannot be underestimated. Fearing a loss of "artistry" is, however, a less tangible fear, based on the knowledge that there may be a loss of optimal balance between the many factors that influence an expressive result. That such a fear is well-founded can be ascertained by looking at the way musical signification is formed, not as a direct projection of an "inner" state, but through the control of sound. I can control the formation of sounds as a vehicle for signification, shaping melodic "gestures" with the intention of conveying a certain expressive nuance, but I cannot ask for a state of complete certainty that by controlling the sound I will produce the precise emotional sense that I imagine. Knowing that I am unable directly to "express" some inner state "through" the music, apart from the manipulation of its micro-structural shaping, is where anxiety may appear. Signs can take on a life of their own, becoming displaced from the meaning intended for them.

Returning to the opening of Tartini's Violin Sonata in G Minor, "Dido's Lament," will illustrate this point. Whatever I may think of Dido's grievous plight at the departing Aeneas, I cannot directly project my understanding into sound. The material I have immediately at hand is an opening motive, which may be shaped as an expressive gesture. Suppose that I can form it in an acceptably authentic Baroque manner, and that, thanks to the many repetitions of practice, I am also well-attuned to my own affective and kinesthetic responses to the gesture. Now, for the performance to "work," I need to form it in such a way that it is stylistically appropriate and yet carries a conviction that comes from knowing its "feel" in the body. I cannot achieve my expressive end directly, giving utterance to a controlled and somewhat halting pathos through the violin, with magical immediacy. I can only control the production of sound, controlling my own movement with that end in mind. This is the point at which "accidents" can occur, to use Dunsby's term (1995: 35). Even small changes in timing or tone production can tip expression toward being too conventional or unconvincingly overblown. Any change in sound will influence the expressive nuance heard, even when that change is not fully intended or fails to match my conception of the movement's emotional tone. A source of anxiety is, then, found in the possibility that things can go wrong, I cannot have complete certainty in controlling the expressive outcome of action on the strings. Practice increases certainty, but never entirely eradicates doubt. Though I may produce the sounds (representata) with an expressive object in mind, I may never grasp that object as a tangible thing.

e. Performers and Critical Loss

Another way of looking at the anxieties of controlling "expression" in a semiotic medium could be found by looking again at how performers' personalities are judged through their performances. The gap between careful preparation and a sought-after accolade of "artistry" is a reality even among professional players, if evidence is taken from reviews of their performances. In a recent review of the Australian String Quartet, performing in London, a critic reminds his reader that "this quartet is acclaimed for its ensemble playing, interpretative skills and fastidious attention to detail," but he is nonetheless dissatisfied with their performance of Schubert's *Quartettsatz*. It is too precise, he suggests, too well-prepared: "even the most professional forensic exercise can sound clinical. . . . What was needed was less clean-cut surgery and more blood and guts" (Cutts, 1996: 825–826). No inadequacy is to be found in the quartet's careful preparation of stylistically appropriate shapings of gesture and phrase, yet the critic felt a lack of embodied energy. It can be presumed that their fastidious presentation gave each moment of the music a precisely controlled contour, making of it a finely honed stylistic gesture. It seems, however, that on this occasion their fervently committed attention to the music's details led to a state of over-control, repressing the energy imagined as possible by the reviewer.

A conventional performance is "boringly correct" and a Romanticized one "laughably self-indulgent." Examples of conventionality have been cited from the 1996 Leopold Mozart competition, but it was not without sufferers from the latter extreme. One competitor played "with the intensity of one possessed, producing a huge sound with a rich, ringing tone" but failed in his playing of Mozart, "the necessary subtlety of style eluding him" (Duchen, 1996: 518). In the first case, the performer's individuation has been lost, sacrificing with it the interest of the work. In the second case, "fantasy" has forgotten its bounds, and created a distortion of stylistic propriety. In both cases, current conventions for "stylistic" performance are forced upon the attention of a listener (a connoisseur of the style), who finds them too slavishly adhered to, or else flouted in a cavalier way. Similar judgments could be made of individual taste in clothing, or choices in social behavior, as more or less conformant to the pressure of a "norm." It is a social skill to know the degree of freedom permitted in different kinds of events, and it is "artistry" to know the degree of freedom permitted by a work or stylistic context, exploiting it without shyness or excess. Projecting individuality is, then, in part a consequence of knowing the domain in which freedom of choice may be exercised and monitoring its degree. It cannot be doubted that competitors in a violin competition would seek to project an individual interpretation of their prescribed works, and yet the absence of that "magnetism" sought by the chief juror suggests that none in the Leopold Mozart round of 1996 achieved a convincing balance between energetic freedom and respectful conformity. Without this balance, the critic's attention was led away from expressive content (the semiotic object) to standards of stylistic execution (interpretants).

The balance between freedom (or "fantasy") and conformance to style is a fragile one, as Dunsby points out, because the standards of performance practice are subject to changes of fashion, while perceptions of historical "authenticity" change. There is no certainty for a performer that they can grasp the skill of expressive balance as a commodity they will never lose, or which they can "sell" to any audience. What counts as "balance" in one place will change, and standards already vary strongly between interest groups. A possible source of anxiety could be found in not being able to "fix" the meaning attributed to a musical sign, because the "interpretants" are multiple, and will change. Errors of judgment about the audience's expectations of stylistic "appropriateness" afflict new and experienced performers alike. A cool critical response greeted the well-established German soloist, Anne-Sophie Mutter, when she appeared in concert at the Barbican Centre in London. Tully Potter, the reviewer, found herself "wishing, not for the first time, that [she] could get more enjoyment out of Mutter's technically secure but rather comfortable playing" and reported a "feeling that the whole recital was being given at arm's length" (T. Potter, 1996b: 829). Mutter failed to project herself, to convey an affective engagement with the music, despite her respected mastery of the violin. She apparently veered too close to the side of conventionality and correctness in rendition, to the point where her individuality seemed to suffocate—at least as far as Potter was concerned.

There seems to be little doubt that it is a hope of performers, and an expectation of reviewers, that an illusion of expressive transparency can be achieved, whereby listeners will not be distracted by thinking about violations (or over-conformance) to conventions, but instead feel the "immediacy" of an emotion that touches them. Further anecdotal support for this claim is provided in a rare comment from a young violinist about his own expressive aspirations. Making a new CD release of virtuoso works, Ioan Harea was so bold as to put himself into print in the CD booklet: "I feel my strength lies in my ability to reach out and touch people at the very core of their being"! Such a self-offering was too much for the critic, who noted that "reaching out and touching cores is exactly what he largely fails to do" (Joseph, 1996: 833). It is easy to ridicule someone making such a bald declaration of his capacity to "touch" others, but how easy is it to sustain the ridicule without it taking a reflexive turn? Can you really dismiss Harea's desire for musical intimacy as a lonely aberration that you do not share? His naiveté is embarrassing because it touches a common desire. It points at an experience recognizable to many musicians and listeners, though rarely named. Try a nervous giggle instead. Or try to define why, exactly, his desire is naive. Why is his confidence so amusingly preposterous? It is because he seems to claim a magical ability, not bestowed on lesser souls. The everyday wisdom that he so effectively insults is a knowledge that a direct communion of performer and listener is not something that can be predicted and controlled. Communication is never direct, without the mediation of musical signs, stylistically organized and interpreted. A musician can think introspectively of his or her own response to a work, and imagine the "inward resonance" he or she would like an audience member to feel, but such thoughts in no way ensure that an effect will be achieved. Intending to "touch" another is insufficient, if the means to touch them is ignored. Focusing on inner states and responses distracts attention from the musical means of expressivity, the material of the sign. This, then, is a central point of musical challenge and frustration for all performers. No matter how "deep" a musician's own response to the work he or she performs, it is not an inward-looking examination of personal emotions, but an outward-looking attention to musical nuance that will allow expressivity to be imbued in the sound. The French violinist and competition judge, Auclair, reportedly made comment on this problem when she expressed the feeling that "young people these days are too much given to 'navel-gazing' and should learn more from 'everything that has gone before'" (Chadwick, 1996: 493). It must be remembered, though, that if navel-gazing is insufficient, it is not corrected by an obsession with "technical" mastery. What is needed is a specific awareness of how music is a pattern of signs, where "inner" states find their character through the molding of audibly material form.

f. Losing and Finding the Self Once More

"The eye at its center is blind." The self cannot be formed in its own imaginary reflection. It is there in the inference of an integrating and controlling capacity, "behind" semiotic forms, but it cannot be seen self-reflexively apart from them. This would be mere sophistry if it did not bear some consequence. How, then, could this view of the self have an impact on a performer's fear? Consider first the problem of virtuosic self-consciousness— "showing off." Where is the virtuoso's "I" except in his rendition of the work? If he seeks attention to his own virtuosity, he has drawn it away from the work, as some examples in this chapter have shown. The work does not then "sing." It fails to "touch" people, and as a result, the performer's own capacities or subjective character are held in doubt. "He" can only touch people if the work does, through him. In trying to prove himself, he has failed to create a musical statement that will point to his interpretive identity. From the point of view of an observer, he does not have a musical "self" apart from its sounding form.

Consider now the rather different problem of scrupulousness and conventionality. A competitor in a violin competition is noted for "being a good girl." Her medals of stylistic correctness shine out. No lack of reverence for the expressive requirements of the work need be noted, as every possible means has been employed to create a carefully manicured rendition. What is the problem then, if not an exaggerated state of credulity before the requirements of being "correct"? If showoffs try to prove themselves, conventionalists try to preserve themselves, and in so doing play their works as if they were the "preserves" of unalterable tradition. An attempt to ensure acceptance by "getting things right" is no more successful as a means of communicating an artistic self than is a misplaced emphasis on virtuosity. Nor can it bring a work "alive." The problem here is a fear of losing credibility by taking risks, its antidote a reappraisal of how the work may gain its own identity. Where is the work, except in the performance? It does not have "life" if the performer fails to risk herself for it. Only by taking the risk of spontaneity, in playing with nuance, can a performer give the work a liveliness that will also convey her own interpretive character.

The problems of the self that are confronted by a performer may be seen as an allegory of those confronted by anyone engaged in a performative act. What is it, really, that you are losing when you take the risk of an act whose outcome is uncertain? Can you really be losing your "self" if your selfhood is formed in activity? If you are constituted in your acts, your performances, you are per-forming yourself through them. Your "self" will appear in the act. You do not yet know fully who you are, but will discover yourself in the action of taking risk, as I discover—or perform—myself in taking the risk of writing this. The cost of creating new meanings is only the risk of "losing" the self if that selfhood is imagined as a static thing.

chapter two

~

Listening Subjects and Semiotic Worlds

THE LAST CHAPTER examined the performer, as subject, acting to form
sounds as bearing signification. This chapter will focus on the subject
positions of listeners, critics, and analysts as they act in various ways to interpret those sounds, either in the particular realization of a performance, or
as potentialities of a score and style. Its task will be to explore some issues
that have arisen in current discourse about interpretation, with particular
concern for the problem of "subjectivity."

1. The Uncertainties of Musical Signification

An initial sense of the way in which judgments of subjectivity can become problematic in musical discourse may be gained by comparing the
conventions of different genres of writing. When the terms "subjective"
and "objective" are placed together as a binary opposition, little doubt need
be entertained as to which one gains more approval in academic writing. To

label an author's text "subjective" is to mark it as self-indulgent and ephemeral, more of interest in disclosing a state of the writer's psyche than in revealing an enduring aspect of the work. It indicates a stance opposite to that of a writer who elides discussion of the individual impressions made on them by a work, attending instead to its enduring attributes of structure and style. "Subjectivity" is not a desirable quality in this genre of text. It suggests a violation of boundaries imagined as marking off private selves from the shared discourse of academic prose. Implicit in the judgment against "subjectivity" is an assumption that aspects of interpretive response that draw attention to the individual subject (the one who listens and interprets) rather than to some attribute of the object (the work) can readily be expunged as of less than peripheral interest. Part of what it is to be initiated into an interpretive discipline is, indeed, to adopt procedures that are shared and can be replicated by other listeners and analysts. Merely reacting to a work or offering reports of an untutored response is no evidence of having understood what it presents.

If, on the other hand, the critic of a performance failed to give an account of the impressions made on him, substituting instead a discussion of the work's enduring properties, he would be seen as failing in his task, except in a circumstance when the work was unknown. His failure would not be described as a "lack of subjectivity," due to the pejorative marking of that term, but it might be noted by other means, as evidence of inattention, or a deficit of skill in conveying the qualities of a particular interpretation. This genre demands evidence of the critic's awareness of his own responses as "subject." It presupposes his attention to the ephemeral moments of a particular performance, whose qualities recede with time, and a willingness to risk evaluative statements about the heard qualities of sound. Membership in a speech community, such as that of the readers of the *Strad* and *Strings,* provides a vocabulary of basic metaphors, such as the violin as "voice." Assuming that the critic is part of such a community, where criteria of judgment are learned, his authority to remark on a given performance is realized only by his attentive presence for a particular, and unrepeatable, span of time. His self-reflexive awareness of how the performance "came across" on that occasion may be given a privileged place as he seeks to convey its qualities. A description of this occasion can be substituted neither by general remarks on the performer's style, as assessed by others, nor by assessments made on previous occasions. The particular moment, and the individual critic's response to it, are the substance of the report. Under these circumstances it is inevitable that attention will be drawn to the critic's own subject position, which might include stylistic preferences, but also circumstantial features such as the effects of his physical location in the performance venue—as when a critic commented on Midori's sound in the Barbican Concert Hall. Such attention to a particular place and time is no longer to be dismissed as evidence of subjectivity in its pejorative sense. The ability to take risks in assessing the affective qualities of a performance is part of what it is to offer a critical opinion, and the individual position of the critic can find a recognized place.

One of the problems to be highlighted in this contrast between two genres of writing is that of dealing with self-reference. Any analysis or criticism involves careful listening with awareness of one's own responses to the work, and an analysis of music need not be directed at a given performance in order to take account of aspects of performed interpretation as potentialities of the score, but explicit references to listening—and to a particular subject position —are much more common in journalistic writing than in academic prose. What, then, is the inhibition that prevents self-reference from appearing more explicitly in interpretive texts whose tone is intended to be formal? Why not say "I hear X as a voice?" An avoidance of the "first person" might be dismissed as a trivial inhibition, but it is not so. It stems, rather, from a concern to substantiate musical judgments by reference to features of the music that are not born merely of projection, through some personal and idiosyncratic response. A statement "I hear it like this" is implicit in most forms of analysis that are not purely mechanical, but it cannot be used to resolve any kind of dispute about alternative readings. If it were offered in this way, it would seem to point to the utterer's own listening experience as a source of final authority, without inviting investigation of the reasons for his having heard in that way. A concomitant problem is that resort to the first person, in a statement "I hear X," comes to imply a lack of certainty, bracketing the proffered aural analysis as no more than an expression of opinion, without any possibility of explanation. Statements made with the strength of a belief do not need to be marked in this way. A preference for certainty—or at least evidence of strongly grounded judgment—may, then, lead analysts to avoid reports of their listening experience, where the first-person appears textually, in order to eschew the temptations of solipsism. Mixed with this commendable concern for interpretive responsibility is, however, a less obvious fear of uncertainty. The "quest for certainty" (as John Dewey named it) can have interpreters avoiding comment on any aspect of musical content for which they cannot find an empirical foundation. Comment on such things as sound quality and its signification, or the affective connotation of a phrase, do, for example, present a greater element of risk to an interpreter who wishes to project the image of secure knowledge, because the factors informing aural judgments of this kind are not always readily accessible (even to one who is convinced of what she hears), and they cannot be specified by reference to a score. The kinds of support that can be offered for such judgments are also inherently less secure than those which might attend the analysis of such things as voice-leading. Whereas systematically ordered conventions exist, to varying degrees, for the application of theoretical systems (for example, Schenkerian theory or set theory) to given works, the habits of speech which exist in a performance community, giving intelligibility to discriminations of such things as quasi-vocal "tone" in a violin, do not follow such an obvious system. They rely more fully on the individual interpreter's having developed a sense of discretion as to when (and to what degree) the given metaphor may be applied.[1]

Once they are opened up, the problems of uncertainty readily multiply. Suppose that an analyst wishes to comment on what it is to "hear" a given passage in real time. Her judgments about the qualities that might emerge in it when performed are necessarily of a hypothetical nature, given that her analysis is offered as an interpretation of the potentialities of the work, without a particular performance in mind as the "authentic" one. Any assessments of the qualities that might emerge at different tempi can only be put forward as possible (based on attributes of rhythm, harmony, or melodic shape), not as fixed and inviolable properties of the score, and a statement of preference among the possible choices will therefore always carry a degree of self-disclosing risk. If this were not enough to discourage the conscientious scholar, addicted to certainty, and determined to justify her stance, the terms of description commonly used among performers and critics, such as references to "voice" or "gesture," may themselves come under attack as no more than "metaphors," outside of the range of terms accepted by a theoretical community as referring to objective properties of a work. Merely using these terms can come to imply an unsupported personal stance. All of these factors together reinforce a polarization of textual styles: "formal" genres of musical analysis avoid the risk of apparent uncertainty; some less elevated genres, such as journalistic criticism, accept judgments of heard qualities without the need for extensive justification; "aesthetic" writings, meanwhile, attempt to unravel the mysteries of metaphoric prose, and to interpret the affective connotations of music without reference to the analytical methods followed by theorists, the relevance of which they have come to doubt.

⌒

Inscribed in the different priorities of interpretive approaches to music is an informal distinction between reports of sensory qualities, which rely in some way on the sensitivity or feeling state of the analyst and on descriptions of conceptual orderings, taken as evidence for the application of formal knowledge. This bifurcation of sensuous recognition from conceptual interpretation may be useful in distinguishing the emphases of diverse genres, but when overextended, it represents a false dichotomy of sense and reason. On the one hand, the discrimination of sounds and their signification demands the acquisition of habits in perceiving which are themselves evidence of learning. On the other hand, an approach to analysis such as that found in Schenkerian theory, although it may seem from the outside to be purely mechanistic (and even capable of formalization in a computer language), is, from the point of view of a practitioner, a means of exploring and articulating perceptions of motion in sound, where felt differences in qualities of motion may guide decisions about the kind of structure being exemplified. In both cases, reasoning is embodied in a sensuous form, when qualities of timbre or tonal motion are heard, and retrospective thought allows the rational content of the perception to be abstracted from it. The uncertainty that is sometimes felt to afflict reports of "sensuous qualities" can never be entirely absent, even in analyses of formal stature (unless they are mathematically precise), but this is no cause for rejecting them. The converse side of this is that structured understanding is never entirely absent even in what seem to be overtly sensuous presentations, although the structure may be formed at a micro-perceptual level which cannot be directly inspected, and must be inferred through observations of descriptive metaphors whose ordering follows a non-arbitrary (even if informal) scale—as in degrees of "warmth" in a tone. In the pragmatic philosophy developed by Peirce, meanings are relational structures that emerge in active behavior, as an individual responds to some aspect of the environment (Rosenthal 1994: 27). Neither pure relational patterns nor purely sensuous data are possible, as both are mixed at every level and evident in functional differences of behavior. Instead of a polarization of sensuous qualities and formal relations of feeling and thought, "criticism" and "analysis," what is needed is a recognition of continuity between these ways of understanding. Giving credence to a continuity between comments on the sensuous and the schematic might serve to dislodge any defensive avoidance of the former, or false sense of security in the latter.

Having come this far, it is no longer obvious that one genre of writing can be judged peremptorily as promoting objectivity and another as drawing attention to the interpreting subject. Nor is it obvious that a responsiveness to the ephemera of performance is the background to critical reports alone. A self-reflexive negotiation of the relationship between something heard and learned criteria for critical analysis is demanded in the interpretation of musical events at any level. The pragmatic demand on any interpreter is, then, to be able to distinguish various moments of awareness and phases of interpretive work, so that neither the experience of listening nor the discipline of testing "what is heard" gets lost. He or she might, for example, listen without self-consciousness, attend to the listening experience itself, seek to describe the object of listening, then relate that description to knowledge of structure and style. A danger in some theorizing is that a concern for the last stage of the process overrules attention to the first, or renders it invisible as the musician-interpreter retreats from a discussion of heard qualities of whose objective status he or she is unsure. It might, for example, seem better to offer strong assertions about identifiable structures than to risk suggestions about ways of hearing which can only be pointed out for consideration, without the conviction of their being necessary, fixed, and exclusive of other interpretations. Suppose a student of analysis were to move through the sequence of moments described above. After listening to a work, she embarks upon a Schenkerian analysis; she represents that analysis graphically and describes it verbally. Another step that she could take would be to make suggestions about how the structures have an impact on the affective qualities she hears in the work. At this she balks. A lack of certainty, she reflects, comes too readily to seem like a loss of intelligibility. She fears that only proposals made with the strength of propositions about structure are capable of carrying any force, and of gaining assent from a reader. She fears, furthermore, that she might be dismissed as relying on ungrounded "intuitions," which carry no authority. Concern about a loss of certainty inhibits her in taking such risks, and her disclosure of what she has heard in the work remains limited. A frustrating split between what she knows as her listening experience and what she reports in writing remains in place.

The next section will look at why some kinds of metaphorical language have been taken as "markers of the mental." Following that, I will examine the problems of self-reference, in a dialogue with an early text by Peirce, "Questions Concerning Certain Faculties Claimed for Man" (Wiener, [1958] 1966: 15–38).

2. Intentionality and Metaphor

Given that it is not uncommon to attribute subjectivity to some kinds of description, it will be profitable to look at the arguments supporting this stance. Consider some examples of critical description, introduced in the last chapter: Kató Havas hears a violin tone as "voice" and various critics hear it as "singing"; Miriam Fried's tone is described as possessing a "full-bodied" quality, and Chang's as "innocent"; the opening of Tartini's sonata, "Dido's Lament," is a typically formed "gesture" of grief, whose nuances can be realized in various ways, influencing its precise affect. These descriptions exemplify the application to music of predicates that do not apply to material things. Instruments are not literally voices, and it would be more usual to say of a person that they spoke with a tone of warmth or innocence, or moved in a way that conveyed the pathos and passivity of grief, than it would to observe these forms of expressiveness in a material thing. Because these forms of description take terms that apply to the subjective states of human beings, observable in their voice or movement, and transfer them to the domain of sounds, they have been classified as "metaphors." Nelson Goodman takes any such transfer as defining metaphor, as distinct from literal terms, which are more "at home" in a given domain (Goodman). A further explanatory step is taken by Roger Scruton, who observes that metaphors such as those cited above identify the object of someone's interested attention, an "intentional" object, rather than an object as a material thing. In the interpretation offered by the phenomenologist, Franz Brentano, and adopted by Scruton, intentional objects must be taken necessarily as "markers of the mental," a clue to the psychological state of the one whose object of thought has been described.

It should be noted that "intention" here has a technical sense that differs slightly from its colloquial use. It refers to an involvement by a perceiver in casting something in a particular light by describing it in a certain way. The speaker's attitude may be differentiated in many ways, according to circumstance. It does not matter whether it is one of amusement or revulsion, of whimsical imagination or considered belief. All that matters is that some distinctive attitude or perspective is implied in the description of an object. When Brentano's phenomenological observations of intentionality are translated into the terms of analytical philosophy, it becomes a property of certain kinds of sentences in which a prefix, "I hope, fear, believe, desire, etc." precedes a proposition "that P" (or may be imagined by the hearer as doing so), with the result that the proposition is heard as an expression of the speaker's state of mind, rather than as asking for a judgment of its truth or falsity (Chisolm: 201). As I have noted in a previous article (Cumming, 1994a) Scruton's argument is that musical descriptions are based on a particular kind of intentional attitude in which "imagination" is the typical state of mind. A further example will clarify why he should suggest this.

Suppose I were to look at a cardboard packing box made damp by standing in the rain, and exclaim "that's rather sad-looking!" The statement would be understood as figurative. I could say the same of wilting flowers, a drooping lettuce, or even a canvas siphon for indicating wind strength, hanging limply on a highway bridge in still weather. In no case could the statement be taken as representing a false *belief* that material things have feelings. I do not attribute mentality to the objects at all, but merely comment with a common cliché on their appearance. Each bears a sufficient likeness to the flaccid limpness of a melancholy person's limbs to make the expression of "sadness" amusingly appropriate and easily intelligible (see also Davies, 1994). Because no false belief is implied, and some heightened form of attention is presumed in the choice to use language like this, Scruton suggests "imagination" as a way of characterizing the mental state involved. I have argued (Cumming,

1994a) that the range of musical descriptive terms identified by Scruton as "metaphors" is far too wide to make recourse to "imagination" a plausible strategy for explaining the states of mind of a listener or critic who uses these terms. He and others have, for example, identified the "motion" of tones as a metaphor. To carry this idea of motion as a metaphor through, much of the discourse of tonal music theory would, however, need to be placed in "scare quotes," as an indication that states of belief are not assumed by theorists, and that their statements about tonal motion are not subject to judgments of truth or falsity but created in an imaginative spirit, and to be received in the same way. This would not only fail to capture the range of attitudes, or degrees of certainty, that may be found in formal analyses, but would extend the range of "imagination" beyond what many would find plausible. An alternative strategy would be to exempt the "dead" metaphors—those that are accepted within the theoretical community as having a literal meaning—and only judge more obviously aberrant or imported terms as "metaphors." Although they would indicate the states of mind of the users, this would not, on Scruton's argument, prevent them from revealing important aspects of the music as an "intentional object."

The difficulty of carrying this proposal through is that it relies on a distinction of the literal and metaphorical taken from a "correspondence" view of language, whereby certain groups of words play the role of labels, directly attached to things in the world, and the state of mind of a person making propositions is taken as typically that of "belief." This view presumes that questions about the "truth" of a description can readily be answered, and that when someone uses language that is not true in an empirical sense, their state of mind can be characterized uniformly under a term such as "imagination." This does justice neither to the variety of ways in which language can be meaningful, nor to the corresponding diversity of mental states that accompany its use. It is, furthermore, cumbersome always to be making guesses about the mental state of a critic or analyst—their "intention"—in the name of understanding their prose. A further problem with recognizing "intentionality" in discourse as a marker of the mental is that it gives insufficient scope for relating subjective states to an intersubjectivity defined through the play of shared discourse. To hear "singing" or "expressivity" in a melodic line played by an instrument is nothing unusual, and it is problematic to suggest that when a listener uses these terms, he or she is displaying symptoms of a "mentality" that is in any sense private. Descriptions of a performance of a cantabile passage in a Romantic work as singing with a particular tone do not suggest the working of an isolated mind, indulging private associations between the violin's lower strings and a contralto voice. Although Conway conveyed a pleasure in the "full-bodied" voice projected by Fried in her performance of Sibelius, and Sainati was charmed by Chang's "innocent" tone as she played Vaughan Williams on CD, their private pleasures are informed by an understanding of the social connotations of vocal timbre, which are readily shared. The terms used correlate with those found in describing varying degrees of maturity in the voice and of differences in tone with changing levels of emotionality. They can be recognized by others, even if they do entertain suspicions that the critics were distracted by reflections on the performers' personal characters, and the common recognition intimates a shared understanding of vocal connotations in instrumental sound. If the descriptions identify an "intentional object," it is, then, a communal one. It suggests the possibility of a form of "intentionality" that is shared, the marker of a psychological attitude that links individuals rather than separating them into private worlds (Short, 1981).

An attempt to fully differentiate attitudes of belief and imagination fails, just as bifurcations of reasoned and sensuous content fail, before they yield any workable suggestions about the development of interpretive discipline. An entirely different approach will then be needed in order to address the fears of subjectivity, and frustrations of interpretive desire, that beset musicians when they attempt to convey verbally their understanding of a musical work. When I use the term "metaphor" in future chapters, I will take it that the distinction of literal from metaphorical language is established within a given community (here, the community of music theorists) and that it discriminates between different levels of description, without having any fixed correlation with belief or imagination.

3. Subjects and First-Person Authority
a. Skeptical Questions
i. Intuition
In his article, "Questions Concerning Certain Faculties Claimed for Man" (1868; CP 5.213–263), Peirce identifies seven questions concerning reference

to selves (or individual minds) as a source of authority. In the process of refuting the Cartesian view that a thinking self is a certainty behind the contents of thought, he inquires about the use of such terms as "intuition" and "introspection." Some of his observations could assist in dispelling concerns such as those felt by some students of musical interpretation, that behind certain terms of description there lurks a black hole of intuitive solipsism. Only his first few questions will be addressed here.[2]

Peirce notes of intuition that "there is no evidence we have this faculty, except that we seem to *feel* that we have it" (Wiener, [1958] 1966: 19; CP 5.214). An intuition (as used here) is a perception that seems to be "immediate," because the cognitive steps that go to make it up are inaccessible. Listening to an LP of Mischa Elman playing the opening note to the slow movement of Bach's Violin Concerto in E Major, a fine and experienced musician (Christopher Martin) found the opening sound to strike him with an immediacy he found compelling for its bare and almost ascetic "presence" (see Cumming 1996b: 135). Hearing it, he stopped the record, and played it again, then commented with great intensity on its affect, questioning "how did he *do* that? Where does the sound come from?" Doesn't it seem to "speak"—just like a voice?" Someone observing this strength of response might assume that Chris Martin possessed a faculty called "musical intuition," which gave him the ability to recognize a special affective quality in that note, without his having to go through an inductive process to arrive at it. (Certainly, the quality of being musically "intuitive" was often attributed to him.) To Martin himself, the expressive quality seemed to have presented itself as a pure immediacy of the sound. He was unable to determine introspectively how he arrived at the perception of its austerity and voice-like tone, and he was puzzled by his inability to reconstruct the manner of its creation from his knowledge of stringed instruments. Whatever longer-term experience as a musician had informed his perception in this moment, he could do no more than report it, excitedly, as a direct perception. He could not have told what (if any) prior cognitions had informed the moment itself. From his point of view, it would not, then, have been unreasonable to say that he had "just heard it." Lacking the capacity to decide by introspection alone where the perception came from, he could, if pressed for further comment, have labeled it an "intuition" of a quality, without even questioning whether "intuition" was a distinct faculty. If he ever questioned what "intuition" might be, he would, as Peirce predicted, have "felt" that he had it, without saying more about what was meant under that name.

Peirce's way of phrasing his question about the "intuitive" should now make some sense. He asks "Whether by the simple contemplation of a cognition, independently of any previous knowledge and without reasoning from signs, we are enabled rightly to judge whether that cognition has been determined by a previous cognition or whether it refers immediately to its object" (CP 5.212; Wiener, [1958] 1966: 18). This question could be rephrased in simple terms, namely, "Can we tell an intuition from other kinds of knowledge?" (Davis, 1972: 6). The question of whether it is possible to have "direct knowledge" of some quality, without going through a process of reasoning to arrive at it, is one that cannot be pursued fully here. At issue, in the discussion of musical writing (or conversation), is whether the kinds of musical perception that people feel are "intuitive" do in fact proceed from some mysterious origin which renders them inaccessible to critical scrutiny, or to intersubjective rapport. Peirce's statement of his question hints at a way of answering this. If "simple contemplation" of heard expressive qualities (in items such as Elman's sound) will not disclose anything of their mental origin, it is useless to proceed along an introspective path. The way ahead, in making these perceptions accessible to scrutiny, is instead to consider the "reasoning from signs" that could have informed them (whether the "informing" occurs in that moment or through the earlier education of perceptual faculties). When Martin has an "intuition" of "restrained speaking voice" in Elman's sound, commenting on it with an excitement that is quite intelligible to another musician, he is displaying a capacity for aural discrimination (and sensitivity to the affective nuances of sound) that is the result of extensive practice at listening to and forming "expressive" instrumental sounds. His "intuition" is an educated one, informed by prior experience. Analysis can reveal quite simply the kinds of learning that could have been involved, and which make his comment intelligible to another whose background of learning is similar. A comparison with other possible ways of performing sounds on the violin shows that this one's bare and thin quality proceeds from an absence of vibrato, with restrained volume. Its sense of "presence" comes from its extraordinary evenness, intimating the violinist's control of the sound. (It is also likely that it has been performed in a high position on a lower string, rather than on the shriller-sounding upper E of the violin, giving it a certain mellowness.) For a musician listening, a knowledge of what *might have been* in the performance of this sound is able tacitly to inform the moment of hearing it. The sound becomes the carrier of an absent fullness, known as possible if "vibrato" had been used, and this control becomes, in its turn, a marker of restraint (as when a speaker conveys intensity by lowering his or her voice). None of this reasoning need have entered self-consciously into the moment of listening, in order for it to have informed what is heard, as part of the background of a musician's "educated discriminatory capacities." Having learned how to discriminate between violin sounds, and also gained a "feel" for what is entailed in their control, a musician like Martin "hears" their qualities with seeming immediacy. Not only the vibrational quality of the sound (e.g., the amount of noise at onset, and the relative richness of its overtone series) but also its affective signification is bound up in this "hearing." What is thought of as musical intuition is, then, the learned capacity to make discriminations of sound and its signification. Although both the acoustic and the signified affective quality may seem "direct" or "immediate," that does not prevent their reconstruction as qualities that are informed by a "reasoning from signs," as the background to the discrimination. An analyst's task is both to develop acuity of listening and, retrospectively, to examine the "reasoning by signs" that informs his or her judgments of heard qualities. To the extent that this kind of reconstruction is possible, it establishes that the discrimination described by a musician, and attributed to an "intuitive" capacity, is not one that is private or inaccessible. It is part of a "play of signs" that can be shared and discussed. In the terms of Peirce's later semiotic theory, these sounding qualities are "qualisigns."

ii. Self-Consciousness

Some musicians and listeners may cherish the privacy of their own musical experience. An enjoyment of privacy—perhaps in forming personal associations while listening—is anyone's prerogative, but the downside of being too credulous about intuitions of one's own "self," including the self-as-listening, is that the supposed intuition of an interior musician self creates a focus "inward" to such an extent that the formation of that self through interactions with the world (or, for a musician, pieces of music) may somehow be forgotten or denied. In the process, the self becomes a mystery, and the self's "musicality" becomes an inscrutable endowment, as if it were an intuited source of the capacity to demonstrate musical skills, itself originary, not formed. A dialogue with Peirce's second question can help to open up the difficulties here, as ones that are not particular to musicians but "common to man." Once it has been established that "there would be no telling of an intuition if we had one" (Davis, 1972: 6), it is not unreasonable to subject some of our most cherished "intuitions" to further scrutiny. A primary one of these is indeed the intuition of the "self" as a source of judgments, reasoning, and perceptions. Peirce's purpose in attacking this notion is not to deny that a phenomenal sense of "self" may be achieved, but to drive a wedge into the illusion that the self may be known directly, without extrapolation from experience with objects in the world.[3] In questioning "whether we have an intuitive self-consciousness" (CP 5.225; Wiener, [1958] 1966: 25) he is concerned with "the recognition of my *private* self," rather than the undifferentiated transcendental "I" of Kantian epistemology (CP 5.225; Wiener, [1958] 1966: 26).[4] It can be taken as given that every perception involves a perceiver, the neutral I. In listening to any piece of music, I can remember myself as hearing it, as the subject of the perception. This kind of subjectivity does not differentiate me from any other listener. It is no more than a presumption of any perceptual act, and is not the kind of self-intuition that is of concern at the moment. What is in question is the process by which a listener may get an impression of him- or herself as an individual listening self, whose response is not the uninflected one of an abstract knower but differentiated in this moment and seemingly particular to the listener. Peirce's idea is that the perception of something as "other" is the essential precedent in anyone for a perception of him- or herself as a distinct entity with individual will. Suppose that I download some electroacoustically altered violin sounds from a web site, never having listened to music of this kind before. I might get a sense of my "self" as a listener at that moment when I confront the sounds as unfamiliar, as seeming to resist description in familiar terms. A sense of struggle with an unknown timbral quality, of finding it "other" than any sound I have heard before, alerts me to the limits of the categories I have formerly applied in explaining timbral qualities. This musical experience is an instance of Peirce's more general observation of how an awareness of "self" may be formed. A failure to encompass some experience in familiar terms, or adequately to predict it, leads to a knowledge of the "self" as one who is over-against something (or someone) in the environment. The "self" becomes apparent as one who had a will to organize things in a way known to it, that will being drawn to attention only by being resisted.

An individual musical "self" appears as having distinctive expectations, based on a particular background in style, at that moment when its expectations are violated in some way. (Leonard Meyer's seminal work, *Emotion and Meaning in Music* [1956], took up this insight as it had been suggested to him by later followers of Peirce's thought, John Dewey and George Herbert Mead; see Cumming 1991.) If this self is an induction from felt "otherness," it is not known as a pure and unmediated interiority, or as an entity having the power to impose meanings on objects that resist. Instead, it is a highly fallible self, discovered only in failures to interpret some aspect of music that resists incorporation in categories already known. This way of viewing individuated responses to music may seem highly deflationary, but it is a very effective antidote to a self-absorbed credulity before the illusion of the "self" as a source of meaning—as one who can determine the content of a musical work through reference to its own supposed "musicality." Rather than suggesting that I may effectively project my own desires onto what is presented in a musical sound (or other musical element), the confronting experience of the music as an "other," resisting classification, can only enforce a sense that I must change to accommodate the experience of listening. Having known my "self" through its denial, I come to know it as capable of change, through the evidence of acquiring new vocabulary in the process of struggle and analysis.

iii. Modes of Consciousness

Even an experience of an event as "other" could be taken as an invitation to interrogate the quality of experience, forgetful of its object. It is not to be denied for a moment that an experience of surprise or shock can be informative, imposing limits on the self and drawing it to attention, precisely as limited. It is, however, important to note that the experience only becomes intelligible by being directed towards some object—a musical sound or other event. It would be easy to assume that attempts to understand a musical experience could benefit from an inward-looking analysis of the states of mind it brings about. In this case, the drawing of attention to a sense of surprise has confirmed that assumption to a degree. It would, however, be mistaken to pursue an analysis introspectively, seeking to discern the difference between varying degrees of felt strangeness, as if they could be recognized independently of attention to the musical effects that bring them about. The danger in doing this would be to fall back on the presumption of an intuitive capacity to distinguish one's own states of consciousness, apart from their objects. Peirce poses a third question in order to forestall this mistake. He asks, in effect, whether "we have any immediate power of distinguishing different modes of consciousness" independently of making distinctions between the things of which we are conscious (CP 2.41; Wiener, [1958] 1966: 31). His answer is strongly negative. A further concomitant of Peirce's position is that states of consciousness—whether of imagination, belief, or desire—can be distinguished only by considering the object at which they are directed, not as pure feeling tones. I might, for example, indulge the conceit of saying "I am in a state of aesthetic imagination," as distinct from a state of "belief," but what it is to make such an assertion remains opaque unless I describe what my attitude is directed at. In a simplified analysis an attitude of belief might be directed towards something like a formal structure, whose derivation can be demonstrated, and an attitude of "imagination" towards affective qualities in sound. Once the objects of musical experience are described, the character of the mental states they imply does, however, become much more complex than a simple distinction of "belief" and "imagination" would suggest. Recall the case of Christopher Martin hearing Elman's opening note as ascetically restrained, yet intense. Although he would not assert a belief in the capacity of immaterial things to *feel*, in any literal way, he *does* demonstrate a belief that the sound conveys those qualities. He demonstrates, furthermore, a conviction that these qualities result from something that Elman has done in producing the sound, and that they have not been imposed by him as a listener, just because he happens to be in an imaginative frame of mind while listening. His attitude could be dismissed as naive, by one who restricts the use of "belief" to propositional sentences of a certain kind. It would not, however, be unreasonable to sustain beliefs about the way that signs function in society, and Martin's description does no more than identify a particular way that a violinist's sound may signify, so a patronizing dismissal of his description would be quite premature. An analysis of the "thought in signs" that would have been the background to the discrimination made has already shown that it draws out a pattern of difference in timbral qualities that is recognizable to others, a shared signification. Attention to the sound, not to some separable "inner" state, allows Martin to describe it as "voice-like" and "expressive yet restrained" and his impassioned conviction of its being intersubjectively intelligible is not unfounded. It is less informative, in a case like this, to become concerned about the mental state (or attitude) of a perceiver than it is to examine the object of his consciousness.

In this kind of case, quibbling over whether the mental attitude of a listener is "belief" or "imagination" (a strategy suggested by Roger Scruton for identifying the special attitude entertained by people responding to artworks) is unproductive. The attitude cannot be identified apart from its object, a sound-as-signifying (voice-like restraint). If it is accepted that *any* use of metaphor is linked with an "intentional attitude founded on imagination, not belief," as Scruton suggests, an "imaginative" attitude must be ascribed to anyone who describes a musical sound as signifying some affect. It is, however, quite possible to hold beliefs about signification, and to express them metaphorically (see Cumming, 1994a). Descriptions of a qualitative sign may be expressive of a belief about it, even if they are not made with the strength of assertion appropriate to more formalized elements. A degree of uncertainty, reflecting the less systematic patterns of timbral connotation, when compared to notated elements, does not remove the possibility of substantiating this judgment by reference to perceptible differences in harmonic spectra and other possibilities of sound production, with their capacities to create different affects. A weakened degree of "belief" may not be inappropriate as a description of the state of mind involved in making this judgment, but that does not exclude it from being "believed" at all.

iv. Introspection

After this dismissal of any intuitive capacity to distinguish states of consciousness apart from attributes of their objects, it would seem that little room remains for self-reflexive activity, in which feelings themselves might be the object of attention, or the self-as-listening come into view. This is not the case. Peirce's denial that self-knowledge is possible through introspection is made not as a denial that anyone might inspect the character of their own interaction with some object, but as a denial that introspection can reveal purely "inner" states without any signified content at all. He asks "whether we have any power of introspection, or whether our whole knowledge of the internal world is derived from the observation of external facts" (Wiener, [1958] 1966: 32; CP 5.265; see also Davis, 1972: 13). His conclusion that "the only way of investigating a psychological question is by inference from external facts" (Wiener, [1958] 1966: 33; CP 5.249), is very strongly stated, and could be read as committing him to the idea that awareness of oneself as a knowing and perceiving entity—an individuated "I"—is discovered only by repeated acts of inference. Such a strong emphasis on inferential acts can become, in common parlance, "counterintuitive." I do not often say, "That was 'strange and uncanny,' so my 'I' must be a person with rather conventional ideas of what is normal." To speak that way would suggest I did not "know" myself, but was trying to catch evidence of the "self's" existence, as if seeking myself in the elusive shadow formed by movements of thought. That kind of searching, self-discovering inference is more an exception than a common experience. More normally, I feel the strangeness and in that moment know also the affront to my "self." The two are given together, without a process of inference. The important point for a musical interpreter to take from Peirce's argument is not, however, an argument about the path to self-consciousness (inductive or not). It is, rather, that the *content* of that consciousness will be formed by thoughts about other things—musical contents of some kind. It will not be given directly as a sense of "self."

v. Signs

Peirce's central hypothesis is that "all thought is in signs" (Wiener, [1958] 1966: 34; CP 5.253, 5.265). Even experiences of music which seem to be "inner" experiences—personal and even intimate—are not unmediated by a knowledge of musical signification as something that is learned within a community, and hence shared. Musical selfhood (whether that of the performer or critical interpreter) is not, then, surrounded by irremediable boundaries, isolating the individual "self" as the origin of insight, but is formed in shared activities, which ensure modes of connection with others. Recognizing this musicianly dependence on others might be felt as a loss, if the idea of a musician as lone creator is valued, but it does have other advantages. Letting go of an attachment to the illusion of selfhood as something to be discovered as a form of pure interiority, without content, the result is a freedom from that fearful isolation which some musicians feel as they attempt to grasp this mysterious "source" of insight, or "musicality," in themselves. Reflective thought about musical signs leads not to the discovery of an inner musical self, imposing meanings on a work as a justification of its existence, but to the discovery that selfhood (even in music) is a contingent formation whose qualities derive from the signs over which it operates. If the kinds of signs that musicians work with most directly are the "qualitative" signs that emerge from work with sounds, hearing them and describing them is also an activity that takes place within a community, where modes of discrimination are learned. Critical texts which deal with these kinds of signs need be no more intrinsically "subjective" than those which deal with aspects of form. No matter what the kind of sign involved, the ability to be conscious of it is one that is learned and shared.

b. Phenomenological Tools

A skeptical approach to intuition has the positive effect of clearing space for a phenomenology in which the learned contents of experience are not excluded. To demonstrate this phenomenology, the examples of listening to violin sounds could be reconstituted as demonstrating three different modes of awareness: an attentive awareness, during listening, of a sound quality for itself; an awareness of a sound as "other," registered with a kind of shock; and an attempt to revise categories of sound or their signification, having become aware of the inadequacy of familiar ways of understanding. The first stance is an attentiveness to quality, which continues for the duration of the sound. It is unselfconscious. Although reflection on the self as the listening subject is quite possible in retrospect, a full attention to the sound precludes a deflection of thought to the self during the act of perceiving. To learn this kind of attention is a discipline, though it may at times occur spontaneously. Just as a performer in training has to learn how to focus on the sound she is actually producing, and to attend to it through time, a listener needs to learn to attend to sound, minimizing distraction. When this kind of attention is sustained in its purest form, no explicit awareness of the self will occur, but the self-as-intending, directed towards the object, is nonetheless active, and can enter into awareness at moments of broken attention, or when listening is complete. That the quality itself can be the entire object of attention, in some moments at least, and the self-as-hearing-it be kept in the background for later attention, is necessary to Peirce's conception of "quality." In an article of 1907, he reflects on an experience characterized by a pervasive feeling which lasts through time with "its own positive quality," a definite intensity (CP 1.306, 1907; see also CP 1.318, 1910). Such an experience is not limited to simple things like colors, but may extend to any quality that emerges as a sustained effect.

A second kind of awareness—that of shock, startle, or a sense of strangeness in the object of perception—brings the self-as-perceiving much more quickly into view. The musical entity perceived is now heard not just as a single quality but by comparison with some possible other. A relationship of the musical sound to a listener's expectancies and to other sounds is brought together. The sense of the sound's "otherness" might elicit a more sustained attention, drawing a listener into a state of absorption in its quality, but another possibility is that it will engender a third moment of awareness, in which an explicit knowledge of the styles of sound production (or in more complex sounds, of harmonic spectra) is brought to bear on what is heard. Modes of representing sounds through scales of warmth and coolness might, for example, be questioned as the need for other means of representing scales of difference becomes apparent.

This series of discriminations between different modes of awareness starts with a kind of listening that might seem to be most familiar as a form of phenomenology: an attentiveness to sound quality as heard, without explicit attention to questions of performance style, or other contextualizing features. Acknowledging a moment of awareness in which the sound seems immediate is not, however, a denial that the qualities perceived in it are learned within a particular "speech community" as conveying different "tones of voice." Their immediacy is apparent, as a phenomenal effect that may tempt a listener to presume his or her intuitive prowess, but it should not cloud the vision in seeing that a previously trained mode of thought has informed the moment. In the second kind of attention, noting "surprise," the relationship of feeling with its object is similarly strong, and need not invite personal ruminations on the deep psychic source of a propensity to respond to startle effects. An element of surprise can alert a listener who is familiar with a style that something unusual has occurred, and is thus informative, but it can best be elucidated by pointing back to the features of the perceived sound which mark it out from those that are more expected. The subjective state remains directly linked to attributes of the sound, as an "event" now rather than just a quality. Questioning the event involves an examination of the regularities brought to it by the listener, no matter how inchoate and unformalized they might be. Expectancies from prior experience of performances may be fallible, even as they are predictive. They are attuned to repeated patterns in an ongoing performance tradition and should be adaptively open to correction or new learning. A flexibility of adjustment is needed, then, without a fear that fallible knowledge is to be rejected as of no practical use. Elman's style, in the romantic tradition of the earlier twentieth century, is commonly re-called as having used excessive vibrato on many notes, with inappropriate "emotiveness." If he surprises by using a bare tone, he prompts a revision of the clichéd view of that style. The idea of "Romantic as excessively warm in tone" is not entirely inaccurate, and hence subjective, but it does require a finer attunement to what Elman presents. This third mode of attention draws out those repeated characteristics that form a "style" and is also adjusted to new information.

Emerging in this sequence of modes of listening is the image of an active relationship with music in which different kinds of awareness correspond to various aspects of the sound. A narrative account of events could be written out. First, I am simply aware of a feeling, without self-consciousness. I hear a sound and am attentive to its felt quality, as yet unnamed. Second, I am struck next by its "otherness" and become aware of myself as reacting to it, making comparisons with other sounds, seeking descriptive terms. Third, at this point, having begun to name what it was that I felt or noticed first, I reason about styles of tone production and their affective connotation, seeking to revise previous assumptions about the limits of possibility for a violin, or a particular tradition of its performance. I have moved, in this process, from a position of attentiveness just to the sound, to a recognition of its otherness. Analytical disengagement follows, with a self-conscious monitoring of response as the self-as-listening comes into view loaded with archaic assumptions. If these phases of awareness are then imagined as occurring not as a slow-moving sequence, but as fluctuations in states while listening, a picture emerges of what it can be like to be actively engaged. For one who is self-reflexively aware, and critically concerned with music, the temporal processes of listening itself, in which modes of attention can change, acts further to inform a considered response, where prior knowledge is brought to bear upon experience, having already been implicit in it.[5] The various modes of listening might be termed a "texture" of experience, unfolding in time.[6] Their object—the sound—is similarly textured: a complex object, the different attributes of which may be drawn out in differing modes of listening. It is a quality and also an event to be encountered; beyond that, it is an element in a style (of performance, and of composition) which loads it with traditions of signification—or perhaps it deliberately eschews a known style and provokes a reconsideration of categories.

c. Categories of Experience

In the last section, a listener's attitude has been portrayed as varying along a scale from passive receptivity to a sound's quality, through reaction to it as an event, to an attempt to rationalize expectancy. Corresponding to these various modes of attention, or thoughtful involvement, are different aspects of the sound: qualitative, eventful, and reflecting conventions of sound production. When a listener attempts to communicate the different attitudes embodied in his or her musical experience, with a sensitivity to these variegated construals of the musical object as they emerge in time, he or she may take on a variety of textual moods: a quality might be simply *presented* for contemplation; an event could be *urged* as having a compulsive effect, in its capacity to stand out from its immediate context or its style; a more considered judgment of signification could be *submitted* as authoritative, based on relevant observations of style. In sum, the interpreter might adopt a suggestive, imperative, or indicative mood (CP 8.371; Short, 1982: 305), to mark the differing degrees of uncertainty or assertoric strength appropriate to each way of responding to the sound (or other musical object). As T. L. Short puts it succinctly, "possibility is known through the passive content of experience, actuality is known through the compulsiveness of experience, and laws are known by the habits of self-control in which they are made" (Short, 1982: 301). None of these attitudes excludes the others from belonging to a given object. They, rather, pick out different moments of experience and facets of its object. If attributes of response, aspects of the object, and interpretive moods are now listed consecutively, a pattern of correlation between them begins to emerge: (1) feeling, (2) reaction, (3) rationalization;

Table 2.1. Categories		
First	**Second**	**Third**
Feeling	Reaction	Rationalisation
Quality	Event	Convention
Possibility	Actuality	Pattern or rule

(1) quality, (2) event, (3) convention; and (1) presentation of a possibility (2) pointing to an event as actual[7] (3) submission of a considered interpretation, showing the sound as reflecting an habitual pattern of performance within a certain school. (*See* Table 2.1.)

The terms listed under "first," "second," and "third" draw out aspects of the very broad set of categories which Peirce developed as foundational for his philosophy.[8] The idea of working in categories was a reaction to Kant's philosophy, which Peirce hoped to supersede, and his names for the New Set of Categories are very simple: "firstness," "secondness," and "thirdness." These terms could suggest an ordering of precedence, with aspects of firstness assuming priority. This manner of organizing the categories is not without justification, as they represent differing degrees of complexity, both in the attributes understood to belong to an object, and in the way of describing it. A brief recapitulation of their musical working-out will demonstrate how this hierarchical view of the categories could work. A felt quality might (first) be contemplated while listening, and described for another's contemplation, without any comparison being made with other sounds, or further interpretive judgment offered. It is then presented as a simple thing, without relation to others, or contextualization within a style. The sound may, on the other hand, be heard and described in its relation to other possible sounds—a dyadic relationship (second). When its manner of attaining difference from possible others is interpreted further, by reference to a performance style, the dyadic contrast between pairs of sounds is brought under the domain of a third element—a somewhat informally derived knowledge of style as habits or patterns of action, shared by a given community (third). The numbering of Peirce's categories then lines up effectively with the number of elements being brought into consideration.

Any ordering of the categories which seems to give primacy to "first-ness," and make "thirdness" an afterthought, does, even so, need to be viewed with some circumspection. One problem is that the attempt to posit an order of priority can result in the categories being given a false independence from one another. Such an explanatory step moves in the direction of reifying them, making them into distinct modes of being, rather than mutually dependent aspects of a world (or object in it) interpreted as meaningful. As the philosopher Sandra Rosenthal puts it, "the categories must be understood as analytic tools for discriminating aspects of a complex, concrete, inseparable unity, not as tools for separating distinct 'realms of being.' No category represents a content that 'is' or 'can be' apart from the others" (1986: 113).

An avoidance of any false separation between the categories is, furthermore, important if Peirce's way of dealing with the illusion of phenomenal immediacy is to be kept in perspective. A quality may seem to be immediate, although the fact that it is already interpreted is evident, most pointedly so in cases when only listeners with trained habits of discrimination (such as members of a community of string players and listeners) are capable of picking up a tonal quality as signifying a particular affect. The intermingling of interpretive activity with perceptions of quality must necessarily be recognized, even if an attention to some quality and the more self-conscious interrogation of the experience are phenomenally distinct when viewed from the point of view of one who listens and then reflects on what they have heard. Peirce tries to avoid any confusion between the phenomenal aspect of his thought and that found in continental philosophy—which isolates phenomenal qualities from any interpretive categories brought to them—by coining his own word for phenomenology, an awkward-sounding "phaneroscopy." Peirce's "phaneron" is unlike the uninterpreted, pure "phenomenon" of European phenomenology, in that it does not exclude the interpretive "meanings" that emerge from ordinary interactions with things. Instead, it reflects the meanings derived from established patterns of interaction (see Rosenthal, 1986: 105). Elman's sound quality, in the example cited, seems to be "ascetic" due to its spare volume, and the conventions for hearing an absence of vibrato as "marked" within a Romantic performance tradition where continuous vibrato is more expected.[9] Peirce's category of "firstness" embraces the "phaneron," as that which presents an (already interpreted) appearance. A concern with this kind of meaning is essential to his "science" of signs, which is designed to account for the meanings attributed to observable things, by ordinary people, without the aid of special instruments.[10]

A criticism that can be leveled against Peirce's broadly defined categories is that they embrace too many different kinds of problems under one set of headings and are hence in danger of muddling issues that should be kept separate. In general terms, it has been asked whether he confounds phenomenology with metaphysics or merely equivocates between them, sometimes emphasizing interpreted experience and sometimes the features of an independent reality (Rosenthal, 1994: 89). Translated into the terms of musical interpretation, the problem to be considered is whether an account of some musical element as signifying (and experienced as such) should be kept distinct from an account of what it is "in itself." A skeptical approach could well be taken, questioning whether "feeling, reaction, and rationalization," as experienced by the listener, do indeed correlate with "quality, event, and convention," as manifested in the work. In answer, an initial step might be to acknowledge that it is, of course, possible to separate an account of the sound-as-signifying from an account of it as an auditory vehicle, with distinctive characteristics of volume, onset noise, and spectral complexity. To distinguish the acoustic conditions for the formation of an aural quality from the name given to it when perceived is not, however, to grasp the intentional force of skeptical questions as they are usually raised. It is most likely that such questions would take the form of a doubt about the "objectivity" of a particular interpretation of the sound as signifying. It might be asked, for example: "Why should a sound that is heard and felt as 'ascetic' be accepted as *really* ascetic? Asceticism is not, after all, a set of practices or attitudes that can be held by a musical entity, or signified fully in something as rudimentary as a sound, and a 'feeling' of having heard a quality of that sort cannot establish that it belongs to the sound, rather than to the listener's projections of what he or she wants to hear." In answer to this line of questioning, it is necessary to review Peirce's understanding of the structure of a sign, and the place of interpretation within it. The roles of "feeling" or "reaction" will then become clearer in their relationship to what is heard as being signified.

Although it is possible to separate a musical sound as a "sign" from its material qualities—the vehicle of the sign (see Lidov, 1999)—it would not make any sense, on Peirce's definition, to distinguish the sign "as interpreted" from what it is "in itself." What it is for an element of music (or anything else) to be a "sign" is for it to be already interpreted, in the very moment of perception, by reference to established practices of discriminating differences and according them meaning. A sign is just a unit of meaning: something that brings to mind an idea, its "object," through the operation of an interpretive response, which may be manifested in a feeling, an action (or reaction), or reference to a conventionalized code. Interpretation is included by Peirce in his very definition of the sign, by the inclusion of a third element—the "interpretant" (see chapter 1)—which is not found in discussions by Saussure. A fondness for neologisms could well be imagined as his reason for coining this, another awkward term, but it does serve a distinctive purpose, despite its ugliness. "Interpretant," it should be noted, is *not* a pretentious substitute for "interpreter." It is that which brings a sign into connection with its object, not depending on any individual mind, or psychological attitude, for its operation. If a sound is "restrained, to the point of intimating an ascetic attitude," it is so because of patterns of difference that can be recognized by more than an individual mind. What, then, to make of "feelings" of quality and "reactions" to musical events as compulsive (or distinctively "other")? It might be objected that these look like psychological responses in interpreters—as the skeptical question above implied. If such feelings and reactions are accepted by Peirce as "interpretants," does not the problem of his admitting a psychological origin for meanings still remain? Another equivocation could be proclaimed. It does not, however, take much examination to discover that the "feeling" referred to in this context is a manifestation of trained discriminations. This was the point of earlier discussion of hearing a sound's quality as able to signify (as in the feeling of restraint in Elman's sound). Illusions of immediacy may perhaps be entertained by a listener who makes intuitive prowess a source of pride, but prior cognitions inform each moment in its felt quality. Attention to the "feeling" of a sound as evoking a certain quality is one moment in a process of interrogation, which can lead to a more fully articulated account of how the sound's place in a style allows it to create this impression. Feeling is informative about a mode of understanding that has not yet become self-conscious, but it does not have the power to create a signification that is not already "given" through a play of difference established outside a particular listener's mind. It does not, then, follow from recognizing a sign as interpreted that its signification has a source in the mental attitude of any individual listener or reflects a special endowment of intuition upon a chosen few, who are able to understand musical elements as "signs." The source of substantiation for felt qualities is not a search in any individual psyche, but reference to the scale of differences applicable to the sound.[11]

4. Regaining an Interpretive "I"

When learning to perform, part of the discipline involved is learning to attend to the sounds being produced, hearing what is given in their material and significatory qualities, rather than what is merely imagined or desired. As commented upon earlier, a similar discipline is involved in the interpretive analyses carried out by a musician-as-listener. If a musician, while playing, can discern the difference between the affective connotations of her sound and those she wishes to project, an analyst should be able to exercise the same kind of discernment while listening. With this discipline in place, interpretive writers need not sustain a position of heightened reticence in commenting about the signification of musical elements as they hear them. If the basic understandings that inform musical feelings and reactions, or judgments of signification within a style, are supplied by a community, beyond that individual, even an explicit reference to a "feeling" need not be the marker of solipsism. The "feeling," in this case, would gain its content from an attribute of the music, and not be a manifestation of some incidental association.

Musical interpretation may be understood as a process taking place in time, as does the process of performance itself. In this process, not every mental state will be of the kind just described—a feeling or other response whose object is a quality of the music. It would be simplistic to pretend that this was the case, and legalistic to rule that only states of mind which are the transparent purveyors of musical content ought to be acknowledged in interpretive texts. One detrimental effect of such a ruling—whether explicit or "understood"—is to create the illusion of dissolving the interpreting agent into the musical text (or performance), as if no individual perspectives brought by the agent to the music could influence what he or she heard as belonging to it. Another difficulty is that the equation of feeling and content, stated too strongly, creates a whitewash over the widely varying degrees of certainty that accompany judgments of "quality" (Peirce's "first-ness"). If the objects of knowledge may be distinguished along a line that includes the "possible, actual, and logically founded," the first element in this line is the least certain, and for good reason. Traditions of performance, such as that of the Classical violin from around the eighteenth century, establish a vocabulary that circulates among members and includes notions such as "voice" and "singing," or degrees of "warmth" in a vibrato, but it is not a tradition whose terms are set in stone, with strong criteria of application. A constant play of language, with gradually changing values placed on its key terms, is characteristic of any tradition extending through historical time, and codes of judgment are all the more vulnerable to change when they relate to aspects of performance rather than to notated compositional elements. When a new work deliberately extends the possibilities of a tradition, as, for example, when an electroacoustic work creates new sounds for the extended violin while retaining some connection with older metaphors such as "voice," a further source for uncertainty is introduced in knowing the degree to which an inherited term is apposite. It might be said "I hear X as a voice, but as disembodied, 'other' than a human projection, uncanny." The struggle for descriptive terms is an indication of the analyst's response to the sound as an event. Hearing a "quality" gives way to a reaction of "struggle," a recognition of the sound in its dimension of "secondness," over-against the listener. If the purpose of analytical texts is to aid others in their process of coming to grips with a work, could it not be as informative to give an account of an interpretive process in which the terms of description are fallible, incomplete, and subject to ongoing reinterpretation, as it is to make assertions of content that have a greater certainty than is possible with the given material? The interpretive agent then reappears, not as one who imposes meaning on signs, but as one who acknowledges his or her place within a shifting discourse and is not afraid of the ultimate incompleteness of any interpretive enterprise.

At this point, a repossession of Peirce's rejected "introspection" might be achieved, without leading to the fallacies he wished to avoid. Rather than being an attempt at looking "inward" to find a self as Subject without any particular qualities, the introspective side of interpretive work could be seen as a process of becoming aware of, and questioning, one's own presumptions about signs—and especially their apparent immediacies. Why does a certain quality seem "immediate" to me? Because I am so contained in the world that created it (that of a Romanticized Classical violin) that I have not even thought to question the priority given to emotionality in this world. The "self" is evident not as an empty subject, but in a set of habitual interpretive responses, previously considered self-evident. If an "I" then appears as ac-knowledgment of positionality, it is not an "I" that seeks to assert the self (or mental state) as an origin of meaning, but to open the possibility that others might "hear" sounds and styles differently, if the worlds of sound into which they have been initiated are different from one's own. This is not "mere subjectivity" but a statement of "subject position." A listening subject cannot only move through different phases while listening, and write with varying degrees of assertoric strength, she can recognize the limitations of the interpretive world within which she operates, and, opening up the way of listening available to her, allow others to respond from a position of dif-ference. Listening, then, is not only a matter of musicality, but of hearing other selves.

chapter three

~

Musical Signs

PEIRCE DEVELOPED HIS theory of signs with reference to his general
categories of thought: firstness, secondness, and thirdness. This connection has often been put aside in semiotic approaches to music, in order to
achieve greater simplicity and ease of communicating an unfamiliar mode of
thought. An awareness of the broader context of Peirce's semiotic thinking is
nonetheless useful in clearing up general problems with the very notion of
"sign" and "object," or their applicability to music. The first section of this
chapter will survey the nature of these problems. The next section will give
an exposition of Peirce's theory of signs (as described in volume 2 of the
Collected Papers), by following through a series of three sets of questions designed by Peirce. General examples will be followed by musical applications.
The chapter is intended to be introductory and accessible to those without
a previous knowledge of Peirce. Later chapters will take up more detailed
points.

1. Signs and Objects

a. What Is the Object of Musical Semiosis?

Attempts at applying semiotic ideas to problems of musical expression have often stumbled at a very early point, due to confusion about what constitutes an "object" or the relationship of a sign (representamen) to an object. The problem hinges on the nature of "reference" itself. If the word "object" is used in its ordinary, non-technical, sense, it is perfectly normal to think of the object as a concrete thing. An "object" is just an observable entity in the world.[1] In its most common uses, the word "sign" refers to an object in this sense: a thing that is absent, to which a reference is being made, in the form of a likeness, a pointer, or an arbitrary (but agreed upon) substitution. If a notion of "sign" is to be borrowed in order to address problems surrounding the interpretation of non-texted instrumental music, some alternative account of "object" will be needed. Even music that is "programmatic," or otherwise titled, does not *refer* to its object in an obvious sense, but rather *presents* it in its own form.

Consider again descriptions such as those made by the critics of violin performances, where terms for "voice" or "singing," modified in various ways, are quite common. These descriptions give a signifying capacity to violinistic sounds comparable to that of expressive tones of voice (Davies, 1994; Kivy, 1986[?]). There is, however, no physically distinct "object" to which the sound refers. When you hear "singing" in a violin's sound, the singing is *in* the sound, not somewhere else. On hearing the sounds, you hear certain properties of singing as belonging to them, whether or not you articulate that thought or make it explicit. "Singing" is not, then, an object to which you imagine they *refer* (although you might be reminded of an operatic singer), but a quality that seems to be presented in the sounds. Thoughts of "singing" or "vocality," as typically experienced in Western traditions of performance, may certainly inform listening, but they do not need to become the explicit objects of thought as you are attending to these sounds. Suppose that a particular quality of "voice" attracts your attention, one that is not captured precisely by another performer, or perhaps even by the same performer at another time (or in a different acoustic environment). A recognition of its individual quality implies that some comparison has informed

73

your listening. That comparison can, however, remain entirely tacit until a moment of critical reflection, when it becomes more articulate. On a similar basis, it would not be fair to say that "innocence" and "emotional warmth" must necessarily be made explicit as the abstract objects of a critic's thought, at the very moment when he or she hears these qualities in Chang's Vaughan Williams or Fried's Sibelius on CD. The critic may conceivably be focused on the moment, noticing the particular qualities presented by that particular performer, in the particular acoustic environment which surrounds her (or is constructed by the CD sound engineers), only later becoming aware of the terms that have informed perception. When Scruton says that "there is a kind of understanding that rests in appearance" he is trying to capture the kind of understanding that is wrapped up in a non-reflective moment of this kind, as a listener attends to the particularity of a performance, or a viewer to the aspects of a visual appearance.

~

In these cases, the semiotic "object" is that which is being picked out by the metaphoric description: the sounds heard as "innocent" or "warm." A simple linguistic experiment can demonstrate the difficulties that arise if this "object" of thought is made into a distinct entity, to be held in mind as something entirely separable from the musical elements (the representata) in which it is conveyed. Try to take the term of description and make it the object of a sentence in the form "X (the music) is expressive of Y (the quality)": "Chang's *The Lark Ascending* is expressive of 'innocence'; Fried's Sibelius of 'warmth.'" The terms "innocence" and "warmth" may be well-enough motivated by a knowledge of differing degrees of maturity or emotionality in women's voices, a sensitivity to which is relevant to hearing violin sounds (whether produced by women or men), but put the observations in this way, and they veer close to seeming like presumptive statements about the performers' states of mind or maturity. The problem occurs due to a difference between language and music in the way that they convey an object of thought. Verbal terms convey the idea of a quality of character, or a state of mind, with some degree of abstraction. "Innocence" and "warmth," as general ideas, can be realized in many different possible ways, unrestricted by one particular manifestation. They can themselves be made the objects of thought, "turned over" in the mind without limitation of concern to only one mode of expression. When musical sounds *present* such qualities, they do so within the limitations of a given moment in time and acoustic space. They do not invite a mode of attention suitable to language, one of reflective thought about the idea conveyed in an abstract term (although that need not be dogmatically excluded). Instead, they ask for a closer attention to their own phenomenology, drawing the listener into the qualities of a sign. An expressivity of "voice," or "singing," is heard as *belonging* to a sound, not as something that can be separately known in all its specificity. It may well be termed "innocent" in its purity or "warm" in its broad timbral palette, leading to subsequent reflection on why sounds have been marked in Western musical culture as conveying such qualities, but these general terms—by their very nature—cannot capture a content that is presented as particular.

The object of a musical sign is specific to its presentational form and is not captured adequately by general words for previously recognized mental states. Despite that, prior knowledge of how these states are manifested in vocal sounds is necessary to their recognition in a musical timbre. A question then arises of what role in musical signification is played by such general ideas, gleaned from participation in musical culture and society. In my application of Peirce, they will be treated as semiotic "interpretants": those ideas which allow a connection to be made between a sound and its particular inflection on "vocality" within a given musical group. The capacity of some violin sounds to convey a quasi-vocal "innocence" or "warmth," as their embedded "object," is established within a community of discourse—one which habitually links "violin" with attributes of "vocality." It is one of a range of potential "interpretants" understood by the string-playing community and realized at the moment of one listener's recognition. Saying that these ideas are "interpretants" does not make them less important or suggest that they should be dismissed as irrelevancies. The "interpretant" is as integral to the sign's functioning as is the sign-object relationship. The interdependence of sign (representamen), object, and interpretant is definitive for Peirce's "sign," which is triadic in all its forms. What the idea of "interpretant" does is to allow a very important distinction between what the sign conveys in the moment of its presentation and what constitute the preconditions of its being understood. General notions of "vocal emotionality" are not the "object" of the timbral signs that have been used as examples here. As general ideas, they do not capture what is conveyed by the sound, but rather the conditions of its being understood.

In sum, remarks on qualities of "voice" in an instrumental sound convey something of how a sound may be heard as signifying. They do not suggest that a given timbral quality *refers* to "voice" as an extra-musical object, or even that it becomes *expressive* of vocal emotionality as an idea that is entirely preconceived. The timbral quality has become a "sign" in giving rise to a mode of listening that goes beyond its reception as an acoustic fact, a case of "hearing *as.*"[2] Its "object" is that quality which is pointed at in the metaphoric description, but not fully grasped by it, or made separable from its sounding form. Its "interpretant" is formed by the general notions of expressive vocality, which allow the sign to be understood.

b. Skepticism about Absent Objects, and an Answer from Peirce

These comments on what it is for a musical sign to have an object should allow some rapprochement with the perspective taken by analytical aestheticians on the question of whether (and how) non-texted instrumental music can be said to be expressive of affective states. Aestheticians responding to a semiotic account of music have been particularly concerned with the apparent collapsing of the object into the sign. Wilson Coker's *Music and Meaning* (1972) is (with Susanne Langer's *Philosophy in a New Key,* [1942] 1982) the best-known example of a semiotic approach to aesthetic questions, and has elicited critical comments against the whole project of musical semiotics, on grounds of Coker's perceived failure to account for music's lack of "object." Ann Clark writes, for example, that "there can be no semiotics of music if by 'sign' is meant one kind of thing which stands for, and hence is read as, another kind of thing. There cannot be a semiotics of music because musical structures cannot support a semantics" (1982: 198). Monroe Beardsley (1982), like Clark, raises doubts that music can "take account of" an object. Stephen Davies adopts their views in a recent exposition of music's aesthetic problems, *Musical Meaning and Expression,* where he rejects the possibility of a semiotic theory for music with the comment that Coker's "sign and signified collapse into each other; [whereas] a successful semiotic theory should be able to maintain their distinctness" (1994: 11). The skeptical questions posed by these thinkers can be reviewed in the terms already given for the discussion of a violin's sound as signifying. "Why say that a violin's sound 'points' or 'refers' to a quality of expressive singing, when it would be very unnatural, if not impossible, for a listener to distinguish the sound from its expressivity? Isn't there only one thing to be heard, a sound-as-singing?" Implied in these questions is a further assumption: "Does not a semiotic theory suggest that music points beyond itself, with the naiveté of a reference to cuckoo calls?" Implicit also is a further concern about the role played by interpreters in understanding signs—or falsely projecting meaning onto music: "Would it not be the case that the "object" ("vocality") is created by a perceiving mind— leading into an idealist trap, where the music's content becomes dependent upon a response from a listener?"

The answers to these questions have already begun to be opened up. For a sign to have an "object," in a Peircean view, does not require "reference" to a concrete thing. It is true to say that the sound-as-signifying is heard as one thing, its "object" wrapped up in its presenting form, but the unity of a moment in perception need not imply a confusion between different attributes of the sign in reflective thought. The sound, in its potential to signify, has many attributes which a practitioner needs to be able to discriminate in order to correct for poor sound production: scratchiness, unevenness, lack of resonance through being "forced," and so on. That quality which it actually signifies, its metaphorically described "object," is an emergent property of the sound-as-heard, irreducible to any of its individual characteristics.[3] As seen in chapter 1, a performer cannot create that "object" except by attention to the medium of the sound, and any over-involvement with an idealized image of what is to emerge can actually be detrimental to its production. Recognizing signification is not, furthermore, a private act, reflecting merely psychological projections, but a realization of ways of hearing established within a speech (and performance) community (as seen in chapter 2).

⌒

This defense of a semiotic view of music against skepticism about the "object" would be incomplete, if it were not acknowledged that the applicability of Peirce's semiotic theory to music has been questioned even by some

Peirce scholars, on similar grounds to those raised by the aestheticians above. Disagreement centers this time on the limitations given by Peirce to "object" in his definitions of the sign. As Peirce tried to create a theory of signs that would cover all kinds of cases, his definitions of "sign" are inevitably inconsistent, reflecting the variety of his subject matter and the difficulty of embracing every mode of signification under one scheme. Signs include natural occurrences, like thunder, or created effects, such as a scratch on a piece of soft metal. In these cases, reference to "an object" could be read in a relatively concrete way. Thunder creates a notion of imminent rain close by, and a scratch on metal leads to a conception of the relative softness of the metallic substance (Peirce, CP 2.257). "Rain" and "soft metal" are objects in the ordinary sense, existent items in the world. Despite the concreteness of these items, it should be noted, however, that Peirce does not treat them as existent "objects" alone. Instead, he distinguishes the "immediate" object of the sign, a notional *idea* of these things, from the "dynamic" object, the existent thing or event. Note that the "immediate object" is not an uninterpreted entity, an object in the concrete sense, but an object of thought. Although not all of Peirce's definitions of the sign make this distinction clear, it is generally implicit in them. When he says, for example, that "by a *sign* I mean anything which conveys any definite notion of an object in any way, as such conveyors of thought are familiarly known to us" (CP 1.540) he points to a notional object, whose dynamic motivation is assumed.

When Peirceans reject the possibility of treating music as a subject of semiosis, they do so from a background of emphasis on empirical uses of signs, where dynamic objects are habitually assumed to be relevant. Two scholars, Justus Buchler and Douglas Greenlee, relying on a concrete idea of reference, draw attention to music as a problematic case, citing it as incapable of a semiotic interpretation due to its inability to refer to objects in the world (1966: 155; Colapietro, 1989: 3).[4] Alternative readings of Peirce that do not limit his idea of the "object" to a concrete thing have, however, been offered both by the philosopher, T. L. Short, and the anthropologist, Richard Parmentier. Short emphatically defends Peirce from the criticism that he "erred in making all signs to be 'signs *of*'—namely, of one or another object," with an observation that "Peirce did not, in fact, limit 'objects' to physical individuals" but used it for anything that could "in any manner be referred to, expressed, represented, or presented in a sign" (Short, 1992:

110–111). Peirce illustrates this expansive view in a late definition of "sign," which at first seems extraordinarily vague:

A Sign, then, is anything whatsoever—whether an Actual or a May-be or a Would-be—which affects a mind, its Interpreter, and draw that interpreter's attention to some Object (whether Actual, May-be or Would-be) which has already come within the sphere of his experience; and beside this purely selective action of a sign, it has a power of exciting the mind (whether directly by the image or the sound or indirectly) to some kind of feeling, or to effort of some kind or to thought. (1911, MS 670)

Peirce's capitalization of "an Actual or a May-be or a Would-be" in this definition is not just a piece of poetic license but signals a covert reference to his Categories, introduced in the last chapter. A "May-be" is categorically First. It is an item of possibility, something which can be imagined and thought about, but which does not necessarily exist in a concrete sense. An act of "seeing" (or "hearing") this possibility need not involve a conscious deliberative process. Some "object," such as a "vocal" violin sound, seems to present itself immediately, though interpretive activity is implicit in the perception. It is "known" as an object (in a world of musical signs) despite its metaphoric description, its apparent "intentionality." Shared habits of description (interpretants) give evidence of shared understandings, and "hearing" vocality in the instrument as a qualititative possibility need not lead any listener to fear that it is merely their own creation, a form of "intentional" projection that reveals their private mind. The object of perception is a "semiotic object," an aspect of a shared sign. An "Actual" is Second, a concrete thing, of which some new notion may be gained through its representation in a sign. Third is a "Would-be." Like a "May-be," it is something conceived as possible, but this time it is arrived at through deliberation, its characteristics conditional on the working of certain conventions: "X would be so because Y (set of conventions) is working here." Significations found in non-texted instrumental music may be taken, in accordance with this scheme, as belonging to a class whose objects are not "actual" but more of a "May-be or a Would-be." They belong, that is, to a class where both signs and their objects display more of the characteristics of Peirce's "first" and "third" categories than they do of his "second" one. Certain qualities seem to have an "immediate" content (in the phenomenological sense), though it is interpreted (firsts). Conditionally established stylistic codes (thirds) also present contents known to those familiar with the style. Possibilities of content, understood either as seeming immediacies, or as conventions, take precedence over reference to actualities which may be stated as "fact."

~

In his *Elements of Semiotics* (1999), David Lidov gives a vivid picture of what it can be of a sign to point to an object that is neither observable nor clearly defined. In Picasso's *Mother and Child*, the child points to an object that was once part of the picture, but has been removed. The figure's pointing suggests an object and gains its "point" by leading the viewer to contemplate one as possible. What that object is does not need to be further specified for the figure to be understood. It is, indeed, in the *lack* of an object that attention is drawn more fully to the sign (1999, ch. 17). Peirce accounts for this kind of active pursuance of a possible "object" in his comment (above) that signs have "a power of exciting the mind . . . to some kind of feeling, or to effort of some kind or to thought."[5] The possible "objects" of musical semiosis may also be experienced not only through the apparent "immediacy" of feeling, or the intervention of thought, but in an active response born of engagement with the music as sign. Further exploration of the kinds of semiosis that may be opened up within Peirce's scheme is needed in order for these modes of engagement to be better understood.

2. Questions and Typologies

As the principal value of a semiotic theory lies in the guidance it gives to the process of interpretation itself, the best way to get to know the theory is to look at the kinds of questions it prompts an interpreter to ask. To make this easier, I will start with a simple example of a road sign. In the Australian countryside, it is fairly common to see a black silhouette of a kangaroo (or other native species) on a diamond-shaped sign with reflective golden backing. To understand the sign, the first and most obvious question is, "What is doing the signifying here?" It is not primarily the diamond shape or the colors black and gold, which form the vehicle for the sign, but the shape of an animal standing out in black-on-gold. It is shape that signifies most forcefully and which invites further interrogation. To elaborate the questioning of this shape as a sign "in itself," it could be asked further, "is it a singular thing, a unique occurrence?" "No," is the immediate reply, "it is a replica of the same shape used everywhere in the road system to convey 'kangaroo.' It would be uneconomical for the municipal authorities to exercise greater originality than that." So this is (in Peirce's language) a token of a type, or a "replica" of a "legisign" (law-governed sign). It is neither a quality, nor a singular thing, but a token. So much being satisfied, it is possible to move from a concern with the thing "in itself" to a consideration of how it relates to its posited "object." The black silhouette conveys the idea "kangaroo" as its immediate object. How does it do so? By presenting a schematic likeness of some brute features of a kangaroo's shape (erect posture, long tail, large hind legs, small paws, ears pricked forwards). These features allow it to present "kangaroo" irrespective of whether any actual kangaroos happen to be in the area at the moment when the sign is noticed by a particular driver. An appearance held by the signifying shape, and accepted as "likeness," is thus the ground of signification, able to hold true quite apart from the position of the road sign in the countryside, or the existence of any real kangaroos. How should a driver then "take" this sign? This third line of questioning has already been anticipated and relates to its "interpretant." Does the sign represent a possibility, an invitation to contemplate kangaroos, without asserting any truth about a situation in the world where they may occur (rhemes)? Or does it point to some definite fact, which can be asserted as true (dicent)? Is it, on the other hand, to be taken as pointing to a general rule of some kind—perhaps one about kangaroos' appearances (argument)? The first question is the only one that can be answered affirmatively, although it produces a comic effect when taken alone. No particular kangaroo has to present itself in order for the road sign to convey its idea of possibility, through its own characteristic shape. It represents a "possible object," not a particular, factual occurrence. If, however, kangaroos on highway signs were no more than an invitation to bored drivers to contemplate the idea of possible kangaroos, they would be of little use. This way of "taking" the shape, as a primary signifying element, has missed its relationship to other aspects of the sign.

"Warning" signs are established conventionally in Australia with the use of the color gold, a purely stipulative meaning. Positioned on the road, they are not to be taken just as likenesses (icons) but as pointers (indices) to the general area in which an occurrence might be thought to take place. The expected behavior of drivers in the "bush" does not depend only on recognizing the kangaroo icon, and contemplating kangaroos as an abstract possibility, but on noticing the sign's position. The recurrent appearance of such signs at moments of entry into forest suggests that drivers might slow down (especially if driving at night) and thus avoid colliding with the animals. The message is "(possible) kangaroos *ahead*" not "think of a generic kangaroo now!" The sign's position indexes a location where kangaroos are known to appear, and requires a response as if the object were a fact.[6] An adaptive response to this index is energetic and asks a driver to assume a relationship with a (dynamic) Object, not as a pure possibility, but as one that might be realized as a fact in a given place. A cynical and self-conscious driver might, of course, take the sign merely as a "sign of law," with the thought that this is "yet another example of the excessive vigilance of the local council," and, as such a driver continues at speed, the sign has become for her no more than a symbolic representation of an archaic legal code. A less cynical appraisal of the sign does, however, take its complex of features, including aspects of likeness, pointing, and conventionality, as inviting some vigilance, even if ameliorated by thoughts of council excess.

a. Qualities, Singularities, Conventions

Peirce's semiotic scheme distinguishes three different kinds of questions about signs. In the first set are questions about the signifying item. An interpreter might start by seeking to identify its most salient features. The advantage of this most general level of questioning is that it allows for an interrogation of musical experience without prejudice from preconceived categories. It constitutes that primary moment when an interpreter asks, "What am I actually attending to here?" "What is it about this moment or passage that seems to give it the capacity to signify?" Rather than starting with a conception of what "ought" to be signified in the moment or work, based on prior analysis of its structural features, this first step encourages attention to the phenomenology of listening. Peirce's typology gives some general guidelines for the kinds of answers that might be forthcoming. Defining a range of possible signifiers, Peirce postulates three types, which again reflect his more general categories of thought: first is a quality, inter-

Table 3.1. **What kind of sign is this?**			
	First	**Second**	**Third**
What is the item that represents, taken alone? (Representamen)	*Qualisign* A quality, colour, timbre.	*Singular Sign* a) An individually occurring item or event; b) a token of a type.	*Legisign* A conventional representation; a type.

preted as a qualisign; second is a singular occurrence, not predicted fully by any familiar patterning of events (a singular sign, or "sinsign" for short); third is a general type, exemplified in a particular token (a legisign, with its particular "replica"). (*See* Table 3.1.)

i. Qualisigns

A quality is any item of consciousness that *seems* simple or unitary, whether it occurs in a single moment or emerges over an extended span of time. It may be an individual sound or the pervasive texture of a movement. When the quality becomes a qualitative sign (qualisign), it is heard *as* something, inviting metaphoric descriptions. The qualisign could not come to attention unless it were embodied in a musical event, or set of events that have become unified into a composite whole. Its signification *as a quality* is nonetheless worthy of attention. Describing the acoustic structures that characterize Elman's sound, the orchestration that enlivens Ravel's setting of "The Great Gate of Kiev" (from Mussorgsky's *Pictures at an Exhibition*), or the contrapuntal properties that make up the first movement of Beethoven's String Quartet in C-sharp Minor, op. 131, could not *substitute* for a recognition of "voice," of expansiveness and majesty, or of controlled restraint, as emerging qualities. All these explanations would be relevant, but not sufficient to characterize the moment. A qualitative sign has emerged when technical features are linked with further attributes. (These have been identified by Monroe Beardsley [1982] as "aesthetic" rather than "non-aesthetic" properties).

ii. Legisigns and Singular Signs (Types and Tokens)

A "singularity" is any item or event that cannot be predicted by reference to a general rule. A "singular" occurrence is, by nature, unexpected. It is informative, rather than redundantly predictable.

In actual music, it is rare that any sound would be entirely "singular," outside of the domain of a vocabulary belonging to the work or style. Context can, however, make a singular moment of an item that also displays conventional attributes. The opening chord of Bach's Sonata in G Minor for Solo Violin is a widely spaced tonic chord, a token of a chordal type whose occurrence at the opening of a movement is not unusual for a Baroque sonata. Merely to spread that chord over the four strings of an unaccompanied violin, and to sustain its top note while allowing the open-string G to continue to resonate, does, even so, make of it an event that invites attention to what is to unfold. The inadequacies of the violin in sustaining four notes together make of the chordal harmony a possibility that is realized in aural imagination and carried through with the mere suggestion of the tonic notes, both in the bass and in the melodic line. What could be "richness" of harmony (perhaps in an organ chord) becomes ephemerality and suggestiveness. An instrument that could, on the other hand, be taken as primarily suited to the unfolding of melodic lines is revealed as endowed with the potentialities of harmonic depth and contrapuntal multiplicity. The event of an opening hovers at a moment of possibility, where the further revealing of these things is sought out. The moment is "overdetermined." It allows of interpretive possibilities (of "poverty" or of "richness" in its harmony) that are not entirely compatible with one another and are yet able to be sustained at the same time. Its "eventfulness" and "singularity" lie in this very lack of closure, its setting up of a unique set of tensions, which will be resolved to some degree as the work unfolds.

A "type" is any category, capable of some degree of normalization, which may be exemplified in a particular "token." Peirce's own neologisms for this relationship of general scheme to particular realization are "legisign" and "replica." Not all types and categories need to be understood as "signs." Just as qualities become "qualisigns" and events become "sinsigns" when they are heard *as* X (described in metaphoric terms), a type becomes a "legisign" when it is heard *as* conveying a content whose description is to some degree metaphorical. A root-position tonic chord might, for example, be characterized generically as "stable." This common description of its tonal role could be taken as a "dead" metaphor, one that does no more than allude to the most common practices of tonal orientation, but it may (in Schenkerian theory) also carry further suggestions, whose connotative dimension is more marked. A background of "stability," contextualizing features deemed "disruptive" at a more local level, is not merely a technical feature of a tonal style, but impinges on the potential mood of a phrase or section in which it is exemplified. The sonorous G-minor chord that opens Bach's Sonata in G Minor for Solo Violin re-sounds at its close, creating a frame of stability around some elegiac melodic explorations. It carries a hint of monumentality, even within the restricted dimensions of a lone violin. Add to that a "pathos," predictable as a potentiality of the minor mode (when marked off from the more neutral major), and the significations of this opening phrase begin to look more complex again. The generic possibilities of a tonic chord and minor mode in a tonal style are realized in this (or any other given) context, where their sense is modified. Just as a quality requires an event in which to be embodied, a type requires an event in which to be exemplified. A qualisign emerges from the event, as a possibility that could not be fully imagined as taking any other form. A legisign is realized in the event as a conceptual possibility that has been imagined through the dictates of a style, but which remains indeterminate in its particular presentation. It may now be seen that these aspects of the sign are not mutually exclusive but complement one another.

In the contrast of the singular and conventional, carried through in this trichotomy, Peirce captures something of the distinction between "natural" and "conventional" meaning, elaborated at length by Davies (1995; see Cumming, 1997b). Most important to note is that not all items that signify do so by virtue of their relationship to formally organized, rule-governed codes. The degree of formalization found in qualities-as-signs, in singular events, or in conventional codes of reference is highly variable. Semiotic theories which emphasize language may fail to give adequate account to qualitative signs, or to singularities that cannot be reduced in their emergent effect to any combination of legisigns. In a semiotic theory derived from Peirce, Umberto Eco tends, for example, to emphasize the word "code," implying that all signs are conventional (as appropriate to language). Some care is, however, needed in using this term within the context of musical interpretation, if it is not to obscure the differing degrees of formality in signs which may be qualitative, singular, or conventional. As seen in the first chapter, the circulation of common metaphors for violin sounds (such as "voice" or "singing"), within a group of musicians such as those who read the *Strad,* does establish a pattern of shared understanding which might loosely be called a "code," but it does not add up to a formal system of reference that could be elaborated with strict rules. An element of social stipulation can be admitted, recognizing that the violin is not "naturally" and "necessarily" to be heard as "voice," but this kind of stipulation does not have the strong sense that can be attributed to, say, cadences (as degrees of closure).

b. Icons, Indices, Symbols

A second set of questions is concerned with the *ground* of a relationship between a signifying unit and its object. How do they get to be connected? Peirce's range of answers is again organized as a set of three—icon, index, and symbol. These are the most familiar of his semiotic terms, and they are commonly summarized as pointing out relationships of "likeness," "causality," and "convention." (*See* Table 3.2.)

Table 3.2. **What is the sign's relationship to its object?**

	First	**Second**	**Third**
What is the ground of signification? What connects the Sign (Representamen) and its Object?	*Icon* a) An aspect of the presentational form giving rise to: b) A putative likeness to some object (either 'naturally' or by convention).	*Index* A 'causal' or directional connection to the object, established by context.	*Symbol* A conventionally stipulated relation (as in most words), requiring knowledge of the convention for its interpretation.

i. Icons

In one place Peirce defines an "icon" in a manner that could seem exceptionally convoluted to someone familiar with the idea of "likeness." An icon is, he says, a

> sign which refers to the Object that it denotes merely by virtue of characters of its own, and which it possesses, just the same, whether any such Object actually exists or not. It is true that unless there really is such an Object, the Icon does not act as a sign; but this has nothing to do with its character as a sign. Anything whatever, be it quality, existent individual, or law, is an Icon of anything, in so far as it is *like that thing* and used as a sign of it. (CP 2.247, my italics)

Resonances of *possibility* should be heard in the first clause, where Peirce denies the need for an actual object, to which an icon is similar. An icon can denote something, in its own character, as a possibility, and do so irrespective of the actual existence of anything to which it corresponds, either in appearance, or in sound, or in any other attribute. It can have the *character* of a sign by being the stipulated "likeness" of a nonexistent thing, although (Peirce equivocates) it does not really "act as a sign" in that case.

Much difficulty in defining iconicity has been found to hinge on the multiple senses that could be given to the notion of "likeness." Eco differentiates five possibilities for a "so-called iconic sign": that it "has the *same properties* as its object"; it "is *similar* to its object"; it "is *analogous* to its object"; it "is *motivated* by its object"; or, in conflict with these, it is "*arbitrarily coded*" ([1976] 1979: 191). If this multiplicity is problematic in a general discussion of the icon, it can seem to become even more intractable when the signifying thing is an element in a piece of instrumental music. In what respect is a violin "like" a voice, a melodic figuration "like" a gesture (Lidov, 1987), or the unfolding of direction in a tonal movement "like" the will of a Subject, who provides a background of control in the chaos of surface events (Korsyn, 1988)? The senses of "like" are rather different in each case. Before becoming entrenched in answering these questions, it would, however, be helpful to review the Peircean framework within which they are here being posed. If an icon can present as its "object" a quality that does not, strictly speaking, exist, why should the degree and nature of the sign's likeness to that thing even be considered a sensible question? This is not to deny that human voices, gestures, and acts of will exist. Nor is it to deny that notions of voice, gesture, and willfulness might inform listening to selected tonal works for violin. It is merely to reinforce the view that generalized notions of things in the human world are not the "objects" of musical signs, but the "interpretants" of musical possibility, which guide recognition of a particular element as signifying. The violinistic "voice" of Elman, Chang, Fried, Midori, or anyone else is not *like* a particular voice in the world, but is understood through a generalized notion of "voice," which guides recognition of each violinistic "voice" as an exceptional (non-human) case.

The problem of how an icon can be "like" its object does not, even so, dissolve with this logical sidestepping. Nor does a reminder of the sign's triadic nature allow escape from the fact that "iconicity" can cover a wide range of different kinds of perceived content. To press the definitional question further, it might simply be re-framed with "by virtue of what do the predicates X Y Z come to be applied to the music, as interpretants?" It is, however, fruitless to seek an answer in the form of a single, common justification for applying the descriptive terms. A seemingly glib response, mimicking an argument developed by Nelson Goodman, could indeed be given in such a way that all commitment to a common criterion of iconicity is avoided: "the predicates X Y Z come to be applied to the music insofar as it is heard as giving metaphorical exemplification to selected characteristics of X Y Z." This may seem vacuous, but it does have some advantages when elaborated on a case-by-case basis. A violin displays "vocality" insofar as it exemplifies certain qualities of a human voice, including a capacity for inflected variation; a melodic figure is "gestural" insofar as it exemplifies the characteristics of direction, emphasis, and speed found in certain brief, expressive motions; a line of voice-leading is "willful" insofar as it exemplifies an apparent compulsion to continue in an established direction, despite impediments. The factors establishing iconicity are qualitative in the first case, singular in the second (although gesture may sometimes be conventionalized), and rule-governed in the third. These distinctions are the ones already established in the first phase of questioning signs. When answers to the two sets of questions are put together, they give rise to more elaborate descriptions: voice as "iconic qualisign," gesture as "iconic sinsign" (but sometimes the token of a type), "willful" voice leading as an "iconic legisign."

One more review of an example will illustrate the value of Goodmanesque circumlocution, when accounting for iconicity in particular cases. The predicate "monumental" has been applied to the quadruple-stopped tonic chords in the opening phrase of Bach's Sonata in G Minor for Solo Violin, due to their relatively large sonority for a violin, their stability, and their use as a framing device—like an architectural object with two stable legs. (The description becomes even more appropriate if applied to a performance such as that by Henryk Schering, who contributes a massiveness of sound uninhibited by the more restricted sonic possibilities of a Baroque violin.) The advantage of putting it this way is that one aspect of the music's tonal structure is identified as exemplifying a quality, "monumentality," without an overly strong statement of "likeness" being made. It would be much less convincing to say directly, "the tonal structure of this phrase *is* an icon of a monument." An aspect of monumentality can be heard in the tonic chords, without that metaphor taking over from the various others that also apply in this overdetermined and complex phrase. An identity of character "X *is* an icon of Y" is avoided by stating that "certain characteristics of Y may be heard in X." This turn of phrase retains a mode of suggesting possibility, rather than asserting fact. The G-minor tonic chord under discussion could be named in composite fashion as an "iconic legisign," one replicated in a particular context where its potential for stability is marked out as bearing the singular quality of monumentality, while the spread texture of the chord suggests a conversely ephemeral incompleteness.

ii. Indices

An icon "presents" its object, making it directly available (Ransdell). Because it has no causal connection with that object, its occurrence cannot be taken to ensure that the object is really an existing thing. It may be something entirely fictional. An index, by contrast, is a sign which, Peirce says, is "really affected by its object." The wind moves a weather vane and needs to be considered as an existent object, with particular direction, when interpreting the vane's indications (Peirce; Short 1982). An index finger "points" and invites a viewer to look actively in the direction indicated. A person says "this" book, and requires of the listener that they look at the one speaking, to see what they hold, or someone out of view says "I . . ." and their identity remains unclear until they have been observed. Non-verbal indices (examples of indexical sinsigns) suggest a factual situation, and the sense of indexical words (indexical legisigns) depends upon the pragmatic context of their use. Both require active responses of seeking out an observable state of affairs in order for their "sense" to be understood. These requirements of indexicality do not look very promising for the exploration of non-texted instrumental music, which does not "point at" anything in particular, unless the music is composed as a fanfare, overture, or prelude to a following event, and played in the appropriate context. Another example will, however, begin to suggest ways in which indexical signs may play a musical role. Peirce describes his experience of hearing an approaching train: the long-sounding whistle of the locomotive suddenly changed its pitch, shocking him out of a state of inertia as it passed by (CP 1.335, 1905). The siren caused a confrontation with this physical thing—a forcefully existent "other." The sounding warning signal was designed to promote the confrontation, compelling any hearer to move from the path of the train. Replicate that same sound on a recording and it will not lose its capacity to confront a hearer with the apparent motion of a large body, but will continue to index the direction and speed of an apparent object, without the train actually being present anymore. The sound, taken away from a real event, retains its indexing properties. Instead of requiring the response of actively seeking a dynamic object, the "cause" of the sound, it is, however, transformed into an aural icon—"approaching train." It now "presents" the train as an object of consideration, its change in tone allowing an illusion of proximity.

This pattern of embedding an index of some physical state within an icon representing that state is quite common in aural signs. Consider Peirce's further example of a shriek (CP 2), a sound that causes hearers to look immediately for the source of someone's pain or distress.[7] It "indexes" an intrusion on the body, or a confronting violation of someone's personal space and momentary expectations. At the same time it "presents" (makes an aural icon of) distress. In a pragmatic context, an understanding of the sign would be evident in someone who sought out a physical cause, but this response would cease to be relevant if the sound were merely a recording, heard in the context of a non-narrative piece involving taped sounds. The shriek would then continue to present "distress," as a possible object for contemplation, without inviting any further seeking-out of the physical cause or living subject of that distress. In both the "live" and recorded settings, an "index" to a physical state of the body (and indirectly to a confronting circumstance) may be heard within the sound, as an "icon" of distress. In less extreme circumstances of vocal production, the indexing of a physical state in a quality of voice remains evident, but ceases to be of concern in itself, as interest is focused on the affective state alone. A raised voice, for example, indexes a level of tension in the vocal chords but, except in a medical setting, would not invite inquiries about shrillness or hoarseness as the symptoms of a vocal problem. It is much more likely that a hearer would respond adaptively by taking the sound as representing anger, alarm, or commanding force, making an appropriate response to the suggested affective state. An index to physical tension becomes the substance of a further iconic sign, which presents an emotion requiring response.

All of these examples illustrate how the indexing in sound of a physical state, or change in state, can become a means of representing that state "iconically" at a more abstract level. When the train sound is removed from its physical source and replicated, it remains an iconic sign whose indexing capacities have lost their immediate purpose. A physically caused shriek can be repeated, without pain, to represent "pain" or "alarm." A shrill sound can be produced as indicative of, say, "anger," irrespective of what the "inner" state of the utterer is. These kinds of effects can be found also in the context of musical sound production, where the embedding of physical indices within icons of affectivity remains salient. A relatively "strong" sound, within a classic tradition of violin playing, may index the high degree of force used by a player; a soft and wispy sound may suggest the position of a violinist's bow—right over the fingerboard. These indices of physical creation are not, however, to be heard simply as indications of the mode of production, except in a didactic setting. When used deliberately, they retain the capacity to suggest altered affective states, even if those states are not explicitly named.[8] A certain range of sound production holds a neutral value (as a "good" sound) within a given style, and departures from it are recognizable as holding an affective purpose (compare Meyer, 1956).

The distinction between indices as symptomatic of physical states (symptoms), and as the basis for an iconic representation of those states, can also be applied more broadly to aspects of "gesture" and of melodic formations heard as "gestural." Physiological changes are accepted as part of the etiology of at least some emotions, observable not only in the altered sound of a voice, but in characteristic changes of movement and activity, as well as the flow of thought (DSM IV, 1994). Expressive "gestures," occurring in verbal interchange, may then be symptomatic of the physical changes accompanying an emotional state, but it is the emotional information they present that is of most interest to an attentive observer. If that state is seen as a visual icon, the energetic aspect may not be as immediately salient as the appearance of drooping or taut muscles, moving with varying degrees of control. An indexing of different degrees of energy, or directions of motion and degrees of pressure in movement, is embedded within the "icon" for the state, without becoming an immediate source of concern. If the state is heard as an aural icon, the energetic aspect becomes more important. When an element of music is heard as expressively "gestural," it suggests the kind of "energy" or directionality commonly linked with an expressive gesture in a person or animal, without the aid of visual cues (Davies, 1994). The direction, force, and timing of a movement (transformed into musical terms) is now the most important aspect of the "icon." It is not so much the *appearance* of the gesture that is informative, as Peter Kivy or Stephen Davies have sometimes implied, as it is the variable attributes of apparent energy and control. It is because the varying qualities of motion do not depend on a visual presentation in order to be recognized that they can be musically presented and transformed in such an effective way. A listener's means of understanding them may include a tacit "feel" for the gesture, or even an energetic response, suppressed to different degrees depending on the style. The energy and directedness of an index is not lost, though they form part of a unit which, as a whole, becomes the aural icon of a possible affective state.

The idea of an iconicity derived from the indexing of different kinds of movement could be carried even further to include aspects of movement formalized in music theories. In their most general definition, indices are context-dependent pointers. Peirce broadens their definition beyond that which is most commonly used, accepting even terms such as "who" and "which" as linguistic indices, words that require a reader actively to seek out the parts of a sentence being referred to. In accepting this extension of the term "index," he implies that the "object" of reference can sometimes be a part of grammar, without its material realization being of concern. It would not be unreasonable to compare this kind of indexical relation with the directional pointers of music, where an actively expectant response is quite appropriate (Meyer, 1956). It is not, however, necessary to introduce the notion of "indexicality" in order to find a language for the directional relations established by voice-leading, rhythm, or melodic organization, and it is more economical to retain the common language of music theory for these functions, while recognizing that they may take on a connotative dimension, becoming embedded within iconic signs. The term "connotation" here refers to a set of structural relations, containing qualities of directionality, which together suggest another interpretive dimension. Tonal voice-leading, taken to connote "willfulness," is an example already discussed under "iconicity." All that has been added here is that it depends on a prior recognition of directional relations which hold some force in promoting an active response of looking for their continuation or eventual completion (see Meyer, 1956).

iii. Symbols

How can something be a sign if it bears no likeness to what it represents and is not physically connected to it? By pure stipulation. A symbol is, most simply, a stipulated sign (Lidov, 1999). Language is the most familiar form in which stipulated signs are found, and nouns are Peirce's favorite example (CP 2.261). Explained in the most rudimentary way (without regard to language games, which change meaning with context), nouns are arbitrary terms for things. A student of a foreign language cannot escape without learning lists of them, with a relatively fixed range of meaning, though greater subtleties of contextual nuance may be acquired in time. What is important in a Peircean definition of "symbol" is that these terms hold their reference through the strength of convention alone. They differ from "shifters" (I, you) and demonstrative pronouns (this, that)—the "indices" of language which rely on pragmatic context for reference—because (Peirce believes) they are able to hold onto their meaning with relative stability, when moved around, referring to their object by pure convention, not by a situated pointing at it (CP 5.249). Both verbal indices and nouns are governed by the conventions of language, and thus belong to the general class of "legisign," but the *ground* of reference differs between them. The reference of indices or "shifters" is grounded in their time and place of use (as "here" and "there," or "this" and "that," can gain no sense without observation) but the reference of nouns is grounded in the conventional stipulation of meaning, without such dependence on observation. The difference between these types is important to grasp, because it makes sense of what can seem like an obscure and hair-splitting distinction between the "legisign" and "symbol," as manifestations of Peirce's third category. A "legisign" is "a law that is a Sign . . . usually established by men" (CP 2.246), and includes any kind of regular ("law-governed") relationship, interpreted as a sign. A "symbol" is a subcategory, embracing arbitrary terms whose reference is fixed by the conventions of language alone, without help from the observation of a practical context of use. Those parts of speech that depend on their pragmatic use as pointers are "indexical legisigns," but they are not symbols because they lack the mobility endowed on a word by a purely conventional allocation of meaning. (In summary, "all symbols are legisigns, but not all legisigns are symbols" [Parmentier, 1994: 9].)

Before moving to musical uses of "symbol," one further point of nomenclature should also be cleared up here. David Lidov notes that Peirce's use of "symbol" to characterize a common term "goes against the grain of dominant usage [which] . . . weights 'symbol' and 'symbolic' with a quasi-magical connotation" (1999, ch. 9: 64). He suggests finding less loaded labels, with "term" being adopted as the noun and "stipulated" as the adjective to replace "symbol" and "symbolic." Lidov's suggested usage will generally be adopted in this book.

The absence in music of discrete units which function like words, with single denotation, has led Davies to warn of strong disanalogies between music and language (1995). If a symbol (stipulated term), in Peirce's sense, is most typically exemplified by a noun, it would not seem to show much promise for musical adaptation. In its broad definition, the symbol is not, however, limited to exemplification in a verbal system of signs. Units with conventionally stipulated sense, requiring particular instantiation, but capable of retaining some stability of meaning through their contextual transformation, can quite easily be identified in music, or in any other art form where some conventional schemata exist. For example, a well-established cue to closure, the tonal cadence, could be seen as displaying a capacity to retain its sense, independently of context. Recognized as such by nineteenth-century composers, it commonly invited a play with its very conventionalization. A feature of Romantic style pointed out by Meyer (1989) is the awareness of many repeated patterns as structural clichés, requiring skill in obscuring them. In this period, a V–I close stands out for its conventionality, to be hidden in various ways (Meyer). Postmodern works take a different strategy, deliberately exploiting a former cause of stylistic embarrassment to great ironic effect. In a postmodern opera by the Australian composer, Andrée Greenwell, one of the characters has her speeches punctuated in the style of an eighteenth-century recitative, with frequent perfect cadences, displaced slightly from their normal rhythmic position (see Kouvaras, 1996). No matter how misplaced the cadence, in style or structural position, it announces itself as a "close." As the character is a woman obsessed with conventionality and correctness in her social arena, the cadential feature, so strongly established as a conventional marker within tonal works of the eighteenth century, has the ironic effect of both reinforcing her conventionality and undermining her credibility, through its apparently inadvertent misplacement. The cadence can thus be relocated without losing its sense, and its conventionality becomes the point of attention, with humorous and ironic effect. Such playing with displaced contextual clues is not new, having been used even in Beethoven's work (see Meyer, 1973, on "Les Adieux"). What it demonstrates is that some features of music may attain a fixed "meaning" which can be sustained even under displacement. Those conventions that display this capacity have a structural commonality with Peirce's "symbol," as a rule-governed sign whose meaning is not context-dependent but freely able to be moved.

c. Possibilities, Facts, Laws (Rhemes, Dicents, Arguments)

i. The Third Set of Questions
A third set of questions raised by Peirce is concerned with how the sign appears to an interpreter or, to put it technically, "from the point of view of an interpretant" (Ransdell, 1997). Does it represent a possibility, a way of seeing things, without asserting any truth about a situation in the world (rhemes)? Does it point to some definite fact, asserted as true (dicent)? Does it represent itself as proceeding from logical relationships (argument)? (*See* Table 3.3.) An initial distinction, between seeing the sign as a "likeness," whose object need not exist, and seeing it as a "pointer" to some external object, is captured by Peirce with a new pair of neologisms: "rheme" and "dicent."

Table 3.3. **How is the sign to be taken?**			
	First	**Second**	**Third**
How is the sign to be "taken"?	*Rheme (rhematic sign)* The sign of a quality; a possibility.	*Dicent (Dicisign)* The sign of an actual occurrence; a fact.	*Argument* The sign of a stipulated set of relations; a law.

A *Rheme* is a Sign which, for its Interpretant, is a Sign of qualitative Possibility, that is, is understood as representing such and such a kind of possible Object. Any Rheme, perhaps, will afford some information; but it is not interpreted as doing so.[9]

A *Dicent Sign* is a Sign, which, for its Interpretant, is a Sign of actual existence.

Iconic representations belong to the class of "rhemes," those signs that yield a knowledge of possibilities irrespective of whether their objects have a tangible form. By contrast, indexical relationships tend to point to actual events, with which they form a dyadic relationship. This distinction of the "possible" and "actual" does not, however, cover all ways of "taking" a sign, and Peirce's preference for threes makes it unlikely, in any case, that he would be satisfied with only two answers to the question of "how to take it?"

As a third option, signs may be taken neither as referring to an object as "possible," nor to an object as dynamically realized in the world, but to their own procedures of production. Floyd Merrell (1997) illustrates this kind of phenomenon with various well-known paradoxes: "This sentence is meaningless"; "I'm telling a lie." The only way of "taking" such a statement is as a demonstration of grammatical good form, with a semantically impossible content, and hence as a reference to the very phenomenon of grammatical formation. Peirce defines the third item on his list as an "Argument": "a Sign which, for its Interpretant, is a Sign of law" (CP 2.250–252). Someone taking a sign as a "sign of law" is aware of its relationship to a rule or convention. He or she is interested in that convention, rather than the phenomenal appearance of the sign "in itself," or its pointing to an object.

This trichotomy accounts for the different kinds of focus that can characterize attention to various kinds of signs, or the shifts of focus that can occur
when attending to a complex sign: from what it "presents" iconically, to
what it points at, to its own conventionality.

ii. Bringing the Three Sets of Questions Together
In order to understand the way in which Peirce's third set of questions relates to the earlier two sets, an initial step is to review each set of questions,
with an eye to how they line up with his categories of thought. Looking at
Table 3.4, it would be easy to assume a straight correlation between the an-

Table 3.4. **Bringing the questions together**			
	First	**Second**	**Third**
What is the item that repre- sents, taken alone? (Repre- sentamen)	*Qualisign* A quality, colour, timbre.	*Singular Sign* a) An individu- ally occurring item or event; b) a token of a type.	*Legisign* A conventional representation; a type.
What is the ground of signification? What connects the Representa- men and its Object?	*Icon* a) An aspect of the presenta- tional form giv- ing rise to: b) A putative likeness to some object (either 'naturally' or by convention).	*Index* A 'causal' or di- rectional connec- tion to the ob- ject, established by context.	*Symbol* A conventionally stipulated relation (as in most words), requiring knowl- edge of the con- vention for its interpretation.
How is the sign to be "taken"? (How does the sign look from the point of view of an interpretant?)	*Rheme (rhematic sign)* The sign of a possibility.	*Dicent (Dicisign)* The sign of an actual occurrence.	*Argument* The sign of a set of conventions.

swers to the three sets of questions. The way of "taking" a sign would then depend on the category it falls under: icons would be signs of possibility (rhemes), indices would be signs of actual occurrence (dicents), and symbols would be signs of a conventionally stipulated set of relationships. These generalizations are not incorrect, and they reflect aspects of the sign that have already been discussed. Peirce is not, however, so bound by a drive for consistency that he avoids discussing more subtle cases, where the question of how a sign is "taken" yields a more surprising result. His third set of questions is actually set up to address the possibility of "taking" a sign in a way that has not been predicted by an analysis of what it is "in itself" or in relation to its putative object (Parmentier, 1994).

Icons are the most consistent group, conforming to the generalization made above. They may be qualities, singular events, or conventionalized patterns, but they are always signs of "possibility," unable to be interpreted as presenting a "fact" or an "argument." Analyses both of how the sign's relationship to its object is grounded, and of the kind of knowledge it yields, reveal aspects of Peirce's *first* category. (*See* Table 3.5.)

The group of "indices" (or indexes) does not reveal such consistency. Consider, for example, a spontaneous cry, a singular event (sinsign) that suggests a cause, without yielding definite information about it. Or, returning to the linguistic arena, think of "shifters" (indexical legisigns), which point at a grammatical object but do not make it determinate without the aid of further observation. Although each sets up a "causal" or directional connection to something, showing that the sign is a pointer, there remains a lack of determinacy in the thing pointed at. This indefiniteness holds such examples apart from more informative indices, such as the weather cock (CP 2) which

	Qualisign (1st)	Sinsign (2nd)	Legisign (3rd)	
		Table 3.5. **Icons**		
Icon (1st) (presentational ground of sign)	#1 Colour as sign	#2 An individual diagram (or a token/replica of a type)	#5 A diagrammatic type (requiring exemplification in a token/replica)	**Rheme (1st) (sign of possibility)**

Table 3.6. **Indices**				
	Qualisign (1st)	**Sinsign (2nd)**	**Legisign (3rd)**	
Index (2nd)		#4 A weather-cock	#7 A street cry (e.g. food here!)	**Argument (3rd)**
		#3 A spontaneous cry, directing attention to an indefinite object	#6 Demonstrative pronouns, linguistic "indexicals" or "shifters"	**Dicent (2nd)** **Rheme (1st)**

Table 3.7. **Symbols**				
	Qualisign (1st)	**Sinsign (2nd)**	**Legisign (3rd)**	
Symbol (3rd)			#10 A syllogism *-Induction* (3rd) *-Deduction* (2nd) *-Hypothesis or Abduction* (1st)	**Argument (3rd)**
			#9 A proposition (stating a fact)	**Dicent (2nd)**
			#8 A noun (a type of possible object)	**Rheme (1st)**

gives a definite indication of the direction of the wind. In this respect, Peirce suggests that they show a dimension of "firstness," of unresolved possibility. Peirce's examples are tabulated in Table 3.6.

Even greater variability is to be found in the category of "symbol." (*See* Table 3.7.) If icons, the "first" category, are signs of possibility, and indices, the "second," are most typically taken as pointing to fact, it might be thought that the "third" group, "symbols" (terms), could be approached most simply as signs of conventionality, of lawfully formed signification. Observing the *ground* of their signification, in a convention, does not, however, provide an answer to how they are "taken." Despite the fact that all linguistic terms are law-governed (legisigns), and hence conventional, it is not, Peirce suggests, always their conventionality that stands out, or draws attention to itself. A noun draws attention, first and foremost, to its object—acting as if it were an icon of that thing. Taken alone, it suggests a possible kind of object, one whose possibility has yet to be made more concrete through the addition of a pointer to some given case. A proposition behaves as if it were indicating something in the world, a pointer to fact. Only an "argument" draws attention to its own mechanisms, an understanding of the conclusion requiring an appreciation of its formal relation to what came before.

A diagrammatic summary of the ten kinds of sign recognized by Peirce is provided by Parmentier (1994: 17) and adapted in Table 3.8. In this diagram, he presents clearly the possible combinations among the three trichotomies. The numbers, 1–10, are the numbers assigned by Peirce to the resulting types of sign. The more detailed examples given in previous tables fill out this general pattern.

iii. How Can Musical Signs Be "Taken"?
If the questions "is it a possibility? a fact? an or argument?" are addressed to musical signs, the most obvious answers are "yes" to the first and "no" to the following. Musical signs belong to a class of interpreted relationships, which present an object of signification, without either pointing to a defin-

Table 3.8. **Summary of Peirce's ten sign-types**

	Qualisign (First)	**Sinsign** (Second)	**Legisign** (Third)	
Symbol (Third)			#10 #9 #8	Argument (Third) Dicent (Second) Rheme (First)
Index (Second)		#4 #3	#7 #6	Dicent (Second) Rheme (First)
Icon (First)	#1	#2	#5	Rheme (First)

ite state of affairs, or making a statement about it. This way of responding to the questions is not completely satisfactory, but it does, at least, affirm the possibility of interpreting music as a signifying medium, without its having to refer to material objects, or to make abstract propositions and arguments about them. It is also consistent with Peirce's idea of "iconicity." Insofar as music presents "iconic" signs, in which different kinds of indexical relations may be embedded, it cannot do more than suggest "possibilities." No icon is able to do more than that, asserting the factual existence of what it presents. Fictive and imaginary presentations are part of the freedom enjoyed by this mode of signifying, and its very freedom ensures that signs in this mode are not taken necessarily as presenting a factual state. Two simple objections to this generalization can be considered briefly. First, it might be objected that the indexing of an action in the creation of sound, as in an aggressive "attack" on a multiply stopped violin chord, yields factual information about a mode of attack in a performance. Second, it might be objected that musical indices of direction point to further events, leading a listener actively to seek out their resolution, and a theorist to describe them as exemplifying certain procedures as facts of the style. These objections can be met by considering how aspects of indexicality become embedded within a more dominant iconic sign. The indexing of an action in performance does not normally invite questions about the facts of production, but becomes part of that sound in its capacity to present an affective connotation, perhaps one of strength, aggression, or assertiveness in the case of a violinist's quadruple stops. The very fact that attention to the physical act of creation can so easily be subsumed under an interest in the connotations of sound provides a source of further "play" for composers in some schools; for example, those working within the school of complexity represented by Brian Ferneyhough. Such composers deliberately draw attention to the performer's physical limitations by presenting a score that is so physically demanding as to be virtually impossible, leading to theatricality in performance, as well as the production of noises that are ambiguously "extraneous" to the score and an intended outcome of its extreme complexity. A foregrounding of physicality (and its limitations) as part of the point of this music is made possible, and interesting, because it is not marked in other styles, where the indexing of action is subsumed under the perception of aural iconicity.

A similar route may be taken in answer to the second objection, that indices of directionality within music may point at coming events as "facts" of a style. As suggested in the discussion of rule-governed indices (indexical legisigns), it is not informative to treat procedures such as tonal voice-leading as "signs" except when they support the formation of musical "icons," as in cases of melodic motion heard as "gesture" or voice-leading as "willfulness." The facts of directional pointing are taken up, in these cases, within the connotative (iconic) dimension, as a possibility of what the music may present.

This mode of answering the objections above could be taken as suggesting that the interpreter must assume, as his or her dominant attitude, a stance of receptivity towards the possible connotations of musical sound, patterning, or structure. It is, however, dangerous to prescribe a single kind of attitude as a dominant one that must exclude all others. Icons are typically signs of "possibility," not yielding "factual" information, and their ability to subsume the indices of material action within themselves, or to emerge from structural elements, allows them to appear in many different guises in a musical work. To understand them, it is certainly necessary that a listener not close his or her mind to the connotative dimensions of any musical element, and that a critic be prepared to deal with the uncertainty of explicating contents that cannot be stated strongly as "facts." A recognition that the domain of understanding being dealt with in musical semiosis as a whole is one that embraces "possibility" (reflecting aspects of Peirce's idea of "first-ness") should not, however, preclude a listener from assuming a number of different attitudes in response to elements of a musical work, among them a response to the materiality of sound, in the sheer facticity of its production,[10] and also an understanding of the directional forces set up by the formal attributes of the style, as an arbitrary set of conventions. Hearing a sound as "harsh," "guttural," or "imposing" presupposes a recognition of the material qualities that make it up—its mode of attack and relative volume—even if that recognition has not been subject to conscious scrutiny. Hearing a dissonance as "striving" presupposes a tacit knowledge of tonal procedures. In any instance of complex signs, where indices are embedded within an icon, it remains possible that they themselves will become the focus of interest.

If Peirce's schematism of signs, as presented above, were taken as limiting use of the word "symbol" to language, there would be little point in pursuing his third trichotomy any further. A view of music as lacking any equivalent to nouns, as units of meaning, will exclude it from participating in the various kinds of tricks that allow language to form its terms into propositions or arguments, and comments on the subtleties of Peirce's analysis of "argument" will then be of little relevance to music. If, however, it is accepted that music has the capacity to set up certain figures as relatively conventional "terms" (as suggested by Lidov, 1999) it remains relevant to ask how their conventionality is "taken" by an interpreter. In one style, the perfect cadence is simply a close, asking no special comment. In another, its conventionality is so patent as to make it the source of deliberate re-contextualization and ironic play. When conventionality itself stands out, the listener has, in Lidov's terms, become "semiotically aware," conscious of the sign as a sign, to be subject to further play. It would be a bit strange to name this kind of awareness as "taking the sign as an argument," but contexts could be found where even this description has some musical fit. In styles such as the fugue, which play systematically with formal procedures, it is not unreasonable to use the image of a formal argument to describe the manipulation of tonal and contrapuntal possibilities. A Subject, Counter-Subject, and figures within them are developed in such a way as to draw attention to their own formal possibilities and manipulations, each combination being an outcome of previously developed structural features of the themes. It is as if the music were presenting an argument, as an icon, without semantic content. The quality of "argument" emerges from its formal procedures, allowing them to be "taken" as logical in some way, though no linguistic logic is involved. To make this use of "argument," as having a quality which can be mimicked without referential content, is to depart from the limitations set by Peirce, who would never subsume a linguistic "argument" under an icon of any kind. It is nonetheless consistent with his general idea that a conventionally ordered aspect of the world (a kind of "thirdness") can be viewed as having its own emerging qualities (aspects of "firstness").

Any schematism holds the danger of coming to look like a strait-jacket, its purpose to restrict movements of thought. The sets of answers to Peirce's questions about signs, arranged so regularly in groups of three, could well yield a restrictive result like this in interpreters obsessed with classification. More productive, however, is an awareness of the provisionality and fallibility of any scheme, its purpose not so much to provide fixed categories for signs as to separate out the kinds of questions that might be asked of them or the directions that answers could take. Many issues have been left unexplored in this chapter, in the hope of making Peirce's lines of thought clear, but they will be followed up in later chapters. Among the more contentious concerns is the issue of how instrumental music, as an art form lacking "propositions," can yield a form of content that may be described as representing ideologies or carrying through a "narrative." Yet to be opened up is the question of how music's various kinds of "iconicity" may be related to categories of thought that are much more explicit in language. Also unresolved are the aesthetic questions of whether and how music signifies "emotion" and of the kind of response that might be appropriate to it. I will return more fully to these questions in chapter 7. The next three chapters will focus more closely on issues that have already been introduced: problems in the description of timbral quality (chapter 4); the boundaries of singularity and convention, especially as exemplified in melodic patterns heard as "gestural" (chapter 5); and the use of tonal theories to explicate such notions as "willfulness" but also (paradoxically) "control" (chapter 6).

chapter four

~

Naming Qualities; Hearing Signs

Qualities and Qualities-as-Signs

Every sign occurs within an interpretive frame. A quality (a "first"), however measured by objective instruments, becomes in Peirce's parlance a "qualisign" when it is interpreted as representing some "object," according to an identifiable ground of "likeness" or association. To put aside some primary forms of skepticism, a first question to ask is whether a "qualisign" can actually have a stable content, irrespective of who the interpreter is, and despite whatever differences in evaluation come from their culture or their physical positioning in relation to what they see and hear.

~

This question can best be addressed by looking at the perception of qualities themselves. Consider the case of color. Though certain sensations, like color, are held in common by all people of normal sight, the cognitive grids placed on them by language vary. The question, then, is how it can be *known* that people of different languages, or different levels of verbal facility, perceive the same thing. Supposing I ask an ethnically heterogeneous group of tourists, on an English-language tour, to name the color of the desert sky, they might be unanimous in saying "the sky is blue." I can see that they are in the same place, dazzled by the same intensely bright azure that has made some don sunglasses, with protection from ultraviolet rays. I cannot assume, however, that they discriminate turquoise, sapphire, indigo, royal, navy, "baby," or even "sky" blue as differences that they can name. Without some kind of representation in language (or an alternative medium, such as a palette of paints), I have no evidence of what it is they do or do not "see." I cannot, then, say with confidence that each one, seeing "blueness" in the sky, has noticed the differences in hue and tone available to someone with greater versatility in their use of English color names, even if I assume that their sensation of color is the same. To allow for commonality of perception between myself and the foreign group, while restricting myself to using simple names, one strategy would be to assume that each of their languages possesses a category of middling generality, with a similar range to that labeled in English "blue," within which it would be possible for them to make comparable discriminations to the one I label "bright azure."[1] By saying "blue," they show that their perception belongs to the same general category as mine, and it remains an open possibility that their language carries a nuance comparable, if not exactly equivalent, to "azure," which would allow them to name more precisely what they see.

Color is not a simple effect of light rays on the cognizant eye, in which divisions of category are universally "given." Nor, on the other hand, is it an entirely arbitrary construction, able to be organized in any way according to cultural conventions, unlimited by psycho-physiology. Without claiming a universality of perception, which would deny the possibility of training eye to see, or ear to hear, with greater perspicuity within a cultural domain, it is possible to find basic qualities that are commonly perceived—like the category "blue"—and to point at objects (the sky) as giving rise to a shared perception, even if all that is held in common between people of different backgrounds is a "surface" view, without more specific associations. Going so far does not deny the fuzzy boundaries of what is perceptually "given"—

the difficulty of drawing a line between a "sensation" that is unsusceptible to alteration and a perception that can be trained to a specific end, in the art or music schools of different cultures.[2] It does not suggest, either, that a common view of the general classes of color will infallibly lead to agreement about what aspects of a scene are worthy of further discrimination, when a particular artistic purpose is held in mind. All it suggests is that general categories can form a starting point for recognizing common perceptions.[3] Beyond this, it is not *labels* but their modification, with various metaphors, that is most useful in moving towards a point of further agreement between people on a quality or colorful "tone." If language is to be taken as a primary medium, providing evidence of what someone is able consciously to perceive (in visual or other senses), it is rather churlish to limit its use to simple names. Suppose a student lacks the English names for tones of blue, but can distinguish a blue pigment as "brighter" or "darker," "warmer" or "more cool." Seeing the work of a visual artist, mixing paint for representational use, she chooses the range most suited to represent the sky as it lightens towards its zenith and deepens in its horizon tones. Although she lacks the relevant words, her discriminations are finely nuanced, and she describes them metaphorically in a way that English speakers also may perceive. In this way, she establishes a finer level of agreement on what has been shared in the perception of a vibrant summer sky. Whatever the finer categories of "blue" used in her own culture (if she were Inuit, they would be many), she is able to communicate in English with modifying words. A lack of shared finer categories between the cultures does not, then, establish a lack of shared perceptions, even at this more discriminating level.

When working within the boundaries of a single language and culture, it makes sense to assume that a common experience is attached to color terms, despite individual differences in discriminating ability. It is a condition of understanding the language to agree on the range of games a color word (or any word) can play. No one actually has access to an idea of color other than through the categories available to them. It is nonsensical, for example, to ask whether an Australian post box is "really red," as if there were some way to name the experience of its color other than through that label. To say "the pillar box is red" in an urban Australian environment is to state a shared fact. Anyone who possesses the required vocabulary—and is not colorblind —would say the same. To imagine an unusual experience when saying "she found the red pillar box on the street corner" is also questionable, unless you wish to weave a story around the event that makes of it some special encounter. For a Subject to recognize a common object, under its normal description, does not individuate her from any other language user.

2. Disciplinary Boundaries: How Does Semiotics Relate to Psychology?

a. Boundaries of Metaphor: When Is "Seeing" "Seeing as"? (Or the Case of the Scarlet Trumpet)

When Peirce introduces "quality" (in 1894), he is engaged in a project of explaining how things are "represented" in the mind. When recent philosophers of mind (e.g., Fodor) use the term "representation," they do so as part of a similar project. A "representation" is simply the outcome of a perceptual process and may be translated into a proposition, stating fact: "The pillar box is red."[4] The interesting cases for semiotic study are, however, those where a quality is interpreted as bringing some other idea to mind, which cannot be stated as a literal property of the thing to which it is attributed. Metaphors are not only the stuff of poetry—and "pathetic" fallacies: "calm and tranquil sea," or "embracing sky." They are evidence that a quality has been transformed into a qualisign. A quality (stillness in an ocean bay) is noticed, hence "represented" in the mind. At the same time, it is seen as signifying another aspect of experience (a calm mind). The idea of "representation" now takes on a new sense, specific to signs. It is that capacity by which a sign brings its object to mind, even when that "object" is an idea conveyed through some quality perceived metaphorically as "inside" or "belonging to" the sign; in this case, a lack of turbulence. It is difficult, in this example, to identify the boundary which makes a quality of calmness in the sea into a representation of a mental state. The difficulty becomes even more evident if an attempt is made to draw any strong line between "literal" language and metaphor. The description of a "tranquil" sea contains just a hint of metaphor, but if you weaken the term only slightly, the metaphor is lost. "Calmness" can apply literally to the sea, without suggesting the tension of a metaphor, connoting a state of mind. It is just normal to describe an absence of wind and waves as a "calm." As seen here, the degree of tension between a descriptive term and its new owner can either be suppressed, to make it do service as a common ("literal") term, or highlighted to draw attention to its allusions.

The color descriptions considered above begin to cross the boundary between a term for a pure sensation, "blue," to a description of color as bringing to mind an idea borrowed from another sensory domain: a degree of warmth or coolness. The level of metaphoricity is subdued, as it is difficult to describe the relative position of a color on the spectrum without using terms which show a measurement of degrees—heat being a convenient scale. A slightly more pronounced leaping of perceptual domains is found in synaesthesia, when a sound becomes a color, or a color a sound. "Is scarlet like a trumpet sound?" asked the blind man. "Yes," says Peirce, and the comparison is sufficiently intelligible to him, who never met the blind man concerned, to suggest that the analogy of trumpet sounds and "scarlet" has a groundedness which makes it open to others' perception too. The most obvious "ground" of iconicity is found by comparing the relative position of "trumpet sound" and "scarlet" on scales of brightness in the musical and visual domains. It is presumably because of this likeness that the blind man has been able to deduce a connection between them, which a person free of visual handicap may grasp spontaneously as answering to his or her own more direct experience. Peirce, however, hazards a guess that their iconicity may have even stronger grounds.

> For everybody who has acquired the degree of susceptibility which is requisite in the more delicate branches of reasoning—those kinds of reasoning which our Scotch psychologist [Thomas Reid] would have labelled "*Intuitions*" with a strong suspicion that they were delusions—will recognise at once so decided a likeness between a luminous and extremely chromatic scarlet, like that of the iodide of mercury as commonly sold under the name of scarlet [and the blare of a trumpet] that I would almost hazard a guess that the form of the chemical oscillations set up by this color in the observer will be found to resemble that of the acoustical waves of the trumpet's blare. I am only deterred from doing so by its being apparently true that our sense of hearing is entirely analytic;

so that we are totally deaf to the wave of sound as it exists, and only hear the harmonic components regardless of the phases at which vibrations of commensurable lengths are combined. (CP 1.312, 1910)

Peirce explains his reticence in carrying through his analogy of visual and auditory wave organization, as a ground for iconicity, by saying that hearing the trumpet's sound color is "analytic."[5] In so doing, he highlights the problem of finding a boundary between "uninterpreted" perceptions and consciously formed signs. The trumpet-as-scarlet seems to be "analytic." I do not need to go through a clumsy process of induction in order to hear "scarlet" in the sound, and I certainly do not have access to the processes by which the overtones within the trumpet's blare combine to form this characteristic timbre. All I know is that it *seems* to be "scarlet." That is just the way it presents itself. I cannot directly compare the perceptual processes that go to make up "scarlet" from those that create a trumpet's characteristic sound. If a skeptical view were taken, the trumpet's "scarlet" might be seen as little more than a substitute for "very bright," a perception that is automatic, involuntary, and unsusceptible to conscious alteration. With less skepticism, "scarlet" could be recognized as picking out the quality of the trumpet's sound more precisely (and poetically) than "brightness." Even so, the problem remains that the perception is "analytic." Peirce reveals a conflict between his desire to recognize this very persuasive case of sounding iconicity, and his theoretical view that the *grounds* of an iconic association ought to be consciously recognized. Two difficulties are actually implied in this conflict. The first problem relates to the justification or grounding of iconicity. Because the perceptual integration of elements in a sound does not reveal itself to introspection (he could have said the same of a color), Peirce finds it problematic to assume that the *ground* of iconicity between a sound and color is a similarity in the perceptual processes they engender. If a perception of sound quality is very close to an uninterpreted sensation, whose elements cannot be inspected or manipulated in any way—even for signifying purposes—any reference to the perceptual hierarchy in explaining the sign must remain speculative. An obvious line of response would be to look at the relative places of color and sound on their spectra, without making any references to the unconscious mind. The second, and more intractable, problem is in maintaining the referential "tension" of a sign. If the sound just *is* scarlet, it is not a sign. Peirce does not write often with reference to the idea of metaphor, but it is useful in explaining this point. To say that the trumpet is *metaphorically* scarlet requires that some tension be maintained between the sound and its description as a color. Here that tension is still rather weak. Some form of spectrum is needed to describe degrees of qualitative difference in a sound, and color seems an obvious spectrum to use, without necessarily implying that "color" stands out in the sound. It *is* nonetheless observable that less specific alternatives (such as "very bright" and "strident") could be found, and the naming of a specific color rather than of the degree of some general property (brightness) seems to highlight the metaphoricity. If the point of view of a listener, in the moment of listening, is assumed, the trumpet's sound might just seem as "scarlet." If an analytic attitude to descriptive language is taken, the tension of the description is found. It seems, then, that a comparative interpretive act is contained in the perception itself. Though close to an uninterpreted sensation, it is nonetheless interpreted.

Peirce's remark about the "analytic" raises more issues than he, at that moment in his discourse, decides to follow through. The main issue to be considered is the relationship between percepts or signs *as they seem* and the processes by which they are constituted. Is it necessarily the case that sounds are first represented in the mind as sensations, then endowed with associative properties? If so, how relevant is the process of perception to interpreting signs? In an early manuscript, Peirce created an analogy for the perceptual process which suggested an infinite regression to lower and lower levels of perception. His picture was of an inverted triangle dipped into water. Thinking about the part of the triangle that is immersed, it is not possible to specify the level at which a "lower" point of immersion is lacking (1868: 26; see Innis, 1994: 11). By implication, another inferential level would always exist in the perceptual process "below" the one that was apparent, and the regress to lower levels could continue indefinitely, receding to a point incapable of being defined. It could not be said that any perception was just "given" uninterpreted to consciousness (as if consciousness were an entity capable of receiving gifts, or observing the arrival of items from the input process), because each perception is based on representing. An interpretation, or lower-order inference, would always be implicit, even it were not accessible to introspection. For Peirce to reason in this way at an early stage in his thinking was a means of avoiding the idea of a pure intuition of content, given to the mind. He needed to avoid any implication that the mind could have contents which did not result from a process of representation, in order to steer clear of a Cartesian splitting between mind (accessible to introspection) and bodily perceptions, which were deemed unreliable. In holding the view that "mind" or "consciousness" was just the representation of contents in the world, he foreshadowed contemporary views, where "representation" is the content resulting from a perceptual process.

When he further develops his ideas about the functioning of signs as a mode of thought, his purpose is no longer to resist the dualism of thought and representation. Its invalidity is assumed in the semiotic thought, and a new or "higher-level" purpose introduced—that of explaining the social functioning of signs.

b. How Things Seem

By the time he wrote on the "scarlet" trumpet sound (CP 1.312, 1910), Peirce recognized that the way things *seem* to a perceiving subject needed to be taken into account in his view of signs. Of course, it would be possible to dispute the point of whether further abstractions might not be made from a perception such as "scarlet trumpet sound." What is important is to recognize that a semiotic account of an experience, as conceived by Peirce, starts with a quality *insofar as it creates an interpretive response.* This view is emphasized also by Lidov (1999).

By locating the study of signs in the public or "normative" domain, Peirce effectively distinguishes the methodology of a semiotic study from that of speculative or experimental psychology. It is not the perceptual process but its interpreted outcome that is of concern. As far as the self-conscious knower is concerned, the auditory sign comes already loaded with its "color" characteristics, without any awareness of the synthetic process that produced them. In a semiotic study, the terms of this ordinary description are taken seriously, and the "colored" sound becomes the datum to be explained. A quality of sound, the "scarlet" trumpet, seems to be "given." Although perceptual processes are multi-leveled, and it is likely that synaesthetic associations are "higher-order" events which occur at a late stage in passing through the auditory hierarchy, none of this complexity is introspectively accessible. The sound-as-colored is, then, the starting point for semiotic investigations, rather than their conclusion.

As seen in chapter 2, a semiotic study takes the outcome of an interpreted perceptual process, an audible quality heard as bearing some additional information, or "signification," to be its basic unit. It assumes, further, that signs are accessible to all who share a domain of competency. A concern with "how things seem" does not, then, commit a Peircean view to the fallacy of "mentalism" or "psychologism." An individual's impressions are not merely "private," held apart from their participation in a shared perceptual domain. "Mind" or "consciousness" is not an entity formed in lonely isolation, as if anyone could create an inner world *ex nullis,* as their own private and god-like creator. If acts of naming are intersubjectively intelligible, as language requires, then perceptions of quality also are shared. Think again of the blind man's hearing a trumpet sound and his noticing that it answers the description given to the color "scarlet." The appropriateness of his color association can easily be tested by considering other possibilities. Does it make more sense to say of the orchestral trumpet that it is a luminous scarlet, like that of the Peircean iodide, or to describe it as a richly warm and deep red-brown? If you agree that "scarlet" has a better fit, you share the perception that Peirce recognized, and that the blind man guessed at from what he heard. (You might point out that when Ornette Coleman plays jazz trumpet, his sound is more soft and mellow, but it is a nineteenth-century orchestral trumpet that is being considered here.) To "hear" the color in the trumpet's sound is not to have demonstrated originality and individuation—or to have descended into eccentricity. It is to have picked out a "sign" which is culturally ratified, as well as being well-grounded in a spectral analogy between the relative "brightness" of colors and sounds. This (weak) sign, just emerging from perception, is part of a shared domain. Holding the confidence that language defines a shared understanding, it is then possible to name feelings in response to music—the means of access to qualitative signs (their interpretants)—and to do so without retreating into a private realm.

The picture I am drawing of the relationship between perceptual processes and signs could perhaps be compared most fruitfully to the relationship of a programming language to the "icons" appearing on a screen.[6] The program sits unobtrusively in the background, inaccessible to the user. What it presents, as the basic units to be grasped, are "icons." Of course, these icons are already "interpreted." They have been programmed to hold a specific place in the system and would have no "meaning" without it. But the mode of their production does not concern the user, who simply names and works with them. Despite the fact that each icon is the result of rules, which govern its function, it presents itself as a single impression and is able to facilitate work precisely because it is "immediately" grasped. Users who have higher-level purposes in mind do not wish to be distracted by going through several stages in order to underline a word. It is more practical to be able to act immediately. The icon, then, is the content of which they are conscious at a particular moment, enabling a quick response. If this is useful to students, it is also ecologically sensible. Organisms wishing to adapt to their environment by carrying out defensive or amorous goals do not need to be delayed by questioning the origin and veridity of their already-interpreted perceptions. A sound reads "danger" or "mate," not "auditory datum which could be associated with certain possible events, given the former experience of your species." It comes as a "sign," hearing X as Y, not just as the representation of a sound in the mind.[7]

c. Raffman: Words, Consciousness, and Musical Nuance

A contrast between a semiotic view of sound color and that offered by a cognitivist psychological account can be found by looking at the arguments put forward by Diana Raffman (1993), in response to other philosophers of mind. Raffman gives a psychological account of musical nuance with the purpose of demonstrating that it is possible to be *conscious* of some quality in a sound, and to respond to its expressivity, without being able to name it. Her agenda is determined by a debate about the relationship between language and consciousness, which I cannot fully open out here. In brief, a number of philosophers of mind (Fodor, Rosenthal, Dennett) assume there to be a special relationship between being *conscious* of something and being able to *name* it. Their point is one already anticipated by Peirce: that when you are conscious of something, you have registered or "represented" it in some way, so that it is available to thoughtful reflection and memory. But how can you be sure someone "sees," or is conscious of, an item, if they cannot name it? In order to avoid any such hints at an "inner" theatrical space, where the products of sense make dramatic (or mundane) appearances, Dennett goes so far as to say that being "conscious" of something is simply having it *"in the speech center"* (see Raffman). "You feel inclined to say 'blue' so you must be conscious of blue. Think no more of *where* that consciousness resides." The obvious problem with this story is that it leaves little space for items that come carelessly unlabeled to the "speech center," leaving you momentarily dumb. It is not possible to be sure that there *is* a conscious representation if it is not given, *well labeled,* to speech (packages unlabeled at the post office do not functionally exist). Considering that musical nuances often lack names, their recognition as consciously perceived entities is in serious trouble. (Do they just not get posted on? Is the mind's eye lurking in another box again, waiting for their delivery?)

Raffman's answer to the problem of ineffability is to posit an additional level of conscious mental activity "before" that which supplies pitches with names and addresses, fitting them into a slot that is capable of being named (see Jackendoff, 1987). In her argument, "nuance pitches" are inflections of pitch more fine-grained than those represented by the chromatic scale degrees. Most notable in her argument is a lack of concern for any forms of nuance that might come under a description of tonal "color." This lack reflects her reliance on experiments in musical perception which isolate pitch from the specific timbral characteristics of an instrument, presenting subjects with pure sine tones generated by a computer under controlled acoustic conditions. In these experiments, the main point of interest is in how listeners organize pitches in relation to one another, and with reference to some idealized chromatic "grid" which defines the ideal size of an interval. The choice of a "neutral" sound is a point of control, a way to limit the number of variables being measured by screening out the information that comes from the sound's quality. Such experimental procedures are not, however, an optimal way of approaching questions about how sounds are understood in a musical context, where additional qualitative cues are in fact available (see Raffman, 1993). The physical resonance of the instrument itself may, for example, act as a clue to the *pitch* of sounds being played (on a violin, sounds that resonate with the "open" strings—G, D, A, E—are more "open" in their resonance than others; many instruments change timbral quality with register) and, as Raffman points out, many other contextual features make "real" musical contexts *less* and not *more* ambiguous than controlled ones.

Notwithstanding her narrowly pitch-based definition of "nuance," Raffman does have an important point to make about the limitation of a view that restricts conscious experience to items which are capable of being labeled with simple terms. She notes, aptly, that judgments of a player's performance—"I like it like that!" "I like the *way* he did that scale"—indicate finer discriminations than those of pure pitch. The chromatic scale may be the lowest level at which pitches are named in a Western tonal system, but there is plentiful evidence that discriminations are much finer than that. A nuance is recognizably "there" for the listener, "in between" the pitches, as a bending of the sound. Anyone who enjoys listening to the "blues" will recognize those special "blue" notes, bent downwards, flattened, feeling "flat." Or think of the opening to the song, "Maria," from Leonard Bernstein's *West Side Story*. Its opening augmented fourth ("Ma-*ri*-a") needs to be stretched, to be exaggerated, as the tensions of this dissonance press towards its resolution on the last syllable with all the urgency that a song of infatuation requires. What Raffman sets out to demonstrate is that these discriminations can justifiably be accepted as conscious, despite a lack of names for the altered pitches involved. It does not seem a big demand that she is making, when she seeks to elicit an acknowledgment that listeners are conscious of these pitch alterations, so effective in creating the impression of expressivity. Even so, those philosophers of mind who see a correlation between the conscious experience of an item and an ability to name it, have a genuine concern. If you want to avoid mystifying statements about "unnamable" experiences in a vaguely located consciousness, you need some account of how representation can occur, and yet resist the application of working labels.

In her reply, Raffman accepts the existing terms of description in one model of the mind, which would not be accepted by all philosophers of mind (e.g., Dennett). The model she adopts is that developed by the linguist and philosopher, Ray Jackendoff, from the functionalist views of Jerry Fodor. It is not so different in its consequences from Peirce's picture of the inverted triangle dipped into water. A line exists where the conscious appears, and below it an unspecifiable number of levels of sensory input are presumed. The point in dispute is where the water line is. Or, to stay with the computational metaphor, the point at issue is "what kind of representation—sensation, perception, sign—is the lowest level of 'input' to reach the 'central processing system'"? Whereas Jackendoff takes the sequence of events notated in a score as the bottom level of *conscious* awareness, proceeding out of unspecifiable events in the unconscious computational mind, Raffman suggests that there must be a *lower* level of awareness, which is yet unnamable. Accepting that the chromatic scale is the lowest level for pitch names, she speculates that there must be a lower, micro-structural level out of which it comes. It is possible, she then argues, to be conscious of this micro-structural level, even without precise names for its range of pitch nuances, because it is composed of items just "below" the level of pitch. The nuances are going in the right direction on the conveyor belt, on their way to the place where pitches are more securely labeled as belonging to a structured scale, but they haven't quite got there yet. (This earlier level could be compared to the two-and-a-half-dimensional sketch, which Jackendoff postulates as existing in the perception of visual phenomena, *before* the visual field is fully resolved into three dimensions.) Raffman suggests that names for things are normally attached to items that fit within some kind of schema (like the scale), and finer discriminations are organized in relation to these more secure items.

⌒

It is possible to accept Raffman's account of why pitch names are the lowest level at which it becomes possible to *name* a distinct item, without accepting her general approach to the explanation of nuance. In the next section, I look at the semiotic alternative, which does not make use of a multi-leveled functional story about perception, or give priority to simple *labels* as the means of identifying conscious items linguistically. If a connection between language and consciousness is required, why restrict language to names? The story of skygazing in the desert comes back again.

3. *Living Sounds and Virtualities*

Try browsing a web site for non-traditional violin sounds. The classical player, Itzhak Perlman, impresses with the depth and verve of his sound as he plays a Jewish theme, "Firn Di Mekhutonium Aheym,"[8] with all the force of his Romantic vibrato. Duncan Chisholm appears as a "fiddle player for Wolfstone, a Celtic rock band that produces an interesting fusion of traditional Irish style with modern rock."[9] His sound is exhilaratingly fresh in its spare and edgy quality. A "cutting-edge" player creates some electronically modi-

fied violin sounds, tantalizing in their ethereal "presence." As the site owner
says, he explores "new spaces." These "living" sounds have complex timbral
characteristics as an inseparable part of their aural presentation. Timbre is
like the wrinkles of their "skin," the surface without which the body of vibration could not possibly be heard. It is "in the sound," as part of its presenting quality, before a deliberative process has taken place to examine
the associations it brings. Because distinctive timbres cannot be identified
with simple alphabetic labels, as pitches can, or named with nouns that belong to them alone, their description has to find a different linguistic mode.
That is why they are most often pointed at with words for action and quality, words that modify the description of a neutral "sound." It has been
noted in earlier chapters that these metaphors are frequently loaded with an
affective association. The sounds are "warm" or "cool," "gentle" (in legato)
or "assertive" (in strong attack). They might be "cool and distant," without
vocal nuance, or, in *sul ponticello* (playing with the bow on top of the
bridge), "thin and edgy."

To interpret the signification of sounds in an acoustic instrument is not,
then, to deal just with abstracted *pitches,* in their nuanced alteration, but
with pitched sounds of definite timbre, duration, and context. If you hear
the sound as constant or interrupted, in tune, sharp, or flat, you are noticing
simple aspects of its duration or frequency, and "representing" it in the
mind (in the sense used by cognitive science), with reference to a standardized grid—just as Raffman suggests. But what about when you hear it as
the index of an action or as a tone of voice? Sounds may come bearing the
mark of actions, or as suggesting voices of various emotional tone. Taking
a semiotic view (and one consistent with the naturalistic account of the
sense given by the psychologist James J. Gibson, 1966), I assume that it is a
basic psychological proclivity *not* to hear sound as an uninterpreted quality,
but to hear it as bearing information that is adaptively useful. In a natural
environment, such information could be about the location and movement
of objects, the position and attitude of another living thing, the affective
state of another as bidding affection or retreat. "Mental representations" of
sound are not, then, aural recordings of pure acoustic properties, but assessments of a sound's source and connection with other moving bodies,
whether inert or living.

In my usage, a pitch's "timbre" is made up of vibrational frequencies that are part of the harmonic series belonging to it, a selection of frequencies that is synthesized to give the impression of a single "colored" sound. Its available "nuances" are more broadly inclusive. They include the "noise" (impure frequencies) that occurs at onset and in continuing surface friction during the production of a sound, as well as dynamic alterations and modifications of pitch.

Forms of analysis that privilege the notated features of music can easily overlook timbre or nuance in their ability to make a substantive difference to the effect of a piece. Davies, for example, emphasizes the pitched sound as the lowest "musical element of identifiable (and re-identifiable) significance" because its tonal function remains stable if it is performed in different ways (1994: 6), but his argument lacks a means of explaining the signification of nuance. To establish that timbre and nuance do bear signification, all that is required is an observation that instrumentation matters definitively in at least some compositions (though others allow for substitutions). The contrasting violin sounds cited above are one kind of case, where sounds define a style, and could not be substituted for one another without creating a ludicrous or ironic effect. To make the contrasts even stronger, the substitution of orchestral instruments for one another might be considered. What would it be like to hear the opening to the Adagio third movement of Mozart's Serenade No. 10 in B-flat, K. 361 (370a), with violins substituted for the oboe, in its long opening note? (This passage is immortalized in *Amadeus* as the first music of Mozart's that Salieri hears.) Substitute another instrument for the oboe, perhaps a more conventional choir of violins, and its restrained and haunting quality would be entirely lost. Or try imagining what it would be like to endure a performance of Ravel's *Bolero* with a single instrument playing its tune over and over again, unrelieved by timbral change. The work relies entirely on changes in timbre for its effect.

Accepting that differences in timbre and nuance of various kinds are important as qualitative signs, another step can be made in response to Raffman by asking whether a story about successive *levels* of representation will do the work of explaining how these qualities relate to notated pitch. Instead of speculating about the auditory hierarchy, one way to work is to look pragmatically at the creation of the sound. A violinist chooses fingering, controls vibrato, and manipulates the bow with altered degrees of friction, arm-weight, pressure, speed, and closeness to the internal sound post, altering both the harmonic expanse of a note and the amount of noise at its onset. Working with these various possibilities, he or she seeks to form sounds in which aspects of timbre and nuance become synthesized to give a single, unified impression (or in a longer note, to create a well-shaped change). If a pragmatic approach is taken to these acts of performing, questions about the ordering of events in the auditory hierarchy move into the background. The actions that create a sound and its "nuance" occur at one time. From a practical point of view, a sound's characteristics cannot be separated from one another on a time line, except to the degree that onset noise precedes the full formation of a regular frequency (the pitch). A "note" is a pitched and timbrally specific sound, with individual nuance. Even its identification as one thing, a "note," attests to its unity. Moving back to the problems of perception, which are Raffman's concern, no effective supposition can be made, even there, that when a performed note is heard, timbral characteristics and nuance *precede* pitch in the auditory hierarchy. It may seem plausible to conceive of a scale of pitches, and have slightly altered pitches related to them as a "lower" level, but this will not work for the specific harmonic structure that goes to make up the pitch itself as bearing a specific apparent "color."

To follow through Raffman's program, and to conceive of all aspects of nuance as "preceding" pitch (or represented at a "lower level"), it would be necessary to consider the psychological processes by which elements of sound are resolved into the impression of a single entity. To do so is to enter another area in the philosophy of mind, where questions of sensory integration are treated as examples of "the binding problem." Only the briefest glance at this area is possible here. It is worth a glance, because the problem of "binding" presents, on a microcosmic scale, some of the issues that arise when thinking about what it is to "bind" the various aspects of a self into any kind of notional unity. To illustrate this problem, David Rosenthal uses the example of a ball being hit by a bat, at some distance from where an on-looker stands. When you are watching, why is it that you "see" the action and "hear" the sound at the *same* moment, despite the fact that light waves and sound waves travel at different speeds? The process of synthesis has happened prior to "consciousness" and you don't have access to it (D. Rosenthal). In the case of listening to musical sounds, the required synthesis of stimuli remains within the aural domain and does not require an integration of information from different senses. Even so, a complex set of different noises and harmonic frequencies does need to be resolved into a single impression of a note, and success in the integration is evident when listeners recognize a pitch with specific characteristics: "a sustained oboe G." (In the film, Salieri's auditory imagination allows him to create this specific note and its quality, as he eulogizes over Mozart's score.) To suggest that what goes by the name "timbre" is a conscious but unnamable level *before* pitch is nonetheless problematic. Is "timbre"—as this implies—a kind of memory for a pattern of harmonic frequencies, as they were in their non-integrated state, *before* they got to be part of a pitch? One of the most ticklish problems explored by Dennett, and taken up by David Rosenthal, concerns the ordering of events in sensory binding. This problem in the philosophy of perception is not one I can remark on in any detail, but it seems doubtful that a simple time line will solve it.

Accepting the boundary suggested by Peirce between the special and normative sciences (of which semiotic is one), it is possible to take a more pragmatic approach to the question of perceiving and naming nuance. No pitch "appears" to the ear without some timbral characteristic, heard as belonging to it. Only when envisaging a special didactic or experimental environment, where a limited number of notes are selected for attention, does it become plausible to insist on the separability of a note's pitch from its timbre and nuance. In teaching an instrument it is, for example, a normal activity to dissect the elements of a sound and to notice the characteristics of sound production that form a player's style. In practicing a passage, or rehearsing a work for ensemble, musicians will deliberately work on the elements of sound. All of this work is, however, "behind the scenes." Its purpose is to produce for the listener an aural "icon" that will convey a specific sense.

~

One of the myths that Raffman is at pains to dispel is that "ineffability" pervades all aspects of music, including its structure, expressivity, and nuance. Her skepticism is directed most pointedly at writings by Susanne Langer and Stanley Cavell, where they become poetic in their descriptions of the depths of unnamable experience music can evoke. Cavell is particularly eloquent in reflecting on the urgency, and apparent impossibility, of communicating the qualities of a musical experience when the style of a work is new and unfamiliar:

> It matters that others know what I see, in a way it does not matter whether they know my tastes. It matters, there is a burden, because unless I can tell what I know, there is a suggestion (and to myself as well) that I do *not* know. But I *do*—what I see is *that* (pointing to the object). But for that to communicate you have to see it too. (1976: 193)

One of the first problems to be encountered in writing of sound qualities, either as single elements or as the pervasive "feel" of a performance, is a conviction that they cannot effectively be described, because they lack distinctive labels. When mentioning "ineffabilities," it is easy to connote, in mysterious tones of reverential awe, that which "must not be uttered." (This, indeed, is one of the senses of "ineffable" mentioned by the *Shorter Oxford English Dictionary* as current in 1597.) Sounds are taken to belong to the "ineffable," that which "cannot be expressed in words," the "unspeakable, unutterable, inexpressible" (*Shorter Oxford English Dictionary*). Cavell suggests that the desire to communicate is, for him, as powerful as his sense of incapacity. For others, an experience that resists naming leads more readily into a willing withdrawal from speech, a privileging of respectful silence. The tendency to withdraw from speaking of experiences whose naming is problematic could be cast in mysterious tones, suggesting a Romantic's awe of the Sublime. There are, in all seriousness, some experiences so exceptional in their potency, and so valued by those involved, that to name them is to cause their degradation. If naming, or even richer description, is inadequate to characterize that which is beyond your common conceptualization, it is perhaps presumptuous to try. It can be enough simply to point at the work (or "other") that has so affected you, and to know even in the pointing that an experience of listening has been shared. A conversation with Leonard Meyer once brought this home to me, on a visit to New York. "You know the 'Cavatina' (from Beethoven's String Quartet in B-flat Major, op. 130)?" I asked with the intensity of an over-keen student. "Yes, I know . . . Don't say more." It is almost sacrilege to name this work's inexorable sadness. Words seem unable to capture its precise nuance. Understanding between people can be achieved, without further naming, if the experience is shared, and the unspoken may then bring greater understanding than a crass attempt to capture a sense of the music in words. Reverence is due to the mutually accepted silence, a gift. But what of prohibitions born of cynicism, in which the unnamed is discredited as lacking any claim to be an object of conscious experience? You have not then reverence, but the degradation and denial of musical experiences labored over by performers in their care for producing sounds. It is as if you may not speak of the sounds that are a musician's stock-in-trade, simply because their timbres have no definite name, and nouns have gained an improper priority in thinking about what can be "known" of the world, or its experience.

The solution I have begun to suggest, to the problem of nuance "ineffability," is to expand the use of language, and revise the idea of nuance perception. First, not all of the contents of experience are *items*—like packages —which have simple names. Someone discriminating auditory nuances may do so with a language of adverb and adjective that points at kinds of action, or even at a state felt in another sensory domain (warmth), in order to convey the otherwise inarticulate qualities that belong to their perceptual experience. Second, it does not make sense to suggest that "nuance" is the same *kind* of thing as pitch, but at a "lower" or more fine-grained perceptual level. Investigating the perceptual hierarchy does not, then, necessarily solve the problem of what it is to recognize and name a consciously perceived nuance. The language of semiotic descriptions starts, instead, with phenomenological data as "given" and, although this might appear as a naive strategy, it can produce results that are potentially informative for psychology. Working simply with observations of musicianly speech and activity, it becomes apparent that nuance is neither separable from pitch (as an earlier part of a perceptual time line), nor resistantly unnamable. The degree of harmonic richness in a (violin) note is registered as a degree of "warmth" (comparable at times to that of a voice), and described with adjectival terms, while its noise characteristics are heard as the indices of action, to be described in adverbs for qualities of action that could be applied equally in other active domains. It is possible to recognize these modes of conscious experience, which cannot be *named* as discrete elements, without either rendering them completely inarticulate, or offering a premature solution to the problem of perceptual "binding."

~

Timbral iconicity is so basic as to be scarcely avoidable. When listening to a performer, you do not hear his or her sounds as disembodied, but as humanly produced (with or without electronic modification), and as carrying a load of onset noise and shaping which gives them their "active" characteristics. Taking it for granted that the instrument has a limited range of potential sounds, it is in the particular performer's choices within that range that interpretive interest may be found. As seen in chapter 1, "Midori" is the sound she makes. The sound forms her apparent identity, quite apart from any explicit intention she may have. It is not only her acting performer's body, and the instrument's natural resonance, but the surrounding acoustic venue that contributes to her "sound," and gives her an apparent "body." Whether it is a materially entered space or the virtual "space" of an electronic medium—sounds present themselves in an acoustic space where they become convincing in their "presence" or "insipid in their lack of projection," "thin and whistling" or "full, like an operatic voice." The performer's acoustic resonance becomes a marker of her apparent self-projection, as if in a social sphere, although that "self" is not something that she could directly project through the sound. While Midori, in the Barbican Concert Hall, suffers an acoustic that condemns, the cutting-edge player creates an acoustic to suit his own ends. Amplified sounds and artificial reverberant properties displace attention from his own embodied actions, to suggest that he has either eluded embodiment or transcended it. Illusions of transcendence need not be filled with mystery, if techniques for erasing the body in sound are used to good effect. And if the electroacoustic can draw attention to such effects, their use in conventional acoustic instruments becomes easier to hear. Players of instruments can make use of well-controlled motions that do not leave their bodily marks in sound, but display a facility in speed through registers well outside the range of a human voice, and establish continuities of tone that defy the limits of human breath (on a wind instrument) without suffering from "breathiness."

Motivations for metaphors, expressing non-arbitrary associations, are easy to find when the effects of modified "voice" or timbral noise are first accounted for. The "distance" of a pure sound without vibrato becomes "ethereality," a transcending of embodiment. (It is an effect like that sought by choir masters in the English Cathedral tradition.) The edginess of a sound full of surface noise becomes "sinister," associated with a certain kind of rasping "voice." Modernists, in repudiating the excesses of subjective investment in sound, have brought with them a sounding palette far removed from that of twentieth-century Romanticism, with more tolerance for harshness of effect. The Polish performer, Wanda Wilkomirska, for example, chooses a spare sound when playing part of a sonata by her national composer, Grażyna Bacewicz.[10] Spareness becomes "control," or "objectivity," a means of conveying a withdrawal from the indulgence of "sensoriness." In New Age music, as seen above, electronically induced reverberance may become a technological transcendence of body, making machinery the paradoxical carrier of "spirituality." It is by playing with the markers of "voice" as a physiological mechanism, and movement as bodily action, that degrees of embodied passion or self-controlled distancing can be conveyed. When techniques of electroacoustic reverberance or traditional virtuosity are introduced to effect an extension or erasure of the virtual "body" in sound, it is as if the boundary between virtual "selfhood" and disembodied "otherness" were being crossed. If "voice" and "body" form a virtual self, giving the sense of subjectivity in sound, any forms of play that alter these qualities can convey a crossing of the boundary out of the subjective, with its illusions of "expressiveness," and into a realm of virtuality where memories of the subjective have been transformed into formerly unknown identities.

4. Worlds of Sound and Subjective Identifications

a. Romantic Yearnings

"She's shifting positions okay, but I don't like her sound."

"Well, take a look at the position of her bow on the string. Is it halfway between the fingerboard and bridge? When she draws the bow forward, does it stay in line with the bridge? Watch her right elbow, and make sure she doesn't move too far back, creating a bad angle."

"I've done all that, but still it doesn't sound quite right. It is kind of scratchy and raw."

It was like serving on the flying-doctor service, except that I was stationary, teaching the violin to a child in a remote town, over the telephone, talking her father through the motions she would need to make.[11] Sandy's desire to "play the violin" as she knew it *could* sound was unremitting, despite distance from the centers of learning. So she scratched down the line, and I attempted to play duets with her—until I discovered the telephone could not transmit two ways at once.

Sandy's aspiration was for a certain "sound," one neither she nor her father could describe, and whose tradition she only vaguely knew, though recordings let her know she had not "got it." That the sound, idolized by a Romantic performing tradition, need not be obliterated by telephone lines, I discovered much later while surfing the World Wide Web (in 1996). When a Gopher search for "violin" turned up a site dedicated to non-traditional performance, and I first heard the thirty-second sound snapshot of Itzhak Perlman playing the Jewish theme, "Firn Di Mekhutonium Aheym," its effect was undeniably compelling. Perlman's album, *Fiddler's House,* is, says the site owner, "high-energy, high-passion Jewish music that you can't avoid moving to in some fashion. Infectious stuff."[12] He is right. Perlman has "got something." He has that capacity to "move people at the inner core of their being" so desired by Leigh Creek's "Sandy" and the hopeful virtuoso on a new CD alike. But what exactly does he have? And how could it be heard in his sound, even through some tiny speakers on a desktop PC? Why could his sound "touch" me, in that least-committed of moments, sampling bits and pieces on the World Wide Web? Did his "fat vibrato" do the trick? Had my teacher, Dunand, convinced me that emotion was in essence a vibrato sound?

The compelling conviction that can come with a "Romantic" sound, whether heard in modern renditions of nineteenth-century repertory, or in the intense passion of a Jewish theme, cannot be denied. Perlman's sound has "depth" and "intensity." It conveys an interiority which could be labeled "soul" if the song were an African-American ("Negro") spiritual. It is the sound of a voice intensified with emotion, declaiming something strongly felt, intimating tragedy, a voice that persuades of subjective "presence" and individual character. Empathy or identification are called for here, a personal response to match the conviction of the sound. "*That's* the sound I want to make!" says the hopeful child. That something special has been recognized by many in Perlman's sound is attested by his fame, but it is not he alone who cultivates this *kind* of sound, the epitome of Romantic self-investment. Its "pathos" may have been labeled a fallacy—the projection of subjectivity into sound—but such "fallacies" are the stuff of signs, and here there is a pathos that carries the ring of emotional truth. Many students of the Romantic repertory would like to convey the personal authenticity in their sound that Perlman has in this thirty-second "snap"—and audiences commonly expect to be "moved" by it. The appearance of emotionality in sound is a *value* for inheritors to a Romantic performing tradition (as conceived in the twentieth century), something to be sought and cultivated, upon which the investment of time and energy in practice is no waste. Just a little excess, however, and you have bathos, or ridiculous sentimentality, postures of the tragic, or a warbling contortedness that conveys no more than nostalgia for something once felt, whose life and conviction have been lost. Or perhaps (in the young) it is a yearning for an emotion not yet known, that aping of pathos which sounds "pathetic" in the wrong way. You cannot buy "soul."[13]

A range of sounds is like a "world," limiting choice. The "Romantic" violin is one such range, which carries with it the baggage of a world view in which personal, individualistic expression is to be valued above almost all other things. It is a world view physically embodied in the set-up of "modern" violins and bows, with eighteenth-century instruments altered to allow for added power and self-projection: catgut replaced with metal-wound strings, a grip at the shoulder giving a stable base both for speed and mobility in the left hand and strength of force in the bow against the instrument, and springy bows which allow for weight and all kinds of staccato virtuosity. To possess a Romantic "sound" is to have realized the potentialities of such an instrument, engaging with its range. Even the physical reproduction of instruments capable of "richness" (in the complex overtone series of their sound) is a reproduction of subjective possibilities—the construction of a shared "subjective" realm. Shared subjectivities do not, however, rule out individuation. The individuality of a hand-crafted violin, which may have passed through many hands to gain the marks of its own history, gives a potentiality for uniqueness to each player. It is not too much to speak of "love" here, as a player comes intimately to know his or her own instrument's particular idiosyncrasies, its strengths and weaknesses, and its reactions to weather change. Havas says she can tell from the *sound* how the instrument itself has been played, with respect for its resonance, opening it out, or with a clumsiness that suppresses sound. The violin comes to bear the marks of its player in the acoustic response of its own wood. In a very real sense, this instrument, whose sound just *is* the material content of a player's sounding identity, may become for the player a part of him- or herself, whose alteration or injury is personally felt. A physical shock that changes the violin's sound is effectively a change in how its player "sounds" in the world. To buy a string with the wrong metal gauge can be as disturbing as contracting a cold that muffles vocal resonance. To have the instrument opened up for work is tantamount to surgery. But to discover a new brand of string that offers more resonant sound (as I did when I found the Gold-stahl E), or to have a seam closed that has opened in the summer heat, to re-gain lost resonance, is to open up the delight of new possibilities. Subjective identification in sound has a cost and reward for the dedicated player that is more than merely casual. The violin carries in it the means of projecting a range of expressivity. To alter it is to influence the range available to a "self" formed in sound, to render her more "muffled" or "open" in her so-cial projection.

b. "Back to the Future": Old and New Sounding Worlds

"Singing," or "speaking," are terms of approbation attached to sound pro-duction within the various traditions of violin playing, and they do not re-flect an intrinsic feature of any one sound. Standing in a position to make comparisons, this seems obvious. It is not, however, so obvious from the pragmatic point of view of a player who must master a given sound world through assiduous practice and thus come to value it as the site of his or her invested energy. If the Romantic violin is the instrument in which a sound-ing identity has been formed (or received by a listener), the value attached to its sound is inevitable, reflecting the work that has been invested in attaining it—or the repeated pleasures of listening. It can, nevertheless, be a source of freedom to discover that identity is not singular, but multiple, and in a post-modern era this discovery is almost inevitable. A simple recognition needs to be made, then, that other tone qualities than the strongly "Romantic" may signify, too—so long as they are well-produced (without unintended crunches, scratches, and squawks). An addiction to one kind of sound, such as that of a wide vibrato on a "Romantically" set-up violin, may actually lead to a cloying of sensitivity to other sounds, with their suggestion of more "contained" or "distant" voices.

Baroque violins, modern ones, or violins with electronic pickup devices and techniques of electroacoustic alteration, all may create "voices" which give the illusion of "presence," or perhaps of an ethereal transcendence of their "materiality"—by covering the sounding evidence of physical creation. It is not only "richness" of sound that "moves," or impresses with vivacity. The advocates of Baroque authenticity have for decades resisted the hegemony of vibrato in Romantic performance styles. Sigiswald Kuijken, playing Bach's solo sonatas on an authentic instrument,[14] is no less engaging than a "Romantic" player; his vibratoless sound has a bare directness and yet a gentle intimacy. Lucy van Dael, another Dutch player, chooses a sound bordering on the raucous when using her violin to realize Heinrich Biber's imitation of seventeenth-century Bohemian farmyard birds, with amusing effect.[15] As previously mentioned, modernists have likewise repudiated the excesses of subjective investment in sound and performers of their work use a sounding palette far removed from that of twentieth-century Romanticism, with more tolerance for harshness of effect. Wanda Wilkomirska chooses a spare sound when playing part of a sonata by Polish national composer Grażyna Bacewicz.[16] Experimenters in *musique concrète*, in their turn, draw attention to the material qualities of sound, trying to force attention away from subjective projections, to get you to hear the sounds without indulging a need for "expressive" satisfaction.

As seen in some examples cited earlier, the makers and players of electronic violins also offer new possibilities in sonic "space," with instruments that rely less on personal intensity than on letting new kinds of "sound bending" and reverberation create an evolving "sonic self." For a performer who is not rigidly committed to an idea of "expressing" his or her existing self in familiar sounds, the discovery of new virtualities in sound can *make* and extend a sounding identity. To a frustrated player, it might be said, "Instead of seeking your own 'warmth' of sound, why not accept its coldness, and experiment with it, to see what it will reveal? Why try to make the sounds 'express' an inwardness you do not have? If you play with their shaping or reverberant forms, you will not lose their signifying power, but discover that sounds can lead you to 'express' a self you have not known. You create it, as you play." And to a listener enmeshed in sentimentality, the opposite suggestion could be made: "Forget your appetite for rich, and culturally overburdened, sounds! Sample the instruments and works of the twentieth century! It is by listening to new sounds that you gain an open-mindedness to enter new worlds, and with it the skill to negotiate the 'difference' of sounding worlds that exist apart from you. To listen, even in stillness, is to gain mobility."

c. Identification, Distance, and Rationalization

The sounds of a Romantic violin, played in the style of Perlman, invite an empathetic response, an engagement with their signified "warmth" (as in Perlman's wide vibrato). For a listener engaged in this tradition, their familiarity permits a state of "immersion" in the sound, or of uncritical enjoyment. A dwelling on quality-as-sign, without critical distance, is an enactment of the attitude appropriate to Peirce's "first" category. Other kinds of sound, where the apparent richness of vocality is restrained, more readily draw attention to their own "otherness." Although it might be possible to hear in the violin's line a kind of "voice," it no longer carries the emotional tone of an operatically trained singer, but instead evokes that of something unknown, "other." (Wilkomirska, playing Bacewicz, uses a spareness and intensity of sound, which conveys a non-indulgent self-control but also strong conviction.) Where bodily onset noise is obliterated, and alternative means of producing sound effects are introduced, the apparent "disembodiment" creates further distance from the idea of "expressivity." A sound without operatic "richness" or assertive attack moves away from being the signification of something familiar. Although the idea of "voice" might be retained, through association with other kinds of playing, the voice is no longer that of a quasi-human utterance. It is "other," and to the extent that a listener retains even the idea of a possible "voice" as its content, he or she begins to negotiate unfamiliar possibilities in subjective experience. This movement might be thought of as an entry into a more "imaginative" realm, if by "imagination" is meant the idea of entering into experiences beyond those normally thought possible to a human being, or outside the domain of waking consciousness. The structure of a musical sign predicts that this extension will take place. The ideas "voice" or "expressive action" on a violin carry with them their own opposites. The "voice" is not a voice, nor the sound of "aggressive" action on the strings that of a destructive act, and it only takes some exaggeration to draw attention to these facts. ("A sign," says Lidov [1999], "is not a sign unless, to some extent, contra-indicated.") If a listener is, then, willing to entertain the idea of a voice or action carrying subjective connotation, while also being aware of its falsehood, he or she is in a position to explore "subjectivities" that are the virtual creations of modified sound. It is as if an identification with quality and an appreciation of its "otherness" have come together, to allow an identification with that which is "other."[17]

A capacity to stand outside the experience of sound, making stylistic comparisons, is implicit in any movement towards tolerance for multiple sound worlds. It does not, however, take away the challenge of being able to submit oneself fully to the sound world of a particular piece, while listening to it. Someone who is obsessed with comparing the rules of play is not him- or herself a player in the game. Being involved demands at least some moments in which you operate "within the rules," accepting them as final, and it is when changing games that you may be more explicitly aware of differences in convention (though you might also have moments of comparison if a spectator at a game). Transitions then become the moments of more marked self-awareness and even of humor at one's own multiplicity. How is it that I can both be enthralled by Perlman, taken up with his sound as if its world contained me and there were no other, and yet move away to relativize the sound as an example of Romanticism? If subject positions are multiple, they reflect a complex or divided self.

⌢

To extol the virtues of mobility, of moving between different sounding worlds, is to assume that ease of sampling can be matched by ease of commitment, an ability to "enter" the experience of different sounds, and to do so with understanding. Does going to an ethnic smorgasbord and sampling the wares allow you to understand the groups who made them? When you attend a festival and move from the Mahabarata to Hamlet, or perhaps some Japanese Noh, do you *really* make a transition that is well-informed? (Or are you not more shocked by your own ignorance?) When you walk through a museum (like the Metropolitan Museum of Art in New York City) and, on passing the threshold between rooms, trip unknowingly across a threshold of a few centuries, not to speak of an impassable land, do you ever recover from the unflown jet lag? When you flip the channels on the radio—or browse the samples on the Web—are you not searching for a place you call "home," and letting all the sounding otherness pass by like so much musical flotsam washing up to your ears? To think that making transitions is easy is to condemn yourself to superficiality.[18] Really to move away from the "Romantic" sound that is the staple fare of symphony orchestras, and their mainstream broadcasts, is—for one who has been "formed" musically in it—to question a sound that has become a central value, the site of endless effort in practice, the medium of many engaging musical experiences.[19] To flip about is one thing, to become engaged in different sonic worlds and allow them to challenge you is quite another. To be a tourist, to enjoy the indulgence of diverse and exotic tastes without being changed in self-understanding, is a virtual reality not now restricted to those of material wealth. You can gain the great opprobrium of being a tourist, almost for free, without even leaving your room. With the virtual richness of free access comes, then, an invitation to inexorable poverty, if the World Wide Web or CD "travel" offers nothing you have the mental wherewithal to possess as your own. (You can be like Albrecht Dürer's engraving of *Melancolia I.* [1514], surrounded by the symbols of the wealth of her time, but unable to engage with them.) But "travel" between the worlds of sound does also invite a more profound questioning, a willingness to take on worlds whose imaginative dimensions you could not earlier contemplate, a dare to sacrifice the strength of adherence even to a sound you hold as "part of yourself." To listen, or to die in a familiar world? That is the question now. You may never understand or fully assimilate the "other," but you can begin to "hear where it is coming from."[20]

chapter five

~

Gesturing

*T*HE PURPOSE OF THIS CHAPTER is to explore more fully those elements of melodic signification that could be described using terms for gesture or bodily motion. Gesture has been widely recognized by writers from a variety of traditions as being pertinent to the expressive content of music. Predictably enough, their emphases vary according to discipline. Wilson Coker's *Music and Meaning* (1972), an early semiotic work, based on the ideas of Charles Morris, places great emphasis on gestural expression. The musical semioticians, Robert Hatten and David Lidov, emphasize the detailed analysis of gestural moments as they are related to style and performance. Carolyn Abbate, a musicologist with a particular interest in how music might suggest "narrative" moments, has suggested that "gesture" is an occasional intrusion in otherwise non-narrative music (1991). Philosophers in the tradition of analytical aesthetics have, on the other hand, been much more reserved about the gestural content they attribute to specific pieces of music. Nelson Goodman, Peter Kivy, Stephen Davies, and Malcolm Budd are more concerned with the very idea of gesture as a means to understanding the expressivity of music, given that it lacks obvious means of reference, and Jerrold Levinson depends on it for his account of complex affective content. My discussion in this chapter will relate mainly to the semiotic literature. Chapter 7 will take up some of the issues raised by aestheticians.

1. Gesture as Performance and Convention

a. Performance and Convention

In his important exploratory article, "Mind and Body in Music," David Lidov proposes that "music is significant only if we identify perceived sonorous motion with somatic experience" (1987: 70). This simple statement makes a radical departure from some formal approaches to musical content in suggesting that a non-formal element—bodily motion—may account for the felt significance of sound. The force of his "only" is not to be ignored. Music bears significance, he suggests, *if and only if* its capacity to convey somatic experience is understood.

Melodic patterns, shaped by a performer to become an expressive gesture, are the kind of musical sign for which Lidov reserves the term "icon," distinguishing them from simple sounds, in which the indices of action are the main source of signification. A review of Elizabeth Wallfisch, playing the neighbor-note pattern that opens Tartini's Sonata for Violin in G Minor, "Dido's Lament," will show that these "icons" also retain a strong connection with the indices of performed action. Wallfisch conveys a halting pathos, as of a restrained and choking grief, through her action with the bow. Taking up various interpretants, a listener might simply recognize pathos; he or she might more dynamically *feel* the movement as if were an inhibited sigh, as if in the impulse to release a breath freely, a stuttering control had been introduced; he or she might also note the figure as a common type, a neighbor-note motif which, though made consonant through a supporting subdominant, retains the melodic association of a dissonant extension to the fifth scale degree. These possible interpretants draw out different features of the motif as a sign more complex than that of a single sound quality. In its capacity to create an haptic image, it is an "icon," yet one that is realized as a unique event through the indexing of the performer's activity —in minute changes of dynamic, tempo, and emphasis. Its conventionality

Example 5.1. Excerpt, Violin Sonata in B Minor, by J. S. Bach

also allows reference to the recurrent patterns for playing motifs of this kind, making of it a token of a type.

As a further example, a feeling of melancholy might emerge in a performance of Bach's Violin Sonata in B Minor. Its repeated drooping appoggiaturas can be performed in such a way that they may be felt as expulsions of breath—like a repeated sighing. (*See* Example 5.1.) It is not enough to know that appoggiaturas are a conventional form of melodic motion, involving dissonance on a strong beat and its immediate resolution. To gain an impression of their affective import, it is necessary to have a feeling for the somatic gesture they convey, as it is specifically enacted in a given moment of time. The figuration is the representamen, or "sign," and a somatic event its "object." Suppose that I recognize the feeling of motion in the figure as like that of a gestural act. I know that it belongs to a familiar kind of pattern, but also recognize it as unique in its presentation. Without a capacity to focus aurally on this particular moment, and to "feel" the shape given to it by the performer, I cannot claim to have responded to this particular enacted sign. Whether or not a movement in my body as listener makes this response evident to another, and whether or not I myself am aware of moving as I listen, I need to have registered the microstructural elements that discriminate this motive from others, in order to have understood the performed somatic sign.

If a melodic figuration must be performed in order to become "gestural," to realize the potentiality for creating the impression of a short, expressive bodily motion, "gesture" cannot be pinned down to a limited set of notated patterns. To suggest that a performer may decide freely on what melodic patterns are to have "gestural" connotation is, however, to underestimate the information that may be derived by looking at patterning in scores, or the constraints of style. Some melodic shapes are more obviously suited than others to the epithet "gestural." They tend to be ones that are relatively autonomous, and which present simply recognized patterns of directional motion, energy (tempo, or degree of pitch change), and emphasis. (Compare the effect of a slow, drooping motion with a weakly emphasized end with a rapid jab at some unseen object, and you can get a simple picture of the different emotional tones of gestural movements.) A tension is set up, in Lidov's account, between "gesture" as an inflected performance of some patterning and gesture as a notated feature. To be realized as "gestural," a pattern must be embodied in an act of performance which conveys a unitary impulse of some kind (1987: 77), or at least be capable of being so embodied. On the other hand, an inflected performance cannot do the trick of rendering just any group of notes a "gesture" without answering to the suggestions of notated melodic shaping, as well as the inflectional instructions (if any) provided by the composer (see Lidov, 1987: 83). Aspects of pitch organization that influence the recognition of melodic grouping (see Lerdahl and Jackendoff, 1983) could potentially limit also the range of items that can effectively fulfill a gestural role. Once recognized as potentially "gestural," a written grouping carries in its own contours some suggestions about the way it might be performed, not determining precisely the tempo and emphasis that will be effective, but still suggesting a range of possibilities that cannot be infinitely extended without loss of "gestural" identity.

A performed inflection selects only one particular manner of "gesturing" and acts it out, while (hopefully) remaining within a range of possibilities that have been circumscribed, but not fully determined, by a notated melodic figure or grouping. A gesture is thus both particular, in its enactment as an unrepeatable moment, and a presentation of a "kind" which does have some limits on its formation. Recognizing this play between performed spontaneity and determination or constraint is important in defining the "gestural." From Lidov's account, it becomes clear that the idea of "gesture" in music cannot be characterized fully without a concern both for its particularity and its constraints. Neither an attention to the particularities of nuance in one given enactment, nor an emphasis on the notated pattern in a score, would allow the idea of the "gestural" as a recurrent "object" of melodic figuration to be captured. This is true not only of attempts at general definition. Where notation alone is being considered by an analyst of a given piece of music, the range of its *possible* performances would need to be taken into account if the "gestural" were to be identified.

A pragmatic resolution to this tension between a need for the realization of gesture in inflected performance and a recognition of the potentialities in the score can be found in observing the process of preparing performance. Resolving tensions between a desire to shape movement in certain ways and the constraints imposed by the actual contour presented in a score is a routine part of practicing, not a theoretical mystery. A performance of a pattern as gestural is (as suggested in chapter 1) a form of "mediation," whereby a performer brings an embodied understanding of gestural motion, acquired through practice and capable of nuanced differentiation, to meet the interpretive requirements of a specific moment in the score. The gesture that emerges is not simply the performer's "spontaneous" expressive movement, but neither is it just a conventionalized enactment of a shaping that is fully determined by its written melodic shape. It is truly a mediation, at a middle point that reflects both the performer's individual characteristics as a musically trained "mover" and also enacts the subjective potentialities of the shaping observable in the score. It thus provides a middle point between the idea of a particular act and that of a notated formation.

When notated melodic groupings are cited as potentially "gestural," they themselves may be particular realizations of some more general type of pattern, such as a "neighbor-tone figure," "suspension with descending resolution," or one of any number of ornaments. A third consideration in addressing gesture (apart from particular movement and written shape) is, then, with the constraints of "style." Some styles select particular figures to do the work of "gestures"; they set up a relatively determinate manner of performance, and also of affective connotation, to go with them. It would not, for example, be possible to perform the descending patterns in Bach's sonata with an emphasis on their second quaver without creating a ludicrous reversal of the stylistically determined relationship of stress and release. Nor would it be appropriate to perform them at a tempo which undermined the seriousness of the affect of "pathos" typically conveyed in passages of this kind (although Romanticized performance tends to go the other way and overemphasize it with a lugubriously slow tempo). Some freedom is nonetheless available, within limits, in choosing the tempo of performance and the degree of stress, so creating modifications in the affective nuance of the passage, while remaining within a familiar expressive "kind."

Once the aspect of style is included, an interaction is set up between three different, but interrelated, senses of "gesture," which cannot be realized effectively apart from one another: a "gesture" is an inflected *performance* of some patterning, uniquely realized in a moment of time; it is a notated feature, closely aligned with a figuration or motif; it is also an aspect of melodic patterning that is systematically developed in some styles, in ornaments or short conventional figurations. The inter-relatedness of these aspects needs always to be retained. To be realized as "gestural," a pattern must be embodied in a specific act, but the inflected performance needs also to answer to the suggestions of notated shaping (see Lidov, 1987: 83), understood within a stylistic milieu. In some cases, that style might determine the form of the realization, as part of the conventions associated with the notated shape.

b. Neurophysiological Determinants

Lidov defines "gesture" in its general sense as encompassing "all brief, expressive molar units of motor activity, be they of the limbs, the larynx, the torso, etcetera, units which are whole but not readily subdivisible" (1987: 77). Drawing on the experimental work and theories of the neuropsychologist, Manfred Clynes, he develops a view of gesture as an action which is neurophysiologically determined to express a specific affective state. Clynes, himself a pianist,[1] was inspired in his study of musical gesture by what he describes as "the profound musicianship of Pablo Casals." For two months, he worked with Casals in Puerto Rico and attended many master classes.[2] A telling story, which he relates in his book, *Sentics* ([1977] 1989), is of Casals instructing an advanced cello student to play with "grace":

> Some years ago, in the house of Pablo Casals in Puerto Rico, the Master was giving cello master classes. On this occasion, an outstanding partici-pant played the theme from the third movement of the Haydn cello con-certo, a graceful and joyful theme. Those of us there could not help ad-miring the grace with which the young master cellist played—probably as well as one would hear it anywhere.
>
> Casals listened intently. "No," he said, and waved his hand with his fa-miliar, definitive gesture, "that must be graceful!" And then he played the same few bars—and it was graceful as though one had never heard grace before—a hundred times more graceful—so that the cynicism melted in the hearts of the people who sat there and listened. That single phrase penetrated all the defenses, the armor, the hardness of heart which we mostly carry with us, and with its power transformed us into people who were glad to be alive. ([1977] 1989: 53)

The question arising for Clynes from this encounter is related to that raised by Dunsby in his search for "artistry." "What was the power that did this?" Clynes asks. What is it that distinguishes a performance of a figure with op-timal "grace" from one which is acceptably competent and yet somehow or-dinary? It seemed to be "a slight difference in shape between the phrase as played by the young man and by Casals. A slight difference—but an enor-mous difference in power of communication, evocation, and transforma-tion" (ibid.).

Clynes sought to address the question of what it was that imbued Casals' performance with such a superior degree of affective precision by investigat-ing the connection between distinctive emotional states and precise physio-logical actions in a limited span of time (no more than a few seconds). His diverse educational background, in engineering as well as neuroscience, gave him the means by which to devise ways of measuring the movements involved in minute gestural activity. A "gesture," he found, was a motion that could be measured as having a shaped contour, with varying direction, levels of pressure (force), and overall length. He put forward an hypothesis that a set of basic gestural motions were neurophysiologically encoded to express basic emotional states: sex (erotic love), anger, platonic love, grief, joy, hate, and reverence (ibid.: 30–31). If this hypothesis were true, it would entail that the basic shapes were not radically modified by cultural habits in the public expression of emotional response, even if the *degree* of their enactment was attenuated in more restrained groups. Clynes argued also that, as a neurophysiological response, gestures could be carried out in any part of the body. He observed their dynamic forms to be expressed in any motor output, including finger pressure, and in his experimental verification of the theory, using varied cultural groups, he measured the dynamic shape produced by a subject's finger on an instrument called a "sentograph" ([1977] 1989; Clynes and Nettelheim, 1982; Lidov, 1987).

Clynes' "gesture" is defined as a performative act which is neurophysiologically determined to express a given affective state.[3] Although aspects of his experimental methodology have been disputed by others, his general idea that gestures have an invariant form across cultures, and that they are capable of being performed with varying degrees of precision, has been independently supported. Research by the psychologist, Paul Ekman, suggests, for example, that universally recognized expressive facial displays have a stable relationship to the autonomic nervous system (see Schechner, 1990: 30). An opposing viewpoint has notably been put forward by the anthropologist, Ray Birdwhistell, who is able to identify tiny differences between social groups in events as small as gestural displays at moments of greeting. As these events occur in microseconds, they are not, he suggests, explicable by reference to physically determined responses, but display social conditioning—or learning—on a micro-scale. In emphasizing nature or nurture respectively, Ekman and Birdwhistell differ markedly on the extent to which non-negotiable or "hard-wired" elements determine the shaping of an emotional response, or its behavioral manifestation. Mediating between them, the anthropologist, Richard Schechner, has suggested that these views could be harmonized, if observations are made of the fine levels of gestural learning undertaken by actors in traditions with a prolonged and disciplined program of training (ibid.: 30). "The culture-specific kinemes [units of motion] that Birdwhistell finds" are, in his view, "built *on top of and out of* the "universal language of emotions." That is, the universal language is neither static nor fixed but transformable—the more so, the more conscious individuals are of it" (ibid.: 32). Ekman's evidence actually supports this approach, as an important part of it is related to emotional learning. Actors instructed by him to manipulate their faces into an emotion, without knowing what it was, could be measured to "feel" that emotion as much in their Autonomic Nervous System (ANS) as those who tried to put themselves into the designated emotional state (Ekman, 1983: 1210). Noting this, Schechner asks whether it might not be the case that an actor performing in a highly controlled dramatic discipline, such as that described in the Sanskrit *Natyasastra* (see chapter 1), could also be effecting changes on their ANS. "If the kathakali displays also elicit changes in the ANS, might this not indicate the human neurological system accepts a very deep emotional learning?" (1990: 31).

One of the directions in which learning can take place is towards an increasing precision in the control of movements which enact gestures on a scale perceptible to others, so that they become free of extraneous or distracting movements. Konrad Lorenz, also an anthropologist, has observed that, even in natural selection, a pressure exists towards the preservation of those kinds of signaling movements that are most precise in conveying information to another member of the species. Like Clynes, he identifies the resulting quality as one of "grace":

> With the elimination of the noise in the movement, when the movement becomes graceful, it becomes more unambiguous as a signal. . . . The more pregnant and simple the movement is, the easier it is for it to be taken up unambiguously by the receptor. Therefore, there is a strong selection pressure working in the direction of making all signal movements, these releasing movements [Innate Release Mechanisms or learned gestalts], more and more graceful, and that is also what reminds us [in animal behavior] of a dance.

If hypotheses about the universality of gestural expression, and its susceptibility to being entrained to greater levels of precision, are correct, some progress may be made in understanding the "gestural" aspect of musical performances. Lidov's theory of musical semiosis offers one means of making progress in this direction.

c. Performed Inflections and Notated Types

The framework within which Lidov develops his basic exposition of musical gesture is that of Peirce's second trichotomy: icon, index, and symbol. Musical gestures are presented as iconic, conveying in their own presentational form the feeling of expressive gestures. Lidov does not elaborate Peirce's full system in "Mind and Body in Music" (1987), although a description of it may be found in his recent book (1999). The distinctions represented by Peirce in other trichotomies are not, however, absent from his description of gesture in "Mind and Body." Most important is his emphasis on particular performed inflections, as suggested by Clynes. An inflected performance is the means by which gestural signification is realized, and without it—even if only as a potentiality—the sense of "gesture" in a figuration is lost. By pointing out the distinction between a particular performance and its notated form, Lidov shows a sensitivity to the discriminations captured in Peirce's first trichotomy, where singular (sinsigns) and conventional signs (legisigns) appear. Sinsigns and legisigns mark two points on a scale of events with varying degrees of conventionality. The "singular" depends on a particular enactment, while the purely "conventional" can be identified readily as a repeated pattern with an assigned connotative range. A performed inflection is a singular event, and an appoggiatura is a conventional ornament, with gestural potentiality, but between them come many degrees of stylistic determination.

If it is accepted that "gesture" can be applied appropriately to some musical events, the next issue is to clarify how its limits might be defined musically. Lidov suggests that any short grouping of notes, such as a melodic figuration, could fulfill the role. One way to pursue this idea would be to look to ornamentation as a source of short, expressive figures, which give the performer some freedom of execution even while taking a familiar form. It is well recognized that, in a Baroque composition, spontaneous ornamentation (or application of the "graces") by the performer is an important means of injecting expressivity into an unadorned melodic moment. Francesco Geminiani, for example, recommends a study of ornamentation in his violin manual, in order that a performer can contribute to the affective content of a work:

To the end therefore that those who are Lovers of Musick may with more Ease and Certainty arrive at Perfection, I recommend the Study and Practice of the following Ornaments of Expression. ([1751] 1951: 6, ex. XVIII)

Without these ornaments, "perfection" is lacking in Geminiani's view. No matter how well-executed the work, its ornaments are necessary to its expressive success. One tempting way to proceed further would be to create a catalogue of ornaments and seek to establish a rule about the nature of their expressive affect. Topoi, such as the appoggiatura, which extend from the Baroque through the nineteenth century, express "pathos" to varying degrees. Scottish snaps are "jaunty," and trills create an increased intensity, often signaling an immanent end to the phrase. Such generalizations are useful in dealing with the third level of gesture—its conventionalized aspect—as it shows that gestures can become standardized as replicable "symbols" or "topoi" within a style. To jump straight to the conventional aspect of ornaments, as expressive devices which take a familiar form, could, however, be a maneuver that overlooks an aspect of spontaneity or freedom in their execution, made possible through a momentary breaking off from the more formal purposes, or regular tempo, of a phrase. The precise timing of an ornament in performance is as crucial to its expressive success as is the conventionalized form it may take.

A simple example may illustrate the continuing role of ornamentations as gesture in the nineteenth century and the importance of exact timing to their effectiveness. (*See* Example 5.2.) The opening phrase to the slow movement of Tchaikovsky's Violin Concerto is formed with the broad brush strokes of an ascending G-minor scale. So familiar, and even mundane, is this formation, so relaxedly unadorned its presentation, so stable its harmony, that it comes across as "distant" and calm, even noble in its unhurriedness. A repeated enunciation of the stable fifth degree, D, forms a moment of tonal stasis in which further events are portended, undetermined but looked-for. Suddenly, this unassuming scalar formation is personalized with a moment of "fantasy," an ornament, including an extended trill, which turns around the goal note, extends above it, and returns. When Ruggiero Ricci plays it, on an old recording,[4] the trill brings gentleness into the grandiosity of this

Example 5.2. Opening to slow movement of Violin Concerto, by P. I. Tchaikovsky

slow-moving phrase. He makes a slight hesitation, with a subtle emphasis on the higher notes that extend the trill before its end. It is like the inflections of a voice, as if a storyteller were to alter his voice, to say "mark this." Descending, afterwards, through the G-minor scale (from dominant to lower dominant), the emphatic figurations (descending thirds C–B-flat–A; B-flat–A–G; F-sharp–E-flat–D) are drawn out to convey a feeling of gestural urgency, pathos, or bitterness, as one who suddenly injects a strong inflection into their voice, though the passage otherwise could be quite mundane. The wind instruments are to reinforce the moment, echoing in sympathy, as if the personal moment could be understood and taken up also by other voices. In this very simply constructed theme, it is the trill, and the changes of inflection in the descending figurations, that convey the performers' expressive purpose.[5] Even a slight inflection away from what is predictable introduces a feeling of individuality, from the soloist and supporting oboists.

Microstructural changes in pace—as well as in emphasis—are thus used to transform a melody constructed of common scale movements, only slightly decorated, into a theme which marks this movement as individual, and the performers as having an input into its expressive result (see Meyer, 1956). If only slight changes in pressure, emphasis, and timing alter the felt affective nuance, their absence is nonetheless conspicuous in poor performances. Without the perturbations that individuate the gestural content here, the oboes' entries can sound like mere redundancies. Well performed, however, the dynamic of gestural moments and broad thematic pace is reminiscent of a novel like *War and Peace,* where grand themes of war are personalized with intimate moments of love and tragedy. The personal is then taken up into the expansive, as if personal intimacies and national movements were somehow intertwined.

d. Singularity and Category Names

It has been seen, when discussing sounds, that a Peircean account recognizes the capacity of singular events to act as signs and that in so doing, it brings a problematic element into interpretive description, since something "singular"—unfamiliar and unrepeated—is not capable of being identified by using a common label. The same kind of problem appears in discussing nuanced gesture. Accepting Raffman's argument that the aspects of music most readily named are those which fall into distinctive categories (as pitches fall into a scale), any aspect of performance which makes use of microstructural nuance will require an extended use of language in order to be described. Performed inflections must necessarily display singularity—at least to some degree. They are not fully determined by the score, and the range of variation in pitch, dynamic, or tempo are seemingly unlimited. As a result, the problems which attend descriptions of "nuance" in sound quality remain at issue when a grouping of notes, whether an ornament or other melodic figure, are inflected to become "gestural." Even when the pattern being considered is a common one ("appoggiatura," "changing note," "emotion-laden turn"),[6] its performance as an inflected "gesture" cannot be characterized fully by labeling the figural type. Although elements in the structural organization of other melodic motifs (those which do not fall under a common name) can be fully characterized in the lan-

guage of technical description, their combination and inflected performance
are each particular. A way into language for the "gestural" attributes arising
from such unique syntheses and inflections has, then, to take an alternative
route, one that does not rely on category names alone but also embraces ad-
verbial terms for performed action and its qualities.

The opening figures of Brahms' Violin Sonata in G Major would be a case
in point, where short melodic incipits have the potential to take on a gestural force but do not belong to a class of ornaments. (*See* Example 5.3.) The
means of describing gestural nuance are not essentially different here from
those used in describing the nuances of sound (see chapter 4), but a preliminary descriptive step needs to be made. Even the notated organization of
the figure has a gestural potentiality, and to describe it, it is necessary to examine the various structural features that contribute to the formation of
its distinctive shape. The intervallic content, direction of pitch motion, and
rhythmic structure all contribute to forming a unitary figure with distinctive quality,[7] although any feature taken alone could be described as an unexceptional example of standard procedures. In the first entry, a descent
through the inverted tonic arpeggio is anticipated with an anacrusis (with C
added to the descent). The next two entries are rising thirds, similarly anticipated. When an attempt is made to capture the quality of motion that
emerges from them, the resulting language is likely to be metaphoric, but
not unmotivated. With the anacrusis of the first entry, moving towards the

Example 5.3. Opening figures from Violin Sonata in G Major, by Johannes
Brahms

beat, an "eagerness" is conveyed, but the subsequent drop brings a relaxation of intensity. This dropping off is to be compensated for in the anacrustic rising figures. Their anticipation of the beat again brings a sense of persuasive "agency," a need to go in a definite direction, but the brevity of the figures, and their spacing with rests, also creates a kind of "hesitancy." These qualities of motion, derived both from the pitch and rhythmic organization, together give the figures their "gestural" content. An idea of gesture does not get imposed on the music, as something external to it, but emerges from the qualities of its own "motion." Implicit in this view of figuration as "gestural" is an acceptance that the combined aspects of musical motion are not perceived as abstract qualities but "through the body."[8]

If gestural potentiality can be observed in figurations which combine elements of pitch and rhythmic motion, it is not realized unless a performer brings to the figuration an understanding that establishes a unitary "kinesthetic" impulse. Imagine the opening of Brahms' sonata played by a novice at a slow tempo, with studied attention to every beat. The anacrusis is very precisely divided (dotted quaver, semiquaver) and each of the beats in the ¾ bar get an audible emphasis. The effect of this careful performance is to break up the figure into smaller fragments, which do not combine to create the impression of a single motion through the descending arpeggio. What could be a gestural moment becomes a piece of pedantry so extreme, it is hard to believe that Brahms could have composed it. Compare that to a performance by Itzhak Perlman. His relaxed, but not sluggish, tempo is effective in balancing the aspects of forward-striving anacrusis and gentle dropping away, with a view to the ongoing spacing in the phrase. Each figure attains a gestural identity, as a single kinesthetic unit, but also begins to relate to a broader context of motion. The peformer's identity is heard in his specific choices about degrees of emphasis to be accorded certain points, so that "gesture" is not only a realization of a notated potentiality, but a marker of his or her own "feel" for the shape.

⌒

In summary, gestures are to be observed as an emergent potential of the qualities of pitch and rhythmic motion in a notated figure, realized in a particular performance when it occurs at a tempo, and with emphases that allow a unitary kinesthetic motion to be conveyed. It may now be asked, "What is the relationship between a functional level of description and a semiotic one in cases such as this?" Techniques such as those developed by Eugene Narmour for the analysis of melodic implication and realization can be called upon to characterize every aspect of pitch and rhythmic organization that makes up a melodic gesture, and they do so in an exact and highly sophisticated way, so (it can be asked again) why would any additional level of description be required? One hypothesis could be that the term "gesture" captures the combined effect of technical elements. But this is not quite enough to justify its use. The synthesis of elements into an individual result, not predetermined by any given stylistic pattern, is already captured very well by Narmour's technique, and resort to the semantic term, "gesture," is not necessary in order to describe each conglomerate. Intervallic size, directionality of motion, the relative metric positioning and duration of notes, their rhythmic grouping, and tonal role: all act together to individuate a given melodic unit from its common formal and stylistic elements and are separately described in Narmour's methodology. The usefulness of this method should not be underestimated.[9] Recognizing the synthesis is essential to understanding the individual character of any melodic moment and, unless a particular quality of motion were to emerge in Brahms' rising thirds, for example, it would be impossible to say that the violin's entry in this sonata was an individual moment, representing this particular work and no other. (Why, otherwise, would this opening be "special" and worthy of the greatest artistry in the shaping of its intervals in performance, not merely a mundane arpeggiation, similar to that practiced every day as part of a technical exercise?) If the combined aspects of pitch and rhythmic organization are able to be considered, using Narmour's analytical techniques, and the distinctive interplay of pitch and rhythmic elements can be well understood in this way, giving strong guidelines as to the range of its possible shapings, what role can reference to "gesture" play in addition to this?

A gestural "semantics" becomes relevant in an attempt to capture the affective connotation of melodic units. To say that a gestural quality "emerges" from the technical features is to suggest that it is something that comes out of the synthesis of elements, but which cannot be understood simply as their combined effect. The idea of a quality "emerging" can, in some fields (such as the biological), imply that it is endowed "from above," magically almost, apart from the information provided by a lower level of organization, but this "danger" is not so heinous in a humanistic context as it is in some cases of physical explanation.[10] The emergence of a gestural effect in a melodic incipit occurs through the synthesis of its structural elements, when they are heard as embodying aspects of movement (in directionality, force, etc.) which, in a human context, suggest expressive agency. An experience of embodied human movement serves to organize perception of the qualities of musical motion, almost in the manner of an "aspect switch," allowing them to be heard in a manner that may carry a signification of affectivity. This effect is achieved because the vocabulary of human gesture, seconded to musical description, still carries with it the connotations of gestural "affect" or emotional communicativeness found in the human domain. A person does not just move towards something but does so with "urgency" or "hesitation." When an agent is in a state of passive movement, away from something, he or she may be either "suffering" an action reluctantly or enjoying the freedom of a moment's release.[11] Gestural movements in music, like human movements, carry qualities of agency, with their associated affects, as evident in the "eagerness" or "hesitancy" of intervallic motions described above. This level of description thus links the descriptions made available in a method such as Narmour's with haptic images and notions of agency which allow for a characterization of expressive content.

Reference to gesture helps, also, in underscoring the role of a performer in contributing to the heard affective content of a melodic unit. The *degree* of any quality—"hesitancy," "forcefulness," and so on—is modified quite radically in performance. Gentleness or intensity is conveyed by volume; relative urgency or dynamism is determined by the chosen tempo. A potential gesture, emergent in the notated form, can either be heightened to the point of hysteria or extinguished by an overly literal reading. How much emphasis is heard on the strong beats in Brahms' opening phrase makes a great difference to whether a gentle persuasiveness or frustrated passion is conveyed in the halting incipits (the rising thirds). If the tempo is taken too slowly, neither will emerge, and the "gestural" potentiality will be less fully realized in the creation of a more "laid-back" mood. For a critic to characterize this level of content in words, recourse is again necessary to a vocabulary for qualities of gesture in human enactments.

e. Repetition as the Degradation or Intensification of Gestural Signs?

In some cases, a group of notes selected as "gestural" may coincide with a motive which is developed within a tonal movement, where it moves between different harmonic contexts, gaining an altered tonal sense. The neighbor-tone motive opening Tartini's Violin Sonata in G Minor, "Dido's Lament," is a case in point. (*See* Example 5.4.) Heard first as formed around the fifth degree in the tonic, G minor, the neighbor tone (on the sixth degree) reinforces the fifth of the minor triad, its semitonal motion creating a strong impetus for return to the fifth. When the same pitches are repeated as the lower part of a double-stopped version (bar 5), the combined neighbor-tone motive implies a relative major triad (B-flat), more "optimistic" in effect, and the whole-tone interval in the upper part considerably weakens the impetus toward return. Repeated further in the context of the dominant chord (bars 7–8), the semitonal neighbor tone in both parts restores the strength of melodic impetus, the instability of the dominant adds further tonal tension, and the immediate repetition of the motif a third higher provides intensification. A description of the motif as "gesture" could perhaps be attempted, for example, as "a single motion that incorporates phases of leaning towards, and falling away from, a point of emphasis, with a sense of incomplete release." For the motive to remain an exemplification of these gestural properties, it needs only to retain the same kinesthetic shape, achieved in performed nuance. But to what extent does it retain its "pathetic" connotations when the motive forming this gesture is tonally recontextualized? This depends largely upon the performer's choice to maintain a consistent pattern of rendition. If the same pattern of realized motion can be heard, the motif remains the "same" gesture, despite its intervallic and tonal alteration. Its original "pathos" might then be heard as being suggested, but reconsidered somewhat whimsically in the light of new tonal "perspectives." If a performer gives some stability of gestural sense to the motive, across tonal contexts, he or she creates the conditions for suggesting more

Facing Page: Example 5.4. Bars 1–10, Violin Sonata in G Minor, "Dido's Lament," by Giuseppe Tartini

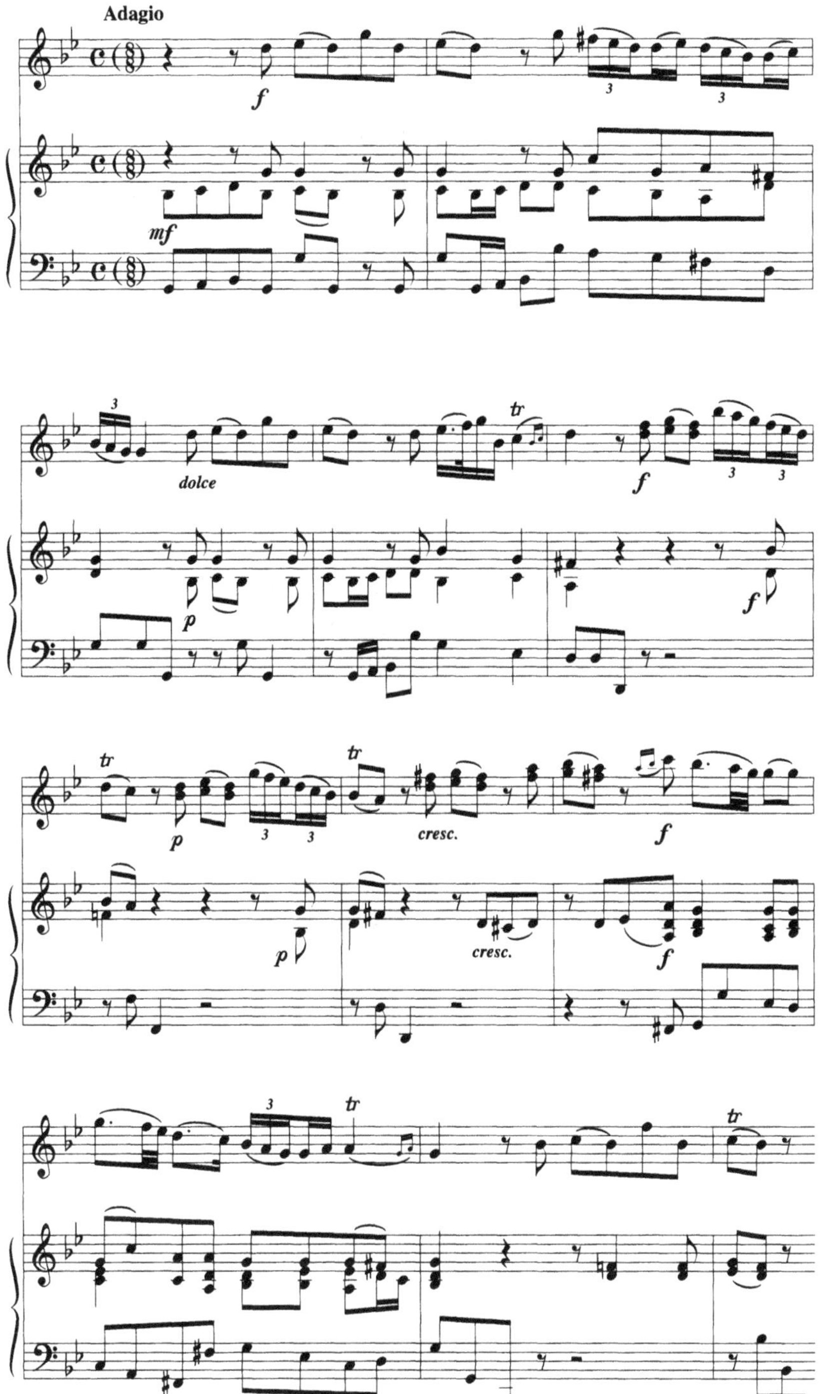
Adagio
f
mf
3
dolce
p
tr
cresc.

than one level of signified sense, as the movement unfolds. Hints of pathos in the gestural shape are by turns ameliorated (bar 5), intensified (bar 6), and rendered more innocuous (bar 10) by the changing tonal value of the pitches that give it motivic identity. On this argument, the shape as gesture remains relatively stable, its motivic identity is retained, but changes in tonal context provide new "interpretants," new perspectives that modify the "pathos" first heard as signified. The group of notes could not be said to carry one essential meaning that remains stable, but neither could they be said to have become completely different in their signification as they move through time.

~

The potential for instability of meaning in verbal signs is a concomitant of their contextual mobility, which allows individual words (cf. nouns) to maintain the appearance of being the "same word" while altering their sense.[12] A mediated awareness of shifting conventions, or altering contextual cues, is necessary to decoding them, just as it is when interpreting the altered effect of an established melodic motive heard in different tonal positions. In contrast to this, indexical signs lack a mobility born of purely symbolic reference because they have a fixed relation to some physical state of affairs, and iconic signs are limited by the need to simulate a likeness to some "object," whether real or only stipulated. A tonal motive heard as a "gesture" embraces aspects of the indexical and iconic, as well as its "symbolic" functions. Its effect cannot be explained purely as that of a pitch formation, transposed to new tonal contexts, because the hearing of "gesture" depends on many factors other than pitch. Musical "gesture" is a perceived indexing of bodily motion, as carrying a definite direction, weight, and degree of impetus, to form a shape felt as "iconic" of gesture in another domain of movement, which may be human and expressive. Because, in many cases, the formation of a motive as "gesture" depends so strongly on the performer's choices of tempo and emphasis when interpreting the motive, the gesture can reasonably be said to index a bodily action quite literally, as it is performed. Heard by a listener, the gestural "likeness" does not depend on how the performance "looks," although a live performance might provide some very useful cues to listening if the performer's movements are not too cluttered with extraneous tics. The gesture can be recognized or (in some styles) dynamically "felt" in sound, in its characteristic directionality, emphasis, and speed, without necessary recourse to an explicit set of conventions. This is not to say that it is completely "natural" and unmediated; rather, to suggest that the kinds of "interpretant" necessary to understanding gesture cannot be limited to an explicit knowledge of stylistic rules, but must include a learned recognitional "feeling" or dynamic response, themselves entrained by conventions of different kinds. (Aspects of Peirce's "firstness" are found in the interpretant of "feeling" and of secondness in a dynamic response.)

The formation of gesture cannot be misrepresented as a direct expression of some state of mind held by the performer, who merely projects it through sound, but neither can the physical states of the performer be discounted as irrelevant to the effect being produced. Insofar as some musical gestures simulate the effects of expressive gesture in people, they are subject not only to the variability of convention but also to neurophysiological constraints, which limit the possible range of movements that can be associated with a given expressive "intent." To what extent can a performer whose actual physical states contradict those to be musically "expressed" succeed in simulating the required gestural form? This leads into a question raised by Lidov.

2. To Perform or to Dissimulate?

a. Can Gestures Ever Lie?

Lidov suggests that gestural signs are unlike words (symbols), in their incapacity to be used as lies. Because gestures are, in normal communication, observable states and movements of the body, which in their expressive capacity are linked to states of the autonomic nervous system (ANS), it is not possible for a speaker to "lie" with them to the degree that is possible with words. ("Lie-detector" machines rely on the fact that states of physical excitation cannot be simulated to fit a speaker's untrue assertion about his or her beliefs.) The degree to which emotional states can be enacted under false pretenses may vary with the states themselves. Manfred Clynes experimented to find out the effects of lying on the expression of (non-sexual) love and anger, respectively, and found that "lying significantly lowered the self-rated intensity of love but not of anger" ([1977] 1989: 195). In effect, he confirmed a common intuition that deceitfulness is compatible with angry but not with loving feelings. This question about the viability of gestural deceit is not inconsequential, as it influences the degree to which the "immediacy" of affect in a performance is illusory. Ekman and Friesen recognize that gestural affect displays in ordinary conversation "can be dissimulated" (1981: 103). Any "immediate" response felt in the ANS is adapted to the demands of "display rules," which incorporate the limitations placed by a culture, social class, or family on which affects are "appropriate for certain settings." The enacted gesture is not, they suggest, an unmediated reflection of a "felt" state, but a form of expression which is modified by social rules, and it may represent a suppression of what is being genuinely felt. At issue, then, is how convincing the social act can be when it masks a state of contrary feeling. Clynes' earlier observation (sentics) that it is impossible to experience and express more than one "basic emotion" at the same time would, if ratified, lead to the conclusion that marked attempts at dissimulation will not go undetected. Of course, it is possible to "assume" a gesture without sincerity, to smile when appropriate, and to act out the movements of a stipulated part without any "inner" conviction; but detecting someone's insincerity, social artifice, or unconvincing propensity to "act" is not an accomplishment that requires great learning. All it needs is what Goleman (1996) cites as "emotional intelligence," a capacity to "read" others' states from their social performances. A disparity between the state being felt by others, as evident in their involuntary movements, and the effect they try to convey in more controlled gesturing, can readily be seen by an observant onlooker. To see and respond to correctly conventional, but insincere, behavior is a normal aspect of participating in what Gadamer (1960) calls the "sensus communis," the cultivated social community.

To gain a concrete image of this point, it may be helpful to imagine a scenario in which welcoming acts are displayed. Suppose I am to respond to the greeting I receive as someone's "formal" guest, where I am not a personal friend, and she is my academic superior.[13] I note that what is in one moment a transparent expression of pleasure is transformed by a subtle shift in expression to a contrived politeness in the other's smile. My perception of her appearance is modified by an awareness that a conventional mode of greeting includes a smile, and that the convention has been manipulated in an overly extended torture to the corners of her mouth. This semiotic consciousness yields an increased "distance." I am less responsive to the "welcome" the gesturer wished to convey because my awareness has shifted to the sign *as a sign*. As the smile has become a token of a type of behavior, I respond to it with a self-conscious awareness of the social game, and my detachment decreases the strength of feeling in my smile of greeting, as it mirrors theirs, making of it a self-conscious mirroring contrivance. This, of course, forms a barrier to empathy and yields a somewhat formal inter-change, but the distance, too, is accepted as part of the game of meeting a stranger with whom emotional "familiarity" is not to be peremptorily assumed.

In this example, semiotic awareness is important for the contextualization of affect and the negotiation of the degree of emotional "distance" between two people. The focus of attention shifts to the form of the representamen (the smile) in such a way that its status as a token of a type of greeting be-comes dominant, rather than its individuated expressivity. An enacted ges-ture is thus capable of behaving like a element of a language, with a stipu-lated meaning. It can be manipulated to produce the appearance of some emotional state as its "object," irrespective of whether that state is being sin-cerely felt, and its opacity as a stipulated unit of meaning can readily be ob-served. In these respects, it is no different from a word, whose slippage of meaning has disarmed the intentions of its speaker. All of this social nuance does not, even so, prove the success of dissimulation. The very fact that it is possible to see the difference between a spontaneous and a contrived greet-ing, in a moment of fleeting and undeliberated attention, suggests that the art of discerning a disparity between a state of feeling and an "affect display" is not a difficult one.

In sum, it appears that the repetition of a gesture, where it represents a state being felt in the ANS, can intensify its affect, but the opposite result is achieved if the repetition is only of a socially stipulated form.

b. Prescriptive Practices in Gestural Performance

If social situations involve a negotiation between sensitivity to the particular, and awareness of conventional constraints on behavior, a similar negotiation could be postulated to exist in response to musical gestures, where both a "natural" awareness of bodily movement and an ear for the conventional in stylistic performance are involved.[14] If it is possible for a listener both to "feel" a movement as gesture, experiencing its affective content, and to be aware of its conventional standing within a style, its "sadness" (or even tragic pathos) may be framed and made tolerable. "Semiotic consciousness," or awareness of context, gives a perspective of greater emotional distance. I may feel intensely the pathos of the series of double-stopped appoggiaturas in Bach's Violin Sonata in B minor, but also recognize the harmonic and melodic conventions which govern their effect. My response is to two different aspects of signification and involves two different kinds of interpretant, an active interpretant mirroring the gesture as a uniquely performed event, and what Peirce would call a "logical" interpretant, contextualizing it as a token of a type. This negotiation of different, but concurrent, levels of awareness occurs also in performance, which involves an ability to split awareness between the shaping of the gesture as an expressive movement, ensuring its appropriate stylistic form (determined by performance traditions), and also making allowances for its context within the continuity of the phrase.

For a performer in a style of music where strong traditions prevail, one of the central tensions to be resolved is that between the freedom of the moment and the prescriptions of a style. The search for authenticity in execution has become a central value in parts of the musical community, starting with the Baroque and earlier works, but now extending itself to music of the nineteenth century, including Wagner. If Schechner's reflections on drama are taken as of any account, the internalization of a highly prescriptive set of rules for the execution of gestures should not, in itself, be incompatible with the production of a compelling performance, in which expressive "immediacy" is by no means absent. The requirement of success is only that prescribed patterns of movement be so well internalized, through frequent repetition, that they become the "performer's own."

3. Voice and Gesture as Virtualities

a. Anyone "Present"?

Jacques Derrida's (1974) discourse against the metaphysics of presence emphasizes that a "sign" can carry out its work independently of its authorial impetus. Rejecting the notion of the sign as a transparent vehicle for some creator's intentions, he places a great pejorative loading on the term "presence,"
a word which may evoke the quasi-mystic aura of an author's intention, hov-
ering about the sign, directing it on its course to a receptive mind. Theolog-
ical notions of God's presence in the Word can be heard in the background of
Derrida's thought, suggestions of immense consequence being imparted to
the hapless mistakes of any naive theorist who would reclaim a notion of
"presence" in a sign. If a case is to be made for a performer conveying his or
her interpretive "presence" through the enactment of a score, it cannot be
made, in the light of this critique, without first taking precautions against
any false assumption that performers can "project" or "express" themselves
in a direct way. A theory of gesture that emphasizes the neurophysiological
determination of some expressive movements could well fall into the trap
of suggesting a direct, unmediated "expression" in music. Lidov's gesture
theory could, for example, be simplified as saying that "if a performer repro-
duces the appropriate expressive shapes as precisely as possible, while exe-
cuting short melodic fragments which take a congruent form, a personal expression is achieved." This summary understates the influence of stylistic
convention on the form a gesture may take, and it downplays also the fact
that every melodic fragment with gestural potentiality is, as a "sign," at one
stage removed from gesture as an unmediated (physiologically driven) gestural expression in a human body. Simply to recognize a notated figure as
"gestural" is already to have engaged in interpretive activity. A brief rehearsal of Derrida's objection to the idea of "presence" in the sign will
reinforce these points.

It is well known that when Derrida rejected the notion of a subjective
"presence," animating elements of language with the intentionality of a
present or imagined speaker, he did so with music specifically in mind, as a
response to some comments made by Jean-Jacques Rousseau on the origin of
languages. Derrida cannot tolerate the excesses of Romanticism, and particu-

larly those of a thinker who imagines the possibility of a pure communion with the soul, who hears primordial utterances in musical sound—the untainted cries of a human creature unmarked by the dampening effects of civilization. To imagine a pure inwardness which can somehow make its way into the sounds of music or language, without the mediation of some conventional ordering, is not, Derrida emphasizes, to appreciate the necessary structure of signs. Nothing can be represented without interpretation. Even sounds created directly by the voice begin to be entrained by social conditions from the earliest infancy. Even expressive movements, existing as a neurophysiological potential in all human beings, require the provision of a specific set of codes if they are to be represented in dramatic or musical form. A pure utterance, leading to an unmediated communion of souls, may have the ring of transcendence about it, attracting people who are sickened by the cloying effects of an overly controlled society and yearning for a "pre-lapsarian" state of intuitive understanding, but the desire to ameliorate the effects of excessive conventionality cannot find its fulfillment in this way, except as a dream. "Cries of the soul," if they are to pass beyond the wailings of an injured child, must find their form in a medium that is shared and to some degree conventionalized. An escape from language into a form that allows a pure and unmediated self-presenting to the world can never be complete.

Once Derrida's anti-metaphysical injunctions have been taken in, do they need to instill a fear into all performers who hold the naive belief that they can "present" themselves on a stage, projecting their character through a dramatic or musical work? Should musicians forget "stage presence" as a quality to be sought? Not at all. The mistake of one excess cannot be corrected by moving to an opposite extreme. An awareness of convention, as the means of entraining bodies in their expressive enactments, should not lead to a denial that people—especially performers—have voices and bodies that are individuated as their own. The fact that utterance or movement has been entrained, especially in traditional artistic forms, does not mean that the voice has been muted or the body erased. Musicians and actors do not become puppets or clones, whose voices and bodies are merely those of their masters and idols on CDs. Presenting a work as a repetition of many others of the type is still making it "present" through bodies that are singular, in a time-space that is unrepeatable. Presenting a performance is not "playing yourself back," like a recording in which you have somehow become entrapped, to be exhausted as the spectator of your own moving, but absent, self. The physicality of a body, even one well trained, is an insistent fact. Tell me, when I'm nervous, that "you're not really here . . . your subjectivity is illusory" and I will be happy to comply with the mystic moment, but the shaking of my body will remind me that, in fact, my presence is required on stage. The individual imprint in a performer's body of conventions of enactment that are shared cannot, furthermore, be denied. The play of language or convention cannot remove the individuated physicality of enactments, or the identity of the "self" as a "subject" who is present in the body that moves. It might, of course, be fun to imagine a roll call of semiotically informed musicians, who answered "not 'present'" when their names were called, but even an impulse to self-denial (maybe from choristers engaged in performing meditative works), would not dissolve the resistant physicality of a bodily performing medium, whose difference from other bodies cannot be entirely dispelled.

Jean-Paul Sartre's (1956) notion of "bad faith" provides an excellent means of grasping the tensions that are here involved, between the need to acknowledge brute physical limitations on one side—with neurophysiological encodings of emotional states in gestures that are adaptive for the species—and to grasp interpretive freedom on the other. Neither denying bodily influence on the gesturally "expressive," nor denying the freedom of the mind to transcend determination, and to engage in interpretive mediation, will work. A denial of the shapings of movement afforded by neurophysiology will lead not to a superior sophistication of performance but to a loss of an essential source of expressive imagery. An opposite denial of the mediating role of a mind will lead to the complementary form of performed banality, in a rendition full of physicality without appropriate shape. A novice might ask, "Why shouldn't any performer who possesses a state of technical mastery and physical individuality impart a personal 'presence' to the sound they produce on the stage, or in a recording studio?" And the answer? "Asserting the simple presence of a performer producing sounds at an impressive rate is not the same thing as hearing 'presence' *in* the sound, any more than being physically present on the stage is the same thing as possessing that elusive quality known as 'presence' in the space. It is not just the presentation of a skilled body but its mediated, interpreted use that is at issue here." In cases of optimal performance, the illusion of expressive "immediacy" might be achieved through the performer's successful negotiation of the mediating space between physicality and interpreted gestural motion. He or she then seems to animate the moment in an individualistic way, and so to "express" him- or herself in it, as Ruggiero Ricci does in playing Tchaikovsky's slow movement on an old recording. Though convention gives a frame to his gestural movement in sound, the moment of performing is made his own, so it seems. What emerges is neither his own subjective identity, nor a reproduction of an affect long predicted in the style, but a "mediating representation"—the "subjectivity" of the work in its particular enactment, unrepeatable and compelling. "Presence" in performance is itself an effect of the sign. Not an authorial voice, not a performer's projection, but an interpreted *effect*. This is what I am claiming, in showing that elements of vocality and of gestural force can appear in a musical performance, as the effect of an interaction between a prepared body and an interpreted score. Hearing voices, and responding to gestures, is entering into a mode of engagement where a virtual "presence" or agency can be felt in the work, without false beliefs being held about its capacity to act as a conduit for the creators' states of mind (composer and performer together). Fears of musicianly delusion could easily be dispelled, if the game of questioning misguided musician's beliefs about their capacity for direct expression were replaced by an attempt to enter a semiotic realm where "presence" is created in the act of interpretive performance itself. Musicians do not need to find strange presences to be born in the music without any conception of its form or conventional constraints. Knowing both the characteristics of their own expressively trained bodies and the demands of a style, they *do,* even so, act as the midwives by whom the "presence" of the music can be brought into the world. Anything less than a fully committed presence to the work would not allow the birth to succeed. It would yield the performance of a stillborn child.

b. Gestural Agency and Subjective "Presence"

If the insistent physicality of the body (and its hardwired responses) is not denied as having an impact on the performed shaping of musical contours as "gestural," neither should the opposite denial be succumbed to, which fails to see the transcending power of "mind" in its capacity to organize, order, and construct the physical. Once the possibilities of "gestural" imagery in music have been recognized as attaching themselves to short figurations of various kinds, nothing is to stop that image from being retained, even when the figurations take on a contour that is disjunct in the extreme and unlike anything predicted either in a catalogue of common human movements, as overtly observed, or in the analysis of neurophysiologically encoded patterns of affective energy (such as those put forward by Clynes). If the quality of virtual "embodiment" and an apparent "presence" or "agency" can attach itself to gestures whose source in human movement is recognized, it can both be suggested and played against in "gestures" of another kind. A number of musical writers name and defend this experience of signified musical agency. Carolyn Abbate uses the image of a performance of a vocal work, the "Queen of the Night" aria from Mozart's *Magic Flute,* in order to describe a situation in which the voice takes on an agency not explicable as that of the performer alone.

The paradox of hearing an emerging musical presence of the Queen of the Night is that its power seems to throw the physically present performer into the background. The *virtual* agency of the Queen in her virtuosic musical utterance so dominates Abbate's hearing of the work as to make the Queen seem bodiless or supra-human. Take away the specific characterization of this operatic part and there remains a vivid picture of what it might be to experience a musical "presence" which is not simply that of a performer on stage:

> She suddenly becomes not a character-presence but an irrational non-being, terrifying because the locus of voice is now not a character, not human, and somehow not present. This same uncanny effect, I would claim, can govern moments marked by a singing voice in instrumental (that is, nonvocal, textless) music. This fear—instilled by voice *without* a physically present human character—might well be kept in mind. (Abbate 1991: 11)

An emergent voice "presents" itself, through the performer's body, and takes on its own distinctive character, not simply that of the performer, although it could not come into being without her. Abbate refers to this kind of emergent presence as that of a "figural subject" and notes that "masking or suppressing perception of individual performers," as when the musicians are hidden from sight in an operatic performance, "serves, in fact, to enhance" a sense of this musical subjectivity" (ibid.: 14). She responds to the "debunking moves" of poststructuralist thinkers by arguing that the insistent "presence" of a figural subject marks music out as being radically different from language. In the terms that have been presented here, the distinctive feature marking music out from purely linguistic utterance is its use of signs (in timbre, or inflection) which are directly connected to bodily states, and cannot be dissolved into a play of pure differences in a manner appropriate to conventional linguistic terms. Musical scores may contain patterns in their melodic organization that are particularly suited to an inflected "gestural" interpretation, and when so realized, it is as if the body becomes inscribed in the sound. Tartini's Violin Sonata in G Minor, "Dido's Lament," or Bach's Violin Sonata in B minor have been cited as examples of melody where gestural expressivity is strong. The "embodiment" heard in these works, when well performed, is not, however, merely that of performers "expressing themselves" but that of the emergent or "figural subject" of the work. When, in cases like the "Queen of the Night" aria, a sense of "disembodiment" is stronger than any embodied state, the structure of the music is such that it seems to "embody" movements which go beyond the capabilities of any human body. The tessitura, tempo, and lightness of the Queen's movement seem to speak of her as a disembodied entity, suggesting a body with an absence of weight and an ease of mobility uncharacteristic of human limitations. It is for this reason that its figural subject can seem supra-human.

Cone describes the virtualities of musical subjectivity by using the term "persona." He is careful to point out that "the persona's experiences are not the composer's experiences but an imaginative transformation of them; the reactions, emotions, and states of mind suggested by the music are those of the persona, not the composer" (1974: 85). In other places he uses the idea of an "agent" in the music. "Unlike real characters, however, instrumental agents move on a purely musical, nonverbal plane, and they communicate solely by what I have called symbolic *gestures*" (ibid., my italics). Cone's reflections do not suggest that a listener ought to be listening *through* the music, as if it were a transparent vehicle of the composer's voice.[15] They imply only that an agency emerges in the themes and "gestures" accorded individual instruments within a work. His idea of "symbol" is not informed by reference to semiotics, but his "symbolic gesture" is more or less equivalent to an iconic sign, which carries its capacity to signify in its own presentational form (see chapter 2). Lidov's description of musical agency, taking on a more specifically semiotic character, allows him to distinguish more readily between the differing attitudes of a gestural "agent"—striving towards a goal, or moving away in passive receptivity—but Cone's sensitivity to kinds of embodied motion is very similar. Finding "motion" in melodic structures is common enough in music theory, but relating this motion to the movements of a body, in breathing, gesturing, or forming a movement "phrase," as these authors do, is an important part of what it is to hear a virtual subjectivity in melodic shapes, the body inscribed in sound.

Hearing certain kinds of melodic movement as "gestural" can be recognized as a propensity that extends well beyond cases in which any likeness to human movement can be realistically claimed. Neurophysiological limitations may circumscribe the range of socialized movements that can be expressive of a given affective state, allowing only a certain range of tempi, degrees of force, or rates of change in physical action as publicly expressive of affective states. A musician's physical movement on his or her instrument is not, however, so circumscribed, nor is a composer's freedom to create melodic patterns that are "gestural" limited to a conception of human expressive gesturing. (The eighteenth-century theorist, Johannes Kirnberger, advised his composition students to observe the characteristic tempi of human movements in various moods and to assimilate them to the composition of musical movements, but the humanistic priorities of the eighteenth century need not be taken as normative.) If a trace of "gesture" and "agency" is retained, even when the range of movement has been extended to include large sudden disjunctions, high degrees of force, durations of motion well beyond that sustainable as a single human impulse, or conversely fast tempi, the effect is one of a "gestural agency" whose notional subject is no longer a human expressive agent, in any simple sense. The second movement of Bartók's posthumous Violin Concerto includes this passage, for example, in which a motive may be heard as "gestural" without suggesting the gross movements of a human body. (*See* Example 5.5.) The passage might be characterized as erratic, skittish, playful, even ironic in its sudden leaps, which distort the motivic shape. If these motivic shapes are "gestural," they are so because their movement suggests a highly mobile but unpredictable

Example 5.5. Solo violin line (bars 131-140), first movement, posthumous violin sonata, by Béla Bartók

agency. It could be that brief movements, in which a single impulse can be heard (even if disjointed), give rise to a recognition of "gesture," and of an apparent agency, even when that gesture is not like anything that could be conceived as the gross physical movement by a human being. If so, they cannot be transparently "expressive" of any affective state which is physiologically instantiated. Without being iconic of any existent thing or state, they suggest an "agent," neither personal in its affective characteristics, nor completely impersonal in its lack of movement and apparent "will," which perhaps embodies the apparent movements of thought, beyond the limitations of physical states.

If no limit can be placed on the kind of motive that could potentially be heard as "gestural," except that it should suggest a unitary impulse of some kind, the idea suffers from an inherent vagueness. Its lack of determinacy does not, however, warrant the conclusion that a notion of gesture lacks meaning. Corresponding views of meaning, which think any word should refer to a unitary thing, are not, after all, the only ones available, and the ability of musical "gesture" to play many games does not discount it from sense. What the variability does warn against is a view that finds in musical "gestures" a simple mapping of human movements, which can be directly "seen" (Davies) or otherwise felt, without respect for the freedom of music's "gestural" patterns to extend far beyond the mimicking of simple expressive shapes. Recognizing gestural virtualities as going beyond the socialized form of neurophysiologically limited expressive patterns could, of course, lead to exasperation for theorists, as the even greater inclusiveness, and hence vagueness in the sense of "gesture," makes a closed definition very difficult. Why not just recognize that "motives" can take an indefinably large number of forms and stop trying to name them as "gestures" at all? The point of describing "gesture" is, however, that it captures the propensity of listeners to hear in short, directed motions the evidence of a sometimes expressive agency in movement. These gestures are like Derrida's decorative "parerga," those elements of a text or structure deemed non-essential, without which "essential" forms and descriptions would be fraught with an insurmountable lack. Take away the most apparently inessential, decorative, vaguely defined thing, and you are left with the certainty of an emptiness that seems to elude your grasp—as the meaning you seek has been defined as non-essential to that which you are willing to see.

chapter six

~

Framing Willfulness in Tonal Law

A TONAL THEORY MIGHT attempt to characterize the structural regularities that give rise to certain kinds of tonal effect, such as varying degrees of virtual instability, willfulness, or desire. It might, on the other hand,
be more concerned with how tonal structures are cognitively mapped in the
broadest sense, without looking at their more connotative effects. Meta-
theoretical questions about the role of rules in different music theories have
been addressed by a number of authors (Agawu, Blasius, DeBellis, Guck,
London, Narmour, Snarrenberg), and a Peircean perspective on some of the
more general issues they raise, relating to the explanatory status of rules (and
particularly to Realism or Nominalism about general properties), may be
found in the Appendix. This chapter is concerned with the question of
structural signification. When it is asked what distinguishes a disciplinary
approach as "semiotic," as opposed to structuralist, one answer (suggested by
Eero Tarasti) is that the "semiotic" draws out connections between at least
two different levels of description, as applied to individual items, and then

seeks to make general observations about the ways in which such connections are achieved. A "sign" might even be described a relationship between levels of description, as an element defined at one level as a "literal" property (of sound or score) is found to support a "metaphorical" description (as an "object"), and to follow a pattern of connotation that may also be observed elsewhere (a repeatedly observed "interpretant"). Previous chapters have considered microstructural aspects of signification: how a combination of nuance and timbral characteristics produces a perception of "voice"; how melodic fragments may have a "gestural" potentiality which is drawn out when they are performed as unitary movements with distinctive shaping (whether that shaping is familiar in the observation of humanly expressive gestures, or newly formed as the image of a virtual moving "body"). In these chapters, both instrumental vocality and gesture have been shown to be capable of suggesting a broader notion of expressive agency as inhering in abstract music, as it is performed. The interpretive activity of a performer has also been found, in each case, to be necessary to the transformation of vaguely defined possibilities into particular events. A *possible* agency in the "vocal" coloration of violin sounds, or in the "gastrula" shaping of melodic groupings, cannot be made actual, unless the agency of an interpreter is involved, bringing the interpretants of "voice" and "gesture" to bear on his or her work with the score. Thus, although a performer cannot directly project him- or herself directly through the score, in acts of direct "expression," he or she can make a performance identity evident in the patterns of choice that he or she makes (see Clarke, 1985). A negotiation between the performer's agency and the potential agencies of the music leads to the formation of something new: a virtual agency in performance which has a particular expressive shaping and a characteristic way of playing with instrumental "voice," realizing one of a range of possibilities in a single moment that will not be repeated precisely at any other time.

In the movement of discussion from "voice" to "gesture," a change could be observed from working with a general possibility of violin performance style, the realization of which is often only loosely specified in written instructions to the performer (such as "parlando" or "cantabile"), to a mode of signification whose manner of realization is somewhat more closely determined, as particular gestural shapings are guided by melodic contour and grouping. This change towards greater determination is a mat-

ter of degree, not of a complete change in kind. As the realization of an ornament, figure, or motif as "gestural" depends on performed nuance, it remains a *possibility* that may not be carried through in a given performance.
"Gestural" signs are not circumscribed by written musical topologies, such
as those of ornament or motif, and although they may sometimes coincide
with them, the circumstances under which a "gestural" moment may appear
cannot be fully predicted by reference to these formal elements. If Peirce's
first set of questions about signs was now brought to bear ("Is the signifying
thing a quality, a singular event, or a general law/convention?"), it would
have to be said that "singularity" is an important feature of moments selected as gestural, despite the relevance of convention to some cases. A further shift is now to be made, to forms of musical signification that are built
on the rule-governed patterns of tonality, that is, from a consideration of
"singular" signs (in which general patterns may sometimes be observed), to
a consideration of rule-governed signs, or "legisigns."

At this point, a renegotiation of disciplinary boundaries needs to occur. It
is the traditional domain of music theory to make generalizations about
tonal procedures that are codified as "rules," while it is the domain of "aesthetics" to consider broader issues in the perception of musical "meaning."
This division is not, however, one that can be comfortably sustained, and the
semiotic analysis of tonal works will tend to bridge the concerns of both
fields. To gain a broad picture of the way that these fields of study have been
divided up in the twentieth century, the definitive comments of the German
theorists, Guido Adler and Hugo Riemann, may be considered in brief. In
defining the makeup of *Musikwissenschaft,* Riemann divides "aesthetics" from
"music theory" in a pragmatic way, on the assumption that the philosophical
approach of "aesthetics" is a foundation for the more detailed work of music
theory. The aesthetic

> is not concerned with passive but with active hearing; individual sounds
> are not, for it, the isolated facts of tonal sensation, but elements of a
> tonal conception. Tonal succession and the connection of chords become
> again for it what they were in the imagination of the composer: forms
> for the expression of mental movements; the medium for the trans-
> mission of the spiritual in an inanimate material, which only serves the

purpose of communication, finding its end and purpose in the spiritual. (Riemann, 1908: 7–8)

By contrast, "syntax" is, in Riemann's view, a practical discipline, which could be thought of as "applied aesthetics," but which must necessarily put aside the study of broad philosophical issues in order to specialize more on the "treatment of details with which aesthetics does not need to concern itself" (ibid.: 9). Riemann's distinction between fields is thus one of emphasis. What he refers to as the composer's "imaginative" or "mental" movements, the concern of aesthetics, remain relevant as the foundation of music theory, without being directly addressed, due to the priority of syntactic detail.[1] Adler works instead with the notion of an historically evolving style, the subject matter of historical musicology, as foundational for any systematic studies,[2] including those of rhythm, harmony, and melody (Adler, 1885: 9–11). "Aesthetic" studies are firmly grounded in this historical milieu, but are more general in their focus, being concerned with the reciprocal relationship between the "highest laws" of art, as extrapolated from historical study, and the "subject apperceiving the artwork" (ibid.: 12).

When the general attributes of tonal music are considered as means of signification, the concerns of "theory" and "aesthetics" are again brought together, within an historical perspective that recognizes the repertory of eighteenth- and nineteenth-century European Classical music both as the source of examples and as the field of application. A concern that comes up repeatedly in the analysis of individual works from this period is with how unfolding tonal processes come to embody properties of virtual agency such as those cited above (will, desire), described by Riemann as the "expression of mental movements" or "the transmission of the spiritual in an inanimate material." Rather than seeking an answer which delves into the creative psychology of the composer, this kind of question is directed toward an understanding of the sense of virtual agency inhering in the work. Generalizing from this interpretive question, a theoretical question is, "How can the aspects of tonal order codified in rules for harmony or counterpoint (and their broader application) assist in predicting the general types of signification that will appear in particular works?" Attributes of gestural "agency" have been observed already as a potential inherent in some melodic contours, to be carried through in performance when microstructural elements are fortuitously adjusted to what is "given" in the notated form. More extended forms of agency, heard as "will" or "desire," can be understood, at least in part, as arising from the organization of harmonic and contrapuntal processes around goal points, which may be anticipated and delayed in various ways. Systematic music theories are largely concerned with setting out the "rules" which govern tonal motion at various levels of generality, and are the principal arena within which detailed questions about the connotations of goal direction and evasion can be considered. Because the interpretive perspective of the Viennese theorist, Heinrich Schenker, has dominated much Anglo-American theorizing about tonal music, due to the subtlety with which it can represent directed motion as occurring on many levels, it will be the first topic of discussion in this chapter. Schenker's language for describing the "will of tones" is quite consistent with the idea of tonal signification. His way of formulating his ideas is not, however, free of aesthetic ideology, particularly in its seeking for hierarchical order and unified deep structures, a priority questioned by theorists interested in the constraints on what listeners can actually perceive. The degree to which listeners notice longer-term connections "below the surface" of a work is a common point of skepticism. Caution needs also to be entertained in taking up a descriptive language which systematically links structural motion between harmonies, or the longer-term unfolding of contrapuntal lines, with "desire," "will," or "mental motion." These general terms can easily become degraded into symptoms of an ideal, lacking connection with the qualities heard to emerge in any particular case, from the interaction of tonal processes with other musical parameters. Rather than discard the general terms, it needs to be asked again "in what way does the general prediction of the theory, concerning the qualities of different types of harmonic and contrapuntal motion, relate to particular instances, where subtle affects can be observed?" American theorist Leonard Meyer's thinking about the goals of music theory will here be taken up as a point of dialogue and contrast with Schenker's thought. His approach to questions of meaning in music seeks to bring together an analytical attention to detail with broader concerns about defining "meaning," which have a line of influence that can be traced to C. S. Peirce. After considering the ideas of music theory developed by these two thinkers, further discussion will be given to how images of "body" have been introduced into more recent semiotic approaches to phrase structure.

1. Theorists: Giving Roles to Rules

a. Schenker's "Real" Ideal

A step can be made in exploring the status of rules in Schenker's theory by examining the role of diagrams in his interpretive practice. In Peirce's philosophy, any diagram is itself a sign, an iconic presentation of selected aspects of some realm of experience, more or less schematically arranged. It presents a perceptual judgment of a given state of affairs as capable of being summarized through a representation of selected elements. An outline sketch of a geographical area or the colored diagram of a city subway system are simple examples. The fact that their visual appearance is selective, and that it in many ways distorts perceived experiences of topography—or the actual distance between stations—is not, in itself, a criticism of the maps' functionality. Maps need to be selective in order to give optimal clarity in their presentation of a set of relationships, and it would make no sense at all to say in a pejorative tone that their production "reduced" the represented area, or the city, to nothing more than an outline, or a stylized web, at the expense of sensory information that was more "immediate" and important to a person in behaving adaptively in a given situation. It is not, furthermore, a criticism to say that the "same" area could be presented differently. It is simply understood that map-makers interested in defining borders will select them for presentation, producing a schematic "world" much different in its appearance from map-makers with interests in topography. Formal analyses of music are no different in their use of diagrams from these cases, where abstraction from experience is necessary. In any formal analysis, perceptual judgments are made of a musical passage as having certain points of structural significance, and these judgments are presented using varying criteria of selection. In the case of Schenkerian theory, the most important features are taken to be harmonic or contrapuntal. The analytical diagram then presents a structure of harmonic progressions on varying temporal scales, linked by linear and contrapuntal motions which may give rise to subsidiary harmonies by means of an adaptation of elements from musical notation.

An act of "tracing the outline" of a given area gives rise to a unique presentation, a "singular" icon in Peirce's terms, not one that follows any preordained pattern. The possibility of creating ad hoc likenesses or diagrams,
perhaps with some spontaneity, to reflect a "feel" for the shape of an experienced thing, is a possibility not to be ignored, as it allows for singularities to
be signified without forcing them into the Procrustean bed of some inflexi-
ble schema. Even the spontaneous presentation of structure in events perceived as unique will not, however, survive uncontaminated by generalities,
if the act is repeated often enough for patterns to begin to appear in the material being observed. This is the route by which Schenker arrived at his generalized schemata for tonal ordering, having observed many examples of linear continuity in melodies and a tendency for descending patterns to prevail
(see William Pastille, 1994). Once patterns emerge in experience, they become the guides for understanding future experience, Generals which do not
have some necessity of their own (like Platonic forms) but which have a
pragmatic role within the experience of a given domain. Although Schenker
might sometimes have used hyperbole in defending his general forms (Ursätze), they are essentially of this kind, modes of contrapuntal and harmonic
unfolding observed to be recurrent in many tonal works. Misunderstandings
are nonetheless prevalent among interpreters of tonal music whose background is not in the disciplines familiar to Schenker—the practical activities
of realizing figured bass, or of working through Fuxian exercises in controlling contrapuntal parts—because the grounding of abstraction in a "feel" for
tonal dynamism is too easily lost, and the schemata themselves come to seem
like a restrictive set of molds into which tonal phrases must somehow be
pushed. It is common, for example, to speak of "reductivism," to assume that
Schenker's interpretive practice "reduces" the surface of the music to a limited set of schemata, with the dismissive statement that X piece is "ultimately no more than 'Three Blind Mice'" (because it exemplifies a form of
structure whose upper line is 3–2–1). To speak of reference to a schema as ne-
cessitating a form of reductionism is, however, to misunderstand the role of
schemata in any domain of activity. All schemata (or types) require a sensory
embodiment in some particular form (a token), through which they might be
perceived. They present a possible sensory content, to be borne out in particular entities, or sequences of event (S. Rosenthal, 1994), an incompletely
defined kernel of sensory possibility, whose general shape has been culled

from previous experience. As such, they will necessarily be empty and incomplete, needing to be made concrete and specific once more, as they are recreated (and reperceived) in some new context. To put the same points in a complementary form, no schema is a "reduction" of content which can make claims to grasping the individuated, concrete textures of artifacts formed and experienced in different contexts. Rather, it is a selective mapping of recurrent patterns which may assist in grasping some elements in a new experience, providing a framework within which more individuating features may be noticed (and sometimes represented iconically).[3]

To review before moving on: in Peirce's thinking, a "type," or general sign (legisign), is necessarily underdetermined, in that it allows realization in many different possible "tokens" (replicas). Tonal schemata are "types," whose notation in a diagrammatic form could be described as "iconic." The notational schemata used in analysis belong, further, to the class of "iconic legisigns," insofar as they follow designated patterns, which guide their general shape. It should not be forgotten, however, that their tokens take on singular features in any given context and are thus not *merely* "replicas" of a preordained type whose qualities are entirely predictable. Reproducing part of Peirce's table (from chapter 3, table 3.5), it will be seen that an "iconic sinsign" (singular icon) and the "replica" of an "iconic legisign" are placed together, drawing attention to the fact that the realization of any general feature will occur in a context that also makes it singular.[4] (*See* #2, Table 6.1.)

Table 6.1. **Icons in Schenkerian analysis**

	Qualisign (1st)	Sinsign (2nd)	Legisign (3rd)	
Icon (1st) (presentational ground of sign)	#1 Colour as sign	#2 An individual diagram (or a token/replica of a type)	#5 A diagrammatic type (requiring exemplification in a token/replica)	**Rheme (1st) (sign taken as a sign of possibility)**
Schenkerian examples	The quality of feeling emerging from structural procedures	Particular realisations of the legisigns	Ursätze; linear descents; types of progression	

To forestall any possible impatience with the terminology involved in this semiotic description, it may, of course, be asked how thinking about the practice of Schenkerian interpretation and its diagrammatic notation in such terms could change the practice of an established discipline in any substantive way. The answer is that no change in practice is intended through the process of meta-theoretical reflection. Where this reflection does have the potential to lead to greater clarity, however, is in understanding the relationship of structure to aesthetic understanding—or signification. It is to this that I now turn. The main concern, in making a link of formal analysis with signification, is to grasp how a generalized notion of the "feeling" conveyed in an abstract structure (such as the feeling of "passing") may be related to the more particular effects of a musical context where it is realized, and combined with many other (possibly contradictory) effects. The problem is, in other words, another manifestation of the issue of relating generals to particulars, couched this time in terms of "quality" or "feeling" rather than of structure alone. Its treatment requires an initial appreciation of how "structure" and "quality" might be related.

Schenker's Ursätze (and derivative passing structures) are "types" whose structure is strictly designated (though indeterminate in its realizations), and whose emerging qualities can only be defined in a general way. The possible qualities of a Schenkerian structure might be described, for example, as an extended "passing," or a feeling of something "unfinished," which can be recognized in tonal movements at many levels, and even (Schenker claims) as extending from the beginning of a movement until the point at which closure in the key of origin occurs. The set of possible, but generalized, "feelings" for passing and continuity may be described further as a generalized "instability," "willfulness," "desire," "propulsion," "necessity," "incompleteness," or "openness," a set of possibilities which will be modified and made more specific by the other musical features of a given context. The qualitative effects of contextualization cannot, however, be predicted within a schematic form. In their lack of full determination, the qualities of harmonic structure and voice-leading may thus be thought of as having a "vagueness of unrealized possibility" about them that reflects some attributes of Peirce's First Category of thought—the domain of qualitative possibility which requires realization in a given case. This is despite the fact that the structures themselves are "rule-governed" and hence "legisigns." Matching the indeterminacy of a general structure's realization (an aspect of its being a legisign requiring replicas) is, then, a necessary vagueness about the qualities that it may assume (an aspect of qualitative possibility). The reciprocal relationship between the "vagueness of possibility" in Peirce's First Category and the "indeterminacy of the general" in his Third Category has been remarked upon by a number of authors (e.g., Merrell, 1997; Rosenthal, 1994) and derives from the fact that both require realization in particular concrete cases: possible qualities need to belong to something concrete in order to become actual, while potential types need to be realized in particular forms in order for the gaps in their definition to be filled out. Indeterminacy and vagueness in these senses are perfectly benign, and, as has been noted above, they do not result from some descriptive inadequacy on the part of the interpreter.

Recognizing the complementarity of qualitative possibility and structural indeterminacy is most helpful in understanding the potentially emerging qualities of a structure. As a point of caution, it should, however, be remembered that these features of signs are held in a complementary relationship to one another and are not two names for one thing. The "possibilities" imagined by Peirce to inhere in the world of yet-unrealized "quality" are very open-ended. This kind of vague "possibility" does not require any kind of specification other than that the given quality is capable of being held in the mind's eye or ear. The indeterminacy of a type is much more directed than this, having the definition of pattern, or "lawfulness," about it. As structural types, Schenkerian voice-leading progressions provide not just a vague possibility, but a shaped potentiality for a succession of states: a moment of stability, a stage of flux, and a point of return. When rule-governed potentialities are described in qualitative terms, they take on a definite pattern, as qualities emerging from structure—though they remain vague in requiring further contextual specification. For Schenker, tonal situatedness, the sense of "being somewhere," gives way to dynamism, or moving on, before the re-establishing of place within a larger perspective, to give what he takes to be the qualitative definition of an "organic" tonal work. This pattern allows for some degree of habituation, or predictability, without foreclosing the details of any individual tonal event. An advantage of keeping in mind the inherent indeterminacy of a structural outline, even while following a broadly conceived pattern such as this, is that it can further ameliorate concerns about the "reductiveness" of analysis. A Schenkerian analysis of a tonal work, presented diagrammatically, gives a particular realization of a general scheme, insofar as it shows the way in which a middleground structure belonging to the work alone emerges from the Ursatz. It does, however, also remain schematic in relation to the "surface" of the music, and, in addition to that, the types of "feeling quality" conveyed in its abstracted structures are not informed by features outside tonality. The patterns of tonal unfolding may, then, be heard as emerging "through" the surface, but it cannot be claimed that the complex surface is reduced to these patterns alone, or that their abstraction from a context retains all of the features relevant to the differentiation of affect. If it is understood that a schematic presentation is necessarily incomplete, the sense in which it "represents" musical content is thus considerably weakened. The diagram is not an attempt to contain the essence of the music but more of a heuristic device, directing the viewer to gain a perception of certain aspects of structure and their qualitative possibilities, which can be translated into a way of hearing connections that might otherwise have been less accessible.

Speaking more generally, the Schenkerian linear descents need not be reified as entities that have their own Platonic reality as ideal forms, even though Schenker might sometimes be read as inclined towards a claim for their necessity. Instead, if a Peircean view of legisigns as real aspects of the world (exemplifying thirdness) is taken to hold, these patterns can be viewed as semiotically "real" in a pragmatic sense, insofar as they can be demonstrated to be part of stylistic organization, and to direct listeners' attention at some levels at least. A comparison that may be useful in grasping the sense in which "rules" are "real" is with the late Wittgenstein's sense of "rule-following," as a capacity demonstrated when someone recognizes "how to go on" in following a certain sequence of events. Knowing "how to go on" demonstrates a practical enactment of rule-governed behavior in someone who sees a general pattern. The General is evident in what is given, not as some supervenient entity, but as the condition of continuity itself.

In the light of the above discussion, it should now be clear that it is not, in itself, a criticism of Schenker's theory to say that the presentations are selective and schematic, or that alternative ways of presenting the same passages of music could be more informative about some aspects of listening experience. Schenker's way of presenting his theory as authoritatively descriptive of the voice-leading in a tonal work (irrespective of its perceptibility) cannot, that is, be countered by saying that alternative patterns are relevant to understanding the same work. Nor can it be rejected simply by expressing doubts about the use of any schematism at all, on the grounds that abstractions are "reductive" of experience. To sustain a doubt about the value of presenting schematic elements in experience, it would be necessary to show how any "theory" could effectively be formed in which generalizations were entirely avoided, in the interests of maintaining a sensitivity to the particular.

The grounds upon which Schenker can be questioned have more to do with a lack of clarity in regard to the role for a listener in his interpretive generalizations. Rules, summarized in diagrammatic typologies, are put forward as "objective" aspects of tonal style, and the question of whether a given composer, performer, or listener is aware of their functions is irrelevant to their governing status, in Schenker's view. In his didacticism, Schenker is not, however, indifferent to how the unfolding of tonal procedures within a work is understood. Far from it. His interpretive practice assumes that tonal structures are analytically discernible by one examining a score, and that they give rise to emergent effects, which may be described in critical or hermeneutic writing as "moods" (see Snarrenberg, 1997). Whether these effects are already recognized prior to analysis, or emerge after it, is not, despite that, of direct concern to him, because his commitment is to a view of the effects *as part of the music,* irrespective of when a given listener becomes attuned to them. He manages, furthermore, not only to be a law-Realist, purporting to describe the content of the music as objectively rule-governed, but also a normative theorist, committed to the value of a complex, temporally extended unfolding of a unified purpose within a work. What *is,* he implies, is also a presentation of what is ideal (in the works he chooses to analyze). In order to understand a work of this optimal kind, a listener needs to confront its many levels of unfolding structure, as occurring independently of his or her own desires, and in this confrontation demand of him- or herself the willingness to extend perceptual understanding through the process of learning how to hear "what is given," in Schenker's view, over extended spans of time. Resonances of conflation between the true, the beautiful, and the good might here be heard. (See Nicholas Cook, 1989a.)

A contemporary interpreter might well view Schenker's equation between certain kinds of tonal procedure and musical value with some skepticism, but this need not prevent them from employing Schenker's theory as a way of exploring tonal formations. To appreciate Schenker's insight into the extended use of voice-leading, or his distinction between structural scale steps and other harmonies, is not necessarily to endorse all aspects of his theory as normative. A point to watch, however, in any attempt to employ Schenker's interpretive practices without a strong commitment to his organicism, is that the wrenching apart of procedure from ideology can lead to a misunderstanding even of his account of tonal continuities. The "will of tones," for Schenker, is a dynamism that proceeds from the "real" necessity of harmonic-contrapuntal unfolding. If a Schenkerian style of interpretive practice is dislodged from Schenker's ideological commitments, it becomes easy to lose sight of this positive side to Schenker's "normative" values, which led him to describe aspects of tonal dynamism, and its disruption, in ways that are by no means lacking in significatory implication. By entertaining such values, Schenker declares that the tonal unfolding of a work, as he sees it occurring on many levels, yields qualities that might be termed "aesthetic." It is easy for an aesthetic interpreter unsympathetic towards formal analysis to make a simple separation of "non-aesthetic" from "aesthetic" qualities (see Beardsley, 1982). "Mere structure," on the one side, then stands opposite the various affects or "moods" thought to inhere in a work, as if it were on the other side of an immutable divide, irrelevant, an empty container. If, however, it is appreciated that Schenker's tonal theory, in integrating harmonic and contrapuntal elements, is capable of great subtlety in the way it differentiates aspects of tonal situatedness or motion, it is only a short step to seeing that it also conveys a subtle variation in kinds of virtuality—"being," "will," "desire," "resistance," "passivity"—which contribute to the formation of emergent affects (the topic of the next chapter). Tonal procedures are not sufficient to account for affects, but they are in some cases necessary to an affect, and in cases where they are less central, they still provide an added dimension to what is conveyed in other kinds of signs.

b. Meyer's Expectancies

Leonard Meyer's beliefs concerning the role of tonal regularities in contributing to the "emotion and meaning" of music could be viewed as diametrically opposed to those of Schenker. With characteristic humor and self-deprecation, Meyer summed himself up in an article of 1991, responding to his critics by saying "I am not a denizen of obscure, abstract depths—a diver after cosmic conceptions and unconfirmable hypotheses. I am content to snorkel along the surface, peering down just a bit to be bewitched by the pleasing patterns of luminous fish and the quiet swaying of colorful coral" (1991: 241). He objected to what he saw as "an almost obsessive concern with the nature of unity in music" and drew attention to the importance of stylistic change. Meyer's skepticism about theories that find hidden depths of structural coherence, beyond the colorfully variegated surface of a work, had led him to place emphasis, in his own theoretical work (Meyer, 1973), on exploring the conditions which create patterning on the "surface" of the music (to continue the diving metaphor), and to investigate the means by which these patterns have changed historically (1989). From his earliest work (1956) he had recognized that approaching diachronic change in a musical style demanded tolerance for uncertainty, both in listening to music and in formalizing its properties, but in all his writings he chose to interpret this uncertainty as a source of meaning, rather than of abject concern. The presence of change might threaten the accuracy of a listener's stylistic expectations and habits of response, but it also provides a challenge to reconsider dispositional traits. Moments of affective reaction (Meyer, 1956; Sloboda) or simple puzzlement then become, upon reflection, the occasions of rationalized meaning. Stylistic change might problematize any synchronic representation of tonality, and determine that even a relatively enduring pattern is mutable, but the moment of uncertainty, when a listener finds him- or herself confronted by a novel patterning, itself brings to light the patterns of understanding that have governed the predictions to that point. These patterns are not arbitrary, but habits of listening that are stylistically formed.

Tonal rules appear in Meyer's (1989) characterization of style as the most general level of musical organization, which may be realized through different "strategies" in the groupings of "dialect," "idiom," and "idiolect." The rules, that is, are "generals" which require exemplification in particular tonal procedures at increasing levels of stylistic differentiation. Where Meyer differs from Schenker is in his engagement with perceptual psychology, evident in his reference to the "laws" of pattern perception as defined by the Gestalt theorists, Koffka, Köhler, and Wertheimer. Implicit in this engagement is a strong but informal concern with issues of epistemology. In what way are "rules" and regularities actually known? A concern with innate perceptual abilities and limitations leads Meyer to question the degree to which "deep" tonal structures (such as those of Schenker's middleground and background levels) can be perceived, but this skepticism does not entail a doubt about the perceptual efficacy of all tonal processes. His earliest formulation of aesthetic ideas (1956) assumes that "tendencies" to respond in a certain way are stylistically formed, and "style" in this account includes tonal process. "Expectancy" is Meyer's typical way of referring to a mental state of anticipation. Expectancies are informed by a knowledge of style and are also consistent with the innate proclivities, identified by Gestalt psychologists, for subjects to seek the "good continuation" toward closure of established patternings, or to look for the "closure" of any patterning perceived as a "gap." Meyer's "expectancies" could also be named as "habits" or "dispositions," fortuitous adjustments of a listener's mind to the internalized constancies of musical ordering. Their openness towards an unrealized future point makes them, furthermore, comparable to "hypotheses" seeking confirmation. All of these manners of description have more than a coincidental association with Peirce's thought, which influenced the writings of the pragmatists John Dewey and George Herbert Mead as well as the behaviorist semiotician, Charles Morris, to all of whom Meyer refers. Peirce finds a correlation between the evolving regularities displayed in some aspect of "the world," and the habits or dispositions of creatures adjusted to it, fortuitously following its "rules." Habitual forms of response are the active embodiment of "beliefs," or states of settled judgment, about some aspect of the world. Dewey, taking up this viewpoint, suggests that when habits, also named by him as "instincts," are frustrated by a collision with some aspect of the world that contradicts their established form, conscious thought or emotional response will arise. He places emphasis on the "uncertainty" that is inevitable when the indeterminacy of some state of affairs makes established habits of reaction inadequate. A volitional drive towards action, frustrated by the novel or indeterminate, leads to a reflective or emotional response before action can resume. This pattern informs the substance of Meyer's aesthetic theory.

It has already been seen that any abstraction of rules or patternings embraces some degree of indeterminacy. Generality in representing possible states of affairs cannot be achieved unless much is "left out," to be filled in by given circumstances. The converse of predictiveness is thus always relative ignorance, a state of uncertainty about whether and how a rule will be carried out or a pattern filled in. The claim made by Meyer, following Dewey, is that situations of musical uncertainty are a key to understanding the occurrence of musical affects. This claim can be cashed out more fully if the notion of uncertainty is seen to be a reciprocal part of any predictiveness, as found in music's "rules." Shock and startle effects, or states of frustration, are not put forward by Meyer as the total repertory of human affect, although this assumption could be read into his text on the grounds that he does not differentiate the affects conveyed in different situations of indeterminacy but merely speaks of "affect" as a general potentiality of the unexpected or uncertain. That his withdrawal from further specification is well-advised should be obvious from the preceding discussion of indeterminacy in Schenker. It is in the contingent realization of a rule, within a given compositional circumstance, that the incompleteness of prediction becomes apparent. As the qualitative possibilities of compositional schemata are schematic, and tonal rules do not themselves determine what effects will arise circumstantially, composers retain freedom to manipulate "incompleteness," "urgency," and so on, by means of strengthening or weakening the use of tonal possibilities. Specific affects are a matter of the circumstantial contingencies arising from such choices, and it is not possible to describe in general terms what affects will be differentiated.

In the process of listening, a subject "lives through" in time the state of not knowing, or of having to wait for a moment of fulfillment whose timing cannot be judged ahead, even if it is "expected" to occur at some point. Such a waiting and anticipation, with frustration of goals, could be taken superficially as the occasion for an affective response (such as annoyance or startle) *in the listener,* but the claim being made by Meyer is more interesting than that, as it points to the response as indicative of an affective moment *in the work.* It would be easy to read Meyer's reference to "expectancy" or to states of "uncertainty" as a confusion of the mental and the structurally given. Continuities implied as part of a structural process are followed "expectantly" and processes whose outcome is relatively indeterminate (when heard in time, without hindsight) are heard in a state of some "uncertainty." Are these not states of mind, rather than a moment in the unfolding of a musical process? To make this kind of split between the musical knower and the moment known is, however, to perpetuate an assumption that what is "given" in music is a material entity, free in its characteristics from the markers of mentality. Suppose that "expectancy" were replaced with "desire," a term preferred by Joseph Dubiel (1990) when describing a Schenkerian view of the way that contrapuntal processes move on. "I desire resolution," or "the moment is expressive of desire." Could they not be equivalent in some way? A state in a listener experiencing "desire" is finely attuned to a condition of the music, which signifies its incompleteness at that point with, say, dissonance and rhythmic instability. Not *all* expectancies and desires on the part of a listener can, of course, claim such attunement, but that does not prevent some examples of these states from functioning as the *interpretants* of some aspect of tonal dynamism. In Peirce's account, it will be recalled, an interpretant could be a kind of feeling, or an energetic response, or a more deliberate reference to a convention known. If it is an emotionally charged feeling of seeking some end that a given listener experiences, that may be his or her most effective way of "knowing" the music (in a weakly conceptual way) without necessarily naming what is known. In this kind of case, a "feeling" is not some purely private matter, whose content can be unraveled only be seeking further information about the individual concerned. It is a state that has been semiotically constructed by the ordering of the music's contrapuntal and tonal processes.

In his later work on melodic analysis (1973), Meyer found some difficulty in maintaining an equation of "expectancy" with a condition of the music, such as "implication" or a "tendency" to move in a certain way. The term "expectancy" did not allow adequately for the kind of forward-looking mental attunement that is capable of synthesizing the conflicting directional tendencies of something like a complex musical phrase. It did not, furthermore, give him sufficient flexibility to withhold judgment about the relative degree of consciousness attending a directed, yet open-ended, perceptual act. Something "expected" is generally expected consciously and single-mindedly. It therefore seemed strange to Meyer to say, as he wanted to, that a listener hearing a complex phrase could be entertaining a set of conflicting "expectations."[5] The state he was after was one of being attuned to a range of possible outcomes, in a state of some predictive uncertainty—not the vagueness of complete ignorance, but the open-mindedness best attuned to predictive indeterminacy. Rather than negotiate the difficulties of finding a language of description in which terms for mental acts would parallel precisely the terms for the structural events taken to form the substance of those acts, Meyer turned to an objectifying language—one which spoke of "tendencies" and "implications" in the music, rather than of mental states. This, indeed, had already been the direction in which his analytical work was going in the thesis published as the book of 1956. He did not, however, make any shift that he himself recognized in his basic epistemological attitude. States of mind were still to have as their substance musical states of affairs, and any affective response in the listener was to be construed as a direct reflection of affect as musically signified, through such things as deflective and delaying strategies, frustrating the virtual "will" or "desire" of an established process of continuation.

c. General Uncertainty

Schenker's desired musical world is a stable one, reflecting the postulated stabilities of tonality. Meyer's musical world is full of instability, with positive appraisal given to changes in style. They differ in important ways on how to "do" analysis, in that Schenker reads from a speculatively extended account of harmony and voice-leading, to give an account of the potential for virtual "agencies" within tonality, and of their subtle realizations, while Meyer relies much more directly upon insights from cognitive psychology, moving from an initial engagement with Gestalt theorists to an absorption of cognitive theories concerning perceptual schemata in order to describe the complex dynamism of a rhythmically and motivically complex tonal phrase. Despite these marked differences of approach, they hold one important feature in common: they observe formal process in order to give an account of varieties of musical "motion" which are presumed to have a mental correlate (whether ideal, or psychologically grounded). A virtual agency in the music, variously construed, takes care of the possible states of any listener deemed competent in a style.

A result of this kind of equation between a musical process and a manner of "hearing" it is that the states attributed to any listening subject must be understood as accessible to others, not as purely personal. Its further consequence is that the "subject" becomes strangely transparent and may even seem to be devoid of real choice. I might feel "desire" for a resolution, and

feel it with an urgency that would make me uncomfortable if it were unfulfilled, but that desire is not a personal thing. I may feel an "expectancy," not
as my personally formed expectation, but as a state predicted by the realization of a style's possibilities. My mental states are not, effectively, my own. A
danger of this presumed equation of structural virtualities with mental states
is that it does, in some cases, allow insufficient space for individual difference
or learning, and even (in a normative analysis) begin to dictate what may be
"heard," without regard for real limitations of perceptual organization or
memory. In order to get a feel for the kind of problem this could pose, it can
be considered in an exaggerated form. Suppose that voice-leading progressions are considered always to signify "desire" or "instability," and to be aurally understood through states of "expectancy," reflecting the openness
of the structures analyzed. If analysis reveals a voice-leading progression at
any level—pointing even to an extended virtual agency—and the analysis is
taken as normative, it would be quite possible to judge the openness of
"desire" as more "real" in the music than any content known through the
other, "merely incidental," feelings experienced by a listener. The "desire"
in voice-leading becomes a signifying fixture, irrespective of whether it is
"heard." Actually feeling expectancy is recognized as appropriate to it, and
as enhancing understanding of the work, but the absence of the right feelings in a given listener is taken to say nothing about the "truth" of the
analysis. This position is one to which Schenker's interpretive practice may
come close, especially if some of his more extravagant rhetoric concerning
the "necessity" of the Ursatz is taken seriously. A conviction of what must
necessarily (and also ideally) be the case in order to fulfill the presumed exigencies of a basic structure (Ursatz), deemed to be a "real" power in tonal
styles, then too easily becomes the touch stone for defining what can or
should ultimately be "heard" and "known," to the point where the stance
seems bullying. In this sort of picture of what is musically real, the "I" of
the listener, even if realized in certain kinds of feelings, shrinks to a vanishing point co-determinate with structural anticipations. Even if he or she has
bodily feelings of anticipation, the body, too, is no more than a puppet of
musical dynamism. Having a body then fails, in a strange way, to make of
the listener a concrete listening self.[6]

These difficulties are not, however, endemic to Schenker's interpretive
practice, but are most likely to emerge with an overstated emphasis on the

more abstract levels of structure, or when it is imagined that the generalized and relatively indeterminate kinds of feeling represented by structural abstractions can be heard in themselves, as pure states. In practice, few analysts would imagine that what it is to "know" or "understand" tonal music is to grasp a pure kernel of structural possibility, or even to hear its outworking in more extended periods. Rather, they accept as fundamental the feeling for "passing," which may be realized in many ways, and on different levels, while being aware of the indeterminacy of sense that this passing has until contextualized. The exaggerated view sketched above gives a false picture of the interpretive assumptions made in formal analysis, then, in that it claims a determinacy in the affective "sense" of passing which it never has in practice. Meyer's elevating the importance of "uncertainty" is a good antidote to this problem, so long as it is understood that this "uncertainty" is not a synonym for ignorance of style, or lack of analytic skill. Vagueness and ignorance are not, of course, states that any interpreter would readily admit or aspire to, but even the most articulate knowledge of structures whose realization is understood with the greatest clarity can well be balanced by an acknowledgment that abstraction is limited in what it can control. To identify the features of indeterminacy that form the shadow side of any knowledge is the job of a contextually sensitive analysis—in any field. General structures do not contain or predict the particularities of a work, but leave a space for its individuation. It is here, when idealized abstractions meet the full gamut of conflicting features, that their own potentialities are either softened or enhanced. "Uncertainty" is thus written into theoretical competence as a necessary part of understanding the nature of generality and of the particular in a work. It is part of what it is to be open to the new.

Once the role of indeterminacy is understood, the recognition that "desire" or "willfulness" are general properties of tonal signification, not in themselves capable of individuating a given passage, can become the impetus for analytical discussion in which the possible senses of context are further explored. The generalized potentialities of tonal unfolding allow for a wide range of different kinds of contextual signification, and of response, all of which can be accessible to others. In an analytical forum, these responses can be made explicit and begin to form the range of "tenable opinions" about a work's content. They are neither fully determined by the music, nor purely personal, but in the space of negotiation in between. (See Narmour, 1977.)

2. The Dialectics of Tonal Semiosis

a. Tonal Structure as Signification

Music theorists who have drawn on semiotics differ in their appraisal of the degree to which formal (especially Schenkerian) analysis can contribute to an account of signification. Giving tonality a high value, David Mosley (1990) and Kofi Agawu (1991) have sought to develop semiotic modes of analysis that are integrated with formal aspects of music. Robert Hatten (1994) and David Lidov (1987), on the other hand, have pointed to the disanalogies and points of rupture between interpretations of structural expressivity, in which tonal formations play a dominant role, and interpretations in which metaphors of gestural embodiment are recognized as having a distinctive derivation. In the latter case, gestures are found not to be reducible to tonal procedures, even though their constitution is—in the broadest sense— necessarily tonal, considering that no event can take place in a tonal work which does not in some way instantiate elements of tonal syntax. These two kinds of approach could be characterized as dwelling closer to the "formalist" or the "expressivist" end of a spectrum, or as leaning towards "structuralism," on the one side, or "hermeneutics," on the other. The ghosts of a "Classical" versus a "Romantic" interpretive preference might even be invoked, in order to place labels on the preference for cognitive, or "felt" and "intuitive" responses. The task of discriminating between theoretical views is, of course, made easier if they are polarized like this, by having their tendencies pushed to an extreme, yet this meta-theoretical act succeeds only in hiding the points of conjunction between views. An exchange of book reviews between Hatten and Agawu dramatizes the challenge of differentiating emphases, without falsely polarizing positions. A dichotomy of "structure" and "expression" is found by Agawu in Hatten's work, and interrogated for its lack of justification, given that most expressive aspects of music have a structural content of some kind (1996: 149). Hatten's references to the "structure of expression" and "the expressiveness of formal structures" (1994: 279) do not, however, resist this question. Instead, they positively invite it, disclosing his own assumption that structure and expressivity are integrally bound together, though they might be viewed from different angles—like the opposing "aspects" of an ambiguous figure. Hatten, in his turn, finds an over-reliance on Schenkerian thought in Agawu's treatment of the play of signs (construed as "topics") in Classical string quartets (1992: 10). He judges that a fuller exploration might have been given to the implications of topical reference, implying (as he does also in reviewing Mosley) that it is not enough to read signification in tonal processes. At the center of this dialectic is a basic agreement that tonal processes have the capacity to signify qualities whose description is metaphorical. This, in itself, is a move away from the earlier stance of Anglo-American "music theory," which, as a nascent discipline, was given to austerity measures against the overuse of descriptive adjectives, leading to the idea that formalist prose was equal to objective virtue. It has not only been semioticians who challenged this reserve. Those interested in questions of signification have differed in the boldness with which they have challenged the cloud of hubris that once made formal descriptions of tonal process seem to be free of metaphoric content, but they have shared a perception that tonality has always (already) been known to signify in some way. Feminists, in particular, have shown the degree to which an ideology of dichotomization between the "cognitive" and the "felt" has led to explicit denials of content that was covertly known (Guck, 1994b; Maus, 1993) and recognized even by the champions of formalism (Maus, 1992). The issue at stake, then, is not whether tonal processes "signify" but whether this form of signification should be given a privileged place in analysis.

Before considering how tonal signification might relate to other kinds of signs, it is important to recognize the variety of ways in which tonality itself may signify. A tonal process might, for example, contribute a sense of "will" and "desire." It might, on the other hand, act as a "container," giving a wider perspective of stability to events taking place in the shorter term. The same kinds of process that act to institute an impulsion to continue can, as Schenker recognized, also act to interrupt, displace, and frustrate a compulsion already underway. Their closure, depending on its level, contains a process, or frustrates the fulfillment of a longer view. Kevin Korsyn compares the unfolding of Schenker's Ursatz to a Kantian agent, whose identity is comprised of the synthesis of moments over time (Korsyn, 1988), embracing the many conflicts encountered in a passage through time within a final unity. This view is not unenlightening, even in its purest and most idealized form. By becoming aware of the subtleties of Schenker's interpretive practice, as informative for understanding the emergent qualities of a tonal work, it is possible to entertain greater subtleties of content, without presuming that formal understanding yields a necessary mastery of what the work has to give. The disadvantage of privileging analyses of tonal significa-tion does, however, become clear when it is seen that any relatively indeter-minate tonal process can only gain a more particular "content" from being worked out in a context where features of rhythm and grouping, of motivic play, gestural shaping, and instrumentation, all have a role to play. In his re-action against Schenker, Meyer was most concerned with the need to take account of rhythmic patterning. Lidov, too, has suggested that any virtual "agency" suggested by a tonal process is radically altered by repetitions of patterning or by interruptions at a local level (Lidov, 1997). Why should the ideal "agency" of an abstract will, unfolding over time, or even a generalized feeling of "passing," be assumed to emerge unscathed through a surface which may be very turbulent?

A consequence of attending to more local levels, and the complex inte-gration of voice-leading with other structural features, is that the unifying power of large-scale tonal processes is given a much weaker role to play. Support for this attitude can be found by recalling, once again, the relation-ship of general principles of structure to particular contexts of realization. The general schema of a voice-leading motion poses with an indeterminate range of possible realizations, the qualities of which can be only vaguely defined under terms such as "desire," "willfulness," or "agency." Suppose that the generalized tonal potential to create a sense of agency has been real-ized in a highly specific context, such as the beginning of Beethoven's Violin Sonata in F Major, op. 24, the "Spring Sonata." Here the rate of harmonic change is very relaxed (no more than one harmony per bar until the ca-dence) and rhythmic interruptions introduce a "breath" in the middle of structural harmonies, contributing further to a sense of unhurriedness. (See Example 6.1.) The individuality of this phrase will not then be eradicated by a simple act of recalling the tonal type from which it comes. There is no reason to believe, either, that an attention to tonal process alone will be sufficient to characterize the phrase, in the absence of observing its rhythmic character. If a "synthesis" of the phrase occurs, offering a retrospective view of its unified agency, it cannot be effective unless it embraces "breaths" and delays, with a locally indirect path through tonal space. A synthesis based on non-rhythmic tonal processes alone cannot, therefore, be assumed as an ideal, even at the level of a phrase. At the level of a movement, it is even less

Example 6.1. First phrase, Violin Sonata in F Major, op. 24, the "Spring Sonata," by Ludwig van Beethoven effective to adopt such a position, where the memory of local contexts will be mandatorily suppressed, to form a unified "agency" as emergent from the whole. Unity of signified "will" cannot be preordained as normative, but only entertained as a vague potentiality of an abstract form, whose modes of outworking are relatively indeterminate. The continuity of the "subject," as signified in the Ursatz (by Korsyn's interpretation), now becomes a tenuous thread to be held onto as a possibility, not taken as a Platonic form waiting to reveal itself.

b. Actoriality and Embodiedness

Having circumscribed the domain of tonal signification, with recognition of the rhythmic factors that modify how a process may signify, the idea of a virtual "agency" may be reconsidered as a signifying possibility that does not depend on tonality alone. This idea has appeared in a number of different forms in theoretical literature. Edward Cone's notion of the "composer's voice" (1974) is predicated on the idea of various agencies being heard in a movement, and a synthesizing intelligence emerging from it as a reflection of the composer. His agencies are not linked directly with analyses of tonal proclivities. Eero Tarasti's notion of "actoriality," elaborated through a series of highly sensitive distinctions between different states of Being and Doing (1994), seeks to characterize many different "modalities" in the apparent movement of a tonal "agent" between states of stability and action. When Lidov (1987) considers the "subject" as being heard in the virtual roles of an "agent" or a "patient," he, like Tarasti, moves away from a concern with the virtuality of tonal process alone, to an attempted integration of melodic and rhythmic factors in creating agency. Virtual "acts" may be heard as being initiated, or as being more passively suffered, through the composite effects of tonal implication, gestural shaping, and rhythmic factors at many different levels. Rather than working from tonal analysis towards notions of a derivative actoriality, these non-Schenkerian interpreters of tonal music place emphasis on the complex of contextual features that add up to a dynamic "feeling" of agency at various levels.

In describing these semiotic approaches to "agency," it would be easy to imply that the only point to have changed is an emphasis on the integration of varied compositional aspects (Narmour's "parameters") in a local context.

This would not, however, give any reason to believe that ideas about music as a play of "signs" have done much more than increase the vocabulary for describing formal features of music, by forcing a stronger recognition of a metaphoric content that was already implicit. The radical point in semiotic interpretation comes with a return to ideas of "embodiment," which lead to a negotiation of the problems of "expressiveness" as proceeding not only from a reading of structure, but from the use of other images. It has been seen that, influenced by the neuropsychological experiments of Manfred Clynes, Lidov postulated "gesture" as a key to melodic signification, going so far as to say that "music is significant only if we identify perceived sonorous motion with somatic experience" (1987: 70). A "gesture," he found, could not just be read off structural units such as motives and figurations, though it could coincide with them. In Peircean terms, the "interpretant" of a figure as gestural would have to be bodily, whether that bodily reference were made self-conscious or not. Observing the process of preparing a performance gives a clear entry to understanding the role that gestural images can play for an active musician, to be contrasted with their role for listeners, and as the idea of "gesture" forms a basis from which to look at more extended uses of bodily images, its interpretive roles will be briefly reviewed here.

Having started with work on "gesture," Lidov (1999: ch. 20) and Hatten (1998) have begun more recently to explore more extended forms of bodily motion in the tonal phrase. An impetus to the extended use of bodily imagery was given in the movement pedagogy of the theorist Alexandra Pierce (1994), who taught Schenkerian analysis to students by inculcating an awareness of different "levels" of bodily motion in space, actively performed. Influenced by Pierce, each has sought to characterize bodily signification in the flow of a phrase. Noting the importance of bodily images, Lidov elaborates his semiotic framework by suggesting that reference to body gives the basis for contemplating two parallel sources of musical organization—a first and second "order" of articulation (influenced by Hjelmslev). The first order is structural, and the second one ordered around metaphors of body, or "haptic" imagery. Hatten, in his turn, complements this suggestion by providing a generously detailed description of the active learning processes involved in "feeling" movement at various levels (1998). A bifurcation of "body" and "mind," such as that suggested by Lidov, cannot be pushed too strongly, if on the one hand, gestures are viewed as being culturally shaped, and, on the other, the phenomenological qualities of mental activity are captured well by physical images of "energy" or "directedness." (Thoughts, not only actions, can be "lively" or "ponderous.") The idea of a double articulation does, nevertheless, fit well with the common distinction between articulatory and tonal phrases. Shaping contour with gestural purpose, evident in the specific speed, direction, and emphasis accorded melodic intervals, is not the same task as achieving tonal coherence in a phrase.[7] The two musical needs may actually exist in a tension, which a performer must resolve when making decisions about tempo and the relative weighting to be given to articulatory events. In extended tonal phrases, a slower tempo and gestural emphasis will tend to increase perceived "expressivity" while reducing the effectiveness of those longer-term sources of tonal coherence which could give a perspective of "purposefulness," "control," or "containment" of affect. In the "Spring Sonata" opening, three elaborately contoured articulatory phrases, each involving a reversal of direction within itself, make up a single tonal phrase (bars 1–10). While each contoured phrase invites careful shaping, too much attention to this kind of content could lead to a performance that lacks a longer-term purpose. It was this kind of problem that led Schenker to discourage too much dwelling on small-scale "expressivity." A feeling for contour should not, he believed, distract attention from coherence in a tonal work.

Having admitted a role to the contrast of "body" and "mind" as a way of grasping the posing of a somatic sense in contour against a purposeful "will" in tonal structure, it is worth considering once more how this "body" has been formed. In the formation of Lidov's gesture theory, assumptions were at first made about the neurophysiological determination of gestural shapes, but no such assumption can be made about more extended phrases of somatically formed motion. I might describe the opening two bars of the "Spring Sonata" as a free, but discontinuous, movement down through space (the tonal space of an octave, on the third degree, A), a movement with a sense of lightness and lack of compulsion about it, as if it were a matter of spontaneous choice when the descents would be made—or delayed by diminution. If a somatic image is implied in this description of "agency" in a movement through space, it would have to be one of a "body" that was highly mobile, flexible, and free of the compulsion of gravity. It descends when it will. A "body" like this is not unambiguously the image of a physically existing thing. If "body" does appear as implicit in the virtual agency of contour, it is a body created by highly ordered structural means, and not the image of a known entity. The space through which it moves is opened up by tonality, in a relationship of identity between the two As at different octave levels, and its "freedom" to move through this tonal space is ensured by the stability of the tonic as an harmonic underlay. An apparent spontaneity or even playfulness of melodic motion is thus made possible by the exemplification of an harmonic generality for tonal music—that spaces within a structural chord will create stability. Rather than expressing some familiar state, whose overt symptoms are readily recognized, the contour of this phrase creates a virtual somatic play which is free of familiar bodily contingencies. In effect, the music creates a bodily possibility that listeners may entertain, as freeing them from known limitations. It is not so much "expressive" of known states as it is "creative" of a virtual subjectivity. If, in this case, the felicitous play on motion through a tonal space creates an image of free movement that can only be congenial, an extension beyond normal capacities, it should be remembered that no law determines that the image of "body" in sound should always be so positive. Just as tonal motion can be frustrated by interruption and delay, the articulated contours of a phrase can be filled with disjunctions which might more readily suggest handicap and disability than they do an optimally functioning body, primed to dance.[8]

With the extension of "body" beyond the limits of small gestures which can readily be "felt" by a listener, a reappraisal is needed of the role in a listener's understanding played by the possibility of movement. When Meyer's student, the jazz musician, Charles Keil, sat in his classes on analysis, the one point that made him fidget was Meyer's apparent forgetfulness of "body," an instrument of understanding very important to a jazz player in being able to feel a "groove" (Feld, 1994; Feld and Keil, 1994; Keil and Feld, 1994). In jazz, having a "feel" for a style of rhythmic performance, which can be made evident in synchronized bodily motion, is an essential part of what it is to understand the music's signification, and attempting to read "meaning" of structure alone is clearly insufficient. Because a jazz groove is regular, yet shaped by a displacement of the performed onset of sound from the center of the beat, it can seem to be "immediate" in its encouragement of a direct bodily response (e.g., swaying, tapping, or nodding in an oscillating motion). The binary rhythms of ordinary human movement could actually be thought of as motivating it. When haptic imagery is created by free movement through a virtual tonal space, it is not, however, possible to assume such ease of bodily response as a necessary interpretant. In practice, the processes of entrainment described by Hatten as central to Alexandra Pierce's manner of teaching physical phrase rhythm suggest that music is being used to shape and extend the body's potentialities, not merely to draw out some previously acquired sense of poise and purpose in extended movement. It seems to be a process not unlike that of learning classical ballet, where bodies are shaped to the requirements of highly stylized movements. In effect, the articulate order of music creates a "body" where one has not been known before, increasing the actual bodily repertoire of one who chooses to learn how to move in an appropriate way. Where such actual motion is absent, a "feel" for the virtual agency in which a "body" is formed has to be acquired by a listener through a process of abstraction, recognizing movement as that of another entity, rather than as a possibility of one's own bodily self.

It remains useful to distinguish the "body" in sound, as formed in a shaped contour, from the "willfulness" or purposeful "desires" of tonal processes. This "body" and "mind" must, however, now be understood as mutually implicative, rather than as dualistic opposites, and the possibilities of a virtual "body," mindfully inhabiting an extended tonal space, must be accepted as taking listeners beyond what is known in familiar corporeal experience to new arenas of transcendence—or disablement.

c. Lawfulness and Spontaneity

A synthetic form of melodic "movement" (derived from a combination of tonal/harmonic, rhythmic, and pitch movements), has been seen as giving rise to haptic images, which may range from the microstructural to the level of a phrase. Although any perceived gesture, or more extended "bodily" agency, can be analyzed by reference to its structural features, a grasp of the image in the first place cannot be gained through analysis alone. No musical item is, by definition, a "gesture" or a "bodily motion through space." As these are images which cannot be fixed to any content, the recognition of where they are appropriate cannot be gained by reference to rules and generalities. It is more a matter of educating the body, or bodily mind, to "feel" musical motion in a certain way. In a musician's studio, this kind of understanding is gained by practice and imitation of a teacher, as one who is already able to draw out the possibilities of a written phrase. A kinesthetic appreciation of how the teacher "looks" may then be translated into a proprioceptive "feel" for performing in a similar way. (For a violinist, much comes down to the use of a variegated speed, pressure, and position of the bow.) In a written semiotic analysis, where kinesthetic understanding has informed the interpretation of some signified content, the challenge is to provide the means for a reader to grasp the haptic images applied to a passage, without the benefit of an audiovisual demonstration of nuanced shaping. The practical difficulty of doing so, and the weakness of assertion that can attend descriptions of this kind, is evidence that this *kind* of image—an "iconic" sign of a particular bodily object, without prototype (not modeled on an existent state)—is characterized by a level of uncertainty even greater than that applicable to the variegated signs of "willfulness" or "desire" that have been seen to emerge in the contextual realization of tonal laws. It is not that any performer, or sensitive listener, need be uncertain of what it is they feel in the shaping of a melodic segment (of whatever dimension). A "feel" for the shaping may, in fact, be so particular, so precise, that the effort of finding a verbal image to convey its character can be sufficiently frustrating to abort the attempt. The lack of any general rules for aligning particular contours with haptic images means, however, that there is no determinacy at all in the language to be used, and inter-subjective understanding is correspondingly harder to achieve. This problem increases with movements over longer temporal spans, where the content being understood is not "gestural" in the familiar sense, with a repertoire of emotion labels linked to observable acts, but is instead an "embodied motion" that is novel in its form. Particularities for which there are no ready labels resist entry into speech, unless that speech is extended by metaphors which are proffered without dogmatic assertiveness. To recall Peirce's semiotic categories once more, these are "iconic sinsigns" as opposed to the "replicas" (or tokens) of "legisigns" (types). Where typology is absent, providing a strong level of publicly agreed content, the sign inhabits a social space with much greater room for mobility of description and ongoing interpretive conversation. Some metaphoric language (such as that used by Hatten) may have the persuasiveness of an apt image in poetry, where it captures a moment or sense that is intrinsically unrepeatable. When support for the image is derived from analysis, it is subject to the range of "tenable opinions" that can be held at that level, but it cannot ultimately be legitimated by the analysis. If it is accepted by another, it is (as Scruton has suggested) because the image captures an experience they share.

These characteristics of singular signs do not bode well for the formation of "theory." If it is the role of "rules" to capture patterns in some realm of experience, reflecting an order that is "given" in some way by the objects being known, any aspect of experience without a consistent pattern will necessarily be excluded from theorization. Lidov's general observation, that melodic understanding is characterized by recourse to haptic images, could nevertheless be thought of as a "rule" whose realization is widely indeterminate. Rather than take this factor of the under-specified as a discouragement from further interpretive thought, it may be embraced as opening the space within which a performer's (and critic's) interpretive freedom may be exercised. If indeterminacies of content are recognized both in the realization of tonal rules, with their general potential for creating virtual agency, and in the formation of "bodily" shapes in the performance of a phrase, a broad arena of choice has been opened up. A composer's choice is exercised at the first level, a performer's at the second (see Lidov, 1987). A listener and critic then find their freedom of judgment in seeking to articulate the particularity of effects achieved. Vagueness in Lidov's "rule" does not then constitute a lack of meaning but a broadly defined space, within which a free interpretive discourse can take place.

chapter seven

~

Complex Syntheses

T HE PURPOSE OF THIS chapter is twofold: to discuss the point at which
the semiotic approach so far developed may be brought to bear on
problems in aesthetics, and to defend the hypothesis that music is capable of
signifying affectively complex states.

1. Expressive Complexity and Musical "Personae"

a. Absolute Music and the Problem of Expression

In aesthetic discussions of music, a central topic of concern is the source of
musical "expressivity." How could instrumental music be capable of expressing emotions, when most emotional states are related to some context
of activity, which cannot be musically observed? The tradition coming from
Eduard Hanslick has most conventionally been read as debarring claims of
musical expressiveness, in the name of promoting an attention to music's

formal properties, but this reading creates a dichotomy of affect and form which, though now well entrenched, does little justice to Hanslick's own descriptions of formal connotation (Maus, 1992). Contemplating the dynamism of tonal harmonic processes does not exclude a recognition of musically signified "feelings," of the kind discussed in the last chapter. Hanslick is, however, skeptical that the feelings aroused in a listener will be very informative about musical effects, given that any number of extraneous factors can influence what someone may feel while listening. "Instead of clinging to secondary and vague feeling effects of musical phenomena, we would do better," he says, " to penetrate to the inner nature of the works and try, from the principles of their own structure, to account for the unique efficacy of the impressions we receive from them" (1986: 6). "Impressions" are not "feelings" in the sense Hanslick implies here, because they are more finely attuned to the contents of the music than to the sensations felt while listening. Recently stated aesthetic positions are consistent with his view when they admit the possibility of "musical feelings," formed by the directionality of tonal processes, while excluding the musical signification of specific emotional states (Raffman, 1993). Peter Kivy's "cognitive" philosophy of musical understanding is a good example. Kivy places emphasis on the mental activities required to follow through the unfolding of musical events in time and, although he recognizes that their description may be metaphorical for someone who lacks a technical vocabulary, he does not see this metaphor as more than a cognitive prop, which could be replaced quite readily with technical terms. Formal events are, he suggests, essentially meaningless in their lack of a word-like reference to conditions of the outside world, and it remains a source of great perplexity for him that listeners would spend so much time engaged pleasurably in meaningless activity (Kivy, 1997). Some steps in the direction of an answer are, however, provided in Kivy's philosophy by the idea of brief melodic moments as capable of mimicking the outward shape of an expressive gesture. Common emotions, whose visible displays are readily recognized, are accepted by him as being translated into sound, through the creation of aural equivalents to visually apprehended expressive movement. Stephen Davies takes this line of thought up from Kivy, to defend the thesis that "emotions are heard in music as belonging to it, just as appearances of emotions are present in the bearing, gait, or deportment of our fellow human beings and other creatures" (1994: 239). An important proviso of this view is, however, that it restricts music's expressive range "to those emotions or moods having characteristic behavioral expressions" (ibid.). Following from this, the surprisingly spartan conclusion is that, in its expressive role, "music presents the outward features of sadness or happiness in general" (ibid.).[1] In effect, it can mimic the appearance of some overt expressive movements, staying within the range of what Kivy calls "garden variety" emotions, but it cannot be informative about emotional states, or present states that are in any way complex, or novel in their content. Without even proceeding to detailed argument, a musician might respond with the question, "then why would playing music be so engaging, so compelling, or rewarding, if it failed so remarkably to pass beyond the most naively obvious of affective states? Why do I waste so much time in the shaping of a particular phrase, if its content is none other than that already known, and equally displayed by other works of its kind? Could it really be just to give someone the pleasure of saying, 'I like the way she does that phrase?'"

The position defended by Kivy and Davies seems, at first, to create its own perplexity in its very denial of a content that is the common experience of musicians engaged in interpretive work.[2] Theirs is not, however, the most ascetic view of musical affectivity. A defense of an even more restrictive view has been offered by Gordon Graham (1995), who argues that instrumental music can invite strong positive evaluations without their depending on music's capacity for expressive differentiation. Graham dismisses even the role of ascriptions such as "light" and "dark" for qualities of tone (ibid.: 143), on the assumption that what music *is* should be decidable quite apart from its description. He thus makes it a premise that metaphoric terms are uninformative about essentially musical content, and in so doing, rules out even the relatively modest idea that a melodic segment might be heard as expressively "gestural" (without being a false perception). The positions entertained by other aestheticians, in their recognition of gestural shaping (Kivy, Davies, Budd), or of other forms of metaphoric content (Scruton), are liberal by comparison. Two denials could be discriminated in their commonly held view that instrumental music is incapable of making fine differentiations of affect, both denials depending on the music's inability to create reference to an objective state of affairs which could show what any expressed state was *about*. The first denial is, implicitly, that music can make differentiations *within* the categories of the "happy" and "sad." If forced to sort the works already mentioned in this book, with only these two available categories, I might say that the first movements of Beethoven's "Spring Sonata" and of Brahms' Violin Sonata in G Major each belong to a positive domain of affect (though "happy" seems a bit trivializing), while the first movements of Tartini's Violin Sonata in G Minor ("Dido's Lament"), Bach's Sonata in G Minor for Solo Violin, and Sibelius' Violin Concerto all display pathos or melancholy of some kind. Although I might alternate between different adjectives, I am not, in this view, making any judgments about the musical content, but just exercising some descriptive freedom without any particular grounding. To be wistful, woeful, lamenting, forlorn, or full of melancholy, grief, or pathos is, it is implied, the prerogative of persons whose life situation can be observed in explanation of their state, not of musical works which lack such reference. I might apply any of those terms, indiscriminately, to works which fit the general attribution of "pathos," without seeking to win any argument that my choice of a term is the optimal one, ruling out others. Why quibble over whether "Dido" in her lament is more "wistful" or "forlorn"? Once the general kind of expressivity has been established, a lack of determinacy about how her state might be described is part of the music's attractiveness. This kind of argument depends on the assumption that, in order for an affective state to be distinct, it needs to determine only one correct descriptive term. "If it makes sense to discriminate musical states *within* the general arena of, say, 'pathos,'" it could be asked, "why is it the case that listeners don't agree about which of the possible set of more nuanced terms for pathos is the right one to use?" "If no consensus can be reached about the term that applies, how do you know that a fine-grained affective discrimination has been made at all?" (see Davies, 1994). No matter how convinced I am that the pathos I hear in Tartini's work is distinct from that which I hear in Bach's, my conviction of there being a difference must (it is implied) be false, unless it is supported by evidence that others will agree on a distinct set of terms for the description of the mood in each work. I will later argue that a full determinacy of sense (or description) is not required in order for discriminations within a category to be intelligibly communicated and grounded in publicly shared features of the music, but before I do so, the second denial needs to be rehearsed.

This second denial is that music can be expressive of complex affective

states, especially those such as "hope" or "remorse," without an obvious behavioral manifestation. States such as this can be understood only by looking
at the external state of affairs being experienced by a person and assessing
their interpretation of that state as one to be desired or regretted. The contextualization of music in relation to some text might serve to turn a passage
expressive of "grief" or "pathos" into one expressive of "remorse," but without that assistance, a greater degree of indeterminacy has to be accepted. The
violin solo opening Bach's aria, "Erbarme dich," from the *St. Matthew Passion,*
is so placed as to specify the expression of a grief tinged with longing, typical of some kinds of remorse (Cumming, 1997a). In another context, the
same passage might be taken as expressive of grief at lost love.[3] These states
are not unrelated, in their combination of a heavy dejectedness with the
apparent striving of an unfulfilled desire or need (for renewed relationship in
this case), and yet a lived context does distinguish them. The music alone
cannot supply that lived context, and its "grief" or "longing" cannot be
pinned down as fitting one circumstance alone. At issue, in response to this
argument, is the degree to which purely instrumental works may supply
their own kinds of contextualization for expressive effects within them. Jerrold Levinson argues, for example, that a theme (bars 57–66) in Mendels-
sohn's *Hebrides* overture is expressive of "hope" (1990: 357–371; 1995), resting
his argument not only on observations of the gestural property of "aspiration" in some rising melodic leaps, but also on the context of the theme
within the movement, arriving as it does as a reversal of the affective turbulence that preceded it (ibid.: 368–369).

In addressing either of the two denials of expressive subtlety in music,
some account is needed of how "expressivity" may be heard in an instrumental work. The position put forward by Davies (1994) gives surprising
emphasis to "appearances." A listener knows how expressive behaviors *look*
and translates that recognition into a way of *hearing* movement in sound.
Such an emphasis on "appearances" gives visuality a strange dominance.
Though not entirely irrelevant to ways of "hearing" music as movement in
space, it remains intuitively at odds with the experience of music as an
acoustic medium, in which movements through virtual space are heard (and
sometimes "felt"—in body or mind), not necessarily seen. The very limitation in the number of visually distinct behavior patterns that can be used to
discriminate affects leads predictably to the conclusion that music, made de-

pendent on mimicking visually observed gesture, is limited in its expressive range. Another approach is needed if subtlety within general categories of expression is to be recognized, or when considering more abstract emotional states, where an "object" is usually needed for recognition.

b. Expressive Personae

A position compatible with that developed in this book is outlined by Levinson, who takes as his starting point the idea of a virtual "persona," a subjective character heard as embodied in the music, as the carrier of an expressive impetus or intent. Levinson does not, however, seek to describe in general terms how that persona might be formed, beyond noting that it could be composed of multiple elements, of both qualitative and structural character. His logical definition of the "persona" simply formalizes some of the notions of virtual agency found in Cone (and later elaborated in Cumming, Lidov, and Tarasti) without seeking to specify the means of their formation:

> P expresses (or is expressive of) a *iff* P is most readily and aptly heard by the appropriate reference class of listeners as (or as if it were) a sui generis personal expression of a by some (imaginatively indeterminate) individual. (1990: 338; see also 1996: 107)

By making the strong proposition that expression occurs *iff* ("if and only if") a group of listeners familiar with some style hears a passage within it as the virtual utterance of a persona (an "imaginatively indeterminate individual"), Levinson excludes the possibility that there could be forms of musical expression that are not so readily explained in this way. He also holds back from specifying the limits for applying some of his terms. In examining the definition closely, questions could, for example, be asked about the "personal" and "individual" as paradigm cases of expression. Such questions are opened up by Levinson's parenthetical admission of an "imaginative indeterminacy" in what might constitute an "individual." The parenthesis might simply be an admission that the Subject of music lacks a particular face. It could be, as Kendall Walton suggests, like the Cheshire cat, who recedes from view while leaving its expressive smile.[4] An impression of individual expression may be gained, in listening to abstract music, without the individual being named. The later naming of the opening slow movement of Tartini's Violin Sonata in G Minor, "Dido's Lament," attests to the desire among listeners to hear the work as if it were a sui generis personal expression of lament by some individual who is now given a possible name. This is, however, an unusual case, and labels for the apparent agent of expression, even if desired, don't always stick. Once the indeterminacy of the agent is accepted, it could be asked why that agent needs to be a familiar kind of individual at all. Does the "individual" concerned need always to suggest humanoid characteristics, in order to be expressive of affective states typically possessed by people, or could it not perhaps be extended to any kind of virtual agency? (A clichéd description of Beethoven's Fifth Symphony has "fate knocking on the door," making an agent of fate, and suggesting that what is expressed is an impersonal threat, carrying with it the sense of foreboding.) If apparent agency may be heard—irrespective of whether it seems to be a humanly personal utterance of not—would this not throw into question also the confidence with which anyone could say that the expression is of "a" (where "a" is presumed to stand for any familiar expressive class)? An agency which is compelling, but deviates from the apparently personal, could be "expressive" of states that are somehow recognized, yet also new and interesting. The agency of the Queen of the Night, as seeming to be disembodied, was discussed in chapter 5. She instills wonder and fear, as her virtuosic fury seems to be beyond that of any human being (including that of the singer). As a different kind of example, consider the "lark" as the agent in Vaughan Williams' *The Lark Ascending.* Its melodic incipits may be suggestive of a "flight," first tentative and restricted in its range, then expanding quickly through larger spaces. The initial segments could then be conceived as "gestural" in the broadest sense, and the longer spans of melody heard as longer phrases of movement by a (non-human) body. The title of the work invites such a hearing, after all. Melodic organization here affords an apparent agency in movement, without suggesting it to be that of a human individual. That does not prevent some passages from being heard, even so, as "expressive" of affects that are, in their usual manifestation, distinctively personal. Its lightness and freedom from being "weighed down" could easily be heard as expressive of a very much heightened positive affect—of joy or ecstasy. Such colloquialisms as "flights" of thought (or even of being "over the moon" with happiness) support the idea of "flight" as an image for the exceptional transcendence of a person's normal range of thought or affect. Hearing the passage as "expressive" in this sense does not, even so, reduce it to a new presentation of psychological states that are entirely familiar, because a recognition of its agency as that of a distinctively non-human kind prevents there being a complete recognition of (or, for some, projective identification with) the affects it conveys. A virtual "agent" in a musical work cannot simply "express" states that are known apart from the form in which they appear, as that agency is formed by the music itself. The sign creates the "subject," not the "subject" the sign.

If a virtual agent may be that of a non-human body, to what extent does it need to be "personal" at all? In some cases, a virtual agent could seem to be making an utterance, with an element of impersonality about it. Metaphors of voice in the violin, of gestural force in some melodic incipits, and of "desire" and "willfulness" are deeply entrenched in Western traditions of performance and listening, to provide some bases from which subjectivity may be musically heard, but their very ubiquity (and reproductive success) has ensured that they carry the codes of their own repudiation. The discussion of a violin's potential to convey the impression of a voice that "speaks" or "sings" revealed that this very potentiality becomes the means of its own reversal, whereby the violinistic "voice" no longer speaks in quasi-vocal tones. A rounded, "expressive," sound (the sine qua non of Romanticism[5]) can be replaced by one that is harsh and guttural, spare and sparse, or electronically modified with a reverberance that is "uncanny" and disorienting, as if the "voice" remained without the normal limits of a (violinistic) embodiment. Transcendence, mockery, or the powerful body blow of asceticism could all be heard in these effects. And again, the very potential to hear a melodic incipit as "gestural" ensures that the virtual "body" can be enhanced or stretched, extended in its apparent capacities, or attenuated in its expressiveness, by the subjection of melodic incipits heard as "gestural" to various kinds of manipulation in tonal space and time. (It is not inconceivable that a musical "body" should by "spaghettified," through the electronic extension of a gestural incipit—like a body imagined by cosmic scientists to be stretched beyond its limits on entering a black hole.) This very possibility of hearing motion in musical space through reference to bodily forms of expressive movement can become a motivating force for modern styles to avoid the overtly "gestural," or to subject it to an abstraction where its alienation is almost complete. Lidov makes this point, in a different context, when he sug-

gests that "music *alienates* its somatic transactions in achieving formal structure" (1987: 71, my italics). As noted in chapter 5, Bartók's posthumous Violin Concerto opens with a phrase from which "gestural" moments could
well be extracted, as a potentiality of small groups of notes whose direction
is uniform. Their place within an extended chromatic phrase ensures, however, that their "expressiveness" is attenuated, or rendered more "distant." A
"sui generis personal expression" might still be heard, but the sense of the
"personal" and "expressive" here is made weaker by abstraction. If a virtual
agent is attributed to this phrase, it might be thought of as "abstracted," in
bodily "denial," overly controlled, or alternatively as moving towards the
"spiritual" in its containment of bodily expressiveness. Certainly the literal
achievement of a higher tessitura later in the movement can be heard as the
"attainment of heights" in more than one sense.

If potentialities for quasi-vocal and gestural expressiveness are subject to
reversal, the means of creating a temporalized sense of "purpose," "will,"
and "desire" are no less so. The very capacity to create musical directedness,
with the virtuality of an "agency" who seeks some form of progress, is also
the capacity to withhold direction, or to weaken it. In Peter Sculthorpe's orchestral work, *Mangrove,* the central theme is, for example, formed in a
Japanese mode, the *ritsu-hyojo,* which has an orientational aspect not unlike
that of the Western Dorian, much weaker than that found in the major/
minor modes. Borrowing the *Isé-no-Umi* theme from the Japanese *Saibar"* (a
genre of *Gagaku*), Sculthorpe adopts it for his own narrative ends by exploiting the very weakness of its directional orientation, its apparent lack of
tonal "will" creating the effect of an agency outside time, without momen-
tum, meditative. The effect of virtual agency is certainly not absent, but it is
not of an agency that is obviously "personal" or "expressive" of an emotional state. Rather, it serves the purpose of questioning an aesthetic where
human subjectivity dominates (see Cumming, 1996a). It is as if there are
other "voices" in the world that should be heard. (Witness Sculthorpe's title
for a later work, *Earth Cry*). The expressiveness of a virtual agent is not,
then, limited to an "individual," to the "expression" of affective states, or to
the obviously "personal." All of those values, central to Romanticism, can be
reversed in other styles.

Hearing some musical passage as suggesting expressive agency does not,
furthermore, require that such agency be singular or unified. A theme

played by a whole section of stringed instruments in an orchestral work can create an "agency" that is at once "personal" and supra-personal, seeming to unite the voices of its constituent instruments. A contrapuntal theme, say, in one of Beethoven's late string quartets, can be distributed between parts to create the sense of a shared affect, created by "agents" whose states are unified. Linking "agency" and "expressiveness" is, in all of these examples, a productive move that leads to consequences well beyond the reproduction of a clichéd emotional expressiveness. The real strength of Levinson's proposition lies not in its exclusiveness (its "expressiveness" occurs 'if and only if' an agent is heard) but in its indeterminacy—its restraint in spelling out its own possible consequences.

c. Non-conceptual Signs

Concerned about the second denial above, the denial to music of a capacity to be expressive of states such as "hopefulness" and "remorse," Gregory Karl and Jenefer Robinson (1995a) have sought to build upon Levinson's position, while strengthening the degree of reference to the large-scale unfolding of a work, which they see as providing the necessary context for subtleties of musical affect. They do not dispute the role of a virtual "persona" as implicit in an expressive affect. What they are skeptical about is the role of "non-cognitive" elements in the differentiation of affective states. "Qualitative feels, desires, and impulses, varieties of internal sensation, degrees of pleasure and pain, patterns of nervous tension and release, [and] patterns of behavior (gestural, vocal, postural, kinetic)" are, in Levinson's view (1990: 196), able to work together to form unique profiles for different affects, which may be quite complex. Even without an understanding of context they could, he suggests, give sufficient information to an observer for the understanding of a complex affective state. To avoid what they see as vagueness in Levinson's account, Karl and Robinson (1995a) argue that any reliance upon the "non-cognitive" should be removed, and that greater emphasis be placed instead upon the large-scale unfolding of a work, as the context within which the persona as a virtual entity is formed and allowed to undergo "experiences" which modify its character. If "personae" are attributed with complex states, such as "hope," that attribution is supported, they suggest, only when the relevant theme has been heard to change in its expressive character, in response to other contextual features within the work. Change itself brings the effect of modifying (or adding complexity and nuance to) a simpler affect already suggested earlier on. Karl and Robinson thus differ from Levinson principally in their skepticism about the capacity of a "persona" to assume a complex state without the assistance of a broadly defined context of musical change. They couch this skepticism in the form of a disbelief that any vaguely defined set of "qualitative feels" could be sufficient to differentiate complex affective states (1995a: 404), but they do not themselves give an account of the virtualities that could form a sense of "persona" in the first place. Their suggestions about musical self-reference (also mentioned by Hatten, 1994) in fact open out an additional dimension of interpretive complexity, rather than repudiating the viewpoint held by Levinson that the "non-cognitive" could contribute significantly to the formation of musically expressive states.

No matter how persuasive the need for an attention to breadth of interpretive context, in commenting on musically embedded subtleties, the need to specify how a given theme attains its character of expressive "agency" cannot simply be put aside. In his description of "persona," Levinson assumes that the place to start is with an examination of what constitutes any experience of "emotion" in ordinary life. It is on this assumption that he makes general suggestions about how musical personae might emulate such states. A very general observation, that various non-cognitive factors, including "affective, hedonic, conative, behavioral, and physiological components" combine to form different "constellations" or "profiles" for complex emotional states (1990: 344), does not, however, move far enough in showing how the transition could be accomplished, between subjectively experienced states and musically represented ones. One solution has been offered by Davies. As noted before, he relies on expressive states that are visually observable in ordinary life, as the paradigm cases of "expression," so that he can point at a direct correlation of the outward shapes of certain kinds of expressiveness—such as the "sinking feelings" of despondency—and their musical instantiation. Davies' account does not, however, go far enough in explaining how the qualities that make up affective states could be taken up musically, because it relies so strongly upon the visual *appearance* of expressivity. It may seem an obvious point, but music is not primarily a visual medium in which "space" is literally displayed, but an auditory medium, which creates its own virtual spaces, as points of orientation that can be heard as directing the flow of movement in time. Sensations may be heard in musical sounds, desires (the "hedonic") attributed to the shaping of melodic intervals or harmonic relationships, and the feeling tone of emotion heard in extended passages, beyond the locally "gestural" or obviously visual. Rather than dismissing these attributions, as an expression of what listeners might *wish* to hear (despite its logical impropriety), some account is needed of how sensations, desires, or feelings can be signified and understood in ways beyond the visual. Levinson, in his article on expression ("Hope in *The Hebrides*" [1996: 336–375]), has noted this problem in Davies' view, but demurred from rectifying it. So it is that Karl and Robinson repudiate Levinson's view, finding that the weakness of his position lies in its very lack of specification, its "vagueness" in referring to the "non-cognitive" as an important part of emotional experience.

It is at this point that a semiotic approach to the analysis of voice, gesture, and agency can usefully intervene in the aesthetic debate. The range of sensations, and of neurophysiologically encoded gestural effects mentioned by Levinson, is broadly consistent with those discussed in this book under the notion of "signs": "qualitative" signs, such as those of voice; "singular" signs for gestures without conventional form, as well as the emergent qualities of rule-governed processes (such as "willfulness," or "desire"). Levinson's idea, that the combined effects of these "non-cognitive" elements could add up to a complex signification (even if it were not possible to derive a complex affect from any single factor, taken alone) (1995: 200), is a view with which I would concur. Skills for analyzing signification, developed through the use of Peirce's categories, provide a means by which to create a detailed picture of those very "non-cognitive" elements, and their complex synthesis in a given work, so that the novel affective character of successive "wholes" (at varying levels) can be grasped. More substance is given, also, to the general thought of a "persona," as including aspects of the "non-cognitive" within its synthetically "expressive" role. In a semiotic account, the "persona" may be understood as comprised of lower-level signs, a kind of provisional reconciliation of their multiplicity into a single impression (no matter how ephemeral). It is not a motivating force "behind" any quality that is heard, but an effect of the combination of other semiotic elements in time—a complex character, with apparent agency and definite affective tone, heard to emerge from other signs. If, as Thomas Sebeok has suggested, the "self"—in its ordinary sense—may be imagined as a "super-sign," an emergent entity negotiating the continuous integration of life representations (affects and memories) in time,[6] this is no less apposite as a way of imagining the musically signified "persona."

Semiotic analysis of the kind described in chapters 4–6 addresses the musical signification of states that Levinson calls "non-cognitive": auditory sensations and nuance, the feeling tone of gestures, or the willfulness and desire of temporally realized tonal processes. Before proceeding it should, however, be questioned whether the very idea of a binary division between the "cognitive" and "non-cognitive" is one that is compatible with a Peircean semiotic view, as developed here. This way of labeling aspects of mental experience presupposes that "understanding" is a state depending upon the use of language, that is, a verbal representation of some state of affairs. On this view, "cognition" is evident *iff* (if and only if) someone uses sentences in the form of a proposition, to make an appraisal of whatever "is the case" in the circumstances surrounding them (Wittgenstein, *Tractatus*). Someone's expressive actions may be presumed to have been informed by an appraisal of some situation, as when a remorseful appearance suggests that they have judged themselves as culpable in a case of loss—but the presumption of cognitive activity cannot be fully "cashed out," or made accessible to another, apart from the linguistic commentary. Only words, it is suggested, could confirm that it is, indeed, a self-judging remorse, and not a simple grief at loss that is being felt by one who displays heaviness of affect. A good reason for maintaining an emphasis on language, as the means of gaining access to interpretive acts, may thus be found in the observation that thought depends on representation—something to think *about*—and language is the most efficient means of designating this "aboutness" accurately. If it is then taken for granted that "names" in language are the principal means of establishing "aboutness" or reference, little option remains but to insist that some object of thought be labeled, before blessing an activity with the accolade of "thoughtful" or "cognitive."[7] This approach offers some degree of security at least. When someone labels their own state, or that implied in another's expressive display, by reference either to a lived context or to observed phenomenal qualities, there can be little doubt that an act of interpretation has occurred. Sensations, feelings, or desires can be experienced passively, and manifested symptomatically, without any active interpretation, so it cannot be taken for granted that someone experiencing such states "knows" what they are about, unless they convey the experience in some way, often with words. Having a state of sensation, feeling, or desire and displaying it is just not enough to establish anyone's self-understanding. Such states are not *themselves* cognitions, but phenomena to be interrogated and appraised, in a process that might also reveal them to be symptoms of unconsciously made judgments, whose content needs to be drawn out and represented—preferably verbalized. An even stronger motivating force for giving attention to language, related to this one, may be found in the desire to avoid any resort to stories about the direct "intuition" of "inner" states, as if they could be directly known. Skepticism about any claims of a directly intuited interiority, mentality, or "selfhood," preceding all contents of thought, is an effective attitude to assume in response to the Cartesian belief in an experiencing "I" who precedes, and hence does not depend upon, language (despite being revealed in thought). If, for Descartes, an "I" became apparent as implicit in thought, but was somehow prior to verbalization, and certainly to the appearance of any sensory form (even in the spoken thought "I am"), no such intuition of the "I" before thought can be accepted in critical response. What is "known" of the self and its states is known in representations (in signs) and not as a shapeless and contentless outside (or "inner") force.

It is not, however, necessary to get stuck on the role of verbal language in order to avoid a Cartesian notion of the "self" as available to direct introspection. Peirce's insistence on the need for a broad range of "signs," as the content of thought, addressed just this point. A consideration (chapter 2) of his skeptical "Questions Concerning Certain Faculties Claimed for Man" (Wiener [1958] 1966: 15–38) demonstrated his repudiation of any approach to the mind based on pure introspection, and showed the role of "signs" as the media of thought. It should now be clear that these "signs" were not, in Peirce's later-developed semiotic philosophy, restricted to language, but could include all of the kinds of representation so far discussed—iconic presentations of qualities, directional indices, or rule-governed conventions. A semiotic view, based on his framework, does not, then, require cognition to be restricted to the most fully developed "symbol"—the prerogative of language. Symbolic modes are only the highest tip of thoughtful, sign-governed activity. The so called "non-cognitive" modes of sensation or desire can be signified in non-verbal ways—through voice or gesture—and when signified, they are implicitly interpreted, hence "cognitive," even if their object is not fully specified in the way that it would be if language were involved. Anyone who is able to consciously manipulate their tone of voice, or the emphasis of their gesturings, in response to a situation in which they find themselves, has displayed "understanding" in their capacity to work with non-verbal signs. If semiotic modalities other than language are to be identified as having a role in mental life distinct from the verbal, that role is not, then, well-captured by relegating them to the domain of "stupid" or uninterpreted reflexes.[8] Peirce proposed another way of capturing the distinction between non-verbal and verbal signs by looking at the differing roles played by the "interpretant" in each. As described in chapter 3, the "immediate" interpretant is that aspect of the sign which allows it to be interpretable, and its "dynamic" form appears when an interpreter actually gets involved in realizing the potential for understanding. Both potential and realized interpretations vary with the kind of relationship a sign (representamen) has to its object. (To review the "second trichotomy" of signs briefly, icons rely to varying degrees on some apparent [or imagined] likeness to their object; indices have a physical connection to it, or are related to a putative object through the creation of a virtual "causality," the sense of "pointing" at something yet to come. Only "symbols" rely fully on convention to gain their meaning.) The "immediate" interpretants of signs do no more than draw out the differing relationships of sign and object, and, as an aspect of the sign, do not say anything in particular about the mental attitudes required of an interpreter. The "dynamic" interpretants do, however, say something about different modes of understanding, as they allow for the varied modes of response in which an immediate interpretant may be realized by an actively interpreting subject.[9] For an "icon," a "feeling" of recognition could be the dynamic interpretant of some putative likeness; for an "index," an "energetic" response of looking for the indicated object could be the dynamic means of interpreting[10] for a symbol, however, only reference to a rule would suffice. "Cognition" is not lacking in any of these cases, from the very fact that all involve an "interpretant" of some kind, but only the last kind of cognition moves towards a form of knowledge that might be termed "conceptual," in its ability to be stated as a set of rule-governed principles.

Levinson's reference to a binary contrast of the "non-cognitive" and the "cognitive" cannot, then, be sustained if cognition is to be given an adequate role in non-verbal signs. No reason has, however, yet been given to do away with a distinction, cited in the last chapter, between the "non-conceptual" and the "conceptual." The latter plays a similar role in Mark DeBellis' philosophy as the "cognitive" in the discussion above, and consists in the capacity to put an explicit functional label on some formal property. DeBellis (1991) argues that it is not evidence of a "conceptual" response to music that a listener would have a *feeling* for certain kinds of continuity, or closure, and be able to label it in metaphoric terms. Knowing that a certain chord feels "open" is not enough, in his view, to show that a student has recognized a "dominant function." Evidence of the "conceptual" is only given when the right name has been attached, no matter how apposite were the qualities previously "felt," and no matter how fortuitously appropriate were the adjustments displayed in performing a dominant chord (for example, by emphasizing the dissonance of a seventh, if present). Denied in this account is the possibility of a purely tacit understanding. The position derived in chapter 6 from a Peircean metaphysic is one that accords a greater role to patterns of adaptive action (musical or otherwise) which display a sufficient attunement to some aspect of the world (or music) such that further activity can be directed purposefully, with a measure of predictive success. (Young musically gifted children may, for example, display tonal orientation, without any conceptual grasp of "key," and may direct the tonal dynamics of their performances in appropriate ways.) A "felt" or "energetic" response was here taken as related in a non-coincidental fashion to the more explicitly conceptual understandings codified in tonal "rules." Implicit in this view is the idea of a "feeling" or "energetic" response as already implying an interpretive act, informed in some way by tacitly known rules. It can be conceded, nevertheless, that this kind of understanding is not "conceptual," and that someone who learns to recognize a chord under its correct label has "heard" something they did not hear before, even if they previously had an appropriate "feel" for the tensions of the chord. A distinction of the non-conceptual from the "conceptual" can be maintained, even if not all semiotic *cognitions* are taken to be "conceptual" (that is, achieved by the application of labels). DeBellis' judgment, that ordinary listeners do not understand music in a "conceptual" manner, does not then prevent them from understanding musical signs which do not depend on an explicit reference to rule-governed (and verbally described) interpretants. (Interestingly, not even a capacity to hear some features of tonal dynamism requires an explicit reference to tonal rules, although the insight gained by learning tonal theory can become "informative" in revealing aspects of structure not heard before.) For Levinson's "non-cognitive" it would, then, be helpful to substitute "non-conceptual," thus allowing for cognitions whose means of signification is not primarily linguistic.

Peirce's more expansive view of thought through signs gives an account of "non-conceptual" modes of thought. If qualitative signs are accepted, which include a strong element of the sensory, they create a thinking self who, through its signs, is embodied—not merely a physically disengaged mentality, and not restricted to the "conceptual" as a means of engaging the world. A consequence of this view is that it refuses not only the empty "I" of contentless thought, but also the disembodied self, knowable without the thought forms of physical life. It is also truer to a developmental view of emotional understanding, which must necessarily allow for some functional discrimination of affective states long before the acquisition of language. The function of tones of voice, of facial displays, and of bodily activity is undoubtedly of central importance in an infant's early reaction to its primary care givers, and although its adaptive and imitative reactions may at first seem quite involuntary, their increased control attests to the early formation of non-verbal sign use. Emotion labels, once learned, provide a conceptual overlay to prior understanding, but do not supplant the use of non-verbal means of affective interchange. Emotional understanding (and its representation) retains a strong element of the "non-conceptual." Any view of musical expressivity that relies upon the apparently "gestural" has made similar observations of the role played by non-verbal displays in emotional communication, without necessarily referring to them as "signs" or even "metaphors," but few seek to elucidate the relationship between different modes of cognition as developmental in origin. Levinson's reference to gesture as a "non-cognitive" aspect of mental activity does, however, stand out from the rationalizing treatment of Kivy or Davies, who see gesture as a communicative display to which the normal response is a *rationalization* of how another feels.

d. Signs of Complex Affectivity

To return now to Levinson's emphasis on non-conceptual elements as capable of differentiating affects, it should be apparent that a Peircean notion of "sign" can make a distinct contribution to the kind of argument he seeks to develop. It may do so both by providing a means of describing how non-verbal forms of expression can be musically signified, in a way that respects their already-interpreted status as a sign within society, and by extending the range of ways in which music may be understood to present contents suggestive of vocality, embodiment, or more extended forms of ("non-conceptual") expressive activity. As noted above, a semiotic account extends the range of elements that can be heard as movements, in which subjective intent is implied. Non-verbal displays may themselves be seen as "signs," open to deliberate social modification, and when some facet of music takes them up, becoming suggestive of "vocality," "gesture," or strength of "desire," it becomes a secondary sign. It does not, however, need to signify through the direct imitation of any determinate tone of voice, visual shape, or form of willful impulsiveness. The musical exemplification of "gesture" may, as Davies suggests, be most obvious in brief, distinctive movements, readily matched to a short list of dominant affects, but it is by no means limited to this kind of movement, and a musical moment heard as "gestural" or as displaying "embodiment" may not always reflect the characteristic of a real (or human) body (or a convincingly "personal" persona) at all. The possibility of recognizing novel musical "voices," "gesturings," or forms of "will" (or, for some, of having a dynamic "feel" for them) can, then, suggest a rejoinder to Davies' emphasis on the visual forms of gesture in human discourse, as a model for musical expressivity. The multifarious forms of instrumental "voice" cannot depend on any naive likeness to actual human voices. If patterns can be recognized as gestural which have no obvious likeness to a visually perceived movement, their understanding cannot be taken to depend upon the presence in the mind of a virtuoso translator of visually perceived forms into an audio/temporal mode. Processes of creative abstraction have gone on both in the composition and hearing of these effects. And if gesturings may be recognized by means other than translation from visual display (perhaps more in grasping a unified pattern of virtual "energies," and their modification), this is certainly true of the forms of "desire" or "will." No obvious form of visuality is here given as a basis for cross-modal signification, and it is not replaced by any direct aural substitute. When the dynamics of "will" or "desire" are musically signified, through formal processes which are directed in time towards some goal, no obvious "likeness" can be claimed between musical process and the "appearance" of a person acting in time. The creativity of abstraction is nonetheless effective in presenting a set of temporal relationships which can be heard to convey the effect of goal seeking with varied degrees of intensity, the necessary basis of these states. A relationship of successive acts, which in "real life" could be spread over large spans of time, can thus be subject to extreme compression in a musical form, and yet remain recognizable (Langer, 1942). Virtual agency, and the passage through different musical "circumstances," provides a means of conveying even more complex states, of "attitude" towards happenings and "reminiscence" of them, as Karl and Robinson have suggested (1995a).

When Karl and Robinson dispute Levinson's treatment of affective complexity in music, they do so on the grounds that he relies too strongly upon the "non-cognitive" (read "non-conceptual"), without extensive reference to the broader context within which musical self-reference could be used as a means of modifying signified states, to a point of perceptible subtlety. These authors assume that the way to substantiate Levinson's position would be to show how a combination of non-conceptual elements (voice, gesture, desire, etc.) could add up to a complex affect in any social context of expression, without reference to its conceptual features. A different way of approaching this problem is suggested by the semiotic account developed so far. Why not start with the basic kinds of signs, already discussed as a means of presenting relatively simple states, and explore the effects of their musical interaction? If music does not depend simply on the imitation of external states of affairs, but can create virtual "affects" which are novel in form (though derived from elements of the familiar), it makes little sense to assume that the only means of understanding a musical work's affective complexity is by analyzing the structure of complex mental states in a non-musical way. This is not to say that parallelisms will be absent between musical and extra-musical states of affairs. It is simply to suggest that a musically based analysis may prove revelatory about complex states of mind, rather than its being assumed that those states need to be "understood" or even "given" in their entirety prior to their musical analysis. If musical signification is a form of thought (implicitly cognitive, in its need for semiotic interpretants), and emotional states depend in large part upon the thoughts that make them up, it is entirely reasonable to conclude that the kind of "emotion" that is musically signified will reflect the musical thought form in which it appears. The musical medium does not render the use of verbal descriptions, and general labels for expressive types, entirely redundant, but neither can it be completely translated into language's propositional forms.

Karl and Robinson suggest self-reference within a work as a means of building the context for complexity. Their example of thematic review is, however, only one of the ways in which "context" can be construed. Another of the ways that an interaction of musical signs could produce a cognitively complex affect might be through the synthesis of elements occurring simultaneously, but in different time frames. The temporal dimensions of gesture, of phrase rhythm, and of larger-scale tonal process are concurrent, but moving at a different pace, so that larger frameworks could be seen to create a "perspective" on more local events, framing them in the context of broader purposes. The processes by which signs of different kinds are related to one another may be termed as kinds of "synthesis." In the next section, the idea of synthesis will be considered and related to the idea of "persona."

2. *Modes of Synthesis*

a. Langer's "Symbols"

A well-known but currently unfashionable defense of music's capacity to signify complex affective states was made by Susanne Langer, whose *Philosophy in a New Key* made explicit reference to the notion of music as comprised of signs. Only one of Langer's claims is of central concern here. It is that the expressive content of a piece of music may be "informative," in the sense that it makes emotional states conceivable, which would not otherwise become available to discursive thought, for the reason that they lack distinctive names. In Langer's terms, "just as words can describe events we have not witnessed, places and things we have not seen, so music can present emotions and moods we have not felt, passions we did not know before" ([1942] 1982: 222). She suggests, further, that the appropriate response to the complex content so signified is not one of emotional involvement, or of excitation of any kind. It is rather an intellectual response, a discursive absorption of what it is that the music has "given" for reflection. "The content has been symbolised for us, and what it invites is not emotional response, but *insight*" (ibid.: 223, my italics).

An immediate source of difficulty in addressing these claims is that Langer seems to underestimate the distinction between non-discursive signs (including icons and some indices), on the one hand, and discursive or "symbolic" modalities, on the other. It has been seen in earlier chapters that the interpretants of these kinds of signs differ quite markedly from one another. The "immediate" interpretant of an icon might include a kind of feeling; an index may provoke a dynamic response; only symbols demand a "logical" interpretant, or process of discursive reasoning. Although these different kinds of sign can occur together in a complex case, neither they, nor the modes of understanding that are operative when they appear, should be conflated or confused. In practice, Langer's "presentational signs" are closer to a complex, emergent "icon" than they are to a "symbol," which performs a systematic role in a language formed of conventions. If she were persuasive in assigning the presentational signs of music to the "symbolic" mode, her emphasis on reasoning as a response would be perfectly coherent, but if these signs do reflect aspects of the "iconic," the kind of response appropriate to them cannot effectively exclude a "feeling" for quality (though the feeling is not of a kind with knee-jerk reactions). Any aesthetic quality extending over a whole phrase or other relatively long passage of music may be thought of as a qualitative sign which "emerges" from smaller, more local signs.[11] (It may be named "iconic," in the broad sense that it "presents" a content, even without having any "real object" as its correlate). As a quality, it fits in with the characteristics of Peirce's "first" category, which includes any single state that seems to extend over time, and may be apprehended in an act of spontaneous recognition, even if examination leads to an understanding of the complexities involved in this act.

An example will serve to show how a combination of different elements could add up to an emergent affect that is complex and subtle yet in some sense singular. In the opening phrases of Bach's Sonata in G Minor for Solo Violin, aspects of "pathos," "reflectiveness," "spontaneity," and "containment" might all be heard. (*See* Example 7.1.) Roger Scruton suggests that if

voice leading framework
- - - - - salient melody

Example 7.1. Score and voice-leading analysis, opening of the Adagio, first movement, Sonata in G Minor for Solo Violin, by J. S. Bach

someone recognizes these descriptive terms as "true" of their own hearing of the work, their recognition is unlikely to have resulted from a process of discursive reasoning. A qualitative term may be assented to, having been "heard" to apply, even when a "likeness" between the musical presentation and a non-musical context has not been established through a process of investigation.[12] It is not, then, necessary for every listener to enter into a self-conscious process of reasoning in order to grasp the appropriateness of the descriptive terms, as they name qualities which the music may be "heard as" exemplifying. That does not mean, however, that someone who is unable to "hear" the appropriateness of the terms would fail to be helped by the provision of an explanatory "story" of some kind, so long as the story was presented as a way of attending to the music, and not as an end in itself. If perception is "cognitively penetrable" and analysis can lead to new ways of hearing, as DeBellis (1991) has argued, there need be little doubt that analytical reasoning will support a listener in acquiring new ways of hearing not only the identity of such things as chords, but also their affective connotations. A student might, for example, have their attention pointed successively to the musical elements which contribute to the formation of each effect, such as "pathos" or "containment," in Bach's phrase, so that they could practice "hearing" it in isolation from other dimensions of the phrase. If this process of learning is successful, its result will be a new awareness of emerging qualities, an analytically informed way of hearing. Learning thus informs listening, but a discursive process is not implied as occurring consciously in every act of hearing a quality.

The kind of story that can be told about the structures of Bach's phrase is very intricate and many-leveled. As the most obvious indicator of "pathos," the minor modality might be pointed out. More subtly, attention could be drawn to the way that the contrapuntal voices interweave with one another, so that the melody, heard to commence on the high G, seems to submerge itself on the "inside" of the harmony, and then to remain there, its dissonant seventh (C of the dominant chord, bar 2, first beat) eventually resolving to the third degree with a decorative twist (bar 2, third beat). The ending of a long melisma on this B-flat, inside the harmony, gives it an element of melodic incompleteness that could be named "wistful" or "melancholy," especially as it is the third degree of a minor key.

To make the moment more poignant, the departure of the opening melisma from the prominent "outer" voice is emphasized by the quadruple-stopped harmonies, which reassert a new "upper voice" (F-sharp–G), one whose registral connection to the opening chord causes it to "take over" from the voice now submerged in an inward part (see Example 7.1, graph). By focusing attention on the decorated line, and allowing the quadruple stops to remain a peripheral effect, Sigiswald Kuijken's performance realizes an air of melancholy. "Containment" and poise are, however, also potentialities of the framing tonic chords (as pointed out in chapter 3), which may, in a less authentic performance than Kuijken's, actually attain some level of monumentality. "Spontaneity" is a product of the notated improvisatory effects of elaborate melismata, which may be performed with apparent virtuosity and some freedom of tempo. "Reflectiveness," meanwhile, is a quality of thought that emerges when someone dwells on a point, and looks at its many sides, without seeking quick progression, peremptory "answers," or revolutionary change. It emerges musically in the very freedom of working around a familiar chordal pattern, unhurriedly, without seeking to challenge a known framework, and yet somehow drawing its "meaning" out. "Hearing" this quality is not a matter of concluding that the phrase is unoriginal, or sluggish in its harmonic rhythm, but of appreciating a level of stillness, related to that of tonal "containment," which gives an underlying stability to the melodically very active train of events. Someone who "hears" all of these qualities recognizes them with a seeming "immediacy," despite the fact that appreciating them depends on having acquired a stock of stylistic comparisons, through listening experience in this and other styles (see Levinson, 1996: 27–41). The discursive explanations that have been given here support judgments of the emergent qualities and may be used to guide others in learning to "hear" them, but assent to the qualitative terms still depends upon there being an experience of "hearing" them realized in the music (or hearing them as a potentiality of the music, in an aurally vivid reading of the score). A discursive description, taken alone, cannot be sufficient to convince another that the qualities inhere in a work. The process of listening to music and recognizing such qualities as emerging in it is, as Levinson has argued, quite dissimilar from the process of working discursively through the stages of a critical argument (ibid.: 60 ff.; Scruton).

Given that emergent qualities are not understood in the same way as language, where a "symbolic" mode of thought dominates, Langer's decision to refer to this mode of presentation as "symbolic" does seem counterproductive for her argument. Equally puzzling in this context is her pointing at "insight" as the outcome of listening. If no problem has been posed and no critical thought has taken place, it is difficult to imagine how "insight" might have been attained at the conclusion of listening. A little historical reconstruction can throw some light on these problems. Before dismissing her terminology out of hand, it should be noted that Langer's initial formulation of ideas about musical signification was made in reaction to the early Wittgenstein's *Tractatus* and discussion surrounding it. In an atmosphere where the binary choice was between a propositional use of language, as the supposed logical correlate of relationships in the world, and "merely expressive" cries (like "ouch!"), Langer was attempting to rescue music from the latter category. It was not a merely expressive cry (somewhat like Peirce's sign type no. 3, a "rhematic index"), but a more complex interpreted sign. Although Langer was aware of Peirce's work, she found his escalating numbers of sign types too complicated and did not pursue them. The closest she could then come to capturing the idea of a non-verbal semiotic modality, where affective qualities could emerge as interpreted entities, was by naming music a "symbol" which presented the "logical form" of affective states. Her hypothesis that the emergent expressivity of music could be novel in its form, yielding insight into contents not otherwise known, does not, however, depend on the retention of this terminology. An emergent quality may be understood as one that proceeds as a higher level (an emergent "first-ness"), out of lower-level signs—including rule-governed signs (displaying thirdness). This complex sign does not need to be named as "symbolic" in order to be understood as involving interpretation. A complex set of inter-pretants must, indeed, be implied, as the conditions for understanding all of the component signs as well as their synthesis into a single quality (no matter how ephemeral); but if the understanding of these signs is labeled "insight," it need not be an insight of a conceptual kind.

Pathos and reflectiveness, spontaneity and containment—these are not qualities that add up to a single familiar "emotion" in everyday situations. Seeking to specify the effect of their musical synthesis, as if it could be cap-tured in a single term, can lead to a sense of false fixity in the description—as if a content specific to the moment were being diminished to a mere re-presentation of something fully known before. "Insight" might be under-stood as the moment of grasping how aspects of experience can be musically connected, though they are often kept apart or perhaps just not "seen." To speak of "grasping" this connection is perhaps to suggest a conceptual domi-nance over it, of taking it for oneself, or possessing it, but the kind of under-standing suggested here is more akin to that of "seeing" differently, of put-ting something in a different "perspective." It is, as Scruton ([1974] 1982) has suggested, an understanding embodied in a perception. The lack of an aural correlate for "seeing," as a mode of understanding, attests simply to the dominance of visual modalities in conversations about thought, but this con-vention of English need not inhibit anyone from having a sense of excite-ment, discovery, or heightened engagement in listening, when they aurally begin to "get the point" of Bach's combination of semantic layers, an on-going synthesis of states in which inherent tensions are involved. "Getting the point" does not consist of accepting one choice of descriptive terms. "Melancholy with sobriety, expressivity with restraint, freedom of play yet an underlying seriousness"—these terms also might capture something of the phrase's sense. No matter which terms are used, they cannot substitute for "hearing" the tensions of a spontaneously unfolded pathos (displayed in melodic melismata and in appoggiaturas in the inner voice) playing against the tonal and harmonic powers of control or constraint. "Getting it" is not, either, taking away a new "conception" of how broadly purposeful acts of will can "contain" the feelings of a moment, by means of their disciplining role. This idea is scarcely original, having been rehearsed in countless ascetic tomes since ancient times. The experience of "getting" the phrase is more like that of gaining a sense of rapport with another person, whose style or self-presentation is unfamiliar. It could involve becoming attuned to their particular way of displaying shifts in mood, learning to notice how they disclose their feelings while maintaining a degree of restraint and to judge the dynamics of that interplay. When such rapport is established, you have not gained a new "concept," but you *have* gained a new relationship. This is a form of "insight," the consequence of which is not so much an ability to generalize, as it is an ability to return to the relationship or to call the person to mind. When I "know" and "understand" a musical work such as Bach's Sonata in G minor for Solo Violin in this sense, I know it as an individual to which I can mentally return at any time. A knowledge like this speaks of some kind of intimacy and respect, terms most appropriate to human relationships.[13] It is a knowledge that values particularity, even while appreciating the way that the more general possibilities of character, as circumscribed by a musical style (or society), have been displayed. It is a knowledge, also, that never presumes mastery of the other but remains open to new discovery.

This discussion has returned, by another route, to the notion of a musical work's content as being captured in the idea of an embodied "persona," whose characteristics unfold in time. Not only the signified content but also the mode of its understanding seem to respond well to personal categories. Langer's elucidation of a work's expression as being that of an "impersonal idea" (1953: 123) does not, however, fit well with this description, and some exploration is needed to discover what she could mean by "impersonality." Her use of the term could be read as, foremost, a means of avoiding the idea that music is expressively restricted to common emotions (merely "personal" states), or to being a "personal" utterance of the composer. It makes little sense to claim, with Langer, that all emotions follow a common "logical form," or that music is the dynamic presentation of "emotion" in general (a form of "impersonal" expression); but if these references to music's emotional "logic" and impersonality are read as part of Langer's dialogue with the early Wittgenstein, they come to appear more obviously as a defense against the idea that music is no more than an expanded personal exclamation ("ouch!"). For Langer, music presents something more than a garden-variety emotion and transcends the most obviously "personal" utterance. Borrowing the term "logic" as a means of describing its dynamic forms, claiming a correspondence between the "logic" of music and that of emotions, seeking generality in the "impersonal," having music be a "symbol" of emotion, and claiming "insight" in understanding it: all are ways of insisting that music not be placed opposite language in a bipartite scheme that links "symbol" with interpretive activity and finds all other utterances as forms of uninterpreted and spontaneous "expression." Langer buys into the very opposition she dislikes, by shifting music from one side to the other of a divide between the "conceptual" and the "non-conceptual" and insisting on its "symbolic" role. As one who protests too strongly, she distances herself also from any recognition that it could at times be expressive of commonly known states, like "happiness." A defensive rhetoric is not, however, necessary to Langer's main point, that music has a capacity to "inform" listeners of otherwise unrepresented affective states. Her concern about its too-easy dismissal into a domain of the non-conceptual can now be allayed, if semiotic formations are recognized which are "interpreted" (and hence cognitive) yet not "conceptual." Once the rhetoric of "symbol," "logic," and "impersonality" has been weakened or dropped, it still remains possible to retain her central insight, that music presents a form of content not otherwise known in its full complexity. If a piece of music, such as the G-minor solo sonata, yields "insight," it does so because its signified content asks for an ongoing synthesis of elements that may not seem compatible, to form a complex (and temporally changing) state without a simple name. Music's capacity to become "informative" about states that are not already known derives from the fact that no individual synthesis of elements can be entirely predictable, no matter how readily identified the signification of some elements. Although this does not make it a "symbolic" form, comparable to verbal languages, a musical work can still stand in the place where names are lacking, a substitute for language in cases where a convenient term for a particular kind of complex expressivity cannot be found. The particular musical piece (or event within a piece) then simply *is* the way that particular concatenation of traits is known, in combination. Reference to a "musical persona" is one way of capturing this notion of a specific character without a particular name—a complex and novel synthesis of signs, occurring either within a theme or over a longer span of time. The idea of "persona" (or of complex "character") does well in suggesting an individuality of affect and agency, which demands to be encountered in order to be known, and which cannot be simply paraphrased or summarized. Langer's interest in music's capacity to present an emotional content not captured in language is served well by this idea. Characteristics of "persona"—including aspects of affect—can be described in non-conceptual language, without music being "symbolic" in the sense that it represents in the same way that language does.[14]

The second part of Langer's reliance on the idea of "impersonality" lies, as mentioned above, in its establishing distance between the states of mind imagined as belonging to a composer's personal life and those embodied in a musical work. Any expressive content that is musically signified may be termed "impersonal" in the sense that it is genuinely separate from the impositions of composer or listener. It "belongs" to the music itself, and it is not a personal "expression" in any direct way. As an element of the music as "other," it can be encountered, confronted, or discovered in the process of listening, not simply experienced by a listener as an image of his or her own subjective desires. One aspect of Peirce's interpretive mode of "secondness" allows this kind of attitude to be drawn out—that which identifies items as existing "in the world" (in this case the semiotic world of music) to be experienced as something "over against" the self, making their own demands for recognition.[15] It does not annul the notion of a work as displaying "persona" to recognize that that persona is truly "other," not merely a projection.

b. Synthesis and Temporal Perspectivity

It has been suggested that a synthesis of musical elements can form a uniquely complex affect, which yet has an element of simplicity or immediacy about it, just because it is resolved in the mind as "one thing." A pervasive mood or texture, as well as a sense of continuity through contrasting moments, might be captured by the notion of a single "persona," which can be heard as acting and undergoing events or as making an utterance. In a Baroque movement, it is not inconceivable for a single "persona" to emerge from the whole, as actor and patient of events, moving through different moments of experience while creating a single "mood." In works of the

Classical and Romantic eras, the image of multiple personae engaging in a drama through their individual themes might be much more apposite (as suggested by Cone, 1974; Maus, 1989b), and it is this sense that is adopted by Levinson (1996). Whichever way it is construed, more still needs to be said about the way that a synthesis of elements into one character can be carried through, if this image is to be useful in addressing concerns about affective complexity. An important feature of synthesizing acts is that they bring elements into association with one another which might otherwise be kept apart, or which might be treated deliberately as distinct processes in order to achieve clarity of analysis. In a semiotic interpretation, it can be useful to start off by distinguishing various kinds of signs, as they appear in a work, in order to appreciate their distinctive contribution. Each sign has its own manner of interpretation. As in cases of complex signification, more than one *kind* of sign is at work; their analysis involves holding them apart, so that they are not falsely assimilated to one another. Identifying a moment as "gestural" is not, for example, the same thing as pointing out the technical features that make it up, whether they be composed of an appoggiatura or other inflection, a brief "arpeggiation," or a rhythmically interesting melodic interval. Nor can it be assimilated to an analysis of broader tonal processes, within which it may play such a minor role that it is scarcely worth mentioning. Starting with an analysis of distinct kinds of signs allows for the possibility that their effects upon one another can be pursued, as effects that are automatically "synthesized" in acts of hearing the work.

The relationship of kinds of signs can be examined by looking at the effect on a moment deemed "gestural" of an increasingly broad context of hearing. In the fifth bar of Bach's G-minor sonata, to give an example to supplement earlier ones, a series of three descending thirds (B-flat–G, G–E-flat, E-flat–C-sharp) may be heard to create and reinforce a sense of gestural "weight." This effect is especially strong if the moment is isolated from its context. (A reader who is well-habituated to Schenkerian modes of listening might hear the fragment in its tonal context straight away, but a "blinkered" attention to gestural shaping is necessary to an appreciation of different kinds of signs as not being assimilated to one another. It is helpful to "feel" the weight of this moment before moving on.) Heard with even the minimal context of the preceding beat, the weightedness of a repeated

Example 7.2. Descending
gestures

Example 7.3. Adagio, bars 5–6

descent is much ameliorated by the fact that these intervals are falling from a B-flat, the highest pitch in the Adagio, but one which had already been reached. This B-flat leaps up from the just-established point of rest E-flat (technically, an inner voice "reaching over" the main linear descent at that point), to fall back to it again, as if free to delay its return. The gestural "weight" of descent thus gains the slightest hint of playfulness in its play between more than one level of voice-leading and its tonally delaying role. (This kind of play could be thought of as offering the "perspective" of distance, or purposefulness, to the moment.) Reinforcing this effect is the harmonic circumstance that the descending intervals form a descending arpeggiation of the E-flat (flattened submediant) triad, with its augmented sixth (C-sharp) added at the end. (*See* Example 7.3.) This triad is typically heard as a strategy of delay or evasion, inserted when tonal movement to the dominant is to be avoided or rendered more interesting just by coming "late." The spare texture of the violin solo tends to suppress the obviousness of this harmonic play but does not hide it altogether. Hints of tonal motion to the dominant (D minor) have already been given by the applied dominant chord (A with raised third, C-sharp) at the beginning of the bar (bar 5), but, as if to avoid letting out the secret of a changed tonal focus too openly, a division of upper and lower parts has hidden the resolution to a D-minor triad (second quarter-note beat), in a texture where the important third degree (F) is registrally isolated from the open strings (D and A) that form its root and fifth. The F is the close of a melodic grouping (also a structural note in

Rhythmic grouping

Harmonic grouping

V/v   v   VI

Example 7.4. Detail of second and third beats (bar 5) with harmonic underlay

the descending voice-leading),★ and the succeeding lower strings become an anacrusis to a new melodic group, so that their harmonic unity is de-emphasized, and the moment of effective resolution to D minor is still awaited. (*See* Example 7.4.) The movement to a triple-stopped inversion of E-flat harmony, with double suspension (the F and D suspended from the second to third beats), presents a form of tonal evasiveness that is very much consistent with a strategy of anticipating a goal point, only to delay its real-ization. The inverted E-flat harmony, its minor sixth (G–E-flat) repeated across the bar line, melds smoothly into the new coloristic effect of an aug-mented sixth (on the flattened sixth degree, E-flat–G–B-flat–C-sharp), but this color is to last only a moment before its identity is transformed by a sin-gle note. An A, in the upper register, stands out as a link to the B-flat that started this melodic grouping, reaching over the structural line. Marked for attention by its register and its linear connection to that earlier B-flat, it transforms the harmonic implication of the immediately preceding C-sharp from that of an augmented sixth (above E-flat) into the third degree of an inverted secondary dominant. The resolution to an inverted D-minor triad (bar 6, beat 2) anticipates the structural sonority (D minor), but does not provide the security of a root position. It then becomes part of a more ex-

---

★Cumming's parenthesis here would seem to refer to her understanding that the voice-leading structure of the Adagio as a whole is guided by a descending octave span from G5 in measure 1 (see Example 7.7, p. 233). Although she refers to the high F in measure 5 as a "structural note," her key point here is that this note is not solidly established. Her interpretation gains further support if we observe that only in measure 7 is the descent to that F decisively linked to the preceding high G. In measure 5, the B-flat intervenes and is still unresolved. In our summary graph, Example 7.7, the first F is black, the second, white. (R.W., D.L.)

Example 7.5. Detail of resolution, bars 5–6

Example 7.6. Voice-leading, bars 5–9

tended process that will lead eventually to the attainment of a structural fifth degree (D, bar 9). (*See* Examples 7.5 and 7.6.)

If the "gestural" descending thirds are interpreted in the light of this broader tonal purpose, they take on a rather more subtle role. Images from conversation could well be sought to capture its effect. They might be found in a politely raised hand, a notable inward breath, an "ah, but wait a minute"—achieved with some emphasis when the "reaching over" inner voice creates an intruding, new upper line, to override basic purposes, and also closes off a grouping of two (quarter) beats by establishing this point of registral return. Such images are suggestive because the moment creates a felt delay; it "speaks" with rhetorical purpose, adding weight to what is to come, without undue vehemence or strength of assertiveness. They are not, however, to be taken as "fixing" the content of the moment in a verbal way, and could be substituted by other, more telling images. Words like these are no more than pointers at an effect that needs to be musically grasped.

In this analysis of a tiny snippet of a phrase, a "gestural" effect comes to be heard in the light of a broader tonal purpose, which gives the local harmony its own felt qualities of evasiveness and delay. Both the haptic image of gesture and the "willful" image of "going somewhere" (or avoiding it) have their own interpretants—the first of apparent embodiment, the second requiring an aural appreciation of tonal "rules." Neither kind of sign cancels the other out, but when they are brought together, they do create a more complex affect, which can be felt as "expressive" even without the convenience of a single term with which to name the moment. It is important to distinguish this kind of interpretation from that which would appear in a more purely structural approach. In an analysis that gives great priority to tonal understanding, it might be tempting to assume that the broader level of tonal process can be given priority and that the graphic representations can absorb more local events within a line that shows their longer-term goals. As indicated in the graph above, a summary of the fifth and sixth bars of the G-minor sonata need only indicate the reaching over of B-flat and the role of the E-flat harmony in the unfolding tonal process. Greater clarity is achieved by this kind of selectiveness, and (as pointed out in chapter 6) it is not to be repudiated simply for failing to include all that appears in the phrase. In understanding the process of synthesis for a tonal work such as this, it is, however, a mistake to assume that a more abstract level of thought, or rule-governed signs, can be taken as absorbing other *kinds* of signs. Tonal process absorbs an arpeggiation as a more local example of the same kind of rule-governed sign, but it does not absorb a "gesture," the interpretant of which is not of the same kind. (This is similar to the point being made by Narmour [1977] when he objects to the absorption of melodic events into tonal processes, although he does not describe the melodic in terms of the "gestural.")

Hearing one kind of sign—a gestural one—"in the light of" another kind, which yields a different "perspective," can be thought of as adding a new interpretant to the one most immediately considered. (See the notion of troping in Hatten, 1994.) If the "perspective" offered by integration is progressively expanded, as it was above—from the most blinkered attention to melodic shaping in a single beat, to a recollection of its immediate registral context, then to a noting of its harmonic role, and its tonal purpose—a progressively more general series of interpretants has been called into the interpretive act, each bringing a more extended context within which the sense of the moment can be "taken." The metaphors of seeing one thing "in the light of" another, of "putting it in perspective," or taking it "from another point of view" are very telling indicators of the dominance of visuality in ways of conceiving processes of understanding, at least in the English language. Staying with this visuality for a moment, the English colloquialisms can be interrogated for what they might suggest about modes of thought which could also be aurally instantiated. Getting something "in perspective" implies a position of more distance from it, an ability to "see further" in entertaining its precedents and probable consequences. Seeing an event "in the light" of something broader tends to change its apparent demeanor, altering the value placed upon what was first seen, or the intensity with which a reaction was first made to it, even to the point of transforming initial judgments of what has taken place. Taking "another point of view" (or a different "angle") on an event is a revisionary process, suggesting a willingness to consider it in ways that were at first not obvious. All of these turns of phrase suggest that understanding is a process in time, where new interpretants can be entertained to bring quite a different "light" on what is known. If these ways of speaking are applied to an individual's actions or character, they suggest a bringing together of knowledge about that person's actions over a long period of time, in order to understand an event in the present. A temporalizing act of interpretation is thus presented in language as a visual phenomenon, "understanding" having been preconceived as a way of "seeing" things. Take away the visual dominance, and the effectiveness of relating events to dispositional traits, as occurring in different temporal dimensions, is not entirely removed. What is lost is an obvious linguistic way of conveying their relationship. Events with differing degrees of temporal immediacy (or longer-term consequentiality) may be held together in the mind, as informing one another, or may instead be considered by turns—in a process of successive revision—but the accidents of language make it difficult to convey the change of attitude that occurs in the process of moving between different temporal stances, without resort to terms for the visual. Even "taking some distance," by considering a new temporal frame, is conceived as a perspectival event. For better or worse, language presents the knowing "I" as located in relation to a visual field, to which temporality is readily assimilated. To "take a position" on anything known is to locate oneself spatially in relation to that thing, as if it were an object in space.

If language and visuality are swapped for a musically presented thought, the problem of displaying a concurrent set of different temporal planes is no longer so pressing. Expressive events and broader purposes simply do occur on different levels, at the same time, in a tonal work and may be heard as informing one another. But try to describe what it is like to attend to these different levels of temporality, and the visual metaphors reappear in quite a telling way. If "gaining perspective" is a revisionary process in ordinary thought, it can be no less so in listening to a tonal work, where earlier events may be reconsidered "in the light of" processes which only begin to become clear over a longer period of time. It is as if tonality is the perspectival force of eighteenth- and nineteenth-century European music, lending a possibility of control or containment to even the most vehement gestural outbursts, so long as a broadly conceived tonal purpose is eventually fulfilled. For a work to have such "control" is for it to retain some point of reference to a tonal "frame," something that encloses events within dimensions that are, in some respects, already known. For a tiny moment, such as the gestural descent in thirds in the fifth bar of Bach's G-minor sonata (above) to be so framed, is for it to be heard as infected with a "distance" that comes from its place in a broader scale of events. Forgoing visual metaphor as a way of placing him- or herself, a listener might say "I am feeling this as only a rhetorical but momentary delay in the unfolding of an intention to reach a new goal." This would be to take a temporalized "position" on the moment, as one interpreted by more distant goals. Alternatively, one might undertake to "forget" the disclosure of purpose, saying "I am just being with this moment, as a gesture given in the present, and feeling its shape." This would be to loosen the hold of any broader interpretive frame and to refuse it an ability to swallow the present in its rule-governed purposes. A listening "I"—who is not all "eye" but also ear—needs sometimes to be *here*, in "present" time. Temporarily forgetting the "I" of longer temporalities, he or she can better appreciate the gaining of more temporally extended interpretants, of retrospective "hearing points" which give previously heard events new resonances. Freedom to shift between the "perspectives" being entertained in time does tend to reinforce the idea that the kinds of signs are interactive, rather than arranged in a hierarchy of progressive assimilation.

c. Synthesis of "Voice" and "Voices" in a Musical Utterance

The bringing of gestural events into the aural perspective of a tonal purpose is an act of "synthesis" between different kinds of signs, which, for a listener highly attuned to the tonal level of organization, might lead to the expressive moment being heard as an ephemeral or passing event, and thus as carrying less affective weight. If a quasi-personal utterance, or "persona," is heard in this combination of signs, it is now of one whose expressive impulse is offered a degree of containment by its relationship to broader tonal goals. The "persona" can be apprehended as a complexly formed yet singular character, whose synthesis as "one" is an ongoing process in musical time, responsive to new information as it is heard, and thus mutable in its emergent qualities—a highly expressive gesture in one moment being quickly contained by a perception of unfolding directional lines, only to reappear at a later time. Hearing a complex musical character as both "one" in its utterance, and as embracing different moments and moods, requires acts of synthesis which are effective in two dimensions: in the bringing together of different aspects of signification as they form a single moment, such as that described above, and in the linking of events over time, with a retrospective (retro-auditive) reconsideration of what has previously been heard.[16] Rather than assuming the ease and obviousness of such integration, it is interesting to attend to the tensions that threaten the formation of any singularity at all, even in Baroque movements where "one mood per movement" and the idea of "music as speech" (or utterance) are well-established as normative.

In the Adagio of Bach's Sonata in G Minor for Solo Violin, one of the ways in which the tensions of plurality and integration are most readily displayed is in the presentation of many contrapuntal voices by a single instrument, as if they were all the utterance of one "voice." In a Schenkerian analysis, priority may be given (especially at middleground or background levels) to the voice deemed "structural," as defining the principal agency or "subject" of the piece. Following this approach, the other voices implicated in Bach's movement may be named as an "inner voice" and as a contrapuntal elaboration of the "bass arpeggiation," tacit dominance being given to the outer voices as carrying the principal streams of virtual agency. Taking a cue from the chords that frame the first phrase, the upper G may be heard as forming a primary voice, to initiate a descending span that is to pass through a large-scale octave, with some interruption. (See Example 7.7.) A strict separation of "outer" and "inner" is not, however, permitted at a "foreground" level. There the two contrapuntal voices intertwine, reaching over one another and sometimes merging. Even after its first florid descent, the melodic line from G (the "outer" voice) seems to remain on the "inside," while a new covering voice is created, to establish the contrapuntal connection G–F-sharp–G. At some points (for example, the last quarter-note beat of bar 3), the "inner" voice has melismata of operatic proportions, to the point of being histrionic. (*See* Example 7.8.) So far does its written-out spontaneity extend the conventions of more formal writing, it is tempting to ask, "is this really counterpoint, or is it an *oratorio* for the inner voice, whose coloratura will not be repressed?" That voice certainly needs attention here. Even if only for a moment, it *is* the agency to be attended to, insisting on the elaboration

Example 7.7. Voice-leading, bars 1–22

Example 7.8. Dialogue of inner and upper voices, bars 3–4

Example 7.9. Detail of bar 4

of its contrapuntally static place. When the upper voice reappears (bar 4), it is as if to cap the excess, interrupting it with a reminder of the direction it, as a higher voice, has already intimated. The upper voice does not, however, dominate now, but instead creates an undulating contour in which the harmonically supported "inner" voice is an equal participant. Dialogue is certainly hinted at in the division of auditory streams, not allowing the two voices to be completely assimilated to one another, but the point at which one voice leaves off and the other begins is not always fully determinate. At the third beat of bar 4, for example, the G-minor harmony that supports the inner voice's B-flat includes the note "D," which also forms the root of the dominant triad, arpeggiated in the upper voice. The succession of pitches B-flat–D–F-sharp–A could be heard to form an aesthetically unpleasing seventh (built on the augmented triad of the third degree), but heard as an elision, the suspension of two voices resolving to a shared note, it becomes quite acceptable. By combining voices, a weakly composite agency is formed, as being allowed a dissonance that would otherwise be impermissible in this style, while also retaining the sense of being separated out into a "dialogue." (*See* Example 7.9.) This gesture, embracing more than one voice, forms an agency that at once moves towards singularity, expanding an expressive range, and also retains a tension within itself.

If a potential for fusion is effective when considering two voices, with harmonic support, it is even more so when the putative "bass" becomes part of the melodic line. At the end of bar 11, for example, a labored passage of ascending double-stopped sixths (with dissonant 7–6 suspensions) gives way to a florid movement of the upper part from an "inner" B-flat to an A-flat which "reaches over" the pitch range both of the immediately preceding passage and the higher structural level (see voice-leading diagram, Example 7.7). Harmonically, a need to elaborate the applied dominant of E-flat is the occasion for this expansiveness. To do so is necessary because E-flat is being set up as a putative temporary goal and the sense of going there needs to be made quite clear, if its subsequent evasion is to be made effective. Purposefulness is already implicit in the harmony as a composite effect, and an abstracted summary of the voice-leading need leave no doubt as to the directional purpose of each contrapuntal voice, as strictly conceived. When, however, the voices are combined (in the last beat of bar 11) to form a single descending line—A-flat, B-flat, D arpeggiated across a diminished twelfth—the result is a melodic expansiveness, or "opening out," which can be heard as carrying the gestural force of a unitary expansive movement, even though the memory of distinct voices within it need not be lost. (*See* Example 7.10.)

Example 7.10. Integration and separation of voices, bars 11–13

Once the bass movement (D–E-flat, bars 11–12) is heard, the distinctive identity of the bass is reaffirmed and that of the upper voice "reaching over" (A-flat–G, bar 12) can be heard also with great clarity, due to its registral separation, but some factor of integration needs still to be retained, as without it the composite melodic shape becomes fragmented, and a sense of a unifying purpose is lost. In the second beat of bar 12, the bass and inner voices are explicitly joined. It is a performer's task to balance between the needs of contrapuntal articulation and of melodic connectedness, in these brief moments before an harmonic accompaniment is reinstated (again on B-flat 7, last two beats of bar 12), to support a newly triumphant melodic "reaching over" to A-flat, in preparation for the point of arrival to come (in bar 13). (*See* Example 7.11.)

d. Drama and Self-Defeat

It is a false "arrival," of course, and a pause is introduced to force reflection on the fact. With all its grand announcement, an E-flat triad would have been welcomed as unexceptional, but instead its major third (G) has been commuted to a disappointing and pathetic G-flat, its insult to expectancies being underscored with a dissonant bass A (suggesting a dominant minor ninth on F). (*See* Example 7.11.) It is a dramatic moment, a decisive "act" of interruption, and it is only in a subsequent outburst of activity, which sweeps from the bass through to the upper voice, that a retrospective

Example 7.11. Detail of bars 13–14

purpose is given to the intrusive dissonance. Interpreted enharmonically as a diminished seventh on F-sharp, it does quite well in preparing harmonically for the G dominant ninth, outlined in the broad arpeggiated sweep across the violin on beat 2. A directional reorientation towards C minor is achieved in this sweeping movement, and its resolution to a C-minor triad, confirmed in the equally florid descending movement of the second half of the bar, anticipates the subdominant return of the patterning that opened the movement (bar 14). The "real" point of arrival is here, in the return of the opening, and yet it enters as if subdued, without any apparent complexity of voicing or overt harmonic accompaniment. It is "quiet" both in its textural presentation and in its tonal role—as the subdominant of the key that structures the movement as a whole. A point of quiescence and relative stability "makes sense," all the same, as compensating for the energetic excess of its preparation (in sixty-fourth notes on beat 3, followed by syncopation on beat 4 of bar 13).

If "personal utterance" is to be heard in this course of events, it is the utterance of one who pursues goals, interrupts them to seek new orientation with frenetic energy, and then sinks into a moment of relative passivity. This "one" is not obviously one, in its capacity for self-interruption and the taking of dramatic turns, but that does not stop it from being "personal" in some sense. Disunity, self-interruption, discordance, and a revision of a directional impulses all lend it a rather more personal verisimilitude. But can all of this be thought of as contributing towards the apparent expression of non-obvious affects? A clue may be found in the ease with which tonal processes may be described in terms not only of "will" and "desire," but also of drama and eventfulness (see Maus, 1988). Acts and events display differing degrees of apparent energy and impulsiveness, of forward directedness or passivity. An agent may be heard in the directional force that seems to initiate and carry through motion towards a goal, but it is also implicit in moments of frustration, freneticism, and rest. These changing levels of energy are themselves observable features of affective states, not necessarily being seen in the obvious manner of a visual gesture, but known nonetheless as characteristic of personal agents as they move through events in time. As Langer suggested, music may demonstrate a remarkable capacity for compression in representing the "logical form" (or energetic pattern) of affective states.

e. Subtle and Non-obvious Affects

If contextualization and self-reference are means of modifying affect, as Karl and Robinson (1995b) suggest, the possibility that music can achieve a subtlety of affect should no longer be held in question, once the multiple ways of creating context are recognized. Speaking in general terms, the Adagio just discussed might be described simply as "melancholy," or as belonging to a class in which "pathos" is exemplified, both of these terms having the potential to be dismissed by a skeptic as no more than synonyms for the generalized "sadness" which some have named a garden-variety affect. A reason for continuing dismissals of more inflected states could found in an ongoing fondness for the idea that emotions are distinguished by their "real-world" objects and by their short-term visual displays. Aaron Ridley, for example, makes a startling reference to the former idea when he questions whether music could distinguish "fear of dentistry" from "fear of Satanism," and predictably answers himself in the negative (1995: 50). If, however, it is accepted that the manner in which music modifies expressive states is neither by the elaboration of a "dynamic" (external) object, nor by the display of contours resembling the visual shape of expressive gestures alone, the way is opened up for recognizing a very subtle compendium of affective states.[17] Among these could be included some relatively nuanced self-reflective attitudes, as displayed by the combined effects of different levels of tonal and semiotic activity. Could it not make sense to say of the Adagio that it presents a "persona" as one who plays with his or her own melancholy, with some moments of spontaneity, and with others of containment and restraint? What about hearing a "dissonance," created by the clash of its own internal "voices," not only as a way of describing a musical technicality, but as a *literal* description of a quasi-subjective state? The major-seventh clash of E-flat and D (bar 3), created by a suspension of the inner voice, or the ninth (bar 10), created in a similar way, would be cases in point. If agency is heard not only in the outer voice's progress but in the inner one, these moments can be heard quite literally as examples of "inward" pain, momentarily heard and then contained. The point is that something as subtle as a self-reflexive attitude is conveyed by the combination of voices with the different temporal dimensions in which they work.

Schenker's rhetoric of "depth" in the creation of long-term tonal processes is well known and has justifiably courted suspicion among readers who do not want to prejudge tonal works as being "deep" just because they demonstrate adherence to a tonal plan. If this term "depth" is now replayed, not as a presumption of a given form but as an effect that can be felt or heard, of what does it consist? It is not to be found in any abstracted skeleton. Nor is it to be labored by a performer, in the endowment of expressive excess upon isolated moments of the melodic surface selected as "gestural." Depth is neither in the "background" nor in the "foreground." It is not in any kind of sign taken alone. It is in the unfolding of a complex musical "persona," who must negotiate conflicts of agency, and deflections of purpose, while moving towards some goal. It is there also (and paradoxically) in the playfulness with which Bach treats the apparent exigencies of harmonic and contrapuntal rules, stretching their limits, teasing the listener with a need to unravel voices in a single melody. How can "playfulness" be attributed to a work that is so sorrowful in its effect? It cannot be a surface effect, or an aspect of the emergent mood, and yet somehow it is there in the "perspective" from which pathos appears. Perhaps it can be accepted by one who knows that the free play of mind need not be choked by the weight of sadness or quashed by impulsive desires. To play with one's own melancholy, with spontaneity and yet restraint: in this is the enlightenment of one who does not run from pain or seek to avoid its experience, and yet who never loses sight of broader purposes.

It has been argued that aesthetic qualities are not arrived at by discursive means (Scruton), that they are not synonymous with technical properties (Beardsley), and that they ought to be readily available to the listener, not requiring a protracted search or repeated listenings (Levinson, 1996). An interpretive analysis, as demonstrated here, does not allow these generalizations to be maintained. It is true that a work might present the general type of its expressivity in a readily accessible way to one who is familiar with its style. It is not, however, true to say that all of the work's affective possibilities can be "grasped" at one time or confined in a general category that serves mainly as an orientational device. Nor can it be presumed that an attention to technical features will not yield a greater appreciation of "aesthetic" qualities. It is for this purpose, after all, that interpretive analysis is undertaken. The analysis above has drawn attention to many aspects of "voice" in order to demonstrate points that are integral to forming an aesthetic effect. Spending time in the contemplation of how the voices work, and how they combine at times to form a composite entity, can be "informative" not only about the structural facts but also about the performative options they allow, with their emergent effects. In this way, it is *expressively* informative. It is not merely coincidental that Hanslick was so attached to the notion of contemplating abstract forms. It is in their very contemplation that new "depths" of expressive play, and subtleties of affect, can be discovered, to yield insight into states not previously "known."

chapter eight

~

Culturally Embedded Signs

1. Emergent Qualities

a. Definitions

In the last chapter, it was suggested that a synthesis of various kinds of musical signs could yield a complex affect that was not reducible to any of them, but a product of a unique contextual synthesis. The terms "subject" or "persona" were introduced in recognition that a complex expressivity, emerging through the play of signs at many levels, could in many contexts be heard as a quasi-personal utterance by some virtual entity — not the composer or performer, but an "utterer" created by the musical passage in question. Just as human subjects are capable of containing conflicts of passion and rationality, or of different emotional states, the musically embodied subject can display features that are in some ways at odds with one another, but which together create a newly compound (if unstable) affect. To say that this affect "emerges" in the play of signs is to call upon a term that is part of everyday language, and yet which cannot retain its semblance of ordinariness when placed in a philosophical context. The idea of "emergence" appears in discussions of the relationship between different levels of organization in many fields. It may be cited in investigating how a biological organism emerges as a whole, formed through the coordinated action of its parts (Roth and Schwegler, 1990). It may also appear in considerations of how the distinctively "mental" characteristics of humans could emerge in evolution (Haldane, 1996), or in any other explanatory project where the question arises as to how a complex entity or behavior arises from simpler or less evolved characteristics. The issue at stake in every case is whether the "higher" (or more complex) level of organization can be accounted for simply as a concatenation of "lower-level" (or simpler) parts, or whether something is added in the process of creating a synthesized whole. One approach to this issue is to focus on the *interactions* of lower-level entities or activities. This approach, named "interactionist," has been judged by one philosopher as "benign" (Spencer-Smith, 1995: 121), because it claims that the emergence of higher levels is not a mysterious process but can be explained as no more than an interaction of identifiable parts. Spencer-Smith's choice of terms is interesting here. It would implicitly be *dangerous* (or even malignant) to look for a "something extra" in a complex entity or behavioral disposition, because if that complex object of attention did *not* arise from the interactions of simpler parts and activities, it would have to be explained as suggesting the arrival of an inexplicable *deus ex machina*. (As Daniel Dennett puts it derisively, "then consciousness happens!") If being "benign" is avoiding mystery, it is, however, the act of creating dangers (or malignancies) that makes the idea of emergence interesting. A view of emerging wholes as no more than an interaction of parts is "consistent with reductionism" (Spencer-Smith, ibid.), because any apparently complex entity could be "reduced" to interacting lower levels. Although "reduction" need not be a dirty word in every case (it would, for example, be difficult to dissent if someone were to "reduce" the qualities of diamonds or graphite to the interactions of carbon atoms [ibid.]), it can become problematic in some kinds of subject matter, where it may not be possible to fully capture the attributes of a complex entity through an analytic reduction of its emerging qualities to the combined effects of its parts. To make claims of explanatory adequacy for any such analysis would be to commit "reductionism" in a more pejorative sense. To avoid this more unsavory kind of explanatory conceit would then be to resort to ideas about emergence which are more "radical," more inclined to accept that factors can appear in a complex idea, which are not causally derived from the interaction of its internally derived, more simply constituted parts.

Emergence in the literature of aesthetics has taken three different, but related, forms. The first is concerned with the ontology of a work of art. What is it to describe a work of art as physically realized and yet as having properties which cannot be explained in terms of its physical features? Roger Scruton's notion of music as an "intentional" construct is stated as an ontological claim, that "music" emerges from mere sound structures when it is linked in some way to a metaphorical description, which reveals the activities of "mind" as intrinsic to its constitution. A semiotic viewpoint is not unlike this, in its claim that "signs" are not merely material entities, but are necessarily interpreted—again implying the activity of mind. It should, however, be remembered at this point that Peirce's approach to signification places emphasis on the shared aspects of mind, not on the supposedly private, or intuitive. Particularly important is Peirce's idea that the "mentality" implicit in a notion of the sign-as-interpreted is not a mentality belonging to any individual, but one that reflects a communal activity, as people sharing a way of life such as musical performance produce signs from material things and allow them to disseminate with an agreed (though sometimes contestable) range of meaning. Thought of in relation to material entities, like notes conceived simply in terms of their material structure as frequencies, a sign is radically "emergent" because it requires the addition of something to the material description, in the form of reference and interpretability. In the case of music, the kind of signification will often be connotative (iconic), as when instrumental sounds are heard as "vocal," but the *kind* of signification does not alter the general point, that signs differ from uninterpreted material things in reflecting shared aspects of mentality. The notion of "sign" itself can then be seen as defining a putative ontological category, neither material, nor belonging to the realm of private mental events, but of interpretable entities whose "meaning" is shared, if contestable. No matter how sophisticated the description of material components becomes, it will never add up to an account of the emergent level of "sign," which is of a different kind.

The second kind of emergence in aesthetics is concerned more directly with the relationship between levels of description as they are worked out in a given artistic medium. What is the relationship of "aesthetic" qualities to the "non-aesthetic" or technical features of a work? Aesthetician Monroe Beardsley's twofold division of levels between the "non-aesthetic" and "aesthetic" reflects a rough disciplinary divide between the more technical disciplines of music (or, say, architectural) theory, as they have been traditionally practiced, and the domain of interpretation, which deals with aspects of expressivity (Beardsley, 1982; see also McErlean, 1990). Terms referring to affective or expressive states, or the qualities of bodily movement characteristic of expressive activity, are taken to represent the "aesthetic," and those couched in the normal vocabulary of a structuralist music theory are taken to represent the "non-aesthetic." The question of emergence then addresses directly the problem of how an interpretation of a work's expressive content relates to a technical account of its structural formation. To restate the problem: can an account of a work's formal attributes reach a sufficient level of contextual sensitivity, and sophistication, that it will add up to an account of expressive qualities? Beardsley would suggest that it cannot. His twofold division could be compared to that made by musical semioticians when they distinguish between the language of formal analysis (restricted to the naming of processes without explicit recognition of metaphor) and the analysis of signification, which seeks to account for the connotative dimension of tonality's apparent "desire" or "will," as they are realized in a given context. A strict binary division of the "non-aesthetic" and "aesthetic" (or "formal" and "semiotic") description can, however, be read as a denial that formal properties can themselves signify (in the form of legisigns). A more inclusive approach, less susceptible to binary oppositions, might be to look at the emerging properties as arising out of the synthesis of signs which are either more local in dimension or more limited in scope. (They could include qualisigns, sinsigns, and legisigns, as discussed in chapters 4–6). What Beardsley calls "regional" qualities could then be defined as emerging from timbral, melodic, and tonal processes, which themselves bear signification, both as notated and as they are microstructurally nuanced in performance. The expressive qualities attributed in the last chapter to a virtual "persona" are of this kind—regional qualities (or higher-level signs) emerging from simpler (more local, lower-level, or parametrically restricted) signs. One kind of novelty discussed in this connection was an expressive state that could not be predicted from a knowledge of its constituents. It was argued that, where aspects of signification conflict with one another in various ways, their interaction is intrinsically creative of a "whole" that is neither stable, nor predictable from any single contributing factor. Such a whole cannot be captured in any single common affective name but adds something to what is known of an expressible state, becoming the unique form of presentation for that which is newly known without sporting a brand-name emotional tag.[1]

A third kind of emergence appears in the relationship of artistic works to broader aspects of cultural life. Joseph Margolis (1974, 1995) is the most prominent analytical aesthetician to have explored this idea, in articles that address the puzzle of an artwork's ontology by defining artworks as "physically embodied and culturally emergent" entities. What it means to declare that a work "emerges" within culture, in Margolis' sense, is more than to state the obvious fact that composers work in a cultural context. It is to say that the organization of a musical work itself depends on categories that structure other aspects of life, and that even abstract instrumental music cannot effectively be understood as the unfolding of pure patterns, sealed off from other forms of experience. The idea of "spontaneity" in written-out ornamental passage work or of "containment" and "monumentality" in a stable tonal phrase would not be intelligible were it not for an awareness of how these terms are used when playing other language games. To say that these qualities are essential to the musical content is implicitly to deny that a purely structural level of description, noting only the scalar organization of Bach's ornaments or the strong stabilizing role of the tonic, is sufficient for capturing what is musically "given." Content is "given" in Bach's opening phrase, which goes beyond what can be described as a compendium of standard scale formulas and triadic frames. This content is given by the position of the movement within a style—an interpretive context which is not extrinsic to it, but constitutive of its basic attributes, including the very important distinction between "spontaneous decoration" and "structural event," as they are appropriate to this style.

A further consideration of the stylistic factors governing Bach's phrase will further establish that a recognition of intertextuality, or the unavoidable embeddedness of a musical movement within its style, is of central importance to musical understanding. In multi-movement Baroque sonatas, it is given as a feature of style that the opening movement will affect the appearance of spontaneity, as a kind of prelude or "playing around" the key, as if to establish a point of orientation before moving on. When possible performances are compared, it becomes evident that intertextual reference is not an added extra, an optional piece of background knowledge available to some extra-conscientious interpreters. When Baroque conventions for melodic ornamentation are left unrecognized, so that every aspect of Bach's elaborate melody is considered as non-ornamental (hence, as carrying equal weight), the result is a "weighty" performance in which the work's aesthetic content is radically transformed. The potentially spontaneous effect in Bach's written-out ornaments is lost as the passage work becomes stodgy in its plodding seriousness—an effect achieved by an overly slow and regular rendition of the melismata. A subtlety of effect in the multiple stops is also lost as the ambivalent play between strong harmonies and timbral brokenness is replaced by a forcedly strong resonance, with a modern bow hitting on metal strings with sufficient force to achieve a momentary simultaneity in triple and quadruple stops. The monumental and serious, the ponderous and "profound," then suppresses the ambivalent, playful, or tentative in Bach's work, to give an overly simple hearing of what could be a more complex set of states. Henryk Schering's Bach was somewhat like this, when presented in a regional recital in Victoria in the 1970s. The image of Bach posing for a portrait, with stern, stolid features and severe, well-powdered wig, could suggest a similar musical image of unremitting gravity.

Stylistic understanding, which links a composition not only with others of its kind but with its historical period, is an essential aspect both of "the music itself," and of what it is to know how to play it. It could, however, be argued that stylistic reference is never absent, even in performances that make no pretense of authenticity. The Romantics liked to create "Gothic" cathedrals, or to simulate a craggy sublimity out of images that were ugly but LARGE and, as Nikolaus Harnoncourt (1995) and other specialists in authentic performance have pointed out, Baroque works have been transformed to a similar end in the persisting Romanticism of twentieth-century performance practice. Whether or not a performance is "authentic," it cannot help but create a reference to other performances of similar style. The intertextuality of stylistic reference is inevitable, even if not controlled, and an avoidance of concern with what might be "authentic" modes of performance does not, in itself, yield a rendition of "the work" as an historically neutral pattern of structural events. Schering's Bach may then be heard in the light of a Romantic preference for the expansively individual and the tragically expressive, and, in being so construed, it is no less situated within a performance style than is Sigiswald Kuijken's Bach, which takes on the more intimate and elegiac resonances of a staged "improvisation." Neither can be claimed as a neutral rendition of "the work" as a pure structure apart from any location within an historical performance style. Pure structures, entering into a play of abstract relationships, may indeed be heard at times (and attributed to a modern performance of Bach), but if Bach is heard in this way, it is under the influence of the dominant aesthetic tradition, which since Hanslick has designated a range of structural events (including the tonal and contrapuntal) as carrying the role of "abstraction," and as being available for appreciation quite apart from the contingencies of their performance. One who sits comfortably within this aesthetic tradition can hear a performance from within the perspective it gives, without relativizing the interpretive frame or becoming aware of the expressive and rhetorical figures of the Baroque as implicit in Bach's musical structures as performed. The idea of "abstraction" in voice-leading and of a neutral "singing voice" in a modern violin sound presents an ideal, which forms an interpretive stance of cool and self-controlled distance from affective rhetoric. For someone who is listening from within that frame, it does not announce itself. It might even become the interpretive vehicle for allowing the presenting forms to seem immutable, profound. Step outside this frame, and it becomes only too visible—and audible. It is not a "pure structure" that you seem to be hearing any more, in an emphatically sonorous rendition of Bach's opening scale, but a structure whose every note is being squeezed for a "meaning" that it does not possess, in the absence of an enactment of its "spontaneous" or "decorative" role. A loss of signification has effectively occurred in the attempt to force "significance" in its honorific and adulatory sense.[2] "Bach," in this performing process, has been elevated to the rank of one who is somehow above the contingencies of his time, the musical structures he has written becoming eternal and disconnected from any gestural enactments that might give them an expressive shape. The composer's persona itself is thus constructed out of an idealized view of his contrapuntal virtuosity.

A comparison of the possible performances of Bach leads to some further insight into the evolution of performed values surrounding ideas of subjectivity in the eighteenth to twentieth centuries. A more "authentic" performance reveals the music as carrying the means to create "depth" and "interiority" as valued attributes of a human self in the European West, but its virtuosity in doing so is contained in a soundscape that eschews the large public arena. The "modern" performance, moved to a grander stage, transforms these attributes into more public declarations of "inner" life. What Albert Einstein referred to as a tendency to "subjective universalism" in the Romantic era gets to be heard as a potentiality of the Baroque work, through a blowing up of its resonances and slowing of its pace, to give great weight and projective force to forms of expressivity that were once intimate. Values placed upon the expression of subjective experience, or even the relative dominance of the self-expressive "subject" within social life, can then be heard as implicit in each of the performances. In this way, the different performed interpretations contribute to a "cultural construction of subjectivity," as Lawrence Kramer (1995) has put it. A performer cannot escape participation in the activities of forming, or contesting, values such as those that surround a subject's "expressivity." He or she can no more bring the work into performance without giving it a set of cultural resonances, through positioning it in a performance tradition, than he or she can play "tones" without embodying them in a particular kind of sound, with specific timbre and nuance. The very fact that the structures need implicitly to be evaluated in some way—as to their relative weight—leads to the conclusion that they can never be "pure" or "uninterpreted" and thus escape patterns of evaluation that appear in a broader arena of life. However performed, values concerning expressivity emerge in structures, and those values are wider than "the work itself."

Whatever decision is made by a performer as to how to render Bach's opening phrase, he or she will draw out aspects of its signifying range (as described in the last chapter). If, now, the potentiality of the phrase to support varying interpretations is considered as an outcome of the many aspects of signification (or kinds of signs) it contains, no synthesizing performance could be imagined as yielding an effect that was entirely devoid of the characteristics of "subjective utterance." As composed, the work contributes to the "cultural construction of subjectivity" insofar as it presents a set of signs whose potential realizations will together yield the effect of a musically embodied "persona," its specific character varying according to the emphases of

a performance tradition or individual interpreter. The work as a set of potential performances is a vehicle of a constructive activity, which does not
only *express* the values of Western humanism, but contributes to their development. It is an inescapable and scarcely controversial fact that musical
structures are situated in historical traditions, both of composition and performance, but a further and less familiar insight is being defended here—that
musical works contribute not only to the expression but also to the formation of a broader set of values surrounding the role of a "subject" and its expression in a given era. When Margolis makes his claims about music as
"emergent" in a culture, it is this idea that he wishes to place on center
stage. A work is not only physically embodied, but also culturally "emergent," because it cannot be understood apart from its place in a broader interpretive web. Its cultural resonances, both as composed potentialities and
as performed realities, are as much a part of "the work" as are its timbral resonances, and they cannot be predicted in a structural analysis alone. Emerging only with contextualization, they "add something" to the minimal account of content that could be given from within a restricted vocabulary of
harmonic and structural types.

b. Musical Personae as Culturally Emergent

Edward Cone's notion of a musical "persona" has been developed (chapter
7) in order to convey the idea of a virtual utterance in music, whose affective
content is a complex synthesis of various kinds of signs. Consistent with
Thomas Sebeok's suggestion that the self is a "super-sign," the "subject" (or
persona) has been found to appear in music as a complex entity evolving
over time, which incorporates conflicting attributes while remaining recognizably "one" in its identity. This musical persona can now be seen as
"emergent" in two senses. It brings a synthesis of signs into a more complex
whole, which could not be predicted from any individual component taken
alone (the second sense above). It also reflects broader values surrounding
subjective expression, made historically available by either its composed or
performed context, and it displays these values in a way that could not be
accounted for without reference to its style and period (the third sense
above). The embodied, affectively complex, and culturally emergent subject,
displayed in Western music of the eighteenth and nineteenth centuries, is no

mere abstraction, like the Kantian subject of apperception. A musical "subject" is a subject individuated, contingent, situated. It is one capable of displaying aspects of "desire" or of its denial, with fine degrees of nuance. If this subject is now observed as one who displays apparent embodiment in gestural moments, and whose degree of expressive display reflects social mores, it could surely not be beyond imagination that it might also display aspects of gendering. To say so is perhaps to mark the place where emergent qualities cease to be "benign" and become instead dangerous—and interesting. When Margolis takes Levinson (and others) to task for staying within the "safe" domain of the structurally derivative, it is not gendered signification in particular that he has in mind, but it does not matter much which set of traits are evoked. Once the potential is recognized for music to signify qualities that are not predictable, either from its structure alone or from a limited range of signs (such as vocality, gesture, will) whose derivation from microstructural and structural elements is relatively simple, the politics of interpretive discourse have already invaded what might have been thought of by some as a safer, more enclosed, interpretive world. The hearing of musical signification at any level requires some reference to a broader cultural frame, where notions of such things as "voice" are constituted, but the domain of reference has here been broadened considerably. Now at stake is the question of how intersubjective agreement can be achieved as to which broad attributes may be heard as inhering in a passage or work. How is it to be known where limits might be set to the multiplying field of interpretants? Should indeed limits be set at all? What distinguishes an arbitrary association from a shared mode of understanding?

An expanding awareness of broad cultural contexts, as the implicit background within which instrumental works gain their signification, can be looked at as an opening up of the interpretive field to an expanding array of possibilities whose extent and means of limitation are unpredictable. A pure tone of violinistic "voice" becomes "innocence" (recall the review of Chang); a melodic leap becomes the embodiment of a desire, its lack of fulfillment a hallmark of Romanticism; a withheld harmonic resolution reinforces the sense of unrealized aspiration. In some instances, an imbricated set of signs, of a kind with these, may add up to a musically embodied "persona" whose characteristics are linked with the conventionally assigned behaviors of different genders. If such a "persona" happens to be heard in the subject of a sonata-form movement, where it reappears in a variety of different contexts, it can also be heard to develop in its character in a way that reinforces (or perhaps ameliorates) the suggested gendering. When Susan McClary makes an analysis of the first subject from Tchaikovsky's Fourth Symphony (1991: 76–77), her interpretive process takes a route of this kind, from observations of the theme's internal signification to reflections on how its position in an unfolding form may influence its characterization. A chromatically "slippery" melodic line, without goal direction, reflects characteristics sometimes ascribed to women, and it is, she suggests, subversive when placed in the position of the conventionally "strong" first theme. Relative position is relative power, and a first theme "feminized" is a denial of power in a position more traditionally codified as "strong" or masculine. In this case, the unusually "effeminate" first theme is placed between an introduction using the military topos and a second theme that is playful and unpredictable. McClary is led to interpret this positioning as suggestive of a narrative sequence of events: "What we have is a narrative in which the protagonist seems victimized by patriarchal expectations and by sensual feminine entrapment: both forces actively block the possibility of his self-development" (ibid.). An explicit statement of the feminist critique of gender stereotypes, as something that is capable of being heard in the character of the personae within Tchaikovsky's score, might lead to this reading's being rejected without much thought, as "dangerous"—an empty projection of one interpreter's difficulties with patriarchy onto a defenseless set of themes. An understanding of the point of McClary's narrative will necessarily elude anyone who believes that she seeks in the score alone a depiction of "patriarchy" or "victimhood." The reading does, however, yield some sense if taken as an account of how the binary contrasts of masculinity and femininity, of martial bombast and playfulness, or of public militarism and private sensuality, may be played out musically within a sonata form. Habits of referring to the two thematic groups as "strong" and "weak," or (in parallel) "masculine" and "feminine," are no more McClary's invention than is the topos of a military march. What she has done is to take these generally recognized oppositions and to use them as the interpretants of the particular characteristics displayed. Although her choice of terms, and development of a coherent narrative, displays some freedom and creativity, it is not merely arbitrary or "subjective." Others could confirm the relevance of the interpretants, even if they were to describe their effects differently.

Readers unused to hearing in music anything like the specific semantic content ascribed to it by McClary may find a sense of affront in a narrative reading of this kind. A reaction like this is not to be ignored, as it draws attention to the shadow side of making any articulate statement of the content to be heard in an instrumental work. One source of restraint might be found in the structure of any sign at all. If a sign presents an "object" of thought as a possibility to be considered, that object is not, strictly speaking, "present." No sign offers a transparent means of knowing its object, without interpretation. No matter what the kind of sign, the "object" is (as Derrida has been at pains to point out) an absent object, displaced by the sign, or suggested by it. When the kinds of signs to be considered are those that display either the vagueness of a possible quality (which does not exclude others), or the indeterminacy of a general pattern (as a potentiality which requires specific instantiation), no particular description of how the quality is realized or the pattern exemplified will manage completely to exclude others or to suppress contestation. "Femininity" might be thought of as a vague quality or specified more carefully as a coded set of behaviors. A social code might, for example, be found in the fact that the "feminine" is often marked off in discourse as standing in a binary opposition to the rationally ordered, purposeful, assertive, and public—the "neutral" or "masculine" (and socially approved). This codification does not, however, make "femininity" a fixed object of concern, which can be ascribed to a musical moment without requiring a careful exploration of whether, and how, the code is applicable. Nor can its musical presentation be assumed to have any fixed form. McClary's strategy is, notably, to look further than the structure of an individual theme when ascribing this property. Her description depends as strongly on the contrasts set up between the theme itself and the preceding military fanfare, or the more playful theme that follows, as it does on the internal characteristics of the theme. In the structure of her argument, she effectively suggests a correlation between the binary contrasts within the music and the binary contrasts typically found in social discourse around gendering. As an interpretive strategy, this is consistent with the one developed by Robert Hatten (1994) from within an explicitly semiotic framework. Marked oppositions, where one term is typically presented as "neutral" and the other as "different," may be found to organize both social life and critical descriptions of musical elements. A strategy like this offers some publicly available checking points, where the workings of oppositionality can be observed. What it cannot do is prescribe the exact vocabulary within which any particular exemplification of a coded set of marked oppositions may be described. It cannot, that is, justify the claim that a particular description of content is irrefutable and capable of being upheld against other possibilities, because no matter what code is in use, the code—as a code—has the character of indeterminacy commonly found in legisigns. The interpretive position that has to result from this is one where descriptions are offered as supportable and yet not maintained as having a final grip on the "truth" of a work, as if that were an object to be grasped. In the domain of qualitative possibilities, more than one object can occupy a single space (see Merrell, 1997). More than one quality can, that is, be observed in a single thing, without ruling others out. In the reciprocal domain of rule-governed or encoded signs, a potentiality always remains for further instantiations to fit "in the cracks" between the recognized ones, disallowing any confidence that the class of all examples can be enclosed, or that a particular way of describing an example is final.[3] When these general aspects of sign use are brought down to the level of music criticism, the result they can most profitably find is a willingness among critics to proffer interpretations that may be contested, as they are opened up for discussion within the musical community. Interpretations may allow of other possibilities, as inherent in what is performed, and yet be based on publicly recognizable qualities, or sets of contrasts, that can be supported in a reasoned account. It is inherent in the exercise of describing emergent qualities that the description can never be final in its authoritativeness. In this sense, the perception of "danger" or risk is well enough founded in the reality of academic and critical discourse. If, however, it is not the defense of a personal and subjective "vision" of the music that is at stake, but the defense of an understanding developed within a community of musicians and listeners, with historical grounds, the need for dialogue should not pose any threat. It is in dialogue itself that such understandings are formed, and the place of a work within a set of performed and culturally embedded styles cannot be established unless it takes place.

2. Skeptical Issues

a. Humpty Dumpty and the New Musicology

At a conference of the International Musicological Society in London (1997), a skeptical paper was partially read (at the Round Table on Philosophy and Musicology) for the absent Peter Kivy.[4] In this paper, Kivy details a number of concerns about the "New Musicology," citing as one of his examples—or culprits—the passage from McClary, above. Taking on the role of the prosecutor, Kivy here posits only limited options as available to the "New Musicologists" in defending what he poses as their intrinsically abortive enterprise of giving semantic descriptions to instrumental works. In the first instance, they might emulate Humpty Dumpty, who tried to convince the literal-minded and rather bewildered Alice that there could be "glory" in the thought of "unbirthday" presents, on up to three hundred and sixty-four days of the year. "There's a nice knock-down argument for you" said Humpty, when Alice questioned how "glory" could apply to such an implausible turn of events (Carroll, n.d.: 246–247). "Glory," observes Kivy, siding with Alice, has been arbitrarily applied. No *rule* or *code* lets you imagine that the plentiful unbirthdays could be glorious. The *rule* is that birthdays just don't have an opposite. *Un*birthdays don't occur. You cannot bluster, boast, and brag over unbirthdays, or consider them a state of high honor, as "glory" would imply. They are not even anything to be glad about. But Alice—and Kivy—are being a bit too resistant to Humpty's humorous reversals here, as if too preoccupied with the absence of a "real" birthday to take notice of how it might be if unbirthdays were allowed—in the Looking Glass world. If Humpty is allowed the step of introducing this complement (but not opposite) to a birthday (an extension to its range), the thought of all those possible presents could certainly be "glorious." And why should that not be "a nice knock-down argument" in favor of liking the days that are not "birthdays" per se? The rules and conventions for generating meaning are not entirely absent from Humpty's argument, as Kivy suggests, but are presented in reversal, through his jiving at the idea of binary opposites. Play his game, and the idea of glory becomes perfectly intelligible. The problem is just that Alice and Kivy don't want to play, and in refusing the game, they don't get to see its point. What they require is a set of conditions that will show when "glory" applies, or not. Humpty's game, they suggest, is a self-indulgence in arbitrariness. The unwritten exhortation to "look at it the other way," in a mirror world, has been bypassed in the name of maintaining academic seriousness.

Kivy finds in the semantics of the New Musicology a lack of "rules and conventions" for generating meaning as palpable as the lack he finds in Humpty Dumpty's arguments. The charge he lays of "Humpty Dumptyism" is, he believes, a serious one that demands some defense—though Humpty's imaginary world might not seem so indefensible to one who knows how to play. One defense Kivy considers is that of viewing the use of words such as Humpty's "glory" as occurring *in a text,* not as isolated occurrences. Following Stanley Fish (1980), a text can, he points out, be understood as finding its own context, within an interpretive community which evolves its own rules of understanding. This is not a defense to which Kivy is sympathetic. His concern is that it gives too much freedom to a particular sub-community (such as that of New Musicologists) to "change the rules" (1997: 10) and impose such outlandish readings as "a sexual interpretation of Tchaikovsky's Fourth Symphony," which would "not have been possible in 1956." Implicit in this concern is a sense that the community could be as susceptible to delusions of grandeur in assigning meanings, as could any individual who wishes to impose his or her own private terms of description on the music, without interest in whether they were publicly intelligible. Neither Humpty Dumpty's "glory" nor McClary's "feminization of the subject" do, however, lack regard for the rules or conventions of interpretation to the extent that Kivy suggests. Their use of oppositionality to generate meaning is a technique in fact used quite commonly (especially in semiotics after Saussure). Changes in interpretive rules are not, furthermore, the kind of thing that can be carried out casually, or imposed by a "new" on an "old" school of thought, without a process of disputation. To the extent that they are accepted, modes of semantic reading (such as the semiotic) may be seen to draw out contents that have been implicit in the historical practice of musicianship, though sometimes inarticulate, and to do so in a way that is as systematic as the topic allows. When read in relation to the comments of musicians in the tradition of violin performance and criticism, described in chapter 1, Kivy's (1997) claim that absolute music can support no semantic terms at all is the one that plays more freely against the musical intuitions of practitioners versed in this historical school. It may be the skeptical voice, doubting in theory what cannot be doubted by a musician in practice, that sometimes needs reigning in.

Kivy dismisses the claim that textual contexts give sense to semantic readings, yet in doing so he misses the importance of context in explicating the purpose of the passages he himself cites as examples of New Musicology. The German musicologist, Hans-Heinrich Eggebrecht (1993: 8), seeks to understand why Bach used the B-A-C-H (B-flat-A-C-B-natural) motive as part of the double discant clausula in the fourth fugue of *The Art of Fugue*. Eggebrecht's reading is remarkably poetic, as he has Bach say, "I am identified with the tonic and it is my desire to reach it. . . . Like you I am human. I am in need of salvation; I am certain in the hope of salvation, and have been saved by grace." A rehearsal of the elements of Lutheran salvitic thought is transparently evident in Eggebrecht's comment, and it is not surprising if someone should at first feel a sense of affront that such articulate and abstract beliefs could be claimed as the content of a musical form. What Eggebrecht has done is not, however, to make a simplistic claim that salvation can be presented as an audible phenomenon. Rather, he has presented something of a sphinxish riddle in quotation form, asking his reader to attend to the tonal properties of the B-A-C-H motive, its lack of closure, and apparent "desire" to reach onwards to a point where its B-natural can be tonally satisfied in the passage to D minor, and in doing so to question what this use of the motive could mean to Bach. If the motto were constructed as a standard changing note figure, B-flat–A–C–B-flat, it would be a tonally complete microcosm, closed, without the need of anything more in order to be a self-sufficient entity. As it is, the B-natural disrupts any such self-enclosure, bringing an incompleteness to the motive that makes it need to reach onwards to something else. The confidence with which Bach reinforces the move towards D, in a double-discant clausula, does give "certainty" to the tonal resolution. Eggebrecht's reading makes of this moment a symbol for the almost-blind composer reaching the end of his life, with a sense of his own fallibility yet confident hope. Bach has written his "I," his name, into the music not without some reason, and, though his intentions are themselves unknowable, this use of his name could well be taken to declare "this is me . . . moving on." Even if only to take up the principle of charity, it should be possible to understand Eggebrecht's reading of Bach's last work before his death not simply as mistaken in its reference to salvitic

thought, nor as willfully rebellious against interpretational rules, but as gen-
erous in spirit, as it risks the contemplation of how a musical formation
around Bach's name could carry a message consistent with the composer's
own beliefs.

A process not unlike this is at work when another musicologist, David
Schroeder, reflects that "the highest form of unity is not the one which
eliminates conflict. On the contrary, it is one in which opposing forces can
coexist" (1990: 88). Schroeder is here thinking about the end of Haydn's
Symphony no. 83, in which he finds a presentation of this very kind of unity
among conflicting elements, as a symbol of Enlightenment tolerance. It is
perhaps his claim that a message of tolerance "can be heard in many of
Haydn's late symphonies" that causes Kivy concern. The sense in which tolerance is an attribute that could be *heard* might well be questioned, as the
manner in which it is behaviorally displayed does not have the apparent immediacy and obviousness of something like a gesture. No rule need, however, be taken as given that only small-scale expressive behaviors are capable
of musical instantiation. When Schroeder refers to the use of themes as "opposed forces" which "coexist" in a single passage, he points to conditions
that could in other circumstances be judged as evidence of social tolerance.
What he is hearing is not a direct display of an abstract quality of character,
but a set of formal relationships which might, reflectively, come to represent
that character. Although his rhetoric suggests that music presents a didactic
message, a moral *ought,* a suggestion that is implausible if taken literally, his
own reflections effectively demonstrate that an engagement with musical
relationships which are, in themselves, relatively abstract, may lead to discursive thought about the values held in a society. McClary's reflections on
gender relationships could also be read in this way.

Each of these writers asks of their reader a willingness to work at understanding language that may be figurative. Although they may seem to be
making the surprising suggestion that music is capable of putting forward
propositions about salvation, social tolerance, or gender relationships, they
are not in fact doing this in a naive manner that makes obvious mistakes
about specifically musical modes of signification. Rather, they are noting a
correlation between sets of relationships, or patterns of opposition, which
may be heard in the music, and those which may be observed in society. In
addition, they are providing an analysis of the structure of certain abstract

ideas. To need "salvation" is to present the self as incomplete; to be "tolerant" is to display an ability to hold differences together, without forcing them to sacrifice their identity; to be "feminized," and oppressed in that role, is to be held as the "other" to an assertive, public, and well-organized way of being—to be represented as lacking that which is expected of one who holds a certain formal role. These ideas may be thought of broadly as cultural "units of meaning" (named by Umberto Eco as "codes"), and their applicability to the passages in question is supported not only by their being structurally apposite, but by their demonstrable role in the historical periods in which the works were composed.

b. Selfish Signs and Their Intentionality

The mode of approach exemplified in naming the semantic contents of music using binary oppositions is characterized by Kivy as "a linguistic model." Having dismissed what he sees as its only possible justification, as being made intelligible within the interpretive traditions of a closed linguistic community, Kivy moves to another model for defending semantic interpretation, which he dubs the "representational" one. In what sense can the contents ascribed to music be "heard" in it? This is, indeed, a valid question. Even if it is accepted that the above interpretations are intelligible and interesting, need it be concluded that their contents are *heard* rather than arrived at in reflection after listening? The simple answer is that none of the examples lacks a basis in formal description, or in the analysis of signification for limited and easily derived elements. It is *these* that are heard, and the more elaborate interpretations are appended in later thought, as an unfolding chain of implication becomes apparent to one who has been immersed in the study of the works. A less dogmatic or purist answer is that any interpretive idea (interpretant), once activated in reflection, can inform what is later heard in a piece. If, as DeBellis (1995) suggests, an advanced course in aural training may transform a listener's perception of vaguely identified "harsh sounds" into specifically named dissonances, such as a "dominant thirteenth" (a change from "non-conceptual" to "conceptual" mode), a course of study in the evolution of musical styles, taught in a manner that shows how they reflect the attitudes of the societies in which they are formed, might well result in (at least some) semantic contents being "heard." This is not to say that abstract ideas suddenly become "immediate," as the transparent content of a work, to be heard in the same way that a scale is heard. It is to say that a listener well-versed in a style gains a new capacity to hear works within it as embodying the values of its culture and contributing to their revision or reinforcement. In some cases, that listening move may be optional, in others—as pointed out by Stephen Feld—it may be quite irresistible. Few North Americans, listening to "My Country, 'Tis of Thee," or English people listening to "God Save the Queen," would *not* hear that same melody as the presentation of a nationalistic theme. Once styles or themes are "tagged" with interpretive ideas, they are not so easily removed.[5]

In questioning what can be "heard" in a work, Kivy is most concerned about establishing the criteria of correctness for any ascription. Taking Richard Wollheim's (1993) theory of "seeing in"[6] as his model for the representational view, he reads Wollheim's reference to the intentions of the artist (Kivy, 1997: 12; Wollheim, 1993: 188–189) as a virtual admission that no criteria for semantic ascriptions can be found, beyond reference to those intentions, when they are explicit and recoverable. The familiar fact that intentions cannot be read miraculously from texts is enough to inhibit acceptance of this view and, Kivy believes, to undermine the activities of the New Musicologists, whom he takes to subscribe to it. His presumption that the search for "intentions" is a naive priority among musicologists is, however, a misrepresentation of the practices of historically informed interpretation. A semiotic mode of approach, taken up more by music "theorists" than historians, will tend to look for patterns of thought or activity, as evident in tangible artifacts and texts, and to use these as the basis for identifying the interpretive codes relevant to a particular society. Peirce's skepticism about the accessibility of a mind "behind" the signs, whose characteristics and motivations can be known apart from them, will dissuade anyone in this school from seeking a mysterious intentionality. No less skeptical about hidden "intentions" is the German tradition of hermeneutic interpretation, which has had a more direct line of influence on ("new") musical historians. Particularly as it has been transformed by Hans-Georg Gadamer (an influence on Eggebrecht), this school of thought is very sensitive to the difficulties in reconstructing the "intentions" of historical identities. Gadamer's *Truth and Method* ([1960] 1992) exhorts practitioners to admit the prejudicial codes of interpretation they bring to any work, and to confront the "horizon" of the past, without assuming that any direct communion with the past artist's thoughts can be achieved. If any use of semantic interpretation is to be put in the expanding basket of New Musicology, it will find in there these already well-formed traditions, each of which resist the presumption of claiming to know the hidden intentions of others' minds. Even the voice of "Bach," whom Eggebrecht finds speaking in his motto, B-A-C-H, is not claimed as a transparent vehicle of Bach's intentional state. Objective structures and units of meaning have been used to reconstruct this putative mind, to give him a "voice" in facing death that he does not have in a literal sense.

The desire for criteria that would ensure the preservation of a word's "correct" meaning in a foolproof manner, quite apart from the context of its use, is a desire for a level of certainty that cannot be attained. Born of a picture theory of language, where every word is a tag attached to some item or state of affairs in the world (or a possible world), it presumes the world to be a stable place and language to be a stable grid upon it. Communities use language, but it does not use them. Such is the common-sense view. Its reversal is not, however, unknown—in the later Wittgenstein, Peircean semiotics, or Derrida's deconstructive mode. Instead of engaging in a quest for certainty and seeking to fix the meaning of every term, as if its stability were immutable, why not think of each new context as providing its own range of interpretants for the words within it? The "meaning" of a word is then deflected and mobile, contingent upon its placement, but not without any code of sense at all. It becomes the task of an interpreter to create a narrative that will capture the richness of the context in determining modifications of sense, or spawning multiplicities of reference. Any assumption that language is an obedient tool then gives way, remarkably, to the drama of self-propagating meanings, which use interpreters as their vehicles. An intentionality has begun to appear, not in the mind of those who would with arbitrary willfulness take up a term and change the rules of its use, but in what could be seen as the fecund "desire" of interpretive codes to reproduce themselves in formerly uncolonized venues. Fanciful language, perhaps, but it points to the self-generating success of common ideas (which include "salvation," "tolerance," and "stereotypical gender difference"), in structuring new domains of experience. Lest this should seem to be an observation restricted to those of literary bent, it has been independently discussed by Daniel Dennett who, under the influence of biologist Richard Dawkins, has extended the idea of the "selfish gene" to the "selfish meme"—or unit of meaning—whose apparent "interest" is only in its own evolutionary success (Dawkins, 1997: 35–54). Signs, it is implied, continue to evolve by making use of the minds that carry them. It could be retorted, without reproach, that the minds of a culture themselves "evolve" or change as they make choices among signs, creating the conditions that make the units of meaning seem so insistently "alive"—and also the conditions of the decadence and death of some unsuccessful specimens. The intentional activity of freely choosing human agents is not smothered by the self-propagating "intentions" of signs themselves. Yet what access to past intentions does any interpreter have, except through the evidence of patterns of meaning that were successfully reproduced? A musical style consists, after all, of such replication, and would not exist unless patterns succeeded in generating copies of themselves (see Meyer). It is the style that can be known, not the motivations of those who choose its forms.

The benefit of locating "intentionality" in the seeming liveliness of play and successive change in a world of signs is that it disarms any false credulity about an individual's intentions as the *source* of meaning. No matter what choices a composer might make in his or her selection of materials, no matter what language a writer might choose in seeking to convey the music's sense, the musical and verbal signs will gain their "meaning" from the play of difference in their respective texts, as read within the cultural milieu of their creation. Recognizing this reversal of intentionality, which gives codes (or established "units of meaning") a virtual agency, is an effective way of dealing with the problem of "intentionalism" pointed out by Wimsatt and Beardsley in their well-known paper, "The Intentional Fallacy" (1976). Kivy (1997) suggests that a performer who seeks to play "authentically," and an interpreter who seeks to elucidate a work's meaning with semantic terms, must be trying to capture the composer's "intentions" as a final arbiter of meaning, justifying their interpretive stance. If they were to do so, they would declare their lack of awareness of Wimsatt and Beardsley's warnings. A performer may, however, seek to reconstruct the kinds of interpretive codes that were most current at the time of the work's creation, in order to give an optimal presentation of the work's signifying potentialities, without giving the composer's voice undue privilege. To speak of fidelity to the "composer's intentions" in this kind of practice is to speak of fidelity to a performance style approximating that of the relevant era, insofar as it is known. A composer's explicitly stated or implied judgments of what a work signifies may then become part of the available data in understanding what could be relevant interpretive codes. They are not, however, the source and justification of signified meanings. As Wimsatt and Beardsley have empha- sized, judgments of the work's emergent qualities need to be made with an open mind to the possibility that the composer him- or herself did not have a God's-eye view of all that was in their own work. The implicit intentions that may be read from context may or may not be carried through.[7] Eduard Hanslick gives an example, now famous, of a composer's failure to ade- quately capture the sense of a context he himself had constructed—the aria of (what could be) abject longing sung by Gluck's Orfeo for Euridice, who has been taken from him. Mournfulness, anguish, and desire are all seem- ingly absent from this harmonious and lilting theme. By contrast, Bach's "Erbarme dich" aria, from the *St. Matthew Passion,* carries through very well the textually disclosed "intention" to convey something of the grief of the weeping Peter, just reminded by the cock's crow of Jesus' prophesy that he would deny their friendship (see Cumming, 1997a). Intentions read from textual contexts may provide a clue to the potential kinds of signification that might be found musically realized, but they cannot ultimately arbitrate in questions of how the music does, in fact, function semiotically. If they could do so, it would be impossible to give an adequate account of occasions when tensions occurred between texts and their musical setting.

c. Fallibilities

Kivy's question remains. How can semantic readings of instrumental music be judged as "correct" or not, if neither the authority of a linguistic com- munity nor that of the originating artist or composer can be called upon to acceptably validate them? It has so far been denied that the behavior of mu- sical interpreters, as a community, is as arbitrary as Kivy supposes, and also that reference to supposedly originary intentions is an ultimate priority among New Musicologists, but the question could still be pressed as to how anyone making a semantic ascription could be sure that they have applied a relevant term, and not merely one that seems to them personally apposite.

If Kivy's question is put to Ruth Katz, as she figures in her paper for the same panel of the IMS conference (1997), the answer he must receive is that questions of truth, or of gaining the "right" understanding of a performance, cannot be decided, in the end, without a respect for the traditions of a performance school, as they are presently embodied in those who have been selected by a community as expert within it. Strains of *Fiddler on the Roof,* with the wonderfully assertive song, "Tradition . . . Tradition! . . . Tradition!" might come to mind, only to be brushed aside by one who cannot imagine how anything so contingent as an historical community could decide on questions so weighty as those of musical "truth." Yet here is the crux of the matter. What it is to be involved in a musical practice, is to be involved in an historically contingent activity, whose significations are not absolute. The transitoriness and ephemerality of past traditions, from which a present interpreter is removed, necessarily makes for fallibility in understanding them (see Kramer, 1995). Make of this a council of despair, if you are so inclined, but to do so is somehow to miss the point that your separateness from others (historically or culturally) is a fact of humanness, and that an occasional experience of "missing the mark" in interpretation (or simply of *not knowing* with final assurance that your understanding is correct) is an experience common to all who are prepared to take the risk of trying to bridge the gaps. In this necessarily fallible exercise, it is the testimony of past practitioners, the "experts" of their time, that stands as the "way across." Francesco Geminiani, Leopold Mozart, and contemporary critical witnesses have here been called to testify about the way that violinistic sound may be understood.[8] Music theorists of various persuasions have been called upon to comment on tonal dynamism as the connotative outworking of "purely formal description." Now to look for some "truth" about the music somewhere "behind," or psychologically "deeper," than what the musicians have to say is to desire again a certainty not appropriate to this domain. Musical signification has its roots in historical practice, not in some ideal.

It would be possible to retort that the problem is not so much in calling musicians as witnesses, but in knowing how far the textual witness of others could be relevant to the analysis of a musical work. Tchaikovsky does not speak directly of sexuality, nor Haydn of tolerance. Bach's religious convictions are not pinned explicitly by him upon the shaping of his fugal theme. Why make such wild associations as these? Is it not possible that twentieth-century preoccupations with matters of gender difference and social equality have created such prejudice as to lead the interpreters cited above to select an historically anachronistic interpretive frame? Such legitimate concerns could most profitably lead to the meeting of semiotic techniques of analysis with the hermeneutic reflections of such as Gadamer. It is, of course, an interpreter's responsibility to be constantly vigilant about the prejudicial effects of their own historical positioning. But that need not cause anyone to die of shame. An *absence* of the sense of historical locatedness is much more harmful, in an interpreter, than an acknowledgment of being conditioned by experiences that bring prejudice and contingency. The denial of being historically embodied will itself bring the unseen prejudice of believing that one can explain the music "as it is" — like a physical object, immutable — but to know one's prejudice is to take it up, positively, as a tool for acknowledging the past (or foreign) work's "otherness" (see Haraway, 1988). All this is the stock-in-trade of Gadamer. To meet the past, he tells us, is to see the horizon of one's own prejudice and then to move through that horizon, to engage imaginatively with the different mappings or perspectives on the world experienced by authors and creative artists of the past, until finally a point of mediation is achieved, wherein your own past mapping of the cultural world has been permanently changed. Those who fear fallibility will refuse to take the first step, failing even to question the interpretive frame which places arbitrary boundaries on the world they are able to conceive, staying within the safety of a solipsistic view — their construction of truth. Trying to remove all prejudice, Gadamer would warn, is something akin to trying to remove your own skin. Your "prejudice" is the condition of your being in the world, of being enculturated within your own society, and of having some boundaries with the world. You cannot just remove it, as if it were a mere contingency, unless you would also like to rub yourself out of the physical boundedness that makes you *you*. Your only option is to work with it, to know that your separation from others is the very condition of your beginning to understand them.

"But slow down!" says the skeptic. "I only questioned the validity of some exceptionally florid metaphors! I didn't ask for a sermon on what it is to be a self! All those injunctions — 'expand your horizons!' — have the ring of paternalistic pronouncements, recalled from childhood. They intimidate those who engage in questioning, while creating the illusion of profundity. But consider this. If knowing fallibility is such a virtue, why not expand it deliberately? Why not take interpretive risks, testing the boundaries of plausibility, that the grace of finding your limitations may abound? You proclaim the paradoxical freedom of knowing your own prejudice, in the very moment making of it a virtue no one should want to emulate! While seeming to speak of limits, you undermine any respect for them, with an endorsement of the 'anything goes' mentality."

And the reply to this questioning, which mimics a Pauline phrase (Rom. 6:1), is the similarly Pauline "No way!" If the "law" being espoused is of "love" — manifest in a genuine desire to understand another's creative work — it cannot be realized in any exploitation of the freedoms discovered in recognizing the inevitability of one's own limitation. To avoid any such self-indulgence, which distorts the value of starting from a place of acknowledged prejudice, it is necessary for every interpreter to subject him- or herself to the disciplines of an interpretive community.

"But now we go around in circles," says the skeptic. "Who is this community, exactly, and what freedoms does it have? Who is to say that self-regulating standards of criticism will work, not merely give rise to a pattern of indulgence and historically entrenched prejudice?"

"The community, in its broadest sense, is composed of all those who share in a musical tradition and are capable of being articulate about it in some respect," replies the musician. "As the competencies of those who are members will necessarily differ, it becomes the responsibility of each interpreter to give an account of the reasons for his or her decisions that will be intelligible to others and open to scrutiny."

"Too vague. If you do not define the boundaries of the community, how can you specify the criteria of judgment used by those within it?"

"Vagueness in defining the boundaries of a community of language users never prevented a language from functioning before, so long as the language is connected with a shared 'form of life,' as the late Wittgenstein puts it. A community of those who compose, perform, critique, theorize, and write histories of Western classical music in the eighteenth to nineteenth centuries is closely enough defined for practical purposes."

"You make a circle around an arbitrary field of play."

"Yes. And by doing so I acknowledge a boundary, a limit to a 'world,' without denying that it may intersect with other worlds, which bring new perspectives to the one I have enclosed."

d. Getting It Right—Maybe!

At this point, we listen in on a conversation, rather than seeking to finally close a case. The substance of this conversation will reappear in the next chapter, as it has a bearing on acknowledging the different positions that a Subject may take with respect to a musical work, but for now it is necessary to revisit the question of how it could be possible to put forward opinions which are supportable, but not testable as truth—to wind the conversation back a bit, slow it down, and dilute its rhetoric. The musician now seeks the aid of one who reflects on "uncertainty."

Skeptic: "If you can't be sure that an analysis is ultimately correct, why hazard putting it forward? Isn't this a mere self-indulgence, a retreat into abject subjectivity?"

Respondent: "It may be that the very terms in which you phrase this question are problematic, in linking truth with certainty and testability. *Uncertainty* is the middle state that you have been unwilling to consider as valuable in any sense. But why?"

Skeptic: "Because uncertainty may be one of two things. If I concern myself with questions of 'being,' it is a state of affairs which, in being merely "possible," has a close affinity with the empirically untrue. If, on the other hand, I concern myself with questions about what it is to 'know' something, it is a state of mind which, in lacking the conviction of belief, just does not qualify as a kind of knowing. The uncertain cannot be deemed to produce 'knowledge.' If I say 'I am uncertain,' in answer to a question, I might just as well have said 'I don't know.' The state speaks of lack, not of positive apprehensions of things."

Respondent: "You link 'truth,' certainty, and the privileged sense of 'knowing,' but I don't think that you have really closed the case. If you say, 'I am uncertain,' could you not be saying, 'I have considered more than one way of describing this phenomenon, and have not decided upon one way as having an exclusive grasp of what it is like.' Or, 'I have noticed general traits as being exemplified here, but they are too indeterminate in what they govern to be able to characterize its particularity.' In either case, your uncertainty would be well-informed, an appreciation of qualities that lack single descriptions, or of complex entities that could not be reduced, in their particularity, to examples of any general type."

Skeptic: "In those cases, I would not say, 'I am uncertain.' I would say that the quality fits within a range of possible descriptions, or that the entity I am observing exemplifies a number of general traits, without its emergent features being captured by any of them. Nothing uncertain there."

Respondent: "Nothing? You have merely slipped from talk of your state of mind as being uncertain, to talk of *knowing* an entity to display elements of vagueness or indeterminacy. In fact, you have admitted to knowing something as uncertain—and yet as acceptably 'true,' insofar as it gives you the conviction of believing what you say about its possible qualities and its presentation of general potentialities."

Skeptic: "Okay, I concede that one may have knowledge of qualities, whose descriptions are multiple, and of tokens of types, which still have not been predicted by their typology. Saying so does not, however, commit me to accepting any piece of vagueness and generality in description as perspicacious about the reality of a musical work. Knowing that some qualities may be described in many ways, or that some musical elements may exemplify general stylistic traits without being captured by them, does not have the power to justify the use of any ascriptions at all. I still want to know what the criteria are for accepting ascriptions of content to instrumental music as 'true.'"

Respondent: "Supposing that I make a concession, too, namely, that certain interpretations have been subject to excess. Is it your purpose to gain a confession of fallibility from those of whose interpretations you disapprove? I ask this, because it seems to me that your fear of excess makes your epistemological concession a very reluctant one. You still read fallibility as failure, and discourse around the uncertain as an exercise in promoting ignorance."

Skeptic: "My caution is fair. A student who gains the message that nothing can be proved will quickly assume that anything is possible. If you admit that fallibility is inevitable in a realm of investigation, such as the musical, you had better be careful that it does not become a weak excuse for irresponsibility."

Respondent: "So, from questions of knowledge, we pass to ethical concerns, but one thing we share is a commitment to doing justice to the musical work. Now stand back a minute and consider the logic of what you have said. You make a universal out of a partial position. The admission of varying degrees of certainty, in the interpretation of music's emergent qualities, does not add up to be a statement that *all* is ambiguous, or that anything goes. You might also consider this: does the refusal to take any interpretive risks in itself ensure infallibility, or give certainty to the representation of a work? Is it inherently *less* self-indulgent to withdraw into a world of the formally secure . . . ?"

~

The dialogic mode could continue. One voice attempts to restrain the excess of interpretive freedom he finds in new practices, tempering it with epistemological conservatism. The other attempts to free the first from what she finds as excessive restraint, a burden of interpretive timidity. In the midst of their argument, Peirce's voice returns. Vagueness and generality are, indeed, both categories of mind and of reality, he will say. You cannot avoid them. But that does not make a moral value out of being vague, nor does it justify a retreat to the mental cloister, where scholars refuse to touch the particular as they rationalize generalities. The works you encounter, which stand up against you in their physically and culturally embodied form, demand to be recognized as individuals in a semiotic world, where they attain their particular characteristics. And then Peirce's voice leaves off with a general notion of signs, a voice making constant reference to a framework of ontology, and of ways of "knowing" what is given in a material and semiotic world—the first category of qualitative possibility, the second of encounter, and the third of general potentiality. At this point, the musical semiotician takes a turn, to say that if you interpret music as a play of signs, you can deal with the imbricated levels of signification, emergent content, and culturally emergent forms, without denying the different levels of certainty that attach to any of them. But the hermeneutic scholar (a follower of Gadamer) interrupts, with further questioning. Is semiotic method an answer at all? Why restrict yourself to typologies, or to the play of differences—as if meanings could be fixed like an array of colorful butterflies in a glass display. The loss of uncertainty—the flutterings of sense—is, he says, a loss of life. Why assume that truth is *method* at all? The semiotician (Merrell, 1997) replies that Peirce had thought of the fringes of certainty. His idea of the sign was wider than any imagined in its common use, and thus the rapprochement of semiotic study with the hermeneutic scholar's historical concerns is indeed possible. But another thinker of semiotic bent (Simpkins, 1997) is uncertain that "semiotics," after Peirce, can make claims to being a "discipline" with a distinctive methodology at all. It consists of no more than a conversation like this, a topic of discussion without systematicity. Whatever Peirce might have said, he has not gained hegemonic control.

In addressing this babble of voices, Peirce cannot be named an ultimate authority or source of all semiotic wisdom, nor can he be dismissed as one who has done no more than put forward a set of typologies. Without becoming obsessed with classification and methodology, or mystified with categories of thought that slip confusingly between the ontological and epistemological, it is enlightening to engage in a dialogue with this philosopher—whose own semiotic reflections were so open-ended—precisely because of his farsighted capacity to open up questions about the kinds of knowledge yielded by signs. Most original in Peirce's thought is the suggestion that factuality inhabits a place between qualitative possibility, on the one side, and general potentialities, on the other. In accordance with this patterning of thought about the world and ways of knowing it, different kinds of uncertainty—and of conviction—can be described. The first kind of uncertainty belongs to an appreciation of qualities that are perceived through an apparently "immediate" feeling (although they are already interpreted), because the inaccessibility of the discursive process leading to their perception makes it more difficult to provide a justifying narrative. When it is considered that Peirce recognizes qualitative possibility (or "firstness") not only as inhering in simple qualities but also as capable of emerging from rule-governed or conventional forms (which display "thirdness"), added nuance is given to the senses of uncertainty provided in this first type. I might hear a quality as emerging in a passage, and do so spontaneously, as when I notice the martiality of the opening to Mahler's Sixth Symphony, only later pausing to consider the set of stylistic contrasts that support this effect. As a quality, the emergent effect is not "certain," but a possibility entertained as capturing something of what the passage is like. Its derivation can be secured, at least to some degree, by reference to conventional patterns of difference, as they are stylistically instantiated and discursively derived (examples of "thirdness"). Another kind of uncertainty belongs, however, to the interpretation of general connotative conventions in music themselves, or to social "culture" more broadly conceived. A wide range of experience is required in order to recognize the forms of social behavior, or the observable dynamic shapes of experiences, which are conventionally associated not only with the "martial," but also with "femininity," "longing for salvation," or "social democracy." These ideas present a set of interpretive potentialities. Their outward forms may be realized or suggested in many different media, without it being at all plausible to give the ideas power fully to control the content ascribed to any given context. The uncertainty of any statement about general ideas such as these, whose implicit forms are so prolific in their self-reproductive capacity, derives from their very capacity to reproduce, with great insensitivity to context. It may become tempting to accord them an explanatory power that exceeds what they are offering, forgetful of the always inadequate or partial nature of the explanations they can give, but an awareness of their very fecundity can only lead the judicious interpreter to caution or "hedging" when ascribing them to a new place. "Knowledge," then, is circumscribed with an admission of differing levels of certainty.

Margolis has expressed the need for what he calls a "many valued" logic (1995: 2), in order to deal both with the many different degrees of certainty or standards of truth that attend analyses of aspects of art works and also with the possibility of incompatible interpretations being equally "true." He suggests that this multivalent view should not be simply an extension of dichotomizing logic, placing "indeterminacy" as a domain between truth and falsehood, but should, instead, take account of the highly nuanced differences in positions or attitudes a person could take when presenting an interpretation; for example, modifying statements with markers that they are varyingly "plausible," "apt," or "reasonable" (ibid.: 6). The form of relativism espoused by Margolis is a strong one, accepting the possibility of incompatible interpretations as having equal claims to "truth." A weaker pluralistic position is put forward both by Stephen Davies (1995) and Robert Stecker (1995), who defend the need for at least a potential consistency between interpretations (mainly of literary works), with a view of differences as drawing out aspects of a work that can be brought together into a single view of it. A Peircean view can supply the basis for a "many-valued logic," through its reading of "uncertainty" as operating simultaneously on different levels, and to differing degrees, according to the kind of sign being interpreted. Qualities that may on the whole be deemed incompatible have also been described as belonging to a single work, and as being reconcilable within it, as a complex state. Recognizing multiplicity, both in a work and in ways of describing it, need not, however, lead an interpreter to throw up his or her hands in a despairing (or perhaps light-hearted) endorsement of the "who knows? anything goes" policy, as Kivy (1997) puts it. The choice being offered is no longer between "getting it right" and throwing all interpretive caution away. A basic level of structural description may allow correctness to be directly "checkable" in most cases, but where this level of certainty is lacking, it is not as if a sudden drop occurs, into the abyss of ignorance and insecure reference which the early Wittgenstein took as a prescription for stoic silences. Rather, the tenability of varied readings needs to be tested within a community (as suggested by Gasking, 1996) taking into account both their responsiveness to historical codes of interpretation, and the degree of certainty being claimed.

e. Uncertain Codes and Multiple Tropes

In this chapter, a more or less systematic opposition of general ideas, which have the potential to be musically instantiated, has been referred to somewhat casually as an opposition of "codes." This term has been defined by Umberto Eco as a "cultural unit" or, in more specifically semiotic terms, "a semantic unit inserted into a system" ([1976] 1979: 67; see also Samuels, 1995: 11). By the very fact that he entitles his book a "theory" of semiotics, Eco intimates a desire for systematicity in interpretative procedures relating to codes, but when dealing with codes or their "interpretants" in practice, it is not the prevalence of system that stands out. Rather, Eco recognizes an ongoing process of deferral, whereby one unit of meaning is interpreted by another. Emphasizing that the implications of codes are virtually unending, he effectively undermines any sense of codified meaning as being singular or contained in a closed theoretical system. No pre-defined limits are set on the possible meanings attached to any given "cultural unit," as it enters the interpretive stream. This kind of openness, referred to by Eco as "unlimited semiosis" ([1976] 1979: 71) is consistent with Peirce's depiction of the "general" in signs, as never fully containing the particular. No general code can account for a presenting entity. More words, further interpretations, will always ensue. An enthusiastic celebration of a sign's buoyancy in the possible stream of interpretants does, even so, need to be tempered with the recollection that not all "interpretants" are equally negotiable. In the first place,

Peirce's scheme does not have all interpretants relating to the domain of fully conventional or "symbolic" meanings. Those signs whose interpretants include a "feeling" (qualitative signs, icons) or an energetic reaction—noting the sign's attachment to its place (indices)—are not naively "immediate" and uninterpreted, but neither are they the kind of sign whose sense can be indefinitely deferred or willfully altered. It *seems* to present itself immediately, despite the analytic fact of a prior conditioning that determines its interpretation. (As Lidov says, "we need our qualia.") Further than that, instances of non-radical "emergence," whereby more complex signs are built on simpler ones (as a "higher" level) can only be understood if it is accepted that the simpler level of description has at least some claims to being more "basic." The priority or privilege of a basic level of description need not be held onto with undue force, when more radically emergent properties are brought into play, but neither can it be simply forgotten. Culturally relative modes of symbolic understanding may penetrate down into the perception even of such things as sound quality, or gestural shapes, since a capacity for interpretability is a condition of their being signifying units at all. Interpretability does not, however, need to be imagined as a free-falling dive, whereby the signs' first interpretants are obliterated by the imposition of later ones. Complex associations do not eradicate the need for new information coming up "from below"[9] or drown relative simplicity in a sea of contextual ambiguation.

Another way of talking about the relationship between different levels of signification is to refer to "tropes" as being formed at a higher level, when an established sign or cultural code is shifted to a new context, where it finds new interpretations, or when previously distinct signs are combined to form new and more complex units. Semiotic anthropology (Feld; Parmentier, 1994: 113–123) can provide narratives of how signs shift in their use within a society, or gain accretions of meaning. Whichever way it is described, one issue does, however, remain. That is, how to deal with varying degrees of complexity, or contextual alteration, in signs without abusing the notion of "levels" or "hierarchies." One abuse may be found in an attempt to dissolve necessary distinctions, making all signs "symbols," and thus losing a sense of simple qualitative icons, or indices of directionality and place. An opposite abuse may be found in calcifying signs into a rigid scheme, outside of which none may even be imagined. Resulting from this is a desire to explain even complex cases reductively, looking "down" for component parts rather than "out" for the network of encoded cultural meanings within which they operate, and then according the status of a superior kind of "knowledge" to meanings so derived.[10] Peirce's own schematisms may be read as promoting the latter fault, but his authority cannot be cited as an excuse for rigidity, especially when his thought about signs is located within his more broadly conceived Categories.

~

chapter nine

'Values and 'Personal Categories

I. Sound and Sensuality

a. Sense and Sensibility:
The Anxieties of Enjoyment in Listening

If a lower-level boundary of semiotics is to be found at its interface with questions of perceptual representation, its upper boundary is touched upon in questions of evaluation. In some of his writings, Peirce suggests that the "final" interpretant of a sign is evident in the formation of a habit of action in relation to it, a considered manner of response. With this move towards an emphasis on the active agent, interacting with signs, he begins to situate the semiotic in a world of choice. I know that I can listen to Bach's cello sonatas played by Anner Bylsma on an authentic instrument, or by Rostropovich in a sensitively Romanticized manner. Which will I choose? What is my *habit* of choice? I know that in writing about music, I can spend time with the description of formal properties, with a focus on how the work reflects the patterns of a style, or choose to pay attention instead to a single performance in its particularity. Is my interest in rule-governed signs, or in singular ones? In his study, *Values and Valuing,* the philosopher, Graham Nerlich (1989), presents a "naturalized" view of values, in which he reflects that values are most evident in choices of activity and domains of committed work. They are "higher-order" representations of items or events, whose interpretation yields to action. I represent an "inauthentic" performance to myself as a distortion of a work's aural style and decide not to listen. Or I place individuality of realization above historical accuracy and listen to Rostropovich's Bach as well as Bylsma's. The value is self-reflexive, as I am aware of myself in the choosing. It has an economic result, if I choose to buy, and an impact on the kind of practical work I choose, in committing myself to one or the other performance discipline.

Nerlich presents values as realized in a "dialectic" between higher-order desires and the awareness of embodiment as an animal that no one can deny. If this dialectic between abstract ideals and sensory desires is enacted in ordinary life, it finds its counterpart also in music. A tension may be found between the dictates of formal order or long-term goals, and the more "immediate" pleasures of sound. Musical sound production, and response to it, then begins to reflect a person's habits of evaluation in other domains of interpersonal activity. The unadorned purity of a sound without vibrato, or the lavishly nuanced variation of a sound, each may be valued. A preference for the first might disclose a pleasure in musical order without distraction from sensuous immediacies, while a desire for the second could suggest a heightened sensitivity to musical moments as they pass, without such emphasis on broader perspectives. Either possibility can, of course, be modified with judgments of style. That the dialectic is a real one is evident in disputes about performance style and also about the priorities of aesthetic writing.

∿

A violinist's sound production scars the body, leaving calluses on the fingertips and marks on the neck. Performance is a physical relationship of artist and instrument, with both the pain and the satisfaction of extended effort and greatly variegated touch. The pleasures of touch and movement, feeling resistance, sensing vibration, hearing nuanced sound, are undeniably sensuous at times. And if they can be so for a performer, why should it be doubted that a listener, too, may be aroused, or vicariously appreciative, as he or she hears the marks of voice or action in sounding quality? Little surprise, then, that anxieties about the sensuous can be heard and met in this musical domain—by performers, listeners, or aesthetes. The materiality of the sound can draw attention to itself—in marks of its physical creation —especially at moments of audible onset noise or excess vibrato. An active assertion of audible power or sensuous pleasurability in sound cannot be entirely ignored or suppressed in listening, as if hearing them were an indulgence that distracted attention from "the music itself"—a substance existing apart from the accidents of sound. To say as much is to state the obvious. Music cannot *be* apart from the sound it makes, except if you conceive of it as pure moving forms in an inner ear.[1] Then what is the anxiety of sense? It is that in taking pleasure in sounding qualities, you will be doing no more than enjoying a sensory state—like the pleasure of ice cream on a hot day. "When the pleasure taken in music is like the pleasure taken in ice-cream, then that pleasure is not, after all, taken in music as such but merely in some aspect of the sound it happens to make" (Davies, 1994: 324). The aesthetician's fear (see Kivy, 1986, 1990; Davies, 1994: 324) is that mere sensory stimulation, the arousal of sense, does poor justice to the "musical" content of the sound—its capacity to support other musical elements. If you pay attention to the pleasures they afford, will you not be failing to recognize the role sounds play in enhancing more serious "content"?

What is odd in this distrust of musical pleasure is its creation of a duality between sensory embodiment and "making sense." It is something like a dualism of body and mind, which assumes that perception is uninterpreted. Musical sounds impinge on the senses, to be perceived as signs of "inner" states. Their "signification" cannot appear apart from its sensory content, for without it the nuanced sign would have no material form. In order to hear anger in a voice, you need to notice raucousness, an edgy sound. To feel love in someone's touch you have to attend, at least subliminally, to the gentle pressure and motion of their hand in yours. To smell a fragrance as "refinement," as Peirce does in response to a woman's perfume, you need to take at least some pleasure in its effect on your discriminating nose. These are not "merely" physical sensations, since they come interpreted as signs. Tangibility is entirely necessary to them, as emotionality and character cannot exist as mere abstractions, but must take a sensible form. The threat of sensuous, nuanced signs is, however, in this very characteristic of "closeness" to the body—as Lidov has identified. Touch and smell may be indulged for the pleasures of sensation alone, and the one who engages in great excess gets labeled as perverted or gluttonous. When sounds become a stimulus, apart from their context, they invite a similar devaluation. The "body" in sound, heard in nuanced effects, brings a form of stimulation that might conceivably distract an indulgent listener from other musical content, allowing him to engage in a pleasure without obvious interpretation. Who might be the culprit of such poor listening? Perhaps the supermarket shopper, relaxed by Muzak, or the rock-music fan, gyrating to a thumping beat. Or is it any listener who chooses for a moment to enjoy a sound? A danger in being too ready to condemn an act of pleasurable listening is that it presumes the separateness of sense and sense-making even in these instances. Even to respond to a sound as pleasant and relaxing requires an active (cognized) recognition. Who said that sense is dumb?

b. Listening as an Act of Love

It is in reaction to some academic inhibitions about the pleasures of sound that feminists in music theory and musicology (Lawrence Kramer, Cusick, Guck, Kielian-Gilbert, Maus) have begun to place an emphasis on a listener's being willing to acknowledge their responsiveness to the sensory elements in musical performances. An imperative may be found in their work, running in the opposite direction from that seen in the aesthetic tradition. Here is no incitement to ascetic self-control and to applying rational constructs while listening. Instead, a challenge is made: Acknowledge your enjoyment! Stop pretending you're in control of your musical experience! Dare to admit the pleasure of a passive listening role! (See Maus, 1993.) Suzanne Cusick (1994a) makes these enjoinments to a rapprochement with sense most forcefully, in a self-searching essay which compares a musician's relationship to music with the attitudes of an attentive lover to one whom she loves. The creation of nuance through sensitive touch, and the pleasurable response it may engender, together lead her to suggest parallels between acts of musical performance or listening and the acts of affection that form a loving relationship.[2] "Intimacy, pleasure, and power" are the central aspects noted by Cusick as needing to be negotiated by the "partners" in each case. A relationship of intimacy cannot allow one partner to assume the position of rational distance and control in relation to the other, whose power to "touch" is denied. To a certain degree, a loss of self-containment and distancing is required of the one who would "know" what it is to exchange the pleasures of touch in relationship. The same is true of listening. Those attitudes, which might form high "values" in contexts of research where the restraint of personal interest is required, become a potential impediment to understanding what it is to be "touched" by a sound.

Though music's personification can easily be carried too far, Cusick's image of a relationship does suggest a reconsideration of the site of musical "depth." Is love in a relationship necessarily "deeper" if lived out as "a commitment," an enactment of abstract union, without the signs of touch? Is your musical understanding "deeper" if you are ignorant of how the music "touches" you, but absorbed in interpreting its form, as of deeper consequence? It may be in the interrogation of your own points of response that you discover what it is that the music has to give. For Cusick, to fail to do so is to "dismember its body," to assume rational dominance and control, to negotiate what could be an intimate relationship of pleasure in music, by overpowering it with analysis. She (as well as Guck [1997] and Maus [1993]) incisively picks up an anxiety among analysts of music about attending to the sensuous and the particular. Both Cusick and Maus equate rational analysis with "control." Analysis engenders an awareness of one's own predictive capacity, or ability to foresee what is coming musically (or in relationship), and to forestall any unwanted reactions with a deliberate act of self-containment. It is in the power of abstraction to be able to place the palpable, and seemingly "immediate," in the context of broader principles. But such is not an attitude that suffices in intimate relationship, where attentiveness to the moment is surely required. The challenge of intimacy is to know how to listen to a tone of voice in the moment of utterance, and to respond without the distraction of evaluative analysis (even if later reflection reveals an awareness of intonations and response that yields well to analytical thought). To borrow a phrase from a Jungian psychologist, Thomas Moore, the "cultivation of depth and sacredness in everyday life" may best be achieved by modest acts of attentiveness to ordinary things—to the qualities of items as they appear to you (1992: 4–5).[3] Instead of rejecting those attractions to sound that you might find less than ideal—if what you seek in yourself is evidence of stylistic knowledge and theoretical understanding —ask what it is that the sound qualities have to offer you.[4] "Why am I so moved by Perlman's Jewish theme? So surprised and enlivened by the 'cutting-edge' player or the violin in a folk band?" Caring for music, and for the continuing formation of your listening self, does not always require an eschewal of sensuous sound. It can be in caring for the surface that you attend most fully to the work. Finding "depth" of understanding may paradoxically require a willingness to attend to the qualities of sound, as they emerge on the "surface," in time. It is, after all, in the formation of that very moment that the musician is investing her energy.

In the writings of Cusick and Maus, it is suggested that gender differences mark out a controlled, analytical stance from a "passive" and receptive one. The "masculine" seeks control while the "feminine" accepts the power of sound, attending to musical content that does not fit well in formal theories. Neither author claims, however, that "gender identity" is a simple equation, where masculinity belongs to male, and femininity to female writers. Positions of analytical distance and predictive control may be contrasted with positions of receptivity to sound in any listener.

c. Resistances

A question of balance needs to be cleared up here. To recommend an attentiveness to the moment is not to imply that you must embrace an attitude of passive enjoyment as a sole listening position. It is simply to draw attention to the need, already recognized, for the "surface" to be heard in its richly expressive depth. The conflict of values that emerges in the resistance of musical interpreters to this level of content is made more acute when the two ways of listening are deemed exclusive, or the (tentatively gendered) positions pitted against one another as opposites. "Are there not 'higher' or more formally and stylistically insightful ways of listening that ought to be cultivated?" Well, yes, it is scarcely possible to deny that an appreciation of form and style are legitimate values. They might even be accepted as "higher" values, in that they involve a gradual learning of ways to hear, demanding attention to less immediately palpable aspects of the music. The German musicologist, Hans-Heinrich Eggebrecht, goes to some lengths in his *Musik verstehen* (1995) to persuade his reader that simply to indulge in enjoying the music, without any appreciation of its style, is not to "understand" it. No claim need be made against him that an attentiveness to the signifying power of sound quality somehow *replaces* a knowledge of style. What is nonetheless to be avoided is the creation of a dichotomy between "music" and "the sound it makes." Even Cusick's account of her relationship with a piece of music may be read as reinforcing this dichotomy. She does not countenance any place for analytical approaches and wants to encourage an awareness of pleasure in sound. It might be assumed, then, that she has displaced the "rational" and sought to create a purely hedonistic passivity in the students who are her nascent listeners. A closer reading of Cusick's text does not, however, permit the sensual to be torn away so flippantly from acts of musical appraisal and analysis. It is just that the mode of understanding she describes is not constituted in "formal" approaches. If mutuality in relationship is taken to be her model, it cannot be carried through without the "negotiations" that bring pleasure into contact with "power." A further consideration is then needed of this conflict which, though not intractable, remains insistent in her text and in Eggebrecht's.

One way of seeking to undo this unhelpful dichotomy between pleasure in the sensory qualities of musical "surfaces" and the felt imperative to be rationally "in control" might be to reconsider the conflict as it presents itself in experiences of relationship, taking a more analytical stance. It would then be possible to look at alternative ways of addressing the interface between sensory awareness and more formal (or rational) elements. The conflict of values involved here is between a striving after the "higher" self, in rationality or distance, and a giving way to the impulses of sensory "creatureliness." The conflict is an ancient one. Plato suggests it in his treatment of humans as being *metaxu,* in the middle between the gods and the beasts, partaking of each of their characters. Many philosophers, in different ways, have addressed the question: how can a rational embrace of the world, which yields an illusion of separateness, be reconciled with a knowledge of being incorporated in that very world?[5] Graham Nerlich takes this conflict and rewrites it in an experiential mode, with a highly sensitive account of values in intimate relationship. He names the conflict a "dialectic of desire and value." Desire draws an individual into bodily experience, requiring, for its fulfillment, that he momentarily surrender to a physical drive. A central "value" in relationship is, however, that each should be self-aware, responsive to the other, able to moderate movement and exercise control in continuing acts of self-appraisal—somehow using the rationality that places the subject "outside." The anxieties that afflict people engaged in intimate sensual contact are born, Nerlich suggests, of this dialectic, which requires moments of spontaneity, and others of self-monitoring. Complete absorption is not a state that can be sustained for any length of time, considering that ongoing acts of appraisal are part of an intimate relationship, but undistracted involvement is, even so, the normal condition of an aroused response (1989: 120, 5.2.1). Neither awareness of sense, nor an hyper-self-conscious effort to control every motion, can then gain undue privilege. Only a mobility of attitude will allow the sensitive negotiations that form such a relationship. If, in this kind of experience, a dialectic appears between moments of absorption, and moments of self-appraising consideration for another's needs, it may be found also in a listener's interactions with a musical work whose sensuous surface calls attention to itself. An absorption in the moment might alternate with an appraisal of the music's unfolding shape or thoughts about its style. Anxieties can afflict a self-conscious interpreter who wants to write about music with the distance of rational control, while remembering her own involvement in the music, similar to those that afflict a self-conscious lover, who cannot quite acknowledge the power of sense.

Elements of "higher" valuing become intrusive when they act not to give further attention to what is being perceived, but to increase self-consciousness while listening. If I interrupt listening to ask myself the question, "Should I be listening for the form right now, instead of enjoying the violinist's sound?" do I thereby enhance my way of listening to the work? It may be so, if my purpose is to develop "structural hearing." It may, however, also be that the question is born of anxiety. Evident in it is an act of continuing self-appraisal, one which admits in the asking that enjoyment has been known. In the act of questioning, a limit is placed on self-abandonment, a checkpoint established whereby sensory response will answer to reason and control. It can be recognized that such limits and acts of self-interrogation are the necessary tools of sociality, but misplaced they become the bearers of an inhibition that stifles anyone's ability to be, or perceive, in the living moment of their experience. It is as if all acts of sensuality were to be carried out with the audience of an evaluating mind. Parallels with the anxiety of relationship remain strong. A dialectic of "desire and value" requires that an awareness of "sensuality" alternate with other ways of being aware or rationally in control. Nerlich points out, poignantly, that the very acts that make for satisfaction in a sensuous relationship are those which require the greatest abandonment of "values" otherwise sustained in the call to "selfhood" through self-consciousness and rational choice. Moments of abandonment are needed for a relationship. Yet without the "higher" values of control, no relationship would be sustained. Instead of looking for an easy answer to this conflict, or railing against those who fall down on one side, it is more effective to embrace it (as Nerlich suggests) as representing different "sides" of the self, neither to be demonized.

~

It might be objected, further, that a state of *arousal* is something stronger than just any sensory feeling for quality. It is a heightened feeling, often indulged in for its own pleasurability. Quite so. It is a matter of degree. But if you must necessarily have a feeling for quality, as part of the process of understanding a qualitative sign, why should you not permit a state of high involvement, or "arousal," as one that can occur at times? If you admit a place to the sensual in life, might you not consider that it has a place in music, too, without imagining that by admitting it, you open the path to utter profligacy and uninformed, self-indulgent listening? Without an allowance for involvement, it is unlikely that you will be open to being impressed by a sound, involved without distraction—even if this is not your primary listening mode. High excitation by sounds may be rare, but that does not make it inadmissible. An obvious trap, which I highlight with this somewhat facetious rhetoric, is the belief that occasional excesses of self-indulgence make *any* response to sound rather suspect. The main problem is not so much one of perceptual knowledge, concerned with what it is to "know" a sound as possessing a certain quality, as it is a problem of evaluation, as discussed above. A retreat from conditions of "arousal" does, nevertheless, hint at a further mistake, of an epistemological character: the false assumption that modes of listening are mutually exclusive, ruling one another out. Partial understandings, or conditions of response, are elevated to a much stronger and more exclusive position than they need hold, then rejected as being too partial, as failing to represent central "values," such as those of stylistic knowledge and self-control. If interpreters allow themselves to become caught in a conflict between a feeling for sound and a felt imperative to objectify knowledge, they merely reenact a poorly adjusted response to the dialectic of sensuality and control, as found in other domains of life. Questions of knowledge and of value meet one another, requiring some further *rapprochement*. A resolution that has been suggested here is to recognize different phases and moments of knowledge as a necessary part of actively engaged and thoughtful listening (or indeed, being). Writing or speaking of what has been heard cannot then pretend to represent an understanding only of "conventions" and "laws" (as if "third-ness" were the only condition of meaning), because those conventions themselves depend on the development of shared feeling.

⌒

Little doubt need be entertained that strong feelings are at stake when questions of value and disciplinary priority come up in the domains of music theory and musicology. A polemical tone is entirely predictable, as acts of evaluation and emotional response are intrinsically linked. Nerlich comments that "emotions can be *of* value only if they are somehow *about* values" (1989: 146, 6.3.1). When Cusick assesses formalistic writing as a "dismemberment" of music, or Dunsby expresses a reverse contempt for the "ecstasy" school, each engages an exaggerated image to convey the strength of their repudiation for what they see as a loss of a valued attitude: a loss of sensitivity; a loss of appreciation for structural order, analytically appraised. When Lawrence Kramer declares formalism "dead," he is comparable in his resort to hyperbole. His concern is to protect the linking of music to other cultural meanings (the topic of chapter 7). When Jonathan Bernard and Marion Guck exchange articles on modes of interpreting the music of Varèse, their conflict centers markedly on the relative values of formally descriptive prose and reference to "how I hear" a certain sound, which is unrepeatable. A dialectic between the sensuous (and its qualitative signs) and the conventionally controlled is not, then, one of philosophical speculation alone. It actually enters the politics of publication and scholarly discipline. To calm the polemic, and reorient music's interpretive disciplines, what is needed is a reappraisal of the processes of valuation themselves. If more than one standpoint can be embraced as not only tolerable, but epistemically *necessary*, the horror of choosing one position alone begins to look more like a fantasy.

2. Encounters

a. Encountering the Boundaries of Subjectivity

Music could be thought of as subverting the boundaries between the material and the personal, commanding an attention more familiar in the encounter with other human beings. So much is evident not only from the ease with which personalizing (subject-related) terms are used in describing aspects of musical signification (chapters 4–6), but also from the sense it makes to explore a relationship with music as being in some ways comparable to a relationship with a person. A musical work, like a person seeking to be understood, demands recognition for its uniqueness, its active role in relationship to the listener, and its formation within a social and stylistic milieu. In case the metaphors of musical subjectivity should become too dominant, the possibility for reversing the musically "subjective" does, however, need to be retained. It is useful to remember that any musical sign of subjectivity—in voice-like tone, gestural shaping, or systematic attributes of "desire" or "will"—gains its status as a sign not by offering an "immediate" sense of subjective "presence" in the music, but by realizing a possibility set up by a play of differences understood within a community (such as that of listeners to classical violin music). The possibilities of a personalized tone, or of a gestural shaping of a notated figure, need not be actualized in any given performance, and only a very small alteration in a performer's movement can, in any case, lead to a loss of the desired effect. (When Derrida chooses to describe signs as relating to "absence" rather than "presence," he captures this sense of a sign as yielding a content that it somehow cannot secure.) More importantly, the very *possibility* of a personal tone yields the counter-possibility of an impersonal one, which takes up the kinds of onset noise, frictional attributes, or alterations in tone available on an instrument and exploits them deliberately to avoid the illusion of a personal voice. If the "personal" is lost, but the memory of "voice" remains, the quality being heard becomes one of an "other" who might seem "strange," "other-worldly," or "ethereal." A sense of encounter with the non-personal, or supra-personal, can thus be created by playing with the possibilities of "personal" sound. An example using even human voices could be found in the vocal practice of some English choirs, such as the King's College Choir under David Wilcocks during the 1970s. Purity of tone and an absence of vibrato here contribute to a construction of what might be heard as the "spiritual"—not as an ineffable presence that descends magically upon the choristers (reinforcing the "angelic" look endowed by frilly robes) but as a quality of sound that belongs to an absence of the overt signs of "subjectivity" or "emotionality." Similar effects can well be emulated on a violin. As a topos of sound production, this way of performing with heightened control of the signs of subjectivity is indicative of a desire to present human potentialities that transcend the "personal." Music has subverted the boundary of materiality and the humanly personal by creating an instrumental "voice." Now it subverts a further boundary—that between the personal and its supposed limitations—by endowing its many voices with qualities that eschew the "subjective," and transcend the expressive potential of an untrained human voice.

It has been seen in earlier chapters that similar reversals attend the treatment of gesture or of "will." The very potentiality for directionality, "willful" pushing towards a goal, or an apparent "desire" to go a certain way, set up systematically within tonal music, can also become the means for creating the very opposites of these qualities—virtual directionlessness, an apparent lack of will, or freedom from overtly expressed desire. An ability to create virtual "personae," expressive of subjective characteristics, carries with it the ability to suggest "personae" with rather more alien character and also the dissolution of subjective unity in postmodern works.

If music can subvert the boundaries set up schematically when seeking to define a human "subject"—boundaries between a material "thing" and a quasi-personal agent, and also between the personal and what is imagined as its "upper limit" or "beyond"—it can also set up possibilities of relationship that subvert the simplest models of interpersonal activity. A passage such as the Japanese *Isé-no-Umi* theme, appropriated in Peter Sculthorpe's *Mangrove,* is able to convey a sense of the "ineffable" or "mysterious," by assuming a weakly directional stance, restrained melodic gesture, and a timbral "voice" depersonalized by the shimmering, mirroring effect of many cellos playing "out of sync" with one another. Its qualities ask not for a presumptive famil-iarity on the part of a listener, but for a recognition of something "other," or alien, a "persona" which demands stillness and attention, without an impa-tient demand for dramatic "events" or forceful movement towards a close. (Sculthorpe's borrowing of a non-Western mode contributes to this demand, softened only by the closeness of the mode to the Dorian, more familiar to European-educated listeners.) Instead of thinking of the relationship with another person as modeling the kind of response demanded of a listener here, a more vivid and apposite image might be created by thinking of a quasi-personal encounter with some feature of a primordial landscape—perhaps a mangrove swamp. In some rare moments, deserving the name of "en-counter," a person might "stop in their tracks" and "listen" to the environ-ment. To do so is not necessarily to assume a voice speaking from behind the landscape. It is, rather, to become attentive to the land, for what it seems to present. It is to enter a relationship in which the humanly "personal" does not hold power, and the desire to project one's own subjective states onto the land around is rebuffed somehow by the very alien nature of what is given, and yet it is still possible to have the sense of being "addressed." Aboriginal dreamings of the land as having its own "voices" may not, on the whole, be well understood by non-aboriginal people, but a point of connection with them may nevertheless be found, if a Westerner remembers moments such as these, when the land seems to "speak"—disclosing its history, its stability or turmoil, its abuse and violation by civilized "man." Not a "subject" in a human sense, the signs of an environment may then yet "speak." Consider an "encounter," in its generic sense—an experience in which some element of personal meeting is evident, its impact on an experiencing Subject made ev-ident in an ongoing sense of having been challenged or "addressed." Now consider an encounter with the "other" in a feature of the land. Does it not remain a very strong case? There, on the cusp between the personal and the environmentally material, the "land" seems to make a demand, to assume the position of one with a voice. Sculthorpe's use of a Japanese theme is capable of creating an effect such as this, where a sense of "voice" is not lost, but transformed from the "personal" in a human sense into a "speech" that is more abstract in its qualities.

b. Encountering Interpretive "Others"

To interpret a piece of music is to engage with it in its capacity to create relationship (see Guck, 1989). It is also, implicitly, to take the risk of noticing
that there is an "I" involved in understanding, without whom the content of
abstract forms would not be known. This "I" of the sign-user, the "interpreter" who brings to bear, or draws out, the "interpret*ants*" of a given set
of signs, can easily be rendered invisible, as no more than one who acts as
the vehicle of interpretation.[6] Allowing a disappearing stunt on the part of
an interpreting subject is not, however, a strategy observed without discom-
fort by those who are sensitive to the effects of how an interpreter is positioned in relation to a large array of possible differences—historically and
culturally, with respect to their gender and sexuality, in relation to their disciplinary background, or to what instrument they play, and in which performing tradition. Any such difference might, at times, influence the range
of interpretants brought to bear upon a sign, or the kinds of signs chosen as
deserving privilege in a given work or style. A given interpreter might, in
fact, not be limited to one dominant position, and in a postmodern era it
would be more realistic to imagine every Subject who is engaged in interpretation as (sometimes informally) circumscribing a set of positions for
him- or herself, and moving between them with some ease. No one can,
even so, stand at any one time at an interpretive point without position, and
presume to present what they see and hear just "as it is"—the "God's-eye
view." Where a point of difference is one that influences the interpretation,
it needs to be made as explicit as is possible in the given case, so that the
prejudices of background can be accounted for (see Haraway, 1988).

Problems are undoubtedly raised in the process of seeking to make explicit the set of circumstances which have influenced an interpretation, or in
attempting to see how, for any interpreter, a characteristic viewpoint is
formed through the intersection of multiple positions on matters of "difference" such as those mentioned above. Chief among them are the problems
of relativism and psychologism, which converge into statements such as
"you see it that way. I see it differently. Neither way is right, or to be accorded greater privilege." In comparing styles, it might be said, relatively
unproblematically, that "you are a white middle-class orchestral violinist,

and I a black jazz saxophonist. Your 'voice' is not mine." Such an observation could only be conceded. From the fact that violins may be "voices" to those who are involved in a Western tradition of string performance, it does not follow that they *must* be voices for those who belong to other traditions, or that their particular way of constructing "voice" is the only one possible. Difference is just part of the fact that the play of signs is historically located in relation to particular practicing communities. More difficult to reconcile are differences of interpretation that occur in what may be broadly conceived as a single tradition. A particular case of this kind of difficulty arises in the opposition of some feminist writers (McClary, Lawrence Kramer) to an interpretive view which suppresses the impact of gendering on a listener's experience. In assessing the significations of tonal hierarchies and their thematic articulation in eighteenth-century European music, a text like this might, for example, be proposed:

> You are socially identified with the empowered masculine mainstream, and I am systematically marginalized as "feminine." You find "profundity" and even "greatness" to be a potential of many tonal movements of the Classic-Romantic era. When you note the triumph over conflicting forces that is achieved through the eventual hegemony of the tonic over the "feminine" second-subject's key, you find satisfaction in this re-assertion of tonic control. I understand the same kinds of relationship as oppressive, mirroring as they do the eighteenth century, aristocratic social order, where to be feminine is to be subject to control. When I hear works of this kind I *hear* them as signifying "oppression"—and as doing so under the guise of "depth" and "normative ordering."

A conservative interpreter, especially one influenced by an hermeneutic tradition, might object to the feminist's comment above by saying that "the interpretation of signs should be attuned to the unfolding of historically apposite descriptive terms. The feminist critique is anachronistic, as far as eighteenth-century modes of thought are concerned." If pushed to an extreme, this objector might even say that "this feminist is doing no more than projecting her own current concerns, and psychological difficulties, onto traditions of the past." In a rebuff such as this, an interpretation put forward as drawing out a currently shared "code" is either relocated in the feminist interpreter's mind as a personal idiosyncrasy, or dismissed as a stance that is ideologically driven. This last move, towards a dismissive extremity, is, however, one that could be avoided, even by a counter-interpreter who wished to restrict interpretations to historically relevant codes. A good reason for doing so (quite apart from avoiding ad hominem objections to an interpretation) might be found in the difficulty of labeling any articulated position as "merely psychological," with the implication that it lacked any publicly available sense. If an interpretation is in any way intelligible, it is so because it invokes codes that are not outside the play of signs, and thus intrinsically inaccessible to public scrutiny (or intersubjective understanding), but are part of a shared discourse. Even if judged "wrong," because the code invoked is not one deemed most apposite, the interpretation cannot be dismissed as evidence of a private psychology alone, even if the individual putting it forward adds to it his or her own personal nuance.

A committed relativist in aesthetics could reply to this disagreement between the feminist and hermeneutic scholar with the comment, "If such different responses to a single set of tonal relationships are possible, it cannot be claimed that there is any stability in the tonal style's signifying potentialities at all. But this does not matter. The logic of 'true' and 'false,' 'right' and 'wrong' is not apposite to this domain of experience. We need a multivalent logic instead" (see Margolis, 1995). Such a stance would be heard as deflationary in the extreme by a person in search of a high level of certainty in assessing the truth of a given "reading" of a work—little short of throwing up one's interpretive hands and saying "anything goes" (Kivy, 1997). A semiotic "take" on relativism might, nevertheless, serve to soften this dis-ease. Couching his or her position in terms only somewhat more guarded than those of a philosophical relativist, a semiotician might say that "any Subject's position in relation to a work's content will differ from that of others, and will be such that the modes of signification drawn out could well be at odds with one another. But that does not make the interpretations "merely subjective." Styles, or works within them, are able to support an analysis of different kinds of signs, as examples of the competing codes available within a single musical—and cultural—community. One kind of sign need not be superseded by another, or embraced within it, so that inconsistency is suppressed. Despite that, it may be possible to distinguish the "troping" of one sign upon another, or the creation of various levels of complexity. "Profundity" in overcoming opposed forces within a single character and "oppression" in suppressing difference are each higher-level "codes" (in Eco's terms), or "tropological" interpretations of a single set of relationships."[7]

~

To gain some purchase on the need to locate an individual "subject-position," or personal point of view, within a broader social and semiotic framework, it may be useful to consider a non-musical case. In common English usage, it is not unusual to find tranquility in references to a "calm" sea, to think of a call to attention, with military connotations, in the stridency of a trumpet fanfare, and to associate fiery colors with danger. If I were, then, to say of a character that he found an expanse of still water disturbing, strident sounds welcoming, and a fiery scene in an artwork as bearing no oppressive connotations, I would be asking my reader to construct a fiction of his past, which would include an account of the alternative set of codes that might have formed his preferences. I would be seeking, that is, to elicit a move to a new level of interpretation, one where it would no longer be the most familiar interpretants of signs that were to be identified, but the factors that could contribute to an alternative set of responses, one of "seeing" the signs differently, or of picking out different possible interpretants altogether. A resort to fiction is not even necessary to illustrate the first case—that of an expanse of calm water as "disturbing" in its effect. An Ethiopian visitor came (in the summer of 1997) to see his son in Melbourne, and was taken by the son's Australian friends on a visit to Port Philip Bay. Never having seen an expanse of water so large in his life, the man's response was not the one expected by the local coast dwellers. For them, it might have been the extreme heat of the January day that stood out as oppressive, the expanse of calm water a welcome invitation to cool off. For the older Ethiopian man, the choice of elements as signifying was markedly different. "Would you like to walk on the jetty?" they asked him. "No," was his reply, "I have my own religion, my own way to die."[8] You see now a subject whose interpretive response is differentiated by the culture, geography, and climate of his own experience, and to make sense of the remark, you need to make a leap into his background, to guess at the process of selection that might have drawn out this watery potential to signify danger of a mortifying extreme. Does water signify an existential threat? Well, it can, if its *extent* leads to visions of engulfment, or the shocked recognition of a merely human person's diminutive size. The comparative stillness of the bay is not, then, the thing that signifies, but the expanse of an ocean that can indeed overwhelm. Here is no trivial mistake about calmness in water as "tranquility," but simply the selection of a different attribute of the water as having the power of a sign. To some extent this response is "personal." The visitor has just experienced a moment of profound confrontation, a disturbance asking not derision from his rather startled audience, but for a more sympathetic response. The very *possibility* of sympathy is, however, created by the fact that the Ethiopian's response is not "merely subjective," in the sense of being inaccessible (or, in Wittgenstein's terms, a "private language"), but a different reading of possible signs. Without descending into psychologism, it could be said that the background of the Ethiopian man, in a land-locked country, leads him to select elements as signifying that would not be selected by locals under the same circumstances, but might be selected if they were imagining a different context, such as a lone yacht voyage in the mountainous waves of the Southern Ocean. Saying this has the advantage, also, of not discounting the powerful *personal* effect of this semiotic moment. The personal can thus be re-centered, as made evident in unique interpretive moments, without being saddled with the pejorative sense of the "merely psychological." Once this renegotiation has taken place, it also becomes less of a temptation to seek the Subject's vanishing act, as if signs could be interpreted without an account of positionality—of where the interpreter is "coming from." It becomes more a point of interest to meet the interpretive "other," the one whose position makes his or her way of seeing and hearing draw upon codes so much different from one's own.

In returning from this general illustration to an artistic or musical case, a first rejoinder might be that in the case of cultural products, all interpretive responses are not equal, and one selection of possible signs just does not carry the authority that another might have. This, again, is the historical hermeneutic scholar's point. "The fact that you're 'coming from' a position that is sensitive to systematic forms of oppression does not entitle you," he or she might say, "to read 'oppression' in every hierarchical structure that you find." "Your reading is 'subjective,'" continues the deflationary analysis, "not because it fails to use any recognizable codes of interpretation at all, but because it draws upon them in a way that reflects the priorities of contemporary feminists, as if their experience had greater authority (in determining significations) than the kinds of terms used historically, or which are maintained within the tradition of a musical community." At this point the hermeneut is not displaying a simplistic "psychologism," which assumes falsely that meanings can proceed from private minds, but is making a more serious objection about the need for an historical rapport in the forms of signification recognized. The problem raised is not only the one hinted at in the last chapter, of "who gets to claim legitimacy, as being part of an historically continuous tradition, or as having authority in interpreting it," but a further one—"can radical, historically critical interpretations, ever be justified?" When looking at the question of authority, it has to be acknowledged that fragmented postmodern communities do not have the closure and autonomy that might be imagined as existing in some more traditional groups (such as the Samaritan community discussed by Ruth Katz, 1997) and, as noted in the last chapter, the practices that make up a tradition cannot be circumscribed in a rigid and exclusive way. Who gets to claim the legitimacy of being part of a practice is not, then, fixed inexorably, and claims of authority cannot be made as absolute. On the other hand, recognizing multiplicity should not lead to a repression of any desire to exercise evaluative discrimination when listening to (or reading) the interpretive responses of others, and an attainment to historically used "codes" is one way of developing the necessary discrimination. When looking at the further question of whether radically critical interpretations of a past style can be accepted within an historically attuned interpretive community, a first move might be to recognize historical works as performed *now*, not as museum pieces, but as events that are capable of gaining resonances with contemporary ways of hearing (or seeing) things—heard as they are, inevitably, in the light of events (both musical and non-musical) that have succeeded them. The main responsibility of an interpreter is then to "flag" the move towards a more contemporary referential frame, rather than working within it as a sine qua non of current discourse.

3. *Rehabilitating the Subject*

a. Semiotic Subjects and the Metaphysical "I"

A single factor creating some commonality between disparate traditions of twentieth-century thought is a reaction against the Cartesian splitting of "mind" from the tangible circumstances of thought—a splitting of mind from body, or the "illusions" of sense. This reaction is as evident in the work of semioticians, hermeneutic scholars, and deconstructionists as it is in philosophers of mind. Understanding between people is taken by Peirce to depend upon the use of signs shared within a community of discourse, the conditions of social life leading to the formation of a "mind" that is shared. His reference to the social context of a sign's usage makes his view of meaning compatible with that of the late Wittgenstein, who rejects the very possibility of a private language and finds any term's meaning to depend upon the conditions of its publicly accessible use. In both Peirce and Wittgenstein, a fundamental concern is with the conditions that allow for the possibility of any meaning at all, and the answer—they find—has to be in the location of "mind" in a social context, where its accessibility does not depend upon lone introspection, or even need it.

When reflection moves out of the philosophical "laboratory," where the conditions of *any* signification or meaning are of concern, and into the diverse contexts of cultural interpretation (whether relating to textual, visual, musical, or performative items), the terms of discussion do not, it seems, radically change. A need remains to see attributes of "mentality," or subjective life, as consisting in, and made accessible through, tangible signs, if a resort to some kind of mysterious inwardness as progenitor of meaning is to be avoided. For Hans-Georg Gadamer, no interpretation of a text or artwork can be judged as merely "subjective," because the very capacity to make judgments of this kind depends upon the interpreter's participation in the traditions of an historical community. The community is given responsibility not only to teach some general criteria for judging artworks, among other things—the conditions for what Immanuel Kant refers to as "taste" (Kant, [1790] 1952: 75 ff.)—but also to supply the neophyte interpreter with examples of good judgment, as the model for his or her own practice (Gadamer, [1960] 1992: 30–34). The irremediable individuality of aesthetic judgment envisaged by Kant is, in Gadamer's reading, a falsely construed subjectivism, which fails to note the formation of even an aesthetic mind within a community of practitioners, where the criteria for judgment are formed.[9] Gadamer's reading of Kant does not do full justice to the relationship of "aesthetic ideas" to "concepts," as Kant envisages them, but it does provide a discursive forum within which Gadamer can assert very strongly that the terms of aesthetic judgment are ones that are shared, having been learned through a practical assimilation of their use in a community. Although he by no means underestimates the personal impact of involvement with historical texts, or works of art (Gadamer, [1960] 1992: 67), the precondition of any more "personal" experience is, he emphasizes, a socially formed understanding.

Although the French movement of deconstructive criticism does not have any strong ties with the hermeneutic priorities articulated by Gadamer, it does have this much in common with them, that the "intentions" of an author are not imagined to be transparently evident in a text. A deconstructive analysis of a text will show that its play of meanings depends upon differences that exceed any overt intentions attributable to its author. As meanings are constantly deferring to later interpretive moves, no originary state can be imagined as fully predicting them and, the analysis might show, the meanings can very well assume a suggestiveness that undermines a sense of authorial control.

One consequence of avoiding the pitfalls of "psychologism" or "mentalism"—imagining the mind as a source of meaning quite apart from its participation in a play of shared signs—is to weaken very markedly the "subject" as lone or autonomous. With a questioning of the role or constitution of a "subject," ideas of the "personal" or "subjective" must necessarily be implicated as potential problems, for the obvious reason that they are extensions of the "subject." To be questioned here, however, is the seeming blindness with which the steps taken in opposing a dualistic metaphysics are so often trodden again as a presumed path to resolving problems of the Subject's role in artistic or ethical activities—problems belonging to the "normative" aspects of philosophy (aesthetics, ethics, logic), and also to interpretive theory (hermeneutic, semiotic, or deconstructive). "Mind" and "creative or interpreting subject" do, indeed, need to be linked. So much cannot be questioned. But (to put it in Wittgensteinian terms) it might be considered also that the metaphysical "I" and the creative or interpreting "subject" might not always be equivalent, as they engage in different language games according to the disciplines within which they operate. A "family resemblance" is established between these terms by the idea of the "I" as "one who knows," but it cannot serve, in practice, to force them into playing equivalent roles. A Cartesian "subject" is a metaphysically isolated figure, thinking himself into being. This isolationist presumption need not, however, be attached to the notion of a "subject" as one who plays a creative role within an artistic tradition, or who offers interpretive perspectives of genuine originality. This latter kind of Subject (a Cultural Subject) is, by definition, one who does not isolate him- or herself. As seen in chapter 1, a performing artist cannot realistically assume a God-like position of originating his or her own performing "persona" through a spontaneous act of thought (or imagined self-projection) without any reference at all to received traditions of performance practice. Nor can a composer create in a vacuum, to put sounds together which have no relation at all to styles previously heard. Even if his or her practice is formed by a reaction against received traditions (as Schoenberg's was), or seeks deliberately to thwart tired Western expectancies (as in the works of John Cage), it will be in its *negation* of the familiar that it will be understood—at least to some degree. To complete the trilogy, a writer about music cannot acquire the first tools of aesthetic discrimination, without participating actively in practices that direct his or her attention towards some differences of tone or style worth noticing. Each of these cultural subjects belongs to a shared tradition (or a set of them). As a Subject, he or she does not, then, originate ideas *ex nihilo,* but takes what is given as a starting place for the work of new presentation, or creative change.

Establishing cultural subjects as socially formed should now make it less threatening to recognize that their creative and interpretive position as Subjects cannot be explained *merely* as reproducing a set of existing signs, without modifying them. Recognizing the metaphysically benign character of the idea of a creative "subject" may have been inhibited by the fact that Romanticism supported the conceit of creative independence, elevating the "artist" to a position of originary power and social isolation where his need to draw upon a shared set of compositional conventions was obscured at all costs (see Meyer, 1989). Reaction to such excess, invigorated as it now is by the impulse to avoid "metaphysical" pronouncements, can certainly provoke a denial of the Subject—even as one who takes up the possibilities of a shared language and realizes them in new ways—but such a denial is a confused one, and brings with it an unnecessary loss of personal categories, or possibilities of relationship. As it is important to avoid reproducing the steps toward confusion, they will be reviewed, and their consequences further contextualized, before moving on (in the next section) to further discussion of what the "personal" could be.

The first step is a move away from a Cartesian position, which assumes the mind as originary, by taking a compensatory stance (exemplified in both Peirce and Wittgenstein) where the shared use of language as the condition within which "mind" is formed is given some emphasis. The step of confusion is to translate this compensatory stance directly into one deemed to dissolve the problem of originality in artistic or interpretive activities. The attitude of an artist or interpreter is then taken to be the contingent result of his or her involvement in a shared social game, and the sense in which either the creator or the interpreter of a work can be thought of as holding a "personal" stance, expressing a "subjective" position, or being "original" becomes problematic. It has to be acknowledged that this result is not destructive in all respects. It may be a positive gain to deny the "subjective" as a position that is intrinsically unintelligible or private, because doing so takes the force out of pejorative uses of that term. A peremptory dismissal of an interpreter's reading of some work as "subjective," before shared interpretive codes had been considered, cannot hold force if the interpreter's subject position is understood to have been socially formed. An insistence on the semiotic formation of understanding and creative activity is also useful in warning against any false deference before a felt "mystery" of creation, with musical contents felt as ineffable, mysterious, or the revelation of the composer's unspeakable "genius." Some ambivalence could nevertheless be felt about the weakening of the creative or interpreting "subject," if it leads to an inability to countenance any evidence of original, creative, and singular work, or of musical experiences that are "personal," in the sense that they cannot be reduced to a stereotypical pattern (Cordner, 1998). It is a paradoxical effect that the "subject" of experience can seem to dissolve into a play of social differences, at a moment in intellectual history when it is those very same sensitivities to difference that make it imperative for an interpreter to assert his or her position as "subject," announcing where he or she is "coming from"—locating him- or herself in the various plays of difference as if to constitute a "position" as subjectively his or her "own" (Guck, 1997).

The problem of locating the "subject" within a Peircean view of the sign is not intractable, as has been foreshadowed in chapter 2, and the interest inherent in doing so may become clearer when it is noted that a weakened or ambivalent sense of "subject" affects all participants in cultural traditions alike. The originating "mind" loses its authority, to be interpreted not as disclosing its own transparent intentions through its texts, but as exemplifying various patterns of shared signification. And if originary intentions become weak in their force, when dissolved into the language of semiotic difference, it would be foolhardy to assume that any interpreter's presumed "mental" or "personal" response could somehow carry a greater authority. Neither in the author nor in the interpreter does the "subjective" carry a weight that it might once have done, when "minds" were understood not as semiotically formed but as somehow *behind* the signs. It is nonetheless possible to find a place in interpretive discourse for the genuinely "original" composition, or "personal" response, and to do so without slipping into the assumption that the originating or interpreting mind is entirely independent of the forms of signification learned in the process of cultural socialization. The answer to "the problem of the subject" does not need, either, to come from some remote place, but is in fact implicit in Peirce's philosophical framework for developing his notion of "sign" itself. As seen in chapter 6, Peirce's framework allows for the indeterminacy of general signs, as a set of potentialities whose realization is never fully determined. And it allows also for possibilities of qualitative signification which may not yet have been realized, and whose description may at times seem "vague," in tolerating more than one possible use of terms as capturing the signified quality—however inadequately (due to the mismatch between musical and linguistic forms of signification). If possibilities for new kinds of quality to emerge are part of the domain of signification, along with a potentiality for new realizations of general signs, this domain is one that embraces the need for *choice*. The apparently self-propagating agency of signs, mentioned in chapter 8, is balanced by the activity of human agents making choices among signs. Where there is choice, there is individuality, not mere determination. Looked at another way, even an apparently passive response to some situation may betray an individuality which suggests interpretive agency, while seeming to present the Subject as being "affected" by what he or she perceives. The life of a world of signs is such that it forms, but is also transformed by, acting and reacting minds, whose interpretive mediation of the world is not "turned off" even in moments of seeming passivity. Uncertainty may be characteristic of the way that signs seem to reproduce themselves, yet that very uncertainty is the condition of a subject's freedom to move among and transform the modes of signification that he or she has received.[10]

The ethicist, Christopher Cordner (1998), has pointed out as an imperative that the "personal" be recognized as something more than a merely passive result of various "social forces," such as those represented in received interpretive codes. The nature of his concern may be illustrated by returning to the story of the Ethiopian man, viewing a large expanse of water for the first time. In viewing the ocean bay, this man selected *expanse* as the signifying factor, rather than noting the relative absence of turbulence. Despite this difference from the more common local response, the motivation for his religious fear was seen as readily restatable in terms that were publicly accessible, as part of another "code"—"water as overwhelming." Because this form of signification is understood by other people in different circumstances, it cannot be taken to reflect a state of mind peculiar to that man. It would, even so, suggest a *lack* of understanding, not a demonstration of semiotic mastery, if someone were to fail to accord this experience a due degree of "personal" power in the life of this particular man, irrespective of the common language he has drawn upon in describing it. To reduce the moment of a man's first confrontation with the ocean to being a token of a type of language use would be to miss entirely its tenor of "significance" for the man. It is certainly true to say that this is an example of reading signs in an unexpected way—selecting an unusual feature in the seascape as bearing the power to signify. Despite that, it cannot be denied that this moment had an intensity and a timing entirely its own, which could only be reported effectively by the man himself, or one who observed him at that time, and although common codes such as "ocean threatening death" must unavoidably be called upon to explain his state, they are generalities which will always remain inadequate to it, as a particular (subjectively extended) moment in time. As pointed out in this book many times before, no general sign (whether legisign or code) can, of its nature, fully predict the particularities in which it will be embodied. It can create a framework, a reference point, or a collection of terms within which to describe an experience, but it cannot contain the precise qualities of that experience itself.

The qualities of an experience do not need to be viewed as "ineffable" by default, and thus to be rejected as merely "private," just because they fail to be captured by generalities. They could be dismissed as such, by one (like the early Wittgenstein) who held a view of language which emphasized labeling, that is, the attachment of general terms to objects, and their description in propositional sentences. In fact, as Peirce (and the late Wittgenstein) recognized, they do not need to gain the ignominy of being positioned "outside language" at all—as if "language" consisted in such a limited set of cases. Instead, they may be seen as exemplifying another kind of sign, a qualitative one which may be described in linguistic terms other than those conceived as "labels" in a simplistic sense (that is, they can be pointed at in descriptions which seek to discern qualities of action, or degrees of intensity). It may be recalled that this kind of sign, which does not consist in generalities but rather in qualitative possibilities, is the kind referred to by Peirce as exemplifying his category of "firstness."[11] One of the chief advantages of his broad view, locating signs within a philosophical framework, is that it extends signification beyond the overt play of "difference" (more typical of conventional signs) to embrace qualities which, though learned socially, may have an apparent "immediacy" of effect. When these qualities emerge in contexts which display a complex of general attributes, Peirce refers to them as presenting the "firstness of a third"—the apparent qualitative synthesis of properties whose conventional organization may be analyzed. The emergent qualities discussed in chapters 7 and 8 were of this kind. The "aesthetic," in Peirce's thought, consists precisely in the qualitative synthesis of disparate properties into an experiential whole, which cannot be grasped simply by paying attention to conventional signs (legisigns and "symbols" within that category).

If the experience offered by a complex artwork (or even an ocean view) may have an emergent quality that cannot be captured entirely by reference to any of the general signs that contribute to its effect, the realization of that possibility may say something of the attitude taken up by the Subject whose experience it is. From the story of the Ethiopian, the aesthetic moment might be understood as uniquely "personal," in that it involves an experience with an intensity and duration quite particular to the individual concerned.[12] Kant captured this possibility well in his definition of the "aesthetic idea" as "that representation of the imagination which induces much thought, yet without the possibility of any definite thought whatever, i.e., *concept,* being adequate to it, and which language, consequently, can never quite get on level terms with or render completely intelligible ([1790] 1952: 175–176).[13] This Kantian sense of an aesthetic moment need not be read as intractable in its "subjectivizing" tendencies, found by Gadamer ([1960] 1992) as distressing because they are destructive of the *sensus communis* (or commonly learned feeling), but can be read instead as offering a positive sense to the "personal" in aesthetic understanding.[14] As Gadamer has set himself up in opposition to Kant on this point, with an emphatically expressed desire to avoid the "subjective" as the presumed content of aesthetics, a brief diversion will be taken here, to address the issues he raises with Kant's position. A place for the "personal"—as Kant describes it as intrinsic to the entertainment of an "aesthetic idea"—can be retained without isolating the aesthetic unnecessarily from the culturally learned, by extending the Kantian notion of "understanding" to include Peirce's non-conceptual signs (which may be learned).

It is true that Kant's judgments of "taste" may seem to be "merely subjective," as Gadamer suggests, and that he encourages such a view by insisting that "taste should be an original faculty" (1942: 75). A reference to mental "origins" is one that throws a spotlight on the Subject's role, in a manner that could cause alarm in its suggestion of ideas coming from nowhere in particular but the Subject's mind. Take this comment, instead, as a slightly overstated observation that judgments of taste need to be "owned" by the Subject, or he or she cannot be said to be having them at all, and it becomes less problematic. The "originary" aspect of taste (or judgment) is essential to Kant's "aesthetic idea" and can be better understood by exploring the ways in which this "idea" is constituted. Kant's way of describing it sets up the "aesthetic idea" in contrast with "thoughts," "concepts," and (implicitly) "understanding," the content of all of which can be described well in language, and hence shared or learned. In an exaggerated reading, Kant might be found to position an aesthetic idea on one side of mental experience —as an idea coming from the "imagination"—and to place more definite "concepts" on the other mental "bank," with the river Styx in between. Aesthetic experience then finds itself standing at an opposite pole to acts of "understanding," unable to be captured in language, or to form any bridge to "the other side," where it might be linguistically shared. The impasse of this polarization then starts to reproduce itself, generating a whole series of binary pairs: the "aesthetic" opposed to the "conceptual," the private to the public, the personal to the inter-subjective, the irrational to the reasoned, the "imaginary" to the objectively given. (It might be tempting, even, to find a reflection of the entrenched polarization of presumed feminine and masculine traits.) An answer to the impasse is not, however, to attempt a crossing of the mental Styx, attributed here to Kant, but to relocate the Styx as an imaginary phenomenon in itself. The opposition will not stand as fixed and impassable and is unnecessary to Kant's constructive point. His point is that an aesthetic moment cannot be contained in or predicted by the "concepts" acquired in learning, no matter how thorough that learning is. By setting a limit on the predictive power of conceptual learning, he makes a space for the aesthetic as another *way* of approaching the world, one that must, as Scruton ([1974] 1982) says, give greater credence to "appearances" and be realized in individual experience. This point is not one that needs to be disputed in itself. To be disputed is only the problematic division of mental "space" that seems to arise out of it, an impassable obstacle, leaving the "aesthetic idea" private and inarticulate—"personal" in a derogatory sense. The answer is in questioning the basis of the division. Once it is seen to rest on a view of "understanding" which is limited in its emphasis on the propositional functions of language, it does not seem so insurmountable after all. The mental division only manages to gain such credence through the implied conflation of "understanding" and "learning" with "verbal proposition," all of them standing on "the other side" from aesthetic experience. Revise your notion of "understanding" to include the non-conceptual and your view of language to include the non-propositional, and you will find a way to cease the imaginary entertainment of an impassable mental divide.

By denying that "concepts" are *adequate* to the formation of aesthetic ideas, Kant does not effectively exclude all rational activity as relevant to the *learning* of aesthetic judgment, although that is the direction in which his argument moves. Kant's presumption that "learning" and "understanding" are irredeemably linked with "concepts," leads him unavoidably to assert that aesthetic judgment cannot be "learned"—and that the aesthetic moment cannot effectively be assimilated to any notion of "understanding" at all. If learning (especially by the imitation of models) is an activity effective for gaining conceptual "understanding," it is not, he implies, an activity that will give anyone a knack for having "aesthetic ideas." But this is where a Peircean view of signs can help, in widening the picture of rational activity, to include a wide range of non-symbolic, non-conventionalized signs (i.e., qualisigns and sinsigns), as well as signs whose dependency on laws for their reference is only partial (e.g., linguistic indices). In Peirce's terms, Kant's aesthetic moment draws out a Quality in some object in the world, or some artistic work. This quality depends upon, but goes beyond, the purely conventional (especially symbolic) forms of signification learned within a community, and attains a singularity of its own. Its interpretant needs to include a "feeling" entertained by the Subject (a capacity for which is learned) and cannot be simply reference to a law. In some cases, the quality may supervene upon various kinds of conventional signs, making unique syntheses of them (as discussed in chapter 7). In that case it still needs to be "felt," and to occupy a particular time in experience. It is no mere abstraction.

This way of framing the "aesthetic" retains in it a positive sense of the "personal," as that which is known in the understanding of a qualitative sign, including those found in moments of synthesis where higher-level qualities are perceived. The aesthetic content does not become publicly inaccessible, because the processes of discrimination allowing the qualities—and their significations—to be understood are learned through participation in an artistic community. "Aesthetic" ideas cannot, then, be taken as entirely removed from the processes of learning that occur within an historical community—or expelled to an arena where they are fundamentally private. They *are* nonetheless realized in individual moments of experience, which cannot be gained secondhand. Kant is right to suggest that they are "originary" in the sense that no one Subject can "do it for" another. Each must *hear* a musical work, and experience its signifying potentialities for him- or herself, in order to make an aesthetic judgment of it. Few readers would be satisfied for long with the judgments of a critic who had not *attended* the performances he or she was purportedly writing about, even if that critic could judge from others' reports of the player's style that "X's playing of Bach accords (or does not accord) with my taste," and could, without even hearing X, elaborate quite reliably upon the attributes of the relevant style, to create a fictional critique—"he aims for authenticity, on an authentic instrument, but tends to calcify the music as if it were a museum piece"; "she presents a clean and stylistically appropriate rendition on a modern violin, but does not give the music any sense of depth"; "his performance style is overly Romanticized, with the affective pretensions of an anachronistic vibrato." Such fictions could be put across as plausible for a time, just because some criteria of taste are learned within the sub-communities of performance, fit within the range of "tenable opinions" about performances in the cited styles (Gasking, 1996), and can be reproduced as pseudo-responses to a performance, while retaining some degree of "fit." They are nonetheless unfair in their failure to attend to the *particular* in the performance, and in their silence about the interpretation of the works performed. This scenario of a critic creating an entirely fictitious report is, hopefully, a rare one, but it does serve to highlight a problem that can occur even in cases where the critic has heard the performance but failed to move beyond a generalized response to it. No matter how long a listener has been exposed to, say, violin music of the eighteenth and nineteenth centuries, he or she cannot claim to offer an aesthetic judgment of a new performer's interpretation of some work, if his or her text does no more than locate the performance in relation to a recognized style of rendition. Judgments of quality need to be "owned" and individuated in some way. A jaded familiarity with many styles of rendition does not guarantee a "feeling" for the quality of a performance and may at times even inhibit it. That does not mean that a naive and untutored response is necessarily going to do better, as if judgment were to be made in an "immediate" way—unmediated by any kind of stylistic understanding— but it does mean that learning typologies is not enough. Acquiring a knowledge of the range of signification available within styles of composition and performance is the precondition of aesthetic judgment, but remains ultimately inadequate in predicting responses to individual performances. The listening Subject reappears, as more than a processing unit for conventionalized signs.

b. Encountering Musical Works Again

The ethical imperative placed by Cordner on the need to recognize the "personal" attributes of another's experience, rather than reducing it to stereotypical patterns, was based on a reading of the passage from Kant cited above. A response to another person that respects the individual textures of their experience may, he suggests, be thought of as one that attains a degree of "depth" absent from more reductive analyses. This reflection is perhaps inspired by Kant's thought, that a principle designated popularly under the name of "soul"—that which is felt as absent in a "soulless" poem or conversation—may be found in "nothing else than the faculty of present-ing *aesthetic ideas*" ([1790] 1952: 175). A person with such an ability is not limited in his or her judgment to pointing out the schematic, the conceptu-ally formulated, or the "pretty and elegant"—as socially defined. Cordner's thought is that an exposure to literature can aid in developing this kind of capacity. The "depth" and "interiority," so questioned in postmodern dis-course (as personal qualities which speak of an unwanted commitment to a "metaphysical" soul), may, he suggests, be rehabilitated without metaphysi-cal excess, if they are seen as qualities that develop through a close attune-ment to the particularity of any situation, without a desire to reduce it to an example of some known pattern, which can never capture it adequately.

Similar imperatives are at work when personal categories are applied to the process of understanding a musical work. The end of interpretation is not to have produced a graphic analysis, a formal classification, a listing of "codes" and topoi relevant to the work, or even a complex discourse on its modes of signification. It is to have gained an "understanding" of the work, through these (and possibly other) modes of approach. To do so demands a willingness to engage with each new work in a manner that is open to the challenges it might bring to preconceptions of any kind. Even if terms for some aspects of human subjective experience are applicable to elements in a musical work, as part of its signification, it has been shown in this book to be just as likely that the familiar will be transformed and the musically "sub-jective" taken across the boundaries between the personal and impersonal. An encounter with a work is not, as Gadamer points out, to be accounted for in an idealist manner, as a meeting of the "human spirit with itself" in a moment of transparent intuition,[15] but is to be approached more as an ex-perience (attained through interpretive work) of an "other" where preju-dices are challenged, leading to change. The ethical imperative drawn out by Cordner in Kant's aesthetic is also elaborated by Gadamer, through the no-tion of an "experience" (*Erlebnis*) demanding integration. "Everything that is experienced is experienced by oneself, and part of its meaning is that it belongs to the unity of this self and thus contains an unmistakable and irre-placeable relation to the whole of this one life" ([1960] 1992: 67). Lest this should seem an exaggerated demand, the experience of a performer could be considered again. To prepare a work, such as Bach's G-minor solo sonata, for performance, is to engage with its many dimensions, to internalize its possibilities, and to allow its complex demands (both technically and expressively) to extend a previously gained capacity. This is no trivial form of engagement. It demands an intimacy with the work which will, indeed, make it an ongoing "individual" in the life of the one who plays. "I do not play the music," it could be said, but "the music plays me," as it demands and produces "soul" in the Kantian sense.

Afterword

~

Robert S. Hatten

$\mathcal{N}$AOMI CUMMING was a remarkable scholar and dear friend. I first met her during the summer of 1989 at an International Musicological Society symposium in Melbourne, where we talked about her work on the theories of Leonard B. Meyer—an important influence on both her work and mine. Over the years we exchanged ideas about C. S. Peirce, musical meaning, markedness, and gesture in such far-flung locales as Berkeley, Paris, and Helsinki. She wrote what I consider to be the most insightful review of my own book (see her bibliography), and I profited from her philosophically informed arguments in papers and articles such as the ones David Lidov cites in his Foreword. But none of this quite prepared me for *The Sonic Self* when I read it for the first time.[1] The range of musical topics is astonishing, traversing the realms of subjectivity, voice, gesture, and voice-leading, and culminating in their ultimate synthesis through emergent acts of interpretation. Peirce's sign categories and Lidov's perspectives on embodied semiotics provide the framework for Naomi's claims about the kinds of significance to be found in qualities and dynamics of sound and inflection, aspects that are too easily ignored as mere variables of performance.

In 1978 I heard a magisterial keynote address by the great linguist and semiotician Roman Jakobson at the University of Michigan in which he stated that for the arts, everything is "emic."[2] Naomi has perhaps most clearly demonstrated the validity for music of Jakobson's claim, but in making the case for neglected qualities of sound, she has not slighted the role of form and structure (from Schenker to Meyer) in the interpretation of musical meaning. She has found a principled place for all kinds of meaning in a semiotic theory based on Peirce's sign types, but her synthesis of meanings at various levels of musical experience moves beyond Peirce's discrete typologies to an understanding of the often multiply motivated character of musical signification.

Naomi's philosophical arguments promise to help bridge the gap between old and new musicologies in situating (and grounding) both stylistic and cultural interpretations as they affect our various cognitions of quality, dynamism, and convention in music. She has thus "minded many gaps" in our understanding of music, bridging between philosophical/aesthetic and music theoretical approaches to musical meaning, and enriching the speculative categories of Peircean semiotics with recent scientific theories of perception and cognition. Her approach to "mediated representation" and "presence," as well as her development of the concepts of "synthesis" and "emergence," exhibit an awareness of the important issues and an ability to add something new to current debates about meaning and interpretation.

Naomi's faith was radiant and durable, sustaining her through difficult personal times. That she completed her "life work" with this book would be a comforting but too easy assumption, as David Lidov reminds us. She would undoubtedly have had much more to contribute along the lines of this book, and it is up to all of us to carry the work forward. I am personally grateful, however, that she was able to enjoy a measure of professional recognition in both the book's acceptance for publication and the Society for Music Theory's Outstanding Publication Award for her article on Bach's *Erbarme dich*.

Naomi's authorial "voice" is preserved in those words she has left behind, an eloquent "thirdness" requiring our careful interpretation. But those of us who were privileged to know her will miss the "firstness" of her gently inflected and confident human voice and gesture, and the community of scholars will miss the "secondness" of her dialogical engagement with their reactions to her ideas. What Naomi Cumming has left behind, if necessarily incomplete, is nonetheless a moving testament to her life. *The Sonic Self* is an intricately textured defense—and celebration—of the varieties of musical experience, the rich potential of musical interpretation, and the profound depths of musical understanding.

~

Theorizing Generals

1. Real or Nominal Rules?

Rules and patterns of event, dispositional structures or habits of response, these are the stuff of any theory, in Peirce's view. Regularity in the world is met with a predictive capacity in observing subjects, who experience the world adaptively by forming habits of response that take advantage of their ability to predict. Consistent correlations of events lead to the formation of expectancies, or forward-looking, anticipatory responses, as a way of "moving with" the world, gaining synchronicity with its movements and controlling the outcome of events. Reflective activities presuppose a desire for such adaptation. Guided by success in predicting how actions will lead to a certain consequence, habits give rise to more abstract generalizations about relationships of cause and effect, as pertaining to the "world." It is the fortuitous adaptive success of habitual modes of action that leads Peirce to maintain a "realist" view of lawfulness. Habitual modes of action are not only adaptive but are, he believes, evidence of tacitly held "beliefs," which must be in some sense "true" if they are to be effective in helping an organism to survive in a changing world. For those unfamiliar with discussions of this kind, a fundamental concern of metaphysics could be summarized in the question: "Do general principles and rules (or Generals, for short) reflect some attribute that is 'in the world,' as part of its intrinsic ordering, or are they to be regarded more skeptically, as constructs derived solely from interpretive maneuvers by human minds?" A Realist about "laws" (for which I will use the term "law-Realist") will accept that the regularities of experience are a reflection of regularities that are "given," independent of any interpretive intervention. A nominalist, by contrast, will see rules as the result of induction from experience, which may be pragmatically convenient in governing further activity, but which cannot lead to any genuine knowledge of the world (or, in this study, a musical style) as an ordered entity. A further possible position is the "cognitivist" one, described by one Peirce scholar as a kind of "fainthearted nominalism" (Potter, 1997: 79). It is a position in which "rules" are seen as a set of constructs, cognitively useful, but essentially disposable as new manners of constructing reality are discovered and found better able to account for observed occurrences. Causality is a common illustration in discussions of Generals (sometimes called "universals"). Is a causal relationship merely a fortuitous conjunction of events (A, B), repeated often enough to convince observers that B must necessarily follow A (the position taken by Hume), or is it a feature of an independently ordered physical world? Peirce is a Realist about laws ("law-Realist") because he maintains that the very adaptive success, in evolutionary history, of rule-governed modes of response is indicative of their attunement to some aspect of an independently ordered reality. The laws are "real" in that sense.

As seen here, metaphysical inquiries raise the issue of what it is for any aspect of the world, or of experience, to display constancy at all. Are the constancies mere constructs, or are they "in the world"? When the artifacts to be considered in answering this question are humanly created, the additional factor of historical change needs to be taken into account, with a reflective examination of what it is to identify constancies in the styles of a given artistic domain, despite the obvious reality of historical flux in creative practices. Music theory cannot escape a concern with this issue, in its historically adapted form, as it is a systematizing discipline which seeks to identify at least some constancies in music, often by treating styles in a ret-rospectively ordered, synchronic way. In its attempt to characterize some general aspects of pitch structure in eighteenth- and nineteenth-century Western music, a tonal theory (my main concern here) is, for example, sub-ject to the same problems that inhabit any attempt at generality in describing other elements in the world, particularly when those elements have evolved over time. Are the rules of a given theory posed as a representation of some aspect of an independently ordered style, or are they presented more tenta-tively, as disposable interpretive props? How can change be accommodated, while seeking to characterize regularities, or constancies, in this domain? If a given tonal theory displays ideological presuppositions of various kinds, in what sense can it be said to represent "rules" of order that are "given" in the style (broadly defined)? Questions such as these about the status of rules (General types) in music theory can be counted as "metaphysical" because they are motivated by a concern with what it is for a rule (or other General) to be "real," or for its description to be "true" of a given style. (It might also be said that they were "ontological" questions, about the kind of exis-tence a general property can be said to have, or about what it is for a style to exist as an entity displaying certain constancies.) They do not, however, sit neatly in a metaphysical domain, which could be dismissed by some as hav-ing no answer in any case. These questions shade all too easily into episte-mological concerns about what it is to "know" or "understand" a rule or to "hear" it as governing a given compositional context. It has been suggested by writers in more than one musically related field that what it *is* for a gen-eral attribute of music to be "real" is for it to be perceptible. Joseph Dubiel (1998) has, for example, given an eloquent expression to the view that a music theory ought to be concerned with what listeners "hear" in music (or can learn to hear with appropriate instruction). As the formalization of rules whose compositional workings out are imperceptible does not satisfy this end, seeking formalization (or becoming committed to a theory-driven ac-count of listening) is, he suggests, a less-than-rewarding pursuit for an inter-preter who seeks to enlighten people in understanding their own musical experience. Participating in this train of thought, it would be quite possible to declare as musically "unreal" any supposed construct that is incapable of being heard. Skepticism about imperceptible properties is not commonly declared in bald metaphysical terms, it is true, but such skepticism is quite familiar in an only slightly softer rhetorical pose, within the "aesthetic" tradition of musical interpretation (as practiced by those of the "analytic" school). Roger Scruton (1997) has criticized much of the enterprise of music theory, on the grounds that what it *is* for some collection of sounds to become "music" is for them to be *heard* in a distinctive way, and that theorists commonly fail to address the question of how the constructs they find in music are to be heard. Imperceptible properties are not, for Scruton, "in the music," because it is the interpretive possibility of being *heard* that defines the category itself.

The variety of ways in which the term "realism" is used could lead easily into confusion, especially when dealing with an art form where metaphysical issues shade, almost unnoticed at times, into epistemological concerns. Reference to Peirce's understanding of signs will assist in addressing some of the concerns raised in the literature of music theory and aesthetics, as stated above, but his own somewhat idiosyncratic use of terms could also itself become the source of more confusion. For now, it is sufficient to understand that Peirce's "take" on the metaphysical tradition of Realism leads him to attribute a strong role to objective laws, and in that sense he is a "law-Realist." The tradition of Realism (derived from Scholastic philosophy) which he takes to be central is concerned with defending the "reality" of rules or general principles (such as causal connection), irrespective of how they are perceived, its emphasis on the Reality of rules or laws making it particularly apposite to an inquiry into the status of tonal "rules."[1]

A theorist of tonal music would be a law-Realist in Peirce's sense (with respect to the status of a theory) if he or she were to claim that its rules described tonal relationships as having had real power to shape compositions in a tonal style. The rules would then be seen as "discovered," rather than made, and as allowing a theoretical knowledge of causal virtualities in the music, even if a given set of (less than ideal) listeners were found incapable of perceiving virtual causality in some given context—perhaps in the operation of voice-leading or chordal progression over larger spans of time. Such a position is not far from that held by Heinrich Schenker. Convinced that his *Free Composition* had successfully described the interaction of middle to large-scale harmonic progression and extended voice-leading in tonal works, Schenker maintained that the capacity of any particular listeners to "hear" the working out of these rules had nothing to do with the success of the theory, and that his own interests did not have a distorting effect upon it. The theory had, he claimed, unlocked the key to the "masterworks" as they were constructed in themselves. This kind of Realism is not incompatible with reference to the work of a community of minds (in this case, it is actually Schenker's mind that is presumed, as representative of the minds of his tradition) in constructing a view of tonal constancies. A group of "inquirers" comes tacitly to understand the recurrent compositional tendencies which have shaped their tradition, to find a spokesman in Schenker for formulating the "rules" of that tradition. Peirce's position could give sense to this view, which relies on a postulated community—and its self-appointed advocate—to formalize the "rules" that govern recognized constancies in tonal style. The kind of reality being made articulate is, Merrell suggests, the "semiotically real," a term he coins in recognition that what is being described is a set of regularities with real power in an enclosed domain of semiotic activity.[2]

Reaction against Schenker's strong claims for his theory has led some more recent theorists to a nominalism that disclaims the objectivity of Schenker's voice-leading rules as an arbitrary construct in which ideology is strongly evident. Eugene Narmour's *Beyond Schenkerism* (1977), for example, seeks to refute Schenker's theory by showing that its rules do not account for many aspects of melodic patterning, and also that historically changing harmonic practices cannot be accommodated within a rigid set of tonal procedures. His objections could be summarized in the question, "If a theory is selective in the features of experience it chooses to codify, and if it is also unable to account for historical changes in patterning (imposing a set grid of stylistic patterns on changing styles), how can it make claims that its rules are "real," an independently operative set of stylistic proclivities?" Narmour presents his metaphysical position as "empiricist," as one that works from the presentations of sense data towards the construction of provisional generalities, without taking a strong view of any supposed rules. (This position could also be named "nominalist," in its skepticism about theoretical constructs as derived.) Narmour's doubts about the value of generality are not aimed at Schenker alone, but at any theory that imposes an order "from above," failing to account for irregularities in patterning, and for the constant intrusion of novelties within the historical flux of styles. Rules of style are, he suggests, at best provisional. Narmour is not alone in placing this emphasis on the provisionality of generalization. A similar defense of nominalism in music theory has been made more recently by Justin London (1998). Starting from the premise that music is not a science (like astronomy), London argues that the ideas of constancy appropriate to its explanation are inherently different from those that apply to the physical domain, where constancies might be considered more inviolable. Instead of entertaining a "realist" belief that certain general structures inhere in some style, to become a reference point for interpreters, he suggests that music theorists seek a manner of referring to perceived constancies that will avoid their false abstraction, and even reification, as something having existence "outside" a given set of observations. The metaphysically "realist" view is, he suggests, "essentialist" (1998: 114), insofar as it creates fixtures of certain kinds of structure. London's nominalism is one in which "the identity of a particular sound-instance flows from the particular instance to the larger musical category in which it is placed" (ibid.). His concern, in sum, is to avoid the reification of general types or structures into items that have a theoretical life of their own, such that they might be allowed to dictate what can be perceived. The central idea of "nominalism," as captured here, is that types or Generals are no more than the collection of their instances, capable of indefinite extension.

More exploration will be needed before it is possible to decide the strength with which a music theory can be held as presenting what is "really given," even while being aware of historical contingencies. It is, however, my speculative suggestion that the sense given by Peirce to "Realism" could provide a model for taking a relatively strong view of theory even while accepting the reality of historical changes in compositional style, as well as of theoretical fallibility. Peirce embraces pluralism in the scientific community, and change in the adaptive dispositions of organisms that display an attunement to the changing world, even while maintaining a belief that "thirdness," or continuity and order, are aspects of "the world," independent of the proclivities of those who would interpret it. What is "given," Peirce suggests, resists the final imposition of arbitrary constructs upon it. Though theories may change in science, they will, he believes, tend towards convergence on a common view, which reflects an objectively given state of affairs. Without necessarily sharing Peirce's optimism about the future unity of any group of interpreters, it would be possible to maintain that some provisional unity may be achieved on key points in a given domain of explanation, and that where a discipline does not allow for certainty of ascription in all facets of its activity, it can at least distinguish appropriate degrees of certainty for different areas.[3] Tonal rules could be seen as retaining a "real" power, in having guided compositional practice for a considerable historical period, as well as in guiding informed listening, even if they are not fully determinate. London's reminder that "listening to music is not quite the same thing as star-gazing" (ibid.) is designed to dislodge any attempt at giving musical categories (such as Schenkerian Ursätze) a false permanence or quasi-necessity, as if they were Platonic forms seeking materialization, which remained unaltered by any of the contingencies of a material world. This fair warning against equating general types of structure with immutable and causally necessary categories does not, however, warrant a complete resignation from the desire London also expresses that "in our theory-making and in our analyses we describe and debate 'real' musical phenomena and 'real' structural relationships" between structures that are "ontologically distinct" (ibid.: 129). It is no more virtuous to shrink from a tenable strength of judgment, where it is warranted (and borders even on a decidable belief at times) than it is to shrink from describing the relatively indeterminate and the personal with a suitably qualified style of prose. Areas of signification, where ascriptions are much less rule-defined, can better be dealt with if greater degrees of certainty are admitted in the appropriate places.

Both Peirce's logic and his tripartite Categories throw into question any tendency among philosophers to assess entities, or interpretations of them, according to a neat pattern of binary distinctions: existence and non-existence, truth and falsehood or fiction, concrete objects and ("mere") possibilities. Peirce's logic includes a domain of the "uncertain" between the true and false, reflecting his understanding that no simple contrast of decidable fact with pure fiction can be made in answering many questions. Instead of seeking such a binary system for judging the success or accuracy of any judgment, he acknowledges a third logical position, which admits a range of possible and tenable opinions. Once this third position is admitted, it draws attention to "uncertainty" as a characteristic of even some judgments which are accepted as provisionally "true." To get a grasp of "uncertainty" is not, however, a simple thing, as the word itself can play so many different roles. And one of the trickiest aspects of this notion of the "uncertain" turns once more around the question of what it is for something to have certainty of "being" (or to be "real" ontologically), and to be known or asserted as such (an epistemic attitude). It would be a simple matter if people could just recognize, and be certain about, things that are objectively "given," and be appropriately circumspect about things that are possibilities alone, but to state this ideal state of affairs does not solve the fundamental problem of how anyone can know what is "given" (or "real") in the first place. To begin to solve this problem, a return to Peirce's three categories can help, as they provide as a tool for distinguishing different aspects both of what is "given" (metaphysically) and of how it is "known" (epistemically). The "uncertain" appears in each guise.

~

Some aspects of Peirce's categories were summarized in chapter 2, and may be reviewed here (*see* Table A.1). In their dual role as metaphysical tools (distinguishing kinds of being) and as epistemological modes (distinguishing ways of knowing), the Peircean categories make it possible to extend an analysis of the "uncertain" to include both an aspect of what is "given" and an attitude held by a knower when he or she acknowledges the provisionality of a judgment. The certainty of the "Real" (described as an attribute of Peirce's "Secondness") may be found at points of friction, in confrontations with the "other," or experiences of a hardness and resistance from some entity, as it seems to place limits on the impositions of mind. This concrete "otherness" is not, however, something that can be understood in isolation. Any event both realizes qualities which were, until that moment, merely "possible" but unrealized (firstness), and it also instantiates general "laws" whose realization was not fully determinate. Suppose I hear an unfamiliar cacophony. On the one hand, it is recognized in a quality of *feeling*—perhaps a feeling that what is given will not yield (a kind of "firstness"), as when I feel that I cannot impose an interpretation on it according to patterns of sound I am familiar with, but must respond instead to its insistent confrontation. On the other, it may give rise to *reflection* on the constancies or "rules" that might govern the felt "resistance"—those recurrent features of harmonic experience that could help predict more occurrences of like kind (aspects of "thirdness"). Every supposedly concrete entity (second) displays

Table A.1 **Categories**			
	First	**Second**	**Third**
Dynamic interpretant	Feeling	Reaction	Rationalisation
Kind of "given"	Quality	Event	Convention
Ontological status of "given"	Possibility	Actuality	Pattern or rule
Qualities or degrees of certainty	Vagueness	Determinate, singularity	Indeterminacy Incompleteness Generality
Degrees of determinacy	Over-determined (excluded middle does not apply; contradictory possibilities can co-exist)		Under-determined (more/other instances predictable)
Temporal dimensions	Pervasive, undifferentiated continuity	Closed, delimited	Open-ended, forward looking continuity
Descriptive attitude	Suggestion	Assertion	Informed Prediction

possible qualities, which may be vague in their description just because they are not merely tokens of types with familiar names. It also realizes (or resists) laws, whose general potentialities do not precisely predict the given case. If the event both realizes a vague possibility and instantiates some kinds of regularity, its explanation cannot be fully given without reference to these. Because "possibilities" are, by definition, non-categorical, their description may be no more than vague and suggestive. (Even when realized, the quality is more than a token of a type, and is not easily grasped by the name for a type of expression.) Because "potentialities" never fully determine the cases they govern, reference to them cannot be sufficient, although it may help. The "uncertainty" of knowledge is a function of the double-edged force of both of these sides.

The moral of this story is, then, that "the uncertain (vague or indeterminate) you will have always with you," even in the apparently durable and rule-governed. The uncertain is pervasive, though differing in degree for different subject areas. Once this is understood, its consequences should be liberating for those engaged in the interpretation of works of art, where qualities of feeling are hard to define, and the regularities of style cannot capture all that is given in a work. Recognizing a degree of uncertainty in some interpretive task is not an admission of defeat. Its occurrence even in judgments of relatively constant features of the "reality" of some domain (like a musical style) need not lead to an overstated doubt about the efficacy of such judgments. Knowledge needs only to be stated with the degree of certainty appropriate to its subject matter (as Aristotle said). In the case of music theory, the kind of knowledge being sought is one that explains regularities, with a recognition of the range of their potential realizations, but it should not be ignored that no event (whether musical or otherwise) can be captured through the formulation of rules alone.

2. Finding Constancies, Explaining What One Hears, or Seeking Enlightenment?

In working towards a clearer response to questions about the role of rules in a music theory, two further lines of inquiry might be initiated. The first concerns the nature of the explanatory enterprise itself. Is the relationship of general "rules" to the particularities of a work, style, or mode of response put forward as a descriptive or prescriptive one? If a theory is descriptive, its rules will be put forward as a way of accounting for observable regularities, whether in a composition, in a style, or in aspects of perceptual organization. If it is prescriptive, the theory will be concerned with dictating the kinds of regularities that *ought* to be formed in composition, acquired through perceptual learning ("ear training" in an advanced sense), or given interpretive priority. Any prescriptive theory reflects a "normative" view of the values to be sought in a given practice, motivated by aesthetic, logical, or even ethical ideals. A second line of inquiry, anticipated above, concerns the relationship between the metaphysical status claimed for a set of rules and its epistemology. What relationship is supposed to hold between the rules of the theory and the states of mind, or even bodily responses, of possible listeners? It has

318

already been asked, in introducing metaphysical questions, whether the supposed regularities are "in the work" (or style) in a strong sense, or whether
they are instead interpretive conveniences, formed "in theory" as a way for
interpreters to account for ephemeral conjunctions of events and thus gain
an illusion of control. This question takes a stronger epistemological turn
when the vaguely defined notion of interpretive "minds," as entities who
delight in regularity, is replaced by a more differentiated notion of how understanding is actually acquired, by listeners who have an identifiable range
of abilities. In addressing a theory, it could be asked "Is the relationship of
the theory's rules to a listener's perceptions left indeterminate? Is a straight
correlation assumed to hold between formal relationships as composed, and
as perceptually understood—as when the governing rules of a language are
believed to be tacitly "known" by a person who can speak the language,
irrespective of their theoretical knowledge? Conversely, is a knowledge of
rules presented as an ideal that can be attained only through a disciplined
process of acquiring the "right" perceptual and cognitive habits?" The difficulties involved in defining the relationship between a structural theory and
processes of understanding may be appreciated by attempting an answer to
this multiple choice question: Which of these statements is most true?

(a) Analysis leads to the presentation of a structural understanding already
possessed tacitly by competent listeners, although a given listener may
not be able to name their understanding in technical terms, or be
capable of recognizing his/her way of hearing a passage when it is
presented diagrammatically.

(b) Analysis takes an inchoate understanding of a musical passage and
"sharpens it up" by leading to an explicit awareness of its structural
features.

(c) Analysis is an interpretive activity which prescribes a way of hearing a
passage and has no consistent relationship with pre-reflective ways of
hearing it.

The points at issue relate both to the kinds of understanding that can be presumed in a pre-reflective listener and to the implicit values of a theory. If a
structural theory is normative, being committed to a particular ideal such
as long-term cohesiveness in assessing the value of a tonal work, the interpretations it engenders cannot be assumed to present what is heard by a pre-

reflective listener. At best, it might exemplify answer (c) above. This could be taken as the position of Schenker's theory. Although the theory has descriptive elements, it is normative insofar as it makes tonal unity, as well as the embedding of many tonal levels within the work, the deciding factors in assessing a work's comparative value with respect to other works of the Western tonal canon. If, as Nicholas Cook (1989a) has demonstrated, Schenker links his aesthetic preferences with a normative ethical code, and undertaking analysis in his school is designed to lead a student to a greater appreciation of a tonal artwork, with new freedom from what he takes to be trivializing or superficial views, it cannot be presumed that the interpretation made possible by analysis does no more than present a content already known tacitly, or one appreciated in an inchoate manner. An understanding acquired through the time-consuming process of analysis must be one which seems "informative" in some way, giving rise to a perception of qualities in the work that were not previously accessible to the analyst (see DeBellis, 1995). But this account is not quite adequate, because it ignores the foreknowledge required to carry out analysis in the first place. If the student's listening had not already been attuned to some degree to the processes of tonal unfolding, or harmonic scale steps, an attunement that could be made evident in an inclination to hear harmony and counterpoint as progressing with some "force," "dynamism," "will," or "desire," or actively to seek certain kinds of continuation, they would not possess the "specifically musical feelings" (Raffman, 1993) relevant to making the analysis. A further phenomenal moment to be accounted for is that at the completion of formal analysis. It would not, I think, be unfair to say that the end of an interpretive process may, at least sometimes, include an element of recognition, of thinking "that is how it is," "that fits," "that makes sense of my experience." If so, it suggests that something of the content was already "known" but inarticulate, or "weakly non-cognitive," in Mark DeBellis's terms. The analysis might seem "informative" because qualities "felt" had never been represented as sentences in propositional form. An example might make these points clearer. I had known and played Beethoven's "Spring Sonata" for some years before studying any formal analysis. As a young performer, I could conceivably have said something like: "I feel the opening phrase as relaxed, spacious, unhurried, and lyrical. It seems to relax down in those descending passages, and yet I also feel it as having some high points which keep wanting to reach up, until it gets to that wonderful apex on C, in the second-to-last bar. It feels kind of expansive as well as relaxed." At this point I had studied enough harmony that I could have figured out the chords if asked to do so from the score, but could not distinguish them aurally, except to know that the phrase closed in the tonic, just as it began.[4] Many years later, having studied analysis, I become interested in how the phrase achieves the effects I hear. I come to understand that its movement through tonal space is, indeed, unhurried, in that the violin's opening gambit is to flow through an octave space, with decorative elaboration, before proceeding to a harmony in minor, whose root is a third away (D minor, the sixth degree), giving a slightly elegiac or wistful tone in the change of mode, reinforced by an appoggiatura. Its feeling of spaciousness is enhanced melodically by an octave leap on F, before a stronger harmonic change (to ii) supports the melody in coming to a point of rest on B-flat. It is enhanced further by having an articulatory gap—an ostensible "phrasing"—at this point, resting within the II harmony, in the middle of the tonal phrase, before the tonally articulating dominant has even arrived. Both here (at bar 4), and when the dominant does arrive (bar 5), the appoggiatura "sigh" effect is reinforced. The phrase reaches its structural apex on C with the reattainment of the tonic, giving it stability in its expansiveness, before a descent to the cadence brings a close that is at once playful and formally correct.

If I ask now what analysis "does," answers (a), (b), and (c) above could all be relevant to some degree. (a) A non-conceptual "feeling" for its qualities was made articulate. That is, aspects of the music that had been "felt," but not represented in symbolic (propositional) form, were supported by the findings of a more formal vocabulary. (b) The naive way of hearing was "sharpened up," in that aspects of "felt" quality which I did not notice or comment on before became more salient. (c) The analysis also reflected a broad theoretical commitment to the idea of a "tonal phrase," as stipulated in a Schenkerian account of tonality, namely, that it should include a stable point of departure, motion through subsidiary chords to a dominant, and a point of close. For this reason, articulations within the phrase were seen as "breathing spaces" rather than as the beginning of a new tonal idea. The formal description would not, however, be readily recognizable to my "naive" listening self. Nor does it account adequately for every aspect of the melodic patterning I perceived, having given precedence to aspects of tonal relationship. In some sense, then, the form of analysis has driven me to exclude features of listening experience that I might otherwise consider important. When I present the analysis, I am aware both of the points it makes salient and of those it excludes.

Reviewed once more, in terms of the multiple-choice question above, the naive listening attitude has been presented as bearing the basis in "feeling" upon which analyses can be made. In the terms of DeBellis, I have presented it as "weakly non-conceptual," and capable of being sharpened up. DeBellis would, however, argue that the disparity between some naive description and that available to a theoretically informed listener is such that the experiences of listening in the two cases have to be accepted as radically different. Not just a "sharpening up" process has gone on during analysis, but the acquisition of new percepts altogether. By comparison with a theoretically driven perception of content (especially one reflecting a strong commitment to a prescriptive theory), the naive listener's view is, DeBellis argues, strongly "non-conceptual," in that it cannot provide the basis in feeling (or any other kind of response) to predict the perceptual content that theoretical learning will provide. Keeping an open mind on this question, would it not be possible to accept that a naive listener's view can include aspects of both the "strongly" and "weakly non-conceptual"? Could not a theoretically informed listener also retain aspects of the "non-conceptual" in his or her own listening experience? My perception of "expansiveness" is not, for example, negated or replaced by a description of the phrase as having "slow harmonic motion, with rests inserted into its main structural harmonies." These are not mutually exclusive ways of hearing, but complementary ones, where the "weakly non-conceptual" prepares for the more articulate way of hearing, and remains an aspect of it, now more self-consciously understood. On the other hand, my perception of the penultimate bar as an "early linear descent, followed by decorative linear motions from the inner voice" is indeed theory-driven, and inaccessible to the naive view. In this sense, that view is "strongly non-conceptual" in its inability to predict the machinations of a theory-driven claim to "hearing."

Justin London worries that the disparity between a "non-conceptual" mode of hearing and a theory-driven one creates a "bombshell" for music theory, as a discipline that seeks to describe musical attributes believed to be "real" in some sense. "Reality" of description should not, however, depend on finding a way to approximate what a naive listener might be imagined to hear—if indeed naiveté could be pursued as an ideal at all. Knowing that I hear a given performer as playing "out of tune," whereas an unmusical listener fails to notice the bad notes, does not lead to the conviction that my perception is "unreal," but rather to the belief that the naive listener needs aural training. Knowing that I hear a tune improvised spontaneously by a non-musician as ending in a different key from the one it began in, while he seems not to have noticed, does not lead to doubt about the tonal reality of "key." From these simple cases, it cannot be taken that the arbiters of what is musically "real" are those whose minds are uncontaminated by aural training or theoretical knowledge. On the other hand, it cannot be assumed that the arbiters of what is "really" to be heard in a musical performance or style are only those with the most specialized theoretical knowledge, or explicit analytical skill, who are capable of hearing in a "conceptual" manner. It may be that musical "realities" include qualitative possibilities, events, and structures which support plural manners of hearing, and that the mapping between "hearing" and forms of theorization is not uniform between listeners.

'Notes

'Introduction

1. The names of my teachers have been changed.

2. In his study of the musical temperament, the psychologist, Anthony Kemp, does, however, confirm that such strong encounters with a specific instrumental sound are familiar in musicians' experience (Kemp, 1996: 140–141). He also cites research (Brodsky, et al., 1994: 103; Pruett, 1991) suggesting that "as young children, musicians attribute intense meaning to sound, hearing and feeling something in music that they cannot articulate verbally and that they experience nowhere else" (Kemp, 1996: 45). The Hungarian violinist and teacher, Kató Havas, reflects that students drawn to the violin are not infrequently seeking a voice and sound: "In many cases it seems to be a psychological urge toward self-expression. But most often I think it is a longing for the preconceived tonal quality which is so characteristic of the violin. After all, violin playing is the nearest thing to singing, which in turn is one of the most primitive, most spontaneous, impulses of all human beings. But how many of us have the voice to satisfy this impulse? So this psychological urge is transferred to the violin and to its limitless possibilities" (Havas, 1961: 55).

3. A popular film, *Meetings with Remarkable Men* (based on incidents from Gurdjieff's book) gives a vivid documentary account of some of the Russian mystics (including Whirling Dervishes) whose ideas Gurdjieff took in.

4. It was only in 1995 that I came across a central symbol in which the Sufi ideas are encapsulated, "the Enneagram," and began to piece together a more coherent view of what was going on in these strangely intense encounters. In its syncretic and Westernized form, the "Enneagram" is used as a tool for eliciting moments of insight into weaknesses of character (Beesing, et al., 1984; Ticker-hoof, 1991: 146–137). It is a nine-point figure which, in the approximation of Western psychological terminology, can be described as representing personality types or dispositions. Each has its strength, but this very strength is represented as a paradoxical source of weakness, as it compels an individual to act rigidly in accordance with it. To change is, then, to see the weakness and move against its "compulsiveness."

5. This is a defect of one Enneagrammatic "type" (Beesing, et. al., 1984: 167–168).

6. Meyer here defines style as "a replication of patterning, whether in human behavior or in the artifacts produced by human behavior, that results from a series of choices made within some set of constraints."

7. Nagel's purpose in writing the article was to hold a place for "first-person" statements (I feel . . . , I think . . .) in a philosophical environment that was motivated by an anti-Cartesian reaction to replace them with "third-person" observational accounts of others' language and activity.

8. The original maxim was stated by Peirce as follows: "Consider what effects that might *conceivably* have practical bearings you *conceive* the objects of your *conception* to have. Then your *conception* of those effects is the whole of your *conception* of the object" (Wiener, [1958] 1966: 204).

2. Listening Subjects and Semiotic Worlds

1. For a hermeneutic perspective on the cultivation of judgment within a community, see Gadamer ([1960] 1992: 19–30).

2. For further discussion, see Apel (1995: 42), Davis (1972: 6–21), Deledalle (1990: 11), Hookway (1985: 20), Murphey (1961: 111).

3. Peirce denies that there can be intuitions of the "self" or of subjective states ("cognitions") without an object (Murphey, 1961: 111).

4. "Pure apperception is the self-assertion of THE *ego;* the self-consciousness here meant is the recognition of my *private* self. I know that *I* (not merely *the* I) exist. The question is, how do I know it; by a special intuitive faculty, or is it determined by previous cognitions?" (CP 5.225; Wiener, [1958] 1966: 26).

5. Both Steven Feld (Keil and Feld, 1994) and Lawrence Kramer (1995) point out that stylistic awareness and interpretation are part of listening, not an afterthought.

6. The use of "texture" here was suggested by S. Rosenthal (1994: 79).

7. An "event as actual" refers here to a musical event within a work. In Peirce's philosophy, actualities are usually concrete occurrences.

8. He drew a set of distinctions between monadic, dyadic, and triadic relationships when developing his logic. For discussion, see S. Rosenthal (1994: 82 ff.).

9. For an account of markedness theory, see Hatten (1994).

10. Peirce (CP 1.238–1.272, 1902) borrowed a distinction made by the English philosopher, Jeremy Bentham (1843), between the "coenscopic" and the "idioscopic" sciences. Its purpose is to clarify the difference between a form of inquiry which relies on unaided observations, and is thus open to every observant person, and one which makes use of special instruments. The "coenscopic" "contents itself with observations such as come within the range of everyman's normal experience, and for the most part in every waking hour of his life" (CP 1.241, 1902). The "idioscopic," on the other hand, depends "upon special observation" (CP 1.242, 1902; see Colapietro, 1989: 52).

11. In order to make the distinction between the potential for interpretation, contained in the play of difference that defines a sign, and the acts of interpretation in which it is realized, Peirce divides the "immediate interpretant" (the sign's signifying potential) from the "dynamic" one (its realization). "It is likewise requisite to distinguish the *Immediate Interpretant*, i.e. the Interpretant represented or signified in the Sign, from the *Dynamic Interpretant*, or effect actually produced in the mind by the sign; and both of these from the *Normal Interpretant*, or effect that would be produced on the mind by the Sign after sufficient development of thought" (Peirce, CP 8.343; Fitzgerald, 1966: 81).

3. Musical Signs

1. The *Macquarie Dictionary* (which emphasizes contemporary Australian usage) gives priority to this sense of the word, as "something that may be perceived by the senses, esp. by sight or touch; a visible or tangible thing." The *Shorter Oxford English Dictionary* also recognizes "object" in one definition (no. 3) as "something presented to the sight or other sense; a material thing."

2. Roger Scruton develops this term from Wittgenstein's *Philosophical Investigations*.

3. Chapter 7 will take up the topic of "emergence" in more detail.

4. Anne Freadman (1993) gives a more extended account of the tensions in Peirce's thought that support this view.

5. This is yet another reference to the "First, Second, and Third" modes in which interpretants may be realized. For readers of Peirce, it is useful to be

aware that any itemization of points in groups of three can indicate the guiding power on his thought of these three broad categories.

6. One sign I saw in South Australia was decorated by a graffiti artist with the instruction "hop to it!" as an alternative, counterfactual interpretation.

7. Peirce cites the example of "a spontaneous cry" (CP 2.256) as an example of an index that is "taken as" presenting a quality. In his terms, it is a "rhematic" index.

8. Even when not intended, changes in sound can indicate physical states with affective connotation, but the states may, in this case, result from performance anxiety, or other problems, rather than from an aesthetic purpose.

9. Actors in an Australian television commercial sing "Install a Rheem! Install a Rheem! Install a Rheem!" while pictured enjoying a hot shower. They are offering gas-heated hot water as a "possible object" for the consumer's desire.

10. Lawrence Kramer (1995: 19) suggests that the material aspects of sound may seem to "intrude" into the more ordered dimensions of musical understanding. He uses the term "semiotic" in Julia Kristeva's sense (referring to an early developmental stage) in order to refer to this intrusion into the "symbolic" stage.

4. Naming Qualities; Hearing Signs

1. Lakoff suggests that people use categories of a "middle" level of generality to label the generic categories, or to identify a generic example of a category. When finer discriminations are made, they belong to the same category but vary in degree of "typicality."

2. For discussion of the Fodor/Churchland debate on perceptual illusion, see Cumming (1993: 54, including notes 18 and 19). See also Fodor (1984), Churchland (1988), and Fodor (1990).

3. See Lakoff (1987).

4. Jerry Fodor (1990) refers to the end of the "input" process that forms perception as being a "fixation of belief." By this, he does not mean that a conscious process of interpretation has taken place, but only that the sensation "red" is fixed, and it is "believed" to belong to the thing holding it. (See Cumming, 1994, 1997f.)

5. His reference is to the Kantian distinction between "analytic" properties, which apply "necessarily," without conscious mediation, and "synthetic" properties, which result from the interpretive processes of conscious thought.

6. Cognitive scientists (for example, Jerry Fodor) have often used the computer as a model for processes of perception and interpretation. Hilary Putnam

first suggested that the mind could be modeled on a computer, instigating the functionalist approach to cognition. (See Cumming, 1993: 42; Putnam, [1960] 1975.)

7. One caveat needs to be considered before moving on. Any model, including the computer one, needs to be treated with some caution because it can throw up unwanted artifacts. Daniel Dennett has been particularly astute in pointing out models of the mind which seem to make consciousness a *place* or "theatre" where sensory experience stages representations before an inner eye (I). Jerry Fodor's computer model does not escape from Dennett's critique, because it suggests that the processes of perceptual input parade the outcome of their operations before a central processing unit—the all-integrating "eye." In any model like this, a trap is laid by the not-so-innocent spatial metaphor, whereby things are presented *to* consciousness, or located *in* the mind. The idea of a user interacting with icons on a screen could also fall into this trap, given that a normal user is endowed with consciousness (or mentality) quite apart from the computer's operations. In order to avoid a Cartesian split between "mind" and its represented content, it is necessary to imagine the different aspects of programming and representation as actually forming the mind. The programming language stands for unconscious mental operations, and the icons form the contents of consciousness.

8. http://www.digitalrain.net/bowed/perlman.htm

9. http://www.digitalrain.net/bowed/chisholm.htm

10. Recording of Wanda Wilkomirska, 1988. *Polnische Violinmusik*, with Paul Dan, piano. Works by Grażyna Bacewicz, 1909–1969; A. Zarzycki, b. 1937; Ignacy Jan Paderewski, 1860–1941. *Ambitus* amb 97 830.

11. Sandy was five hundred kilometers away, in Leigh Creek, a mining town in the Northern Flinders Ranges of South Australia (I had checked it on the map, to find a little place between the salt lakes, Lake Torrens and Lake Frome), while I was in my home on a peak of the Adelaide hills, sitting with a music stand in front of me and a chair with a speakerphone at my side. Sandy, unlike me, was familiar with distance learning. (I had figured out that placing the telephone on the chair beside me, like a person, was more effective than putting it on the table and leaning over to play, but the enlightenment had taken several weeks.) This weekly lesson, on a Saturday afternoon, occurred after the Leigh Creek football match. Sandy's father, the high school's headmaster, rushed away from watching his sons play Aussie Rules to set Sandy up in the distance-learning lab and telephone me for a half-hour call at this pre-established time. It was to him that I was at this moment giving instructions on how to check for symptoms of poor sound production. I had already taught Sandy how to shift

her left hand into "third position" on the violin, no mean feat by remote control. Diagnosing a problem in making her sound "sing," against the distortion of a radiotelephone, was, however, more challenging.

12. http://www.digitalrain.net/bowed/perlman.htm. Recording copyright © Angel Records.

13. Once, in my teens, I spent a whole summer trying out vibrato sounds. At the end, my mother said, "I don't like your sound. It is like Mrs. K. with a rose in her bosom!" Mrs. K was an elderly music teacher who wore a red rose in the cusp of her low-cut outfit to a concert of her protégés, the bosom of her love.

14. Recording of Sigiswald Kuijken, 1987. *J. S. Bach, Sonatas and Partitas,* Editio Classica (Deutsche Harmonia Mundi) GD 77043 (digitally remastered from recordings made in 1983 and 1990). Kuijken plays a violin by Giofanni Grancino, Milano c. 1700, using a bow by an anonymous maker of the first half of the eighteenth century.

15. Recording of Lucy van Dael, 1993. *Baroque Violin Sonatas,* with Bob van Asperen (harpsichord) and Wouter Möller (cello continuo), on period instruments. Philips 434 993-2. The bird sounds are on the first track: Heinrich Ignaz Franz von Biber (1644–1704), Sonata violino solo representativa in A, "Representatio avium."

16. See Note 10.

17. In an electroacoustic composition, Trevor Wishart transforms a vocal sound into the sound of a flight of bees, forcing a recognition that the "human" and the "other" are not so distinct.

18. A concert with musical items from many cultures is a symbolic statement of a desired state of inter-cultural harmony. Celebrations of high art are no indication of inter-cultural understanding, as something that already exists. They are enactments that attempt to create what they represent.

19. For a discussion of the "value" of something, as measured by the effort expended on pursuing it, see Nerlich (1989).

20. In his 1996 "Boyer Lectures," commissioned by the Australian Broadcasting Commission, the French-Australian Sinologist, Pierre Ryckmans, spoke of the "naive faith in the transforming power of travel" as having "persisted well into our own century" (1996: 56). He quotes the French poet and Sinologist, Victor Segalen, as saying "Let us not pretend that we can assimilate customs, races, nations—the others; on the contrary, let us rejoice in our inability ever to achieve such an assimilation: this very inability is a guarantee that we shall continue to enjoy diversity for ever" (ibid.).

5. Gesturing

1. Manfred Clynes (b. August 14, 1925, Vienna, Austria) immigrated to Australia at age 13, having studied piano under the auspices of the Liszt Ferenc Academia in Budapest, and then became known as a pianist, winning the ABC State Concerto Competitions in 1943 and 1944 and the National Competition in 1946. As an undergraduate, he undertook majors in both music and engineering (B.EngSc, University of Melbourne, 1946). He studied piano with Raymond Lambert. Following his 1946 National win, he was awarded a graduate fellowship to Juilliard, where he studied with Sascha Gorodnitzki and Olga Samaroff-Stokowski (September 1946–May 1949). A Fulbright Scholarship and Smith Mundt award allowed him to undertake graduate work at Princeton University under Oliver Strunk and Arthur Mendel (1952–1954). During this time, he also took a master class with Edwin Fischer (1953). He was best known as a pianist for his performances of Bach's *Goldberg Variations* (Melbourne and Sydney, 1950; London, 1953). (This information was provided by Manfred Clynes.)

2. Email from Clynes, October 1996.

3. One principle, reflecting his experience of Casals, is that *"The power of essentic form in communicating and generating a sentic state is greater the more closely the form approaches the pure or ideal essentic form for that state"* ([1977] 1989: 53). Other principles are as follows: "A sentic state is a single-channel system; only one state can be expressed at any one time. (Exclusivity Principle)" (ibid.: 18); "A sentic state may be expressed by any of a number of different output modalities. (Equivalence principle)" (ibid.: 18); "Regardless of the particular motor output chosen to express a sentic state, its dynamic expression is governed by a brain program or algorithm specific for that state which shall be called its essentic form. (Coherence Principle)" (ibid.); "The production and recognition of essentic forms are governed by inherent data processing programs of the central nervous system, biologically coordinated so that a precisely produced form is correspondingly recognized. The recognized form in turn generates a sentic state in the perceiver. (Complementarity Principle)" (ibid.); "The intensity of a sentic state is increased, within limits, by the repeated, arrhythmic generation of essentic form through E-actons" (ibid.: 25); "Sentic states may be experienced as pure qualities or identities, without reference to specific auxiliary relationships to generate or receive these qualities" (ibid.: 43). That is, it is possible for the subject in an experiment to imagine a sentic state without having to act out the movements associated with it. Clynes uses the term "elogize" to indicate feeling a state without forming mental images. These principles are taken up in modified form by Lidov (*Elements of Semiotics*, 1999: 148–149).

4. Ruggiero Ricci recorded Tchaikovsky's Concerto in D, op. 35, for violin

and orchestra, with the New Symphony Orchestra, conducted by Sargent (London LL172; Richmond R19011), and with the London Symphony Orchestra, conducted by Sargent (Ace of Diamonds ADD 126, SDD126. Decca LXT5641, ND373, SXL2279).

5. This is Meyer's point (1956).

6. Peter Dennison, the late professor of music at the University of Melbourne, was fond of identifying "emotion-laden turns" in Wagner and Mahler. Students would assiduously write "emotion-laden turn" at the appropriate point in their scores.

7. Eugene Narmour's (1990) theory of melodic analysis is designed to capture the subtle effects that arise from changes in each of these parameters.

8. Support can be found for this interpretive stance in the work of the philosopher, Mark Johnson, both individually and with George Lakoff, which suggests that reference to the body is a normal way of understanding not only human movement in space, but other things that can be viewed as "moving" in some way.

9. My own review of Narmour (Cumming, 1992) was perhaps too critical of his concern with characterizing the particular.

10. For further discussion of emergence, see chapter 7.

11. See Tarasti (1994) and Lidov (1999) on agents and patients.

12. Peirce's observation about "symbols" (terms) was that their reliance upon convention for the allocation of meaning was the very condition of their mobility, allowing them to be independent of the need to simulate any "likeness" to their object (the lot of icons), or to engage in any real-world "pointing" at it (as in the case of indices).

13. This paragraph has been taken from my article, "Keeping Up (Musical) Appearances" (Cumming, 1997b: 341).

14. This paragraph has been adapted from my article "Keeping Up (Musical) Appearances" (Cumming, 1997b: 328–329).

15. See the special review section in *College Music Symposium* 29 (1989): 1–80, containing reviews of Edward T. Cone's *The Composer's Voice* (1974) by Fred E. Maus, Marion A. Guck, Charles Fisk, James Webster, and Alicyn Warren, and concluding with a response by Cone.

6. Framing Willfulness in Tonal Law

1. Riemann's complete scheme is: acoustics, tone physiology/psychology, musical aesthetics, musical syntax, music history (Riemann, 1908).

2. "Der zweite Haupttheil der Musikwissenschaft ist der systematische: er stützt sich auf den historischen Theil" (The second main category of musicology

is Systematic: it rests on the historical category and falls under three headings) (Adler, 1885: 11).

3. Schemata are recognized by cognitive scientists as a way of organizing experience (Schank and Abelson, 1977: 41, 70).

4. Note that when "icon" is used here to describe the signifying capacity of an analytic notation—its ability to represent some aspect of the musical structure—its use is quite distinct from that found in contexts where an aspect of the music itself is said to be "iconic."

5. See Meyer (1973). Meyer has also confirmed this explanation of his own decision to me in conversation.

6. Readers familiar with the early Wittgenstein might recognize this predicament as one that he espoused there enthusiastically as the necessary consequence of a metaphysical "realism," properly developed. To be a realist is to be a solipsist, because what is known is taken to be "given," and is not to be knowable in any other way (*Tractatus*, 5.64). A structure recognized is simply "what is," and individual selves must adapt to it.

7. On tonal phrases, see William Rothstein (1989).

8. I am grateful to Craig Ayrey for drawing my attention to this point.

7. Complex Syntheses

1. In defense of an emphasis on affective types, it may be observed that when people use labels for emotions, they organize them into prototypical classes, under which more detailed levels of discrimination can be grouped (see Shaver, et. al., 1987). Cross-cultural studies of how expressivity is recognized in facial displays also confirm a broad agreement among people of different ethnicities about the most basic types.

2. Jerrold Levinson defends the relevance of a musician's normal experience to questions such as this, when he says that "the proof of expressiveness, ultimately, is in the aural pudding: qualified listeners must be reliably prompted to hear that emotion, or its expression, in the music" (1995: 200).

3. I am told that it has been used in a movie to that end, but was not informed of which movie.

4. See Marion Guck (1993, 1994a).

5. Harnoncourt (1995) discusses how a uniformly rounded sound took over from the more variegated sounds of the Baroque.

6. Sebeok made this suggestion at the Summer Institute for Semiotics, Imatra, Finland, June 1996.

7. In representation-based cognitive science, the content is some kind of

representing unit like the digits in a computer language, over which logical manipulations could take place.

8. Such as Fodor's inputs.

9. "It is likewise requisite to distinguish the *Immediate Interpretant,* i.e., the Interpretant represented or signified in the Sign, from the *Dynamic Interpretant,* or effect actually produced in the mind by the sign; and both of these from the *Normal Interpretant,* or effect that would be produced on the mind by the Sign after sufficient development of thought" (Peirce, CP 8.343; Fitzgerald, 1966: 81).

10. Peirce referred to icons and indices as "degenerate," due to their incomplete reliance upon rule-governed conventions.

11. This conception of aesthetic qualities is influenced by Monroe Beardsley's distinction of the non-aesthetic (or technical) from the aesthetic, but it does not entirely embrace it, because the lower-level signs are not deemed "non-aesthetic."

12. Levinson also concurs with the view that an aesthetic feature should be recognizable without the assistance of a discursive process.

13. Marion Guck first suggested to me the idea of knowing music like a person. (*See* Guck, 1997.) It appears as well in Suzanne Cusick's article (1994a).

14. Lawrence Kramer (1995) has expressed concern that music not be situated outside language, as an "immediacy" that cannot be described. By distinguishing musical signification from linguistic symbolization, I do not deny that elements of music are capable of being described and linked with other aspects of culture.

15. It is this aspect of Peirce's categorical thought that is also taken up in Jacques Lacan's characterization of stages in interpersonal development.

16. These two kinds of synthesis are taken from Immanuel Kant (see Kitcher, 1990).

17. Opening up the understanding of expressivity in this way is not a revolutionary move. The actual practice of emotional observation psychiatry, as described in a standard diagnostic text, clearly involves an attentiveness not only to overt movements, but to the flow of thought (including its relative intensity and goal-directedness) and the level of activity of an individual. (See "Depressive Disorders" in DSM IV.)

8. Culturally Embedded Signs

1. To contrast "mere interaction" with "emergent novelty" may itself be an unnecessary binary contrast in this kind of case. If analogies with material processes are to be used, it may be less helpful to think of a simple mixing of elements than of a chemical reaction that yields a new substance, with different

qualities from its constituents (so long as the notion of substance is not grasped with undue tenacity).

2. A speaker once described a "bar form" in Wagner by saying slowly, with great warmth and emphasis, "Its form is A . . . A . . . B!" The effect of squeezing meaning out of an empty structure, without interpretive context, is similar to this.

3. A logician might see in these observations a resistance to the laws both of non-contradiction (which insists that a thing should be "either P or not-P") and of "excluded middle" (which disallows the recognition of middling cases, falling between the cracks of a recognized set of classes). Merrell takes these issues up at length.

4. The paper was read by the musicologist, Lewis Rowell. As it was shortened due to time constraints, not all of its arguments were actually heard.

5. See Treitler ([1995] 1997) against symbolization. Note the sense of "symbol" here is expanded. Lidov mentions the Maple Leaf as a "symbol." Musical listening is *not* the same as decoding. Hearing symbolizations is *possible*, but not an imperative to decode.

6. This theory is not unlike Roger Scruton's Wittgensteinian theory of "seeing as," except that Scruton does not emphasize the intentions of an artist or composer when discussing fictive seeing.

7. It should be noted that to speak of "intentions," in this sense, does not imply an unmediated knowledge of the composer's mind, made transparently accessible through the text he or she provides. The textually constructed "intention" is all that is available, but no text is a pure transmitter of another's mind.

8. On knowledge from testimony, see Anthony Coady (1992).

9. This point, in different form, was made by Eugene Narmour (1977) when he defended the need for attention to new combinations of pitches, durations, and directional motions in forming a melody, quite apart from the "style forms" of which they become part.

10. James Buhler (1998) criticizes Robert Samuels (1995) for falling into this trap.

9. Values and Personal Categories

1. To pursue questions of ontology, see Ingarden (1989). Hermann Hesse's novel, *The Glass Bead Game*, pictures music in this way.

2. When Cusick explores the notion of a relationship with a piece of music, she does so as part of an exploration of lesbian sexuality. I seek here to generalize her idea of mutuality in a relationship with music, but do not thereby presume that I can appropriate the subject position described by Cusick. For a

general discussion of how aspects of sexuality could be seen as relevant to epistemology, see Code (1991).

3. Moore writes of observing the signs of "soul" (Moore, 1992: 4). His "soul" is not a mysterious thing, but a way of speaking of the self who is formed by choosing among available signs. "Soul-caring" is an observation of his patients' daily preoccupations, of activities with signs, those things which form a semiotic "self." "'Soul' is not a thing, but a quality or a dimension of experiencing life and ourselves. . . . Care of the soul begins with observance of how the soul manifests itself and how it operates. We can't care for the soul unless we are familiar with its ways" (ibid.: 5).

4. I follow Moore's suggestion that even aspects of self that people want to reject or eradicate are necessary to them (1992: 5–6).

5. I am indebted to lectures on "Human Nature" by Christopher Cordner, at Melbourne University (March 1997), for this point.

6. In some youthful ruminations on the pronouns "I, It, and Thou" ([1861] 1982), Peirce reflected on the possibility that "the I may be IT—as when we think of ourselves objectively" and "the THOU may become IT—in cruelty or rather hardness." This manuscript predated Martin Buber's *Ich und Du* by some sixty-two years.

7. On tropes, see Hatten (1994) and Parmentier (1994).

8. I am indebted for this story to Anna Hutchinson.

9. A process of learning how to judge wines by acquiring a "taste" that follows the criteria accepted in a group of connoisseurs could well fit with this image of the public nature of taste. Douglas Gasking's discussion of "tenable opinions" (1969) makes a similar point, using examples of this kind.

10. The idea of the semiotic as fundamentally a domain of freedom was suggested to me by David Lidov and is explored by him in chapters 4 and 22 of *Elements of Semiotics* (1999).

11. The need for some sense to be given to the notion of a personal response, or even a form of "inner" life, was raised by Iris Murdoch in *The Sovereignty of Good*, where she defended the idea of a reflective change in attitude against the behaviorist reduction of all thought to possible action.

12. Duration and intensity as belonging to an aesthetic (imaginary) experience are pointed out by Roger Scruton. He also cites "subjection to the will."

13. This formulation of Kant's was drawn to my attention by Cordner (1998).

14. This reading was suggested by Cordner (1998).

15. Gadamer summarizes Hegel on this point. "To recognize one's own in the alien, to become at home in it, is the basic movement of spirit, whose being consists only in returning to itself from what is other" ([1960] 1992: 14).

Afterword

1. In August 2000, when I also proofread the manuscript and tracked down several missing references. I am grateful to Indiana University Press for the kind invitation to write an afterword. The various editors involved in bringing the manuscript to publication (especially copyeditor Penelope Mathiesen) are to be commended for their careful and respectful work.

2. *Emic* is a term coined by the linguist Kenneth Pike (from the suffix to phonemic, referring to the minimal linguistic unit whose invariant oppositional features discriminate meaning, as opposed to *etic*, from the suffix to phonetic, referring to those variable features of performance that are not relevant to the basic oppositional structure of the phoneme). Analogous relationships between invariant and variable features exist for any defined units of a code, but composers and listeners can generate types out of the variable features of a token and categorize singularities that do not require conceptual labels (see Hatten, 1994, especially chapters 2 and 10).

Appendix: Theorizing Generals

1. This emphasis on laws or rules does, however, distinguish Peirce's Realism from that of metaphysical thinkers whose way of framing questions about the reality of general things is focused more on general types of concrete entity (e.g., chairs), than it is on general patterns of event. The disadvantage of Peirce's way of framing his position is that it can lead, if pushed too far, to a kind of Platonism, which finds General patterns to be more "real" than particular things (see Potter, 1997: 76–86). This exaggeration of a strong view of lawfulness is not, even so, a necessary implication of Peirce's thought. Ameliorating any tendency toward Platonism is a counterpoised evolutionary perspective, with a generously optimistic view put forward of the scientific community, as they work together to form ideas of the "real." If, as Floyd Merrell points out (1997: 123), reference is made to the community of inquirers as the source of general ideas, the general cannot be assumed as something that presents itself as an a priori necessity. Insofar as knowledge of the general is seen as being derived only by the formation of ideas within the community, who observe constancies in the behavior of particular things, the Realism being espoused retains an "idealist" sympathy, removing it from a Platonic view of the real as "given" a priori. This way of expanding notions of the real to include regularities known and recognized within a community may lead it to be rejected as a form of realism at all. Peirce's refusal to pit conceptions of the "real" against an "idealist" reference to minds is not one that is easily grasped, especially by those who view these as

antinomies, and even Merrell's critique is skeptical of its success. The apparent friction of allegiances does, even so, make sense within Peirce's evolutionary perspective (sometimes named "fallibilist"). His "realism" consists primarily in the faith that the explanatory generalities arrived at by a community do indeed reflect laws, which have genuine power to govern experience in a given domain, irrespective of the fact that the ideas of the general have been formed by human minds. The main opponent, against which Peirce poses this position, is not that of "idealism" but that of "nominalism," the view that any identified constancies are no more than explanatory constructs, whose power to direct experience is limited. (This position is also idealist in its view that constructs are all that can be known.) He wants to deny neither the role of a community of interpreters nor the objective efficacy of "laws" they identify.

When the term "realism" appears as part of epistemological inquiries, its sense is again modified. An epistemic realist is concerned with defending the "real" connection of perceiver and perceived. He or she therefore accepts the data given to sense as "real," putting the subject in touch with "the world," rather than in touch with his or her own "representations" alone. Metaphysical and epistemic realism may dovetail strongly in the semiotic study of human artifacts, where any entity X is said to have its "existence" by virtue of being "knowable," having been created as the product of a human mind. It can be useful, nonetheless, to distinguish epistemic concerns from metaphysical inquiries in some instances; for example, when defending the theoretical formalization of some non-obvious musical structures as having had genuine constructive power in a given style.

2. Jamie Kassler argues that "Schenker's theory of music is based on the hypothesis that the only reality we may know is that of our own conscious experience." This is an idealist stance, which she refines with the observation that "experience . . . is to be understood not in an individual sense, but as an experience of a whole species (particularly the German species)" (1983: 229). A Peircean "law-realism" does not deny that a community of inquirers is involved in formulating the rules that govern regularities in any domain, but it emphasizes that those rules have real power in shaping reality (and experience of it) independently of a particular formulation. Although a given community may be fallible in their formulation of generalities, the scientific community will (it is suggested) arrive "in the long run" at an understanding of rules that reflects their real power. Floyd Merrell (1997) has suggested that Peircean realism is tainted with an idealist flavor, for the reason that it refers to the community of minds.

3. "Decidable questions," the Australian philosopher, Douglas Gasking, has suggested, can be distinguished from a range of "tenable opinions," where a community negotiates the boundaries of possible interpretation, and these in

Example A.1. Bars 1–3, Violin Sonata in F Major, op. 24, the "Spring Sonata," by Ludwig van Beethoven

turn can be distinguished from judgments made more on the basis of personal taste or inclination (see Gasking, 1996). It could, for example, be accepted that tonality has "real" power in directing the compositional practices of the common-practice period, insofar as it is evident as a driving force within them, and a broad consensus may be reached on its more central attributes (or "rules"), so that basic descriptions at least can be judged fairly as "right" or "wrong." Chord labels, in most Classical cases, would be "decidable." At greater levels of complexity, theorists may differ about structural descriptions in some cases, but there will still be a limited range of options that could be supported as tenable. (Semiotic interpretations, also, would enter this area of requiring support by reference to a range of interpretants familiar to others in the community, without being entirely decidable.)

4. If a musician working with a score is to understand a melodic segment as "gestural," he or she must gain a feel for the "fittingness" of a particular image of bodily motion in bringing together aspects of tempo, rhythmic grouping, pitch organization, and harmony towards an "expressive" end. Having gained a "feeling" for how the moment could be realized, a set of microstructural adjustments —in tempo, and in emphasis—become the practical means of acting it out. I might feel the third bar of the opening to Beethoven's "Spring Sonata" as "expanding," with an image of a relaxed intake of breath, leading to a very slight expansion of tempo while performing the octave leap on F. (See Example A.1.) A structural analysis has already identified that point as linking motion in two octaves, but it has not been informative for showing just how the moment of the leap should be performed, and for this the image of "inward breath" is a help. For a listener, the bodily interpretant plays a somewhat different role. Although a

musician's reference to a bodily image in preparing an interpretation may be overt, listeners should be able to get a "feel" for a passing expansiveness such as this without noticing any actual movement in their body, or needing to interrupt the flow of listening in time in order to capture the moment with a name. Due to its ephemeral and transient role, a gestural moment may not be named at all, or isolated from the phrase of which it is part. That does not mean, however, that it would fail to contribute to the overall effect of the phrase. Whether a "feel" for the moment as gestural is acted out in overt movement, or abstracted into a figure of speech ("having a 'feel' for x" as coming under a certain description) does not matter, so long as it is recognized that a somatically formed "understanding" of movement may be brought into play, even at a subliminal level, and later integrated with other factors to contribute to the understanding of a complex signification in the phrase.

·Bibliography

Abbate, Carolyn. 1991. *Unsung Voices: Opera and Musical Narrative in the Nineteenth Century.* Princeton: Princeton University Press.

Adler, Guido. 1885. Umfang, Methode, und Ziel der Musikwissenschaft. *Vierteljahrsschrift für Musikwissenschaft* 1, 9–11.

Agawu, Kofi. 1991. *Playing with Signs: A Semiotic Interpretation of Classic Music.* Princeton: Princeton University Press.

———. 1996. Review of Robert Hatten, *Musical Meaning in Beethoven* (1994). *Current Musicology* 60/61, 147–161.

Apel, Karl-Otto. 1995. *Charles S. Peirce: From Pragmatism to Pragmaticism*, trans. John Michael Krois. Atlantic Highlands, N.J.: Humanities Press. Originially published as *Der Denkweg von Charles S. Peirce: eine Einführung in den amerikanischen Pragmatismus.* Frankfurt: Suhrkamp Verlag, 1967.

Auspitz, Joseph Lee. 1994. The Wasp Leaves the Bottle: Charles Sanders Peirce. *American Scholar* 63 (4), 602–618.

Ayrey, Craig, and Mark Everist, eds. 1996. *Analytical Strategies and Musical Interpretation: Essays on Nineteenth- and Twentieth-Century Music.* New York: Cambridge University Press.

Bakhtin, Mikhail M. 1986. *Speech Genres and Other Late Essays*, trans. Vern W. McGee, ed. Michael Holquist and Caryl Emerson. Austin: University of Texas Press.

Barnett, Dene, with Jeanette Massy-Westropp. 1987. *The Art of Gesture: The Practices and Principles of 18th Century Acting.* Heidelberg: Carl Winter Universitätsverlag.

Beardsley, Monroe. 1982. What Is an Aesthetic Quality? In *The Aesthetic Point of View,* ed. M. Wreen and D. Callen, 93–110. Ithaca: Cornell University Press.

Beebe, Beatrice. 1982. Micro-Timing in Mother-Infant Communication. In *Nonverbal Communication Today: Current Research,* ed. Mary Ritchie Key, 169–195. Berlin: Mouton—de Gruyter.

Beesing, Maria, et al. 1984. *The Enneagram: A Journey of Self-Discovery.* Denville, N.J.: Dimension Books.

Berenson, F. M. 1993. Interpreting the Emotional Content of Music. In *The Interpretation of Music: Philosophical Essays,* ed. Michael Krausz, 61–72. Oxford: Clarendon Press.

Blasius, Leslie David. 1996. *Schenker's Argument and the Claims of Music Theory.* Cambridge: Cambridge University Press.

Blum, Stephen. 1993. In Defense of Close Reading and Close Listening. *Current Musicology* 53, 41–54.

Brodsky, W., et al. 1994. An Exploratory Investigation into Auditory Style as a Correlate and Predictor of Musical Performance Anxiety. *Medical Problems of Performance Artists* 9, 101–112.

Bryson, Norman. 1991. Semiology and Visual Interpretation. In *Visual Theory: Painting and Interpretation,* ed. Norman Bryson, Michael Ann Holly, and Keith Moxey, 61–73. Cambridge: Polity Press.

Buhler, James. 1998. Review of Robert Samuels, *Mahler's Sixth Symphony* (1995). *Current Musicology* 60/61, 86–103.

Burkhart, C. 1978. Schenker's "Motivic Parallelisms." *Journal of Music Theory* 22 (2), 145–175.

Carroll, Lewis. n.d. *Alice's Adventures in Wonderland, Through the Looking Glass, and the Hunting of the Snark,* ed. Alexander Woolcott. New York: Modern Library.

Cassirer, Ernst. 1953. *The Philosophy of Symbolic Forms.* Volume 1, *Language,* trans. Ralph Manheim. New Haven: Yale University Press.

Cavell, Stanley. 1976. Music Discomposed. In *Must We Mean What We Say? A Book of Essays,* 180–212. Cambridge: Cambridge University Press. Originally published in *Art, Mind, and Religion,* ed. W. H. Capitan and D. D. Merrill. Pittsburgh: University of Pittsburgh Press, 1967.

Chadwick, Evelyn. 1996. Woman of Substance: An Interview with Violinist Michèle Auclair. *Strad* 107 (1273) (May), 493–497.

Churchland, Paul. 1988. Perceptual Plasticity and Theoretical Neutrality: A Reply to Jerry Fodor. *Philosophy of Science* 55, 178–179.

Clark, Ann. 1982. Is Music a Language? *Journal of Aesthetics and Art Criticism* 41, 195–204.

Clarke, Eric F. 1985. Structure and Expression in Rhythmic Performance. In *Musical Structure and Cognition,* ed. Peter Howell, Ian Cross, and Robert West, 209–236. London: Academic Press.

Clynes, Manfred. [1977] 1989. *Sentics: The Touch of the Emotions,* intro. by Yehudi Menuhin. Bridport, Dorset: Prism Press.

Clynes, Manfred, with Nigel Nettelheim. 1982. The Living Quality of Music: Neurobiologic Basis of Communicating Feeling. In *Music, Mind, and Brain,* ed. Manfred Clynes, 47–82. New York: Plenum Press.

Coady, C. A. J. 1992. *Testimony: A Philosophical Study.* New York: Oxford University Press.

Code, Lorraine. 1991. *What Can She Know?* Ithaca: Cornell University Press.

Coker, Wilson. 1972. *Music and Meaning: A Theoretical Introduction to Musical Aesthetics.* New York: Free Press.

Colapietro, Vincent M. 1989. *Peirce's Approach to the Self: A Semiotic Perspective on Human Subjectivity.* Albany: State University of New York Press.

Cone, Edward T. 1974. *The Composer's Voice.* Berkeley: University of California Press.

———. 1989. Responses. *College Music Symposium* 29, 75–80. In special review section, "Music Criticism: Edward T. Cone's *The Composer's Voice: Elaborations and Departures,*" 1–80.

Conway, Joe. 1996. Review of CD, *Sibelius: Violin Concerto,* Miriam Fried and Helsinki Philharmonic Orchestra. Finlandia 0630–12999–2. *Strad* 107 (1276) (August), 833.

Cook, Nicholas. 1989a. Schenker's Theory of Music as Ethics. *Journal of Musicology* 7 (4), 415–439.

———. 1989b. Music Theory and Good Comparison: A Viennese Perspective. *Journal of Music Theory* 33 (1), 117–141.

———. 1998. *Music: A Very Short Introduction.* Oxford: Oxford University Press.

Cordner, Christopher. 1998. Literature, Morality and the Individual in the Shadows of Postmodernism. *Literature and Aesthetics: Journal of the Sydney Society for Literature and Aesthetics,* 60–77.

Cumming, Naomi. 1991. Analogy in Leonard B. Meyer's "Theory of Musical Meaning." In *Metaphor: A Musical Dimension,* ed. Jamie Kassler, 177–192. Sydney: Currency Press.

———. 1992. Eugene Narmour's Theory of Melody. *Music Analysis* 11 (2/3), 354–374.

———. 1993. Music Analysis and the Perceiver: A Perspective from Functionalist Philosophy. *Current Musicology* 54, 38–53.

———. 1994a. "Metaphor" in Roger Scruton's *Aesthetics of Music*. In *Theory, Analysis, and Meaning in Music*, ed. Anthony Pople, 3–28. Cambridge: Cambridge University Press.

———. 1994b. Measures of Meanings. Review of Robert Hatten, *Musical Meaning in Beethoven: Markedness, Correlation, and Interpretation* (1994). *Semiotic Review of Books* 5 (3), 2–4.

———. 1996a. Encountering *Mangrove:* An Essay in Signification: An Analysis of Signification in a Symphonic Work by Australian Composer, Peter Sculthorpe. *Journal of Australasian Musicological Research* 1, 193–229. Republished in a slightly altered version in *Signs in Musical Hermeneutics*, ed. Siglind Bruhn, a special edition of *American Journal of Semiotics* 13 (1/4), Fall 1996 [1998], 61–102.

———. 1996b. Musical Ineffability and the Fear of Smiles. Review of Diana Raffman, *Language, Music, and Mind* (1993). *Semiotica* 111 (1/2), 117–141.

———. 1996c. Review of Lawrence Kramer, *Classical Music and Postmodern Knowledge*. *Musicology Australia* 19, 75–77.

———. 1997a. The Subjectivities of "Erbarme Dich." *Music Analysis* 16 (1) (March), 5–44.

———. 1997b. Keeping Up (Musical) Appearances. Review of Stephen Davies, *Musical Meaning and Expression* (1994). *Semiotica* 116 (2/4), 319–349.

———. 1997c. Review of Warren Shibles, *Emotion in Aesthetics* (1995). *Australasian Journal of Philosophy* 75 (3), 434–436.

———. 1997d. Music Theory and Analysis. In *Oxford Companion to Music in Australia*, ed. W. Bebbington, 403–406. Melbourne: Oxford University Press.

———. 1997e. Manfred Clynes, Neuroscientist and Pianist. In *Oxford Companion to Music in Australia*, 131–132. Melbourne: Oxford University Press.

———. 1997f. The Horrors of Identification: Reich's *Different Trains*. *Perspectives of New Music* 35 (1), 129–152.

———. 1998. On Tuning the Self: Musical Models of Human Nature in the Seventeenth Century. Review of Jamie C. Kassler, *Inner Music: Hobbes, Hooke, and North on Internal Character* (1995). *Semiotica* 119 (1/2), 209–220.

———. 1999. Musical Signs and Subjectivity: Peircean Reflections. *Transactions of the Charles S. Peirce Society: A Quarterly Journal in American Philosophy* 35 (3), 437–474.

Cusick, Suzanne. 1994a. On a Lesbian Relationship with Music: A Serious Effort Not to Think Straight. In *Queering the Pitch: The New Gay and Lesbian Musicology*, ed. Philip Brett, Elizabeth Wood, and Gary C. Thomas, 67–83. New York: Routledge.

———. 1994b. Feminist Theory, Music Theory, and the Mind/Body Problem. *Perspectives of New Music* 32 (1), 8–27.

Cutts, Paul. 1996. Concert Review of the Australian String Quartet. *Strad* 107 (1276) (August), 825–826.

Dahlhaus, Carl 1989. *The Idea of Absolute Music*, trans. Roger Lustig. Chicago: University of Chicago Press.

Davies, Stephen. 1994. *Musical Meaning and Expression*. Ithaca: Cornell University Press.

———. 1995. Relativism in Interpretation. *Journal of Aesthetics and Art Criticism* 53 (1), 8–13.

Davis, William. 1972. *Peirce's Epistemology*. The Hague: Martinus Nijhoff.

Dawkins, Richard. 1997. The Selfish Meme. A talk available on *Life of the Mind*. Videorecording. Los Angeles: Into the Classroom Media.

DeBellis, Mark. 1991. The Representational Content of Musical Experience. *Philosophy and Phenomenological Research* 51 (2), 303–324.

———. 1995. *Music and Conceptualization*. Cambridge: Cambridge University Press.

Deledalle, Gérard. 1990. *Charles S. Peirce: An Intellectual Biography*, trans. Susan Petrilli. Amsterdam: John Benjamins.

Dennett, Daniel. 1991. *Consciousness Explained*. Boston: Little, Brown.

———. 1996. *Kinds of Minds: Towards an Understanding of Consciousness*. London: Phoenix.

Derrida, Jacques. 1974. *Of Grammatology*, trans. Gayatri Chakravorty Spivak. Baltimore: Johns Hopkins University Press.

———. 1982. *Ousia* and *Gramme*: Note on a Note from Being and Time. In *Margins of Philosophy*, trans. Alan Bass. Chicago: University of Chicago Press.

Dewey, John. [1929] 1960. *The Quest for Certainty: A Study of the Relation of Knowledge and Action*. New York: Putnam.

DSM IV. 1994. *Diagnostic and Statistical Manual of Mental Disorders, Fourth Edition*. Washington, D.C.: American Psychiatric Association.

Dubiel, Joseph. 1990. When You Are Beethoven: Kinds of Rules in Schenker's Counterpoint. *Journal of Music Theory* 34 (2) (Fall), 291–340.

———. 1998. Hearing, Remembering, Cold Storage, Purism, Evidence, and Attitude Adjustment. *Current Musicology* 60/61, 26–50.

Duchen, Jessica. 1996. Wanted: One Lion Tamer: Jurors at the [1996] Leopold Mozart Violin Competition Were Not Just Seeking Amadeus Experts. *Strad* 107 (1273) (May), 518–519.

Dunsby, Jonathan. 1982. Editorial: A Hitch-hiker's Guide to Semiotic Music Analysis. *Music Analysis* 1 (3), 235–242.

———. 1995. *Performing Music: Shared Concerns*. Oxford: Clarendon Press.

Dunsby, Jonathan, and J. Stopford. 1981. The Case for a Schenkerian Semiotic. *Music Theory Spectrum* 3, 49–53.

Eco, Umberto. [1976] 1979. *A Theory of Semiotics*. Bloomington: Indiana University Press.

———. 1984. *Semiotics and the Philosophy of Language*. Bloomington: Indiana University Press.

Eggebrecht, Hans-Heinrich. 1993. *J. S. Bach's "The Art of Fugue": The Work and Its Interpretation*, trans. Jeffrey Prater. Ames: Iowa State University Press.

———. 1995. *Musik verstehen*. Munich: Piper.

Eisler, Edith. 1993. The Suzuki Method, Pro and Con. *Strings* 8 (3) (November/December), 22–27.

Ekman, Paul, and Wallace V. Friesen. 1981. The Repertoire of Nonverbal Behaviour: Categories, Origins, Usage, and Coding. In *Nonverbal Communication, Interaction, and Gesture*, 57–105. The Hague: Mouton.

Feld, Stephen. 1994. Communication, Music, and Speech about Music. In *Music Grooves: Essays and Dialogues*, ed. Charles Keil and Steven Feld, 77–95. Chicago: University of Chicago Press.

Feld, Steven, and Charles Keil. 1994. Dialogue 2: Grooving on Participation. In *Music Grooves: Essays and Dialogues*, ed. Charles Keil and Steven Feld, 151–180. Chicago: University of Chicago Press.

Fish, Stanley. 1980. *Is There a Text in This Class? The Authority of Interpretive Communities*. Cambridge, Mass.: Harvard University Press.

Fisk, Charles. 1989. Questions about the Persona of Schubert's "Wanderer" Fantasy. *College Music Symposium* 29, 19–30. In special review section, "Music Criticism: Edward T. Cone's *The Composer's Voice: Elaborations and Departures*," 1–80.

Fitzgerald, John J. 1966. *Peirce's Theory of Signs as Foundation for Pragmatism*. The Hague: Mouton.

Fodor, Jerry A. 1984. Observation Reconsidered. *Philosophy of Science* 51, 23–43. Reprinted in *A Theory of Content and Other Essays*, 262. Cambridge, Mass.: MIT Press, 1990.

———. 1990. Appendix: A Reply to Churchland's "Perceptual Plasticity and Theoretical Neutrality." In *A Theory of Content and Other Essays*, 231–251. Cambridge, Mass.: MIT Press.

Frankl, Viktor. [Cumming may be referring to *Man's Search for Meaning*, Boston: Beacon Press, 1962.]

Freadman, Anne. 1993. Music in Peirce. *Versus: Quaderni di studi semiotici* 64, 75–95.

Fyk, Janina. 1995. *Melodic Intonation, Psychoacoustics, and the Violin*, trans. Joanna Ciecierska, ed. Zygmunt Rybczierska. Zielona Góra, Poland: Organon.

Gadamer, Hans-Georg. [1960] 1992. *Truth and Method*, trans. and rev. Joel Weinsheimer and Donald G. Marshall. New York: Crossroad.

————. 1976. *Philosophical Hermeneutics,* trans. and ed. David E. Linge. Berkeley: University of California Press.

Gasking, Douglas. 1996. Tenable Opinions. In *Language, Logic, and Causation: Philosophical Writings of Douglas Gasking,* ed. I. T. Oakley and L. J. O'Neill, 32–41. Carleton South, Victoria, Australia: Melbourne University Press. Original paper delivered at a meeting of the Victoria Branch of the Australasian Association of Philosophy.

Geminiani, Francesco. [1751] 1951. *The Art of Playing on the Violin,* ed. and intro. David D. Boyden. New York: Oxford University Press.

Gibson, James J. 1966. *The Senses Considered as Perceptual Systems.* Boston: Houghton Mifflin.

Goleman, Daniel. 1996. *Emotional Intelligence.* London: Bloomsbury.

Goodman, Nelson. 1968. *Languages of Art.* New York: Bobbs Merrill.

Graham, Gordon. 1995. The Value of Music. *Journal of Aesthetics and Art Criticism* 53 (2), 139–153.

Green, Barry, with W. Timothy Gallwey. 1987. *The Inner Game of Music.* London: Pan Books.

Greimas, Algirdas Julien. 1987. *On Meaning: Selected Writings in Semiotic Theory.* London: Francis Pinter.

Grosz, Elizabeth. 1988–1989. Feminism and the Critique of Representation. *Sounds Australian* 21, 29–33.

————. 1990. Contemporary Theories of Power and Subjectivity. In *Feminist Knowledge: Critique and Construct,* ed. Sarah Harasym, 59–120. New York: Routledge.

Guck, Marion. 1989. Beethoven as Dramatist. *College Music Symposium* 29, 8–18. In special review section, "Music Criticism: Edward T. Cone's *The Composer's Voice: Elaborations and Departures,*" 1–80.

————. 1993. Taking Notice: A Response to Kendall Walton. *Journal of Musicology* 11 (1), 45–51.

————. 1994a. Analytical Fictions. *Music Theory Spectrum* 16 (2), 217–230.

————. 1994b. A Woman's Theoretical Work. *Perspectives of New Music* 32 (1), 28–43.

————. 1997. Music Loving, or the Relationship with the Piece. *Journal of Musicology* 15 (3), 343–352.

Gurdjieff, George I. 1974. *Meetings with Remarkable Men.* New York: Dutton.

Haack, Susan. 1997. Science, Scientism, and Anti-Science in the Age of Preposterism. *Skeptical Inquirer* (November/December). Link through the website "Arisbe," http://www.door.net/arisbe

Haldane, John. 1996. The Mystery of Emergence. *Proceedings of the Aristotelian Society,* 264–265.

Hanslick, Eduard. 1986. *On the Musically Beautiful,* trans. and ed. Geoffrey Payzant from the eighth edition (1891) of *Vom Musikalisch-Schönen.* Indianapolis: Hackett.

Haraway, Donna. 1988. Situated Knowledges: The Science Question in Feminism and the Privilege of Partial Perspective. *Feminist Studies* 14 (3), 575–599.

Harnoncourt, Nikolaus. 1995. *Baroque Music Today: Music as Speech,* trans. Mary O'Neill, ed. Reinhard G. Pauly. Portland, Or.: Amadeus Press. Originally published in 1982 as *Musik als Klangrede.*

Hart, Kevin. 1989. *The Trespass of the Sign.* Cambridge: Cambridge University Press.

Hatten, Robert. 1992. Is Music Too Definite for Words? Review of Agawu (1991) and Mosley (1990). *Semiotic Review of Books* 3 (2), 10–11.

———. 1994. *Musical Meaning in Beethoven: Markedness, Correlation, and Interpretation.* Bloomington: Indiana University Press.

———. 1998. Musical Gesture, Lecture 3: Embodying Sound: The Role of Movement in Performance. Cybersemiotic Institute Course. URL: http://www.chass.utoronto.ca/epc/srb/cyber/hatout.html

Havas, Kató. 1961. *A New Approach to Violin Playing,* foreword Yehudi Menuhin. London: Bosworth.

Herrigel, Eugen. 1971. *Zen in the Art of Archery,* trans. R. Hull, intro. D. T. Suzuki. New York: Random House.

Herzog, Patricia. 1995. Music Criticism and Musical Meaning. *Journal of Aesthetics and Art Crticism* 53 (3), 299–312.

Hookway, Christopher. 1985. *Peirce.* London: Routledge & Kegan Paul.

Houser, Nathan, and Christian Kloesel, eds. 1998. *The Essential Peirce: Selected Philosophical Writings,* vol. 2 (1893–1913). Bloomington: Indiana University Press.

Ingarden, Roman. 1989. *Ontology of the Work of Art: The Musical Work, the Picture, the Architectural Work, the Film,* trans. R. Meyer. Athens: Ohio University Press.

Innis, Robert. 1994. *Consciousness and the Play of Signs.* Bloomington: Indiana University Press.

Jackendoff, Ray. 1981. Generative Music Theory and Its Relation to Psychology. *Journal of Music Theory* 25 (1), 45–90.

———. 1987. *Consciousness and the Computational Mind.* Cambridge, Mass.: MIT Press.

James, William. 1967. The Emotions. In *The Emotions,* ed. C. Lange and W. James, 93–135. New York: Hafner.

Jelgerhuis, J. 1827. *Theoretische lessen over de Gesticulatie en Mimiek.* Amsterdam:

n.p. Quoted in *The Art of Gesture: The Practices and Principles of 18th Century Acting*, Dene Barnett with Jeanette Massy-Westropp, 39. Heidelberg: Carl Winter Universitätsverlag, 1987.

Johnson, Mark, 1987. *The Body in the Mind: The Bodily Basis of Meaning, Imagination, and Reason*. Chicago: University of Chicago Press.

Joseph, Jeffrey. 1996. Review of CD, *Ballade: Works by Paganini, Sarasate, Kreisler, Ravel, and Others*. Ioan Harea, violin, James Wright, piano, and Dina Namer, piano. CCD CD 51106. *Strad* 107 (1276) (August), 833–834.

Kallberg, Jeffrey. 1988. The Rhetoric of Genre: Chopin's Nocturne in G Minor. *19th-Century Music* 11 (3), 238–261.

Kant, Immanuel. [1790] 1952. *The Critique of Judgement*, trans. James Creed Meredith. Oxford: Clarendon Press.

Karbusicky, Viktor. 1986. *Grundriß der musikalischen Semantik*. Darmstadt: Wissenschaftliche Buchgesellschaft.

———. 1987. The Index Sign in Music. *Semiotica* 66 (1/3), 23–35.

Karl, Gregory, and Jenefer Robinson. 1995a. Levinson on "Hope in *The Hebrides*." *Journal of Aesthetics and Art Criticism* 53 (2), 195–199.

———. 1995b. Shostakovich's Tenth Symphony and the Musical Expression of Cognitively Complex Emotions. *Journal of Aesthetics and Art Criticism* 53 (4), 401–416.

Kassler, Jamie C. 1983. Heinrich Schenker's Epistemology and Philosophy of Music: An Essay on the Relations between Evolutionary Theory and Music Theory. In *The Wider Domain of Evolutionary Thought*, ed. D. Oldroyd and I. Langham, 221–260. New York: Reidel.

Katz, Ruth. 1997. Paper presented at the Round Table, "Philosophy and Musicology," International Musicological Society, Sixteenth International Congress, London, August 14–20, 1997.

Keil, Charles, and Steven Feld. 1994. *Music Grooves*. Chicago: University of Chicago Press.

Kemp, Anthony E. 1996. *The Musical Temperament: Psychology and Personality of Musicians*. Oxford: Oxford University Press.

Kendon, Adam. 1983. Gesture and Speech: How They Interact. In *Nonverbal Interaction*, ed. John M. Wiemann and Randall P. Harrison, 13–45. Beverly Hills: Sage Publications.

Kielian-Gilbert, Marianne. 1994. Of Poetics and Poiesis, Pleasure and Politics: Music Theory and Modes of the Feminine. *Perspectives of New Music* 32 (1), 44–67.

Kirnberger, J. P. 1979. *The True Principles for the Practice of Harmony*, trans. David W. Beach and Jurgen Thym. *Journal of Music Theory* 23 (2), 163–225. Originally published in 1773.

Kitcher, Patricia. 1990. *Kant's Transcendental Psychology.* New York: Oxford University Press.

Kivy, Peter. 1986. Live Performances and Dead Composers: On the Ethics of Musical Interpretation. In *Human Agency,* ed. J. Daney, J. M. E. Moravcsik, and C. C. W. Taylor, 219–236. Stanford: Stanford University Press.

———. 1990. *Music Alone: Philosophical Reflections on the Purely Musical Experience.* Ithaca: Cornell University Press.

———. 1997. "Absolute Music" and the "New Musicology." Paper presented at the Round Table, "Philosophy and Musicology," International Musicological Society, Sixteenth International Congress, London, August 14–20, 1997.

Korsyn, K. 1988. Schenker and Kantian Epistemology. *Theoria* 3, 1–58.

Kouvaras, L. 1996. Andrée Greenwell. Unpublished Ph.D. Dissertation.

Kramer, Lawrence. 1995. *Classical Music and Postmodern Knowledge.* Berkeley: University of California Press.

Kraus, Joseph C. 1991. Tonal Plan and Narrative Plot in Tchaikovsky's Symphony no. 5 in E Minor. *Music Theory Spectrum* 13 (1), 21–47.

Kraut, Robert. 1993. Perceiving the Music Correctly. In *The Interpretation of Music: Philosophical Essays,* ed. Michael Krausz, 103–116. Oxford: Clarendon Press.

Kristeva, Julia. 1984. *Revolution in Poetic Language,* trans. Margaret Waller, intro. Leon S. Roudiez. New York: Columbia University Press.

Lakoff, George. 1987. *Women, Fire, and Dangerous Things: What Categories Reveal about the Mind.* Chicago: University of Chicago Press.

Lakoff, George, and Mark Johnson. 1980. *Metaphors We Live By.* Chicago: University of Chicago Press.

Lamb, Warren, and Elizabeth Watson. 1979. *Body Code: The Meaning in Movement.* London: Routledge and Kegan Paul.

Langer, Susanne K. [1942] 1982. *Philosophy in a New Key: A Study in the Symbolism of Reason, Rite, and Art.* Cambridge, Mass.: Harvard University Press.

———. 1953. *Feeling and Form: A Theory of Art.* New York: Charles Scribner's Sons.

———. 1967. *Mind: An Essay on Human Feeling.* Baltimore: Johns Hopkins University Press.

Laredo, Jennifer. 1996. Concert Review of Marat Bisengaliev. *Strad* 107 (1276) (August), 829.

Lazarus, R. S. 1982. Thoughts on the Relations between Emotion and Cognition. *American Psychologist* 37, 1019–1024.

———. 1991. Cognition and Motivation in Emotion. *American Psychologist* 46 (4), 352–367.

Legg, Cathy. 1997. Existent Universals or Real Generals. Unpublished manuscript. Public domain version, available at the website "Arisbe," http://www.door.net/arisbe

Lerdahl, Fred, and Ray Jackendoff. 1983. *A Generative Theory of Tonal Music.* Cambridge, Mass.: MIT Press.

Levinson, Jerrold. 1990. *Music, Art, and Metaphysics.* Ithaca: Cornell University Press.

———. 1995. Still Hopeful: Reply to Karl and Robinson. *Journal of Aesthetics and Art Criticism* 53 (2), 199–201.

———. 1996. *The Pleasures of Aesthetics: Philosophical Essays.* Ithaca: Cornell University Press.

Lidov, David. 1987. Mind and Body in Music. *Semiotica* 66 (1/3), 69–97.

———. 1997. Our Time with the Druids: What and How We Can Recuperate from Our Obsession with Tree Graphs. In *Musica Significans,* ed. Raymond Monelle, 1–28. London: Harwood.

———. 1999. *Elements of Semiotics.* New York: St. Martin's Press.

Linge, David E. 1976. Editor's Introduction. *Philosophical Hermeneutics,* Hans-Georg Gadamer, xi–lviii. Berkeley: University of California Press.

Liszka, James. 1998. Peirce's Discursive Realism. Paper presented at the Symposium on Pragmatism and Idealism, Académie du Midi and the Institut für Philosophie, Alet les Bains, France, June 1–5, 1998. Public domain version, available at the website "Arisbe," http://www.door.net/arisbe

London, Justin. 1996. Review of Mark DeBellis, *Music and Conceptualization* (1995). *Current Musicology* 60/61, 111–131.

———. 1998. Musical Genre and Schenkerian Analysis. *Journal of Music Theory* 42 (1) (Spring), 101–124.

Margolis, Joseph. 1974. Works of Art as Physically Embodied and Culturally Emergent Entities. *British Journal of Aesthetics* 14 (3), 187–196.

———. 1995. Plain Talk about Interpretation on a Relativistic Model. *Journal of Aesthetics and Art Criticism* 53 (1) (1995), 1–7.

Maus, Fred Everett. 1988. Music as Drama. *Music Theory Spectrum* 10, 56–73.

———. 1989a. Introduction: *The Composer's Voice* as Music Theory. *College Music Symposium* 29, 1–7. In special review section, "Music Criticism: Edward T. Cone's *The Composer's Voice: Elaborations and Departures,*" 1–80.

———. 1989b. Agency in Instrumental Music and Song. *College Music Symposium* 29, 31–43. In special review section, "Music Criticism: Edward T. Cone's *The Composer's Voice: Elaborations and Departures,*" 1–80.

———. 1992. Hanslick's Animism. *Journal of Musicology* 10 (3), 273–292.

———. 1993. Masculine Discourse in Music Theory. *Perspectives of New Music* 31 (2), 264–293.

McClary, Susan. 1989. Terminal Prestige: The Case of Avant-Garde Music Composition. *Cultural Critique* 12, 57–81.

———. 1991. *Feminine Endings: Music, Gender, and Sexuality.* Minneapolis: University of Minnesota Press.

McErlean, Jennifer. 1990. Critical Principles and Emergence in Beardsley's Aesthetic Theory. *Journal of Aesthetics and Art Criticism.* 48 (2), 153–156.

Mead, George Herbert. 1934. *Mind, Self, and Society.* Chicago: University of Chicago Press.

Menuhin, Yehudi, and William Primrose. 1991. *Violin and Viola.* London: Kahn & Averill.

Merrell, Floyd. 1997. *Peirce, Signs, and Meaning.* Toronto: University of Toronto Press.

Meyer, Leonard B. 1956. *Emotion and Meaning in Music.* Chicago: University of Chicago Press.

———. 1973. *Explaining Music: Essays and Explorations.* Berkeley: University of California Press.

———. 1979. Toward a Theory of Style. In *The Concept of Style,* ed. Berel Lang, 3–44. Philadelphia: University of Pennsylvania Press.

———. 1980. Exploiting Limits: Creation, Archetypes, and Style Change. *Daedelus* 109, 177–205.

———. 1982. Process and Morphology in the Music of Mozart. *Journal of Musicology* 1 (1), 67–94.

———. 1983. Innovation, Choice, and the History of Music. *Critical Inquiry* 9, 517–544.

———. 1985. Music and Ideology in the Nineteenth Century. In *Tanner Lectures on Human Values* 6, ed. S. M. McMurrin, 23–52. Salt Lake City: University of Utah Press.

———. 1989. *Style in Music: Theory, History, and Ideology.* Philadelphia: University of Pennsylvania Press. Paperback reprint, University of Chicago Press, 1996.

———. 1991. A Pride of Prejudices; or, Delight in Diversity. *Music Theory Spectrum* 13 (2), 241–251.

———. 1992. Nature, Nurture, and Convention: The Cadential Six-Four Progression. In *Convention in Eighteenth- and Nineteenth-Century Music,* ed. W. A. Allanbrook, J. M. Levy, and W. P. Mahrt, 473–516. Stuyvesant, N.Y.: Pendragon.

———. 1995. Response to Charles Keil's Essay, "The Theory of Participatory Discrepancies: A Progress Report." *Ethnomusicology* 39 (1), 84–87.

———. 1998. A Universe of Universals. *Journal of Musicology* 16 (1), 3–25.

Meyer, Leonard B., and Burton S. Rosner. 1982. Melodic Processes and the Perception of Music. *The Psychology of Music*, ed. Diana Deutsch, 316–341. New York: Academic Press.

———. 1986. The Perceptual Roles of Melodic Process, Contour, and Form. *Music Perception* 4 (1), 1–39.

Modi, Sorab. 1996. From Bruch to Bengal: Sorab Modi samples traditional and more exotic [string] fare in Washington DC. *Strad* 107 (1273) (May), 529–531.

Monelle, Raymond. 1991. Music and the Peircean trichotomies. *International Review of the Aesthetics and Sociology of Music* 22 (1) 1991, 99–108.

———. 1992. *Linguistics and Semiotics in Music*. Chur, Switzerland: Harwood.

Moore, Thomas. 1992. *Care of the Soul: A Guide for Cultivating Depth and Sacredness in Everyday Life*. New York: HarperCollins.

Morris, Charles W. 1964. *Signification and Significance*. Cambridge, Mass.: MIT Press.

Mosley, David L. 1990. *Gesture, Sign, and Song: An Interdisciplinary Approach to Schumann's Liederkreis opus 39*. New York: Peter Lang.

Mozart, Leopold. [1756] 1948. *A Treatise on the Fundamental Principles of Violin Playing*, trans. Editha Knocker, pref. Alfred Einstein. Originally published as *Versuch einer gründlichen Violinschule*.

Muller, John P. 1996. Developmental Foundations of Infant Semiotics. In *Beyond the Psychoanalytic Dyad: Developmental Semiotics in Freud, Peirce, and Lacan*, John P. Muller, 43–60. New York: Routledge.

Murphey, Murray. 1961. *The Development of Peirce's Philosophy*. Cambridge, Mass.: Harvard University Press.

Nagel, Thomas. [1974] 1979. What Is It Like to be a Bat? In *Mortal Questions*, Thomas Nagel, 165–180. Cambridge: Cambridge University Press. First published in *Philosophical Review* 83 (October 1974).

Narmour, Eugene. 1977. *Beyond Schenkerism: The Need for Alternatives in Music Analysis*. Chicago: University of Chicago Press.

———. 1990. *The Analysis and Cognition of Basic Melodic Structures: The Implication-realization Model*. Chicago: University of Chicago Press.

Nattiez, Jean-Jacques. 1975. *Fondements d'une sémiologie de la musique*. Paris: Union Générale d'Editions.

———. 1982. Varèse's "Density 21.5": A Study in Semiological Analysis, trans. Anna Berry. *Music Analysis* 1 (3), 243–340.

———. 1989. Reflections on the Development of Semiology in Music, trans. Katharine Ellis. *Music Analysis* 8 (1/2), 21–75.

———. 1990. Can One Speak of Narrativity in Music? trans. Katherine Ellis. *Journal of the Royal Musical Association* 15 (2), 240–267.

Nerlich, Graham. 1989. *Values and Valuing*. Oxford: Oxford University Press.

Nicoll, Maurice. 1984. *Psychological Commentaries on the Teaching of Gurdjieff and Ouspensky.* Boulder: Shambhala.

Nubiola, Jaime. 1996. Scholarship on the Relations between Ludwig Wittgenstein and Charles S. Peirce. In *Studies on the History of Logic: Proceedings of the III. Symposium on History of Logic,* ed. Ignacio Angelelli and María Cerezo, 281–294. Berlin: Walter de Gruyter. Public domain version, available at the website "Arisbe," http://www.door.net/arisbe

Ouspensky, Peter D. 1977. *In Search of the Miraculous.* New York: Harcourt, Brace, Jovanovich.

Papouček, Mechtild. 1996. Intuitive Parenting: A Hidden Source of Musical Stimulation in Infancy. In *Musical Beginnings: Origins and Development of Musical Competences,* ed. Irène Deliège and John Sloboda, 88–112. Oxford: Oxford University Press.

Parmentier, Richard. 1994. *Signs in Society: Studies in Semiotic Anthropology.* Bloomington: Indiana University Press.

Pastille, William A. 1994. *Ursatz: The Musical Philosophy of Heinrich Schenker.* Ann Arbor, Mich.: UMI Press.

Peirce, Charles Sanders. [1861] 1982. "I, IT, and THOU: A Book Giving Instruction in Some of the Elements of Thought" (MS 65, Spring 1861). In *Writings of Charles Sanders Peirce: A Chronological Edition,* vol. 1 (1857–1866), ed. Max Fisch, 45–46. Bloomington: Indiana University Press.

———. 1868. On a New List of Categories. *Proceedings of the American Academy of Arts and Sciences* 7, 287–298. Public domain version, available at the website "Arisbe," http://www.door.net/arisbe

———. 1931–1958. *Collected Papers of Charles Sanders Peirce,* 8 vols., ed. Charles Hartshorne, Paul Weiss, and Arthur W. Burks. Cambridge, Mass.: Harvard University Press. Reference to *Collected Papers* (CP) is by volume and paragraph number.

———. 1940. Logic as Semiotic: The Theory of Signs. In *The Philosophy of Peirce: Selected Writings,* ed. Justus Buchler, 98–119. London: Kegan Paul.

———. Reference to the collection of Peirce manuscripts in the Houghton Library, Harvard University, is abbreviated (MS) and follows the numbering in the *Annotated Catalogue of Papers of Charles S. Peirce,* ed. Richard Robin. Amherst: University of Massachusetts Press, 1967.

Pierce, Alexandra. 1994. Developing Schenkerian Hearing and Performing. *Intégral* 8, 51–123.

Potter, Tully. 1996a. Concert Review of Midori and Joshua Bell. *Strad* 107 (1275) (July), 734–735.

———. 1996b. Concert Review of Anne-Sophie Mutter. *Strad* 107 (1276) (August), 829.

Potter, Vincent G. 1997. *Charles S. Peirce: On Norms and Ideals*, intro. Stanley Harrison. New York: Fordham University Press.

Powers, Harold S. (1993). Three Pragmatists in Search of a Theory. *Current Musicology* 53, 5–17.

Putnam, Hilary. [1960] 1975. Minds and Machines. In *Mind, Language, and Reality*, Hilary Putnam, 367. Cambridge: Cambridge University Press. First published in *Dimensions of Mind*, ed. Sidney Hook, 143. New York: New York University Press, 1960.

Raffman, Diana. 1993. *Language, Music, and Mind*. Cambridge, Mass.: MIT Press.

Rahn, J. 1993. Differences. *Perspectives of New Music* 31 (2), 58–71.

Ransdell, Joseph. 1989. Is Peirce a Phenomenologist? Published as "Peirce est-il un phénoménologue?" in *Études Phénoménologiques* 9/10, 51–75. Public domain version (in English), available at the website "Arisbe," http://www.door.net/arisbe

———. 1997. On Peirce's Conception of the Iconic Sign. Revised version of a paper published in *Iconicity: Essays on the Nature of Culture: A Festschrift for Thomas A. Sebeok,* ed. Paul Bouissac, Michael Herzfeld, and Roland Posner, 51–74. Tübingen: Stauffenberg Verlag, 1986. Public domain version, available at the website "Arisbe," http://www.door.net/arisbe

Ridley, Aaron. 1995. Musical Sympathies: The Experience of Expressive Music. *Journal of Aesthetics and Art Criticism* 53 (1), 49–57.

Riemann, Hugo. 1908. *Grundriß der Musikwissenschaft*. Leipzig: Quelle & Meyer.

Robin, Richard. 1997. Classical Pragmatism and Pragmatism's Proof. In *The Rule of Reason: The Philosophy of Charles Sanders Peirce*, ed. and intro. Jacqueline Brunning and Paul Forster, 139–152. Toronto: University of Toronto Press.

Robinson, Jenefer. 1994. The Expression and Arousal of Emotion in Music. *Journal of Aesthetics and Art Criticism* 52 (1), 13–22.

Rorty, Richard (1979). *Philosophy and the Mirror of Nature*. Princeton: Princeton University Press.

Rosenthal, David M. [Cumming may be referring to one of the essays in *The Nature of the Mind*, ed. David M. Rosenthal. New York: Oxford University Press, 1991.]

Rosenthal, Sandra. 1986. *Speculative Pragmatism*. Amherst: University of Massachusetts Press.

———. 1994. *Charles Peirce's Pragmatic Pluralism*. Albany: State University of New York Press.

Rosenthal, Sandra, and Patrick L. Bourgeois. 1980. *Pragmatism and Phenomenology: A Philosophic Encounter*. Amsterdam: B. R. Grüner.

Roth, Gerhard, and Helmuth Schwegler. 1990. Self-organisation, Emergent Properties, and the Unity of the World. *Philosophica* 46 (2), 45–54.

Rothstein, William. 1989. *Phrase Rhythm in Tonal Music*. New York: Schirmer Books.

Ryckmans, Pierre. 1996. Boyer Lectures. Australian Broadcasting Company.

Said, Edward. 1991. *Musical Elaborations*. New York: Columbia University Press.

Sainati, Edward. 1996. Review of CD, *Sarah Chang with Royal Concertgebouw under Charles Dutoit and London Philharmonic Orchestra under Bernard Haitink*. Lalo, *Symphonie Espagnole;* Vieuxtemps, Concerto no. 5; Vaughan Williams, *The Lark Ascending*. EMI Classics 5-554872. Strad 107 (1275) (1996), 749–750.

Samuels, Robert. 1994. Music as Text: Mahler, Schumann, and Issues in Analysis. In *Theory, Analysis, and Meaning in Music*, ed. Anthony Pople, 152–163. Cambridge: Cambridge University Press.

———. 1995. *Mahler's Sixth Symphony*. Cambridge: Cambridge University Press.

Sartre, Jean-Paul. 1956. *Being and Nothingness: An Essay on Phenomenology*, trans. Hazel E. Barnes. New York: Philosophical Library.

Schank, Roger C., and Robert P. Abelson. 1977. *Scripts, Plans, Goals, and Human Understanding: An Inquiry into Human Knowledge Structures*. Hillsdale, N.J.: Lawrence Erlbaum Associates.

Schechner, Richard. 1990. Magnitudes of Performance. In *By Means of Performance: Inter-cultural Studies in Theatre and Ritual*, 19–49. Cambridge: Cambridge University Press.

Schenker, Heinrich. 1990. *Free Composition*, ed. and trans. Ernst Oster. New York: Schirmer. Originally published as *Freie Satz*.

Schroeder, David. 1990. *Haydn and the Enlightenment: The Late Symphonies and Their Audience*. Oxford: Clarendon.

Schubert, Emery. 1996. Enjoyment of Negative Emotions in Music: An Associative Network Explanation. *Psychology of Music* 24, 18–28.

Schwarz, D. 1993: Listening Subjects: Semiotics, Psychoanalysis, and the Music of John Adams and Steve Reich. *Perspectives of New Music* 31 (2), 24–56.

Scruton, Roger. [1974] 1982. *Art and Imagination: A Study in the Philosophy of Mind*. London: Routledge and Kegan Paul.

———. 1983. *The Aesthetic Understanding: Essays in the Philosophy of Art and Culture*. London: Methuen.

———. 1987. Analytical Philosophy and the Meaning of Music. *Journal of Aesthetics and Art Criticism* 46 (1987), 169–176.

———. 1997. *The Aesthetics of Music*. Oxford: Clarendon Press.

Sebeok, Thomas A. 1998. The Cognitive Self and the Virtual Self. In *New Approaches to Semiotics and the Human Sciences: Essays in Honor of Roberta Kevelson*, ed. William Pencak and J. Ralph Lindgren, 307–321. New York: Peter Lang.

Shaver, Philip, Judith Schwartz, Donald Kirson, and Cary O'Connor. 1987. Emotion Knowledge: Further Exploration of a Prototype Approach. *Journal of Personality and Social Psychology* 52 (6), 1061–1086.

Shibles, Warren. 1995. *Emotion in Aesthetics*. Dordrecht: Kluwer Academic Publishers.

Short, T. L. 1981. Semeiosis and Intentionality. *Transactions of the Charles S. Peirce Society* 17, 197–223.

———. 1982. Life among the Legisigns. *Transactions of the Charles S. Peirce Society* 18, 285–310.

———. 1992. Peirce's Semiotic Theory of the Self. *Semiotica* 91 (1/2), 109–131.

———. 1996. Interpreting Peirce's Interpretant: A Response to Lalor, Liszka, and Meyers. *Transactions of the Charles S. Peirce Society* 32 (4), 488–541.

Silverman, Kaja. 1983. *The Subject of Semiotics*. New York: Oxford University Press.

———. 1988. *The Acoustic Mirror*. Bloomington: Indiana University Press.

Simpkins, Scott. 1997. Lecture One: The Lingua Franca of Semioticians. *Critical Semiotics*. Series of Lectures. Cybersemiotic Institute Course. URL: http://www.chass.utoronto.ca/pc/srb/cyber/simout.html

Sloboda, John A. 1985. *The Musical Mind: The Cognitive Psychology of Music*. Oxford: Clarendon Press, Oxford University Press.

Smalley, Dennis. 1986. Spectro-morphology and Structuring Processes. In *The Language of Electroacoustic Music*, ed. Simon Emmerson, 61–93. London: Macmillan.

Snarrenberg, Robert. 1997. *Schenker's Interpretive Practice*. Cambridge: Cambridge University Press.

Spencer-Smith, Richard. 1995. Reductionism and Emergent Properties. *Proceedings of the Aristotelian Society* 95 (2), 113–129.

Stecker, Robert. 1995. Relativism about Interpretation. *Journal of Aesthetics and Art Criticism* 53 (1), 14–18.

Stich, Stephen P. 1983. *From Folk Psychology to Cognitive Science: The Case against Belief*. Cambridge, MA: MIT Press.

Tarasti, Eero. 1994. *A Theory of Musical Semiotics*. Bloomington: Indiana University Press.

———. 1997. On the Paths of Existential Semiotics. Unpublished manuscript.

Tickerhoof, Bernard. 1991. *Conversion and The Enneagram*. Denville, N.J.: Dimension Books.

Tomlinson, Gary. 1993. Musical Pasts and Postmodern Musicologies: A Response to Lawrence Kramer. *Current Musicology* 53, 18–24. Tomlinson Responds, 36–40.

Treitler, Leo. [1969] 1989. The Present as History. In *Music and the Historical Imagination,* Leo Treitler, 95–156. Cambridge, Mass.: Harvard University Press. First published in *Perspectives of New Music* 7.

———. [1995] 1997. Language and the Interpretation of Music. In *Music and Meaning,* ed. Jenefer Robinson, 23–56. Ithaca and London: Cornell University Press. Expanded version of What Obstacles Must Be Overcome, Just in Case We Wish to Speak of Meaning in the Musical Arts? In *Meaning in the Visual Arts: Views from the Outside. A Centennial Commemoration of Erwin Panofsky (1892–1968),* ed. Irving Lavin, 285–303. Princeton: Princeton University Press [Institute for Advanced Studies].

Van Baest, A ., and H. van Driel. 1995. *The Semiotics of C. S. Peirce Applied to Music.* Tilburg, The Netherlands: Tilburg University Press.

VanNess, Peter H. 1992. *Spirituality, Diversion, and Decadence: The Contemporary Predicament.* Albany: State University of New York Press.

Walton, Kendall. 1988. What Is Abstract about the Art of Music? *Journal of Aesthetics and Art Criticism* 46 (3), 351–364.

———. 1993. Understanding Humor and Understanding Music. *Journal of Musicology* 11 (1), 32–44. Also in *The Interpretation of Music,* ed. Michael Krausz, 259–269. Oxford: Oxford University Press, 1993.

———. 1994. Listening with Imagination: Is Music Representational? *Journal of Aesthetics and Art Criticism* 52 (1), 47–62.

Wang Yang-ming. 1963. Inquiry on the Great Learning. In *Source Book in Chinese Philosophy,* ed. Wing-tsit Chan, 659–667. Princeton: Princeton University Press.

Warren, Alicyn. 1989. The Camera's Voice. *College Music Symposium* 29, 66–74. In special review section, "Music Criticism: Edward T. Cone's *The Composer's Voice: Elaborations and Departures,*" 1–80.

Waterman, Mitch. 1996. Emotional Responses to Music: Implicit and Explicit Effects in Listeners and Performers. *Psychology of Music* 24, 53–67.

Webster, James. 1989. Cone's "Personae" and the Analysis of Opera. *College Music Symposium* 29, 44–65. In special review section, "Music Criticism: Edward T. Cone's *The Composer's Voice: Elaborations and Departures,*" 1–80.

Weeks, Thelma. 1982. Intonation as an Early Marker of Meaning. In *Nonverbal Communication Today: Current Research,* ed. Mary Ritchie Key, 157–168. Berlin: Mouton.

Wiener, Philip P., ed. [1958] 1966. *Charles S. Peirce: Selected Writings.* New York: Dover.

Wimsatt, W. K., and Monroe Beardsley. 1976. The Intentional Fallacy. In *On Literary Intention: Critical Essays,* selected and intro. David Newton-de Moline, 1–13. Edinburgh: Edinburgh University Press.

Wishart, Trevor. 1994. *Audible Design: A Plain and Easy Introduction to Practical Sound Composition.* 83 Heslington Rd., York, England: Orpheus the Pantomime Ltd. (The author's private publishing company). Book, two appendices, and CD.

Wittgenstein, Ludwig. 1958. *Philosophical Investigations,* trans. G. E. M. Anscombe. New York: Macmillan.

———. [1922] 1972. *Tractatus logico-philosophicus.* German text and trans. D. F. Pears and B. F. McGuinness; intro. Bertrand Russell. London: Routledge & Kegan Paul.

Wollheim, Richard. 1993. Pictures and Language. In *The Mind and Its Depths,* Richard Wollheim. Cambridge, Mass.: Harvard University Press.

Zeitlin, Zvi. 1995. The Pitfalls of Young Performers. *Strings* 10 (2), 26–29.

Index

Note: An italicized page number indicates an illustration. An italicized letter *t* indicates a table.

Abbate, Carolyn, 133, 161
abstraction, 247
acrobatics, music and, 23, 24
actoriality, 190–94
actors, 34–36
Adler, Guido, 168, 169
aesthetics, 168, 169, 178, 294; emergence and, 243–45; socialization and, 302; subjectivity and, 300
affect. *See* emotion (affect)
Agawu, Kofi, 166, 186–87
agency, 149, 160–65, 167, 169–70; in Bach, 234–35; expressiveness and, 206; repetitions of patterning and, 188; tonality and, 190; within tonality, 183
Amadeus (film), 119, 121
analysis, 48, 57
anthropology, 140, 141, 272
anxiety, 36–37, 39

arguments, 95–96, 103
Aristotle, 318
Art of Fugue, The (J. S. Bach), 256
artistry, 31–32, 36–37, 38, 39, 139
asceticism, 66, 67, 68, 204
Auclair, 40
Australian String Quartet, 38
authenticity, 246–48
autonomic nervous system (ANS), 141, 153, 154, 155

Bacewicz, Grazyna, 125, 129, 130
Bach, J. S., 138, 221, 239, 246, 263, 307; *The Art of Fugue,* 256; cello sonatas, 274; performances of, 247–48; *St. Matthew Passion,* 201, 262; Sonata in G Minor for Solo Violin, 84, 85, 89, 200, 217–19, *218,* 222, 223; Violin Concerto in E Major, 53; Violin Sonata in B Minor, 135, *135,* 138, 156, 162; voice of, 260. *See also* Sonata in G Minor for Solo Violin (Bach)
ballet, 30, 194

Repin, Vadim, 25
replicas, 81, 84, 173, 195
representamen. *See* signs
representation, 106, 108, 112, 116,
274; consciousness and, 114–15;
levels of, 119
resistances, 279–84, 316
resonance, 128
restraint (reserve), 11–12, 59, 68, 187,
221, 222, 252
rhemes (rhematic signs), 95–96, 98t,
100t, 173t
rhythm, 46, 147, 188, 194, 216
Ricci, Ruggiero, 143, 160
richness, 127, 130
Ridley, Aaron, 238
Riemann, Hugo, 168–69
"Ring o' Roses" (nursery rhyme), 1
Robinson, Jenefer, 206–207, 208, 215,
216, 238
Romanticism/Romantic compositions, 2, 125, 225; Classical compositions *versus*, 186; creative isolation and, 295; desire and, 250;
expressivity and, 204; modern
performance practice and, 246;
repeated patterns in, 94–95; sensuous tone and, 11; singing of, 52;
subjective identifications and,
125–28; the Sublime and, 122;
universalism and, 248; values of,
205; vibrato in, 5, 66; violin and,
3; virtuosity in performance of,
25; warmth of tone and, 63
Rorty, Richard, 15
Rosenthal, David, 121
Rostropovich, Mstislav, 274, 275
Rousseau, Jean-Jacques, 157

Said, Edward, 1
St. Matthew Passion (J. S. Bach), 201,
262
Sandra, Rosenthal, 66
Sartre, Jean-Paul, 25, 159
Saussure, Ferdinand de, 68, 255

Schechner, Richard, 35, 36, 140–41,
156
schemata, 172, 177, 181
Schenker, Heinrich, 170, 171, 172,
177, 238–39; on expressivity, 192;
Realism of, 312–13
Schenkerian theory, 47, 48, 85, 191;
ethical code and, 320; real ideal
of, 171–78; structural voice and,
232–33
Schering, Henryk, 89, 246, 247
Schoenberg, Arnold, 295
Scholastic philosophy, 312
Schroeder, David, 257
Schubert, Franz, 38
science, 121, 314, 326n10
scores, 46, 177
Scruton, Roger, 49–50, 51, 59, 74,
196, 217–18; on aesthetics, 239; on
appearances, 301; on music as intentional construct, 243; on music
theory, 312
Sculthorpe, Peter, 205, 285–86
Sebeok, Thomas, 208–209, 249
Sebistik, Démon, 5–7, 8
secondness (Peircean second category), 65, 70, 79; dicents (dici-
signs) as, 96t, 97t; index as, 86t,
97t; personae and, 224; the Real
and, 316; singular signs as, 97t
self ("I"), 41–42, 71; disembodied,
213; of Kantian epistemology, 56;
lost and found, 41–42; metaphysical "I," 292–303; as a mystery,
55–56; temporality and, 231–32.
See also personae; subject
self-awareness, 10
self-consciousness, 55–57
self-knowledge, 32–34, 59
self-reference, 45, 216
semiosis, 73–76, 80, 102, 141, 186–96
semiotics, 16–19, 243; agency and,
190–91; boundaries of, 274; meaning and, 255; psychology and,
108–17

www.ingramcontent.com/pod-product-compliance
Lightning Source LLC
Chambersburg PA
CBHW070450100426

42812CB00004B/1255